Melvin B. Tolson, 1898–1966

MELVIN B. TOLSON

1898-1966

Plain Talk and Poetic Prophecy

Robert M. Farnsworth

University of Missouri Press

Columbia, 1984

Library of Congress Cataloging in Publication Data

Farnsworth, Robert M.
    Melvin B. Tolson, 1898–1966.

        Bibliography: p.
        Includes index.
        1. Tolson, Melvin Beaunorus. 2. Poets,
American— 20th century—Biography. I. Title.
PS3539.0334Z69   1984   811'.54   83–21571
ISBN 0–8262–0433–3

All photographs included in this book are reproduced
with the permission of the Tolson family.

Nor can I, like that fluent sweet tongued Greek,
Who lisped at first, in future times speak plain.
By art he gladly found what he did seek,
A full requital of his striving pain.

Anne Bradstreet
"The Prologue"

Consciously or unconsciously the black novelist
and storyteller and poet sees this struggle between
white and black as the ancient human struggle
between the past and the future, between that
element in human nature that holds on to the
primitive and the superstitious and the inherited
and the oppressive, and, on the other hand, that
prophetic element in man which seeks to bring
to birth the New. Black authors see in this struggle
between blacks and whites a struggle between
those who wish to perpetuate the Traditional Man
and those who wish to bring to birth the New Man.

Lance Jeffers
"Afroamerican Literature: The Conscience of Man"

PREFACE

Late in 1972 Roy P. Basler sent his essay "The Heart of Blackness—M. B. Tolson's Poetry" to *New Letters*. David Ray, the editor of *New Letters*, asked me to read it. The article was accepted and published. Basler, at the time Chief of the Manuscript Division of the Library of Congress, was negotiating with Ruth Tolson to place the Tolson papers in the Library of Congress and told Ray of the manuscripts. David Ray recommended that I edit them. I visited the Tolson home in Washington, D.C., and reviewed the manuscripts. I happily agreed with Ruth Tolson to assume responsibility for seeking appropriate publication for them.

It was not until 1978, after I had placed several Tolson pieces in literary magazines and *A Gallery of Harlem Portraits* had been accepted by the University of Missouri Press, that I first thought of writing a critical biography of Tolson. By then I had come to know all the immediate members of the Tolson family and was more familiar with Tolson's writing, both published and unpublished. With the aid of a Senior Humanist Fellowship from the National Endowment for the Humanities, I began deliberate biographical research in the summer of 1979, taping interviews with Tolson family members, colleagues, and students and visiting Wiley College and Langston University.

That summer I also read all of the *Caviar and Cabbage* columns on microfilm. My original interest was biographical. However, I quickly became fascinated with the thought that many of these pieces deserved a new audience. My biographical ambition was thus temporarily suspended to prepare a collection of *Caviar and Cabbage* columns for book publication. The two interests were, however, ultimately compatible.

I have received much generous assistance from the Tolson family, from old and new friends, and from several institutions. Roy Basler's praise of Tolson's writing awakened my critical and scholarly interest. Ruth Tolson was ever gracious and generous with her time and hospitality until her death in January 1982. Ruth Marie added a professional librarian's interest to her daughter's pride in her father's work. She cared for and organized the manuscripts prior to their being housed in the Library of Congress. She was of inestimable value to me, and her untimely death from cancer in 1975 was a tragic loss. Helen Tolson Wilson, Tolson's sister, was an energetic

Preface

and effective ally in bringing her brother's achievements to public recognition.

All three of Tolson's sons have been extraordinarily helpful and supportive. Melvin, Jr., has critiqued much of my work in manuscript. He has been informative, insightful, and demanding. Arthur shared invaluable memorabilia and gave me the support of that remarkably zealous Tolson energy. Wiley Wilson, usually at his mother's side in Washington, was readily available with easy and efficient support and hospitality. I met these men many times in many places over the years. Knowing them, I came to know their father far more personally than I ever could have working only with the manuscripts.

David Ray has ever been ready with personal and professional support. *New Letters* has taken special pride in publishing Tolson's writing. Joy Flasch generously made the notes from her biographical research available and arranged for me to meet colleagues and students of Tolson's at Langston University. Maggie Daniel introduced me to colleagues and students at Wiley College. James Farmer, Benjamin Bell, and Hobart Jarrett, former students of Tolson's who later became close friends, were all generous and helpful with anecdotes and information.

Samuel R. Shepherd, the editor of Omega Psi Phi's *The Oracle*, uncovered much valuable information for me. Sophie Cornwell of the Langston Hughes Memorial Library at Lincoln University was warmly gracious and helpful. Thomas Webster, Kansas Citian, Lincoln alumnus, and friend, was a substantial resource, particularly of information about Tolson's schooling in Kansas City. My own former student, Rita Norton, who by most unexpected of coincidences worked as an archivist with the Horace Mann Bond papers at the University of Massachusetts, introduced me to correspondence between Tolson and Bond that I might never have found on my own.

In addition, much of my research depended upon many professionally experienced and resourceful librarians and staff members at the Library of Congress, the Moorland-Spingarn Research Center, The Schomburgh Collection of the New York Public Library, the Missouri Valley Room in Kansas City's Main Library, the Missouri State Historical Society, and the General Library at the University of Missouri—Kansas City. Their help was collectively enormous. This book would be substantially diminished without them.

For time and money to support my research I must also thank the National Endowment for the Humanities for a summer Senior Humanist Fellowship and the Graduate Faculty Research Council of the University of Missouri–Kansas City, which awarded me a semester's research leave and smaller travel grants when needed. More particularly, Robert F. Willson, my department chairman, Herwig G. Zauchenberger, former Dean of the Graduate School, and Henry A. Mitchell, Associate Vice-Chancellor, have provided welcome and generous administrative support for my research.

Preface

It is virtually impossible to acknowledge all who have helped me in this project. Help was characteristically given in memory of a great man and a great writer without thought of personal return. I hope that the merits of this book will in some sense serve as a sufficient statement of my gratitude to all I have not mentioned. I owe a great debt, and it is a pleasure to acknowledge it.

Robert M. Farnsworth
Kansas City, Missouri
December 1983

CONTENTS

I

JOCKEYING DOWN THE
YEARS ON PEGASUS

In 1935, from the far vantage point of Marshall, Texas, Melvin B. Tolson witnessed the Italian invasion of Ethiopia with anger and sorrow. Haile Selassie's warning to the League of Nations—that Italy's blatant disregard for international law combined with the League's disinterest or impotence threatened the future peace of the world—was for Tolson a persuasive prophecy. He observed the events of the next four years, which threatened to consume centuries of civilization, with indignation and sad disbelief. He wondered at man's persistently barbarous worship of that false idol of the tribe, *race,* which Sir Francis Bacon had warned against centuries ago. The racism that black Americans had struggled against for many generations had crystallized during these war years into Adolf Hitler's theories of the master race of Aryans. By 1939 this fascist concern with purity of race caused Tolson to muse on the racial origins of his own family and his youthful awakening to their significance. He noted sardonically the dangers that "certain high-placed German and Italian families" experienced when their family trees were shaken. Then he reminisced:

> In my boyhood I discovered that something was amazingly wrong with my family tree. That was twenty years before Mr. Hitler started shaking non-Aryan skeletons out of everybody's genealogical tree but his own. I have a vivid memory of the time when my little walnut-hued mother took me for a visit to the old Mark Twain country, which was the Promised Land of my ancestors and relatives.
>
> The clan which had produced so many gun-toting preachers and God-fearing badmen gathered to meet us. I was puzzled and shocked. I saw a variety of racial stocks: whites, half-whites, dark yellows, walnut browns, golden browns, reddish blacks, pot blacks, and some indescribable colors. They ranged in size from a 200-pounder who stood six feet and seven inches to a runty backwoods circuit rider.
>
> I saw blonds with wooly hair, blacks with silky hair, and browns with

1

curly hair. I saw eyes that were black, blue, brown, and gray. My Aunt Hilda's rich black tresses were so long that she could sit on them; and my Aunt Sarah's kinks were so short and tightly woven that she had to use a comb with long wide teeth. . . .

Add to these diversities a confusion of dialects, and you can imagine how difficult it was for my boy's mind to grasp the amazing fact that these were my "kinfolks." And these were also Negroes. Would a man from Mars believe it? What is a Negro? It is obvious that only a prejudice-blinded person would attempt to use scientifically the term *Negro* to include Walter White, the blond secretary of the NAACP, and Paul Robeson, the Sudanese-featured baritone and actor.[1]

The questions about the meaning of race raised by this early visit to his mother's relatives stayed with Tolson throughout his life, for they are questions intimately and durably woven into the fabric of American culture. For himself and for other Americans, white and black, he repeatedly tried to conceptualize these questions and their requisite answers. American culture characteristically makes its black writers sooner or later feel this as a major portion of their professional task. Like Sisyphus, Tolson toiled up that hill over and over, knowing that the question was clouded by such a variety of cultural interests and needs that a clear and compelling answer was virtually unattainable. But he at least resolved to attack the unreason that surrounds the issue, the same unreason vividly imaged in the boy's introduction to his own extended Missouri family, to attack it with telling wit and compelling moral appeal. Thus, twenty-six years later in "Psi" of *Harlem Gallery*, the epic poem that stirred some critics to claim greatness for Tolson, the Curator, who like Walter White is blond and light enough to be white when and if he chooses, but who chooses to live as an Afro-American, slyly points up the absurdity of race in America when he notes that he and Black Boy, who "is the color / of betel-stained teeth,"

> (from ocular proof
> that cannot goof)
> belong to races
> whose dust-of-the earth progenitors
> the Lord God Almighty created
> of different bloods,
> in antipodal places.

Then, turning to address White Boy, the Curator wryly suggests that white folks have created racial stereotypes according to their various appetites:

> The Negro is a dish in the white man's kitchen—
> a potpourri,
> an ala-podrida,

Jockeying Down the Years

a mixie-mashie
a hotch potch of lineal ingredients:
with UN guests at his table
the host finds himself a Hamlet on the spot,
for, in spite of his catholic pose,
the Negro dish is a dish nobody knows:
to some . . . tasty,
like an exotic condiment—
to others . . . unsavoury
and inelegant.

But the Curator also strikes a more somber note, a note that must have re-
verberated with personal memories of Tolson's Missouri youth. He points to
the mix of race and sex that dramatizes the barbarous inconsistencies of
American racism:

The dark hymens on the auction block,
the lord of the mansion knew the macabre score:
not a dog moved his tongue,
not a lamb lost a drop of blood to protect a door.
O
Xenos of Xanthos,
what midnight-to-dawn lecheries,
in cabin and big house,
produced these brown hybrids and yellow motleys?
White Boy,
Buchenwald is a melismatic song
whose single syllable is sung to blues notes
to dark wayfarers who listen for the gong
at the crack of doom along
. . . that lonesome Road . . .
before they travel on.

The ironic reference to Buchenwald suggests how deeply and persistently
World War II burned into Tolson's imagination the kinship of racism to
fascism both at home and abroad.

Little is known about Melvin Tolson's family prior to his father and
mother. Tolson seldom shook his family tree, and secondhand memories of
surviving family members contradict each other. Tolson's father and mother
were clearly both strong positive influences in his life, but there is only the
briefest mention of other family members of his parents' generation. The
only reference to any grandparent in Tolson's writing is the often repeated
sentence in *Caviar and Cabbage*, "I am the son of a preacher, who was the
son of a preacher, who was the son of a preacher," and this statement seems
more likely to be a deliberate fiction than a literal truth.

The earliest known record of Tolson's father, Alonzo, is a listing in the 1880 census. He is there described as a boy of ten under the name *Lanner*. The nicknames *Lon* and *Lonner*, as substitutes for *Alonzo*, later appear in church records of his early years as a Methodist minister. In 1880 Lanner lived with his older sister, Chaney, twenty-six, who was married to a Thomas Robertson. Robertson is listed as a farmer, and the family lived in Chariton Township, Howard County, Missouri, less than fifty miles from Moberly, where Melvin was born eighteen years later. Also listed in the household are Alonzo's brothers, Charley, twelve, and Chock, eight, and Thomas and Chaney's son, William. Three other Tolson siblings are remembered in the family—Mollie, Susie, and George—but they are not readily identifiable in the 1880 census. There is a possible listing of Susie in Prairie Township. It reads *Susan Tol*——, but the portion of the last name crossed out does not seem to be *son*. She lived with the family of Cliff and Ellen Hooten. She was black, nineteen, married, and "works in house."

Helen Tolson Wilson, Melvin's sister, remembers that Alonzo was one of six or possibly seven children born to the union of Suzie Tolson, once a slave, and her former white master, who characteristically goes unnamed in family discussion. This story indicates that the relationship began before the Civil War and continued after it. The failure to identify the father suggests an irregular relationship all too common in the time of slavery. The 1880 census information is consistent with this family memory. It indicates that Alonzo was raised in the household of his older sister. It is also part of the family memory that one of the sisters, Susie, passed for white. Melvin's feelings about this part of his family legacy were carefully guarded; however, at one point in a *Caviar and Cabbage* column concerned with color prejudice within the race, he indicates their intensity with pregnant understatement, "I had an aunt who was a good woman. But she believed that black persons are evil." He closed his column, "I've got Caucasian blood in my veins, but I'm ashamed to tell you how it got there."

In the obituary notice of Rev. Alonzo Tolson's death, his father is named Adam. No Adam Tolson appears in the 1880 census of Howard County. In 1870 there is an Adam Tolson listed, but he is black, seventy years old, living with his wife, Polly, and an unlikely father of Alonzo. By 1870, the year of Alonzo's birth, two branches of the white Tolson family, who had originally settled in Howard County after moving from Kentucky in 1819 and 1823 respectively, had achieved considerable prominence. One family in particular had at one time owned several slaves. Probably because of the prominence these families had achieved, by 1870 the Tolson name appeared frequently in Howard County, too frequently for all its bearers to be credibly biological heirs of these two families. Following the Civil War the Tolson name was probably assumed or assigned for a wide variety of reasons. But if Alonzo's father was white and was a member of a slave-owning Tolson family, he probably belonged to the family whose origins and development are thus described in *A History of Howard and Cooper Counties*, published in 1883:

> The Tolson family represents a type of citizenship that constitutes the substantial, intelligent element in every community. Industrious, conservative and energetic, they generally achieve a substantial success in whatever pursuit they follow, and appreciating the advantages of a reasonable knowledge, at least, of the information that can be derived only from books, they are almost invariably friends of education, and commonly rank among the more intelligent in their respective communities. Being usually well-to-do in life and satisfied with the conditions that surround them they are the first to go to the defense of the state against threatened invasion or violent changes in the form or methods of government. Such has been the character of the Tolsons from their first settlement in this country, prior to the revolution. . . . John Tolson, son of William, and the father of Judge Benjamin Tolson, was born February 3, 1791, in Stafford county, Virginia, where his grandfather first settled, but emigrated to Madison county, Kentucky, in 1810. After the close of the war of 1812 he returned to Madison county, and in a short time afterwards, January 12, 1815, was united in marriage to Miss Rebecca, daughter of Benjamin Howard, of the distinguished Howard family of Kentucky. Of this union nine children were born, of whom Judge Tolson was the eldest, and he was born in Madison county, Kentucky, January 10, 1816. In the fall of 1819 the family came to Missouri and settled in Howard county, where they made their permanent home, and here John Tolson died January 9, 1870, his wife having preceded him in death eight years—September 6, 1862. Speaking of the lives led, it has been said of them: "They both lived and died in the fellowship of the Baptist church. They lived peaceable and exemplary lives, and an old pioneer said of Mr. Tolson, that he was the best man he had ever known."

In 1966, the year of Tolson's death, Dan McCall made a perceptive observation about what distinguishes Tolson's poetry from much of the modern American tradition. Paradoxically, however, McCall's statement also indicates what Tolson's major contribution to that tradition was. McCall wrote particularly of Tolson's *Libretto for the Republic of Liberia*, but his observation applies broadly to all of Tolson's poetry:

> While the verse seems to be that of Pound in the *Cantos* or Eliot in *The Waste Land*, Tolson does not really belong in the modern American tradition of poetry. His main difference stems, first of all, from his refusal to accept a primary assumption of those who have shaped the tradition: poetry is an art of privacy. Tolson restores to the poet his function of singing to the community. There is a profoundly personal voice in his poetry, but it is not a private one: in the *Libretto* he addresses himself to the Republic. That poetry of such difficulty should be intended for a wide audience indicates that

> Tolson conceives of his poem as a kind of master singing-book for the country, a storehouse of education for the Futurafrique. His achievement is that he can write about it without becoming hollowly official.[2]

Throughout his life Melvin Tolson discounted and at times denied the significance of merely personal experience. He did not savor the intimate personal detail about himself or others, the "art of privacy," unless it had relatively clear public significance. His concern for the social, the public, well-being was persistent and praiseworthy. It eventually became, as McCall correctly observes, a notable characteristic of his mature poetic style. One can only speculate on the extent to which this characteristic is rooted in his father's early family history. It is apparent that Rev. Alonzo Tolson deliberately established a most publicly respectable and responsible family and equally deliberately repressed any family awareness of or concern with the intimate private responsibility of his white father.

Tolson's mother's maiden name was Lera Ann Hurt. She was born in Missouri in December 1877, but she is not identifiable in the 1880 census. Melvin's sister Helen remembers both of Lera's parents as Cherokee Indians. She remembers that Lera's mother had a home in Moberly and that Lera's father lived out from Moberly, only visiting the family for short stays because he disliked white men. Lera loved music and sang beautifully and enthusiastically. She was also an accomplished seamstress.

Melvin remembers his mother's origins differently, but, like his sister, he remembers her with pride:

> She was a descendant of varicolored fugitives who hid themselves on the islands in the Mark Twain country in the gloom of the Ozarks, from which they raided the slave populations along the Missouri and the Mississippi. They were a taciturn, hot-blooded clan that produced gun-toting preachers and praying badmen. One joined Jesse James and disappeared in the Bad Lands; another, unfrocked, blew the lock off a church door, defied the Law, and preached the gospel of Jesus Christ with his Forty-Five on one side of the pulpit and his Bible on the other. The little walnut-hued woman was fiercely proud of being an American Negro, although in her veins flowed Irish, French, Indian, and African blood.

Tolson's parents were citizens of the midwestern frontier at a time when racial boundaries were only erratically proscribed by custom. Slavery was still a recent historical issue, and it had left a legacy of strong and violent convictions. Missouri entered the Union as a slave state. Howard County, as its name implies, had particularly strong associations with the southern tradition of Virginia, although most of its original white settlers had stopped in Kentucky before moving to Missouri. Most of the state was controlled by Union forces during the Civil War, although the federal troops continually had to resist the attacks of local guerrilla forces as well as the challenge of the Rebel army. Slavery was abolished as a consequence of the Civil War, but the restrictive conventions of racial segregation, which became increasingly institutionalized during Reconstruction, were often yet matters of open contention. Nonetheless, individual freedom was a frontier theme of deep conviction for both black and white, and it was defended with the Gospel and the .45 with rough equality.

Lera Hurt and Alonzo Tolson were married in Salisbury in 1893. They lost two children before Melvin was born. In his middle age, as he became increasingly well known as a public figure, Melvin listed his birthdate as 6 February 1900 and his place of birth as Moberly, Missouri. His own family accepted that date until Melvin, Jr., in the summer of 1978, discovered with surprise that the 1900 census lists the Tolson family as living in the town of New Franklin, Franklin Township, Howard County, Missouri. Melvin, Sr., is listed as two years old. Helen, Melvin's sister, is listed as four months old, and Lera's sister, Victoria, as fourteen years of age, living with the family, and attending school. Tolson's transcript from Lincoln University corroborates the date of his birth as 1898. There is no obvious explanation for Tolson's claiming 1900 as the year of his birth, although there are numerous other discrepancies of dates and places in Tolson's memories of his youth.[3]

In the 1900 *Journal of the Fourteenth Session of the Central Missouri Conference of the Methodist Episcopal Church*, Lon A. Tolson is listed as having been received on trial. A year later, in the fifteenth session, he is listed as "in studies of second year." This would indicate that Alonzo formally joined the Central Missouri Conference shortly after Melvin's birth. Whether he preached earlier under less formal sponsorship is unknown. As a Methodist minister, Alonzo was compelled to move his family often during Tolson's childhood. His assignments after Melvin's birth included Higbee, New Franklin, New Bloomfield (in the St. Joseph district), De Soto, and Slater, Missouri. Then the family moved to Oskaloosa and Mason City, Iowa, both of which were considered a part of the St. Joseph district of the Central Missouri Conference of the M. E. Church, before returning to Missouri for a post in Independence, probably in 1916.

The Methodist tradition with which Alonzo vigorously identified himself supported the values of learning as well as those of morality. Alonzo lived according to that tradition and passed those values on to his son. Although he only completed the eighth grade, he took a number of correspondence courses and taught himself Latin, Hebrew, and Greek. His independent educational efforts apparently made him skeptical of the value of a formal college education, and Melvin always credited his mother with encouraging him to go on to Fisk and Lincoln universities.

Later Tolson was to follow a similar pattern with his own children. As a faculty member with only a B.A. degree, he was often rather defensively scornful of the pretentiousness of others who claimed status because of their advanced degrees. He insisted that learning was not a matter of degrees but of individual achievement, and he was ready at the drop of a hat to test his own learning against any and all comers, especially Ph.D.'s. Nevertheless, he early impressed upon his sons the advisability of earning "that union card, the Ph.D." The Great Depression of the thirties, when his sons were growing into manhood, underscored his fears for their futures. All of them remember that it was assumed from early adolescence that they would earn Ph.D.'s, and they did. Ruth, Tolson's wife, finished her B.A. and earned an M.A. after their marriage, and Ruth Marie, his daughter, completed an M.A. Degrees were a matter of social utility. Learning, however, was prized for the power and insight it gave the individual to live his own life.

Joy Flasch, Tolson's colleague and first biographer, to whom he provided invaluable information in frequent conversations, gave this picture of Alonzo as a caring father:

> His [Melvin's] father was a good provider who gardened, kept the cellar full and was handy around the house. He enjoyed hunting but one day when his four small children [Rubert and Yutha were born after Melvin and Helen] were standing in front of him stairstep fashion, watching him clean his gun, it suddenly discharged and a bullet whizzed directly over their heads. He never hunted again.[4]

In "The Odyssey of a Manuscript," Tolson pays tribute to his mother as the inspiring force of his poetic career and as a counterforce to Gertrude Stein, who cavalierly dismissed the historic legacy of black Americans:

> In Paris, the pleonastic Gertrude Stein wrote at 27 Rue de Fleurus that Negroes suffer from nothingness. Years and years before, my mother had made the same discovery in a small town on the upheaved flats of Iowa. An old Bantu scholar with tribal holes in his ears and an Oxford accent, used to come to our house. Mother cooked chicken pie so that he would regale her children with tales of black heroes and poets and artists. The emaciated Bantu paraded across the dinner table the dramatic figures of Alexander Pushkin, El-Hadj Omar, Crispus Attucks, Alexandre Dumas, Antar, Estevanico, Toussaint L'Ouverture, Menelik, and Frederick Douglass. At such times she watched closely our childish expressions, her black eyes avid coals in the mask of her Mongolian face. When the little Bantu scholar had departed with his inevitable satchel of books and manuscripts, mother would exclaim, "Hitch your wagon to a star!" The ancient proverb became a thing of living eloquence. Mother was bed-ridden with cancer for a year. In the room was a terrible stench . . . and her serenity of spirit. One night as I

sat holding her fleshless hand, she said to me: "Son, I always wanted to write. I had many things to tell people. But now that I am going to die, you'll have to do it for me."[5]

Lera died 1 April 1934. Tolson was then writing A *Gallery of Harlem Portraits,* his first book of poems and the true beginning of his professional poetic career. His mother's death at that time strongly underscored his associations of her with his hopes and ambitions as a writer.

In an interview published in *Anger and Beyond,* Tolson was reminded of another moment of his childhood by the interviewer's suggestion of the close association between his poetry and the art of painting. He remembered painting pictures by the age of three or four, and by the age of ten he was framing and selling his paintings for "big money for a little black boy." At twelve he had a tent show with Claude, a prodigy who could versify anything and invent mechanical toys. Tolson painted the scenery and played Caesar to Claude's Macduff, but because of Claude's interest in girls, their profits frequently came up short. The tent show took place in Slater, Missouri, where Alonzo's church and parsonage sat across from the old Chicago and Alton tracks.

I remember that there was a big roundhouse in Slater at that time. One afternoon, a crack train had a "hot-box" across the road and down the embankment from our house. I was in the yard painting a picture. I don't know whether it was Coleridge's "Inspiration" or Cocteau's "Expiration." Anyway I forgot about the stalled express train and was in the middle of my artwork when I felt, yes, sensed something behind me. I turned suddenly and there stood, leaning on the fence, the very artist I had seen in my art books. He had bushy hair and a magnificent beard. He wore a Byronic collar, an artist's jacket, and an artist's beret. His eyes fixed on mine, he said in Frenchified English, with a grandiloquent flourish: "Marvelous! Marvelous! You must go to Paris with me! Where is your father?" At last my dream had come true! As I ran to the house, I could see in the mind's eye the studios and cafes on the Left Bank of the Seine. I blurted out the good news. My mother stood aghast for a moment. Then she parted the curtains and took an angry look at the bizarre figure leaning on the fence. Suddenly she began to lock every door in the house. As she raced from room to room she said not a word. That was just like my mother—part Negro and part Indian. After that boyhood tragedy, I never painted another picture. For days and days, I brooded. Now, my mother was always making up verses in her head. She was highly intelligent and imaginative, but had little formal education. Like my father, I was a bookworm. Later, much later, I began scribbling verses on tablets and scraps of paper. I repeated, over and over and over, Shakespeare's immortal words in Sonnet 50:

> Not marble, nor the guilded monuments
> Of princes, shall outlive this powerful rhyme.

So, at twelve, I decided to join the immortal poets in a future Paradise.[6]

Tolson told this story on several different occasions. Ostensibly he told it to explain the interest in the visual arts that runs so explicitly throughout his poetry. Yet the story also reveals another theme. Tolson always loved to travel, both intellectually and geographically. He loved trains and the adventures they promised. He belonged to a generation of writers of whom some received a fabled Bohemian artistic education on the Left Bank in Paris. He envied their freedom to live primarily for their art, but he also came to resent their distance, their escape, from the racially and economically oppressed world that he knew. On one occasion he referred to the expatriates in Gertrude Stein's circle as "spiritual nudists." Tolson early chose to be committedly married to his wife, to his family, to his community. He consistently defined art in terms of its function within the social world. In the above story he treats his mother's fear of the stranger with affectionate humor. Her decision, however, turned him fatefully from being a painter to being a poet. One could stay at home and be a poet. The painter's world seemed so temptingly, yet threateningly, exotic and free.[7]

Reconciling the world of the artist and the world of the citizen became a constant struggle for Tolson. For him, the artist at his best inspirits the social world through his insight and his talent for vividly expressing his vision, causing the world to strive toward a nobler and more just realization of community. At his worst, the artist loses touch with the real needs and problems of his community and becomes narcissistic either by himself or in coterie. But Tolson's early intense concern with art sometimes caused him to represent the Parisian Left Bank post–World War I experience in sharply contrasting ways. In *All Aboard*, a novel Tolson began writing in the thirties, he created a German character, Herron Stafen, whom Duke Hands, the novel's protagonist, meets on a Pullman coach. Describing Stafen's history, Tolson fervently revealed the Parisian artistic world as an idealized fantasy of a truly democratic artistic community. Indeed this Paris seems an extension of the happy cultural pluralism of the Harlem of the Renaissance, which Tolson was to discover belatedly but treasure in his imagination all of his life:

> The three summers young Herron spent in Paris were the happiest days of his life. In the Butte Montmartre he came to know Apollinaire and Picasso, and the latter, whom he considered a god, gave him a slap on the shoulder and a word of praise. Among grubby artists and poets, dancers and playwrights, he found the kinship of spirit he had hungered for all his life. In the cafes, the bals musette, the gin mills, the night clubs, he lost the norms

of his caste and discovered freedom in the melting-pot of races and isms. Arm in arm on the street, elbow to elbow in the bistro, nobleman and prostitute, Jugo-Slav and Harlem Negro—the boon companions, bearded vagabonds, drank piccolo and beer and rum while vociferating the issues of Art and Literature.[8]

Joy Flasch has recorded another story that Tolson often repeated of his youth. The story concerns an instance of racial realization precipitated by a sensitive and motherly white woman:

About the time that Tolson was discovering the arts, he became acquainted with Mrs. George Markwell, a white lady who made her library available to the youngster who read everything to which he had access. In her home he had his first experience with racial prejudice when Mrs. Markwell's daughter told him one day that "The only Negro of worth is Booker T. Washington, and the only reason he excelled is that he is half white. He would have been greater if he had been white." When Melvin asked her mother if this statement were true, Mrs. Markwell did not reply; instead, she sent him to the bookshelf for a copy of Thomas Carlyle's *French Revolution* and told him to look through the illustrations until he found the answer himself. As he scanned the pages, he came to a picture of a magnificent white stallion on which was mounted a jet-black man resplendent in uniform—Toussaint L'Ouverture. He never forgot the lesson, and in the years ahead racial pride became one of the chief themes of his conversations, lectures and poetry.[9]

Not all of Tolson's memories of his Missouri youth were so dramatic. More subdued impressions stayed with him only to be fully realized later. Such memories indicate how strongly his life became marked by the midwestern environment of his early years. In a *Caviar and Cabbage* column he recalled a Missouri farmer, "an ordinary man to most people, who was a great hero to me."

One day I saw the old man plowing in his field. He was trying to whip Nature. Now, the poets, in most cases, have painted Nature as something beautiful. But I have seen Nature in her ugly moments. So had that old farmer. He had to fight Nature all day. Nature was bent on the destruction of the crop that would feed his children. While he slept, Nature tried to choke the corn and wheat, with evil weeds. During the day Nature scorched the old farmer's acres and burnt his crops. I heard the old farmer sing to himself:

Hold on, hold on!
Keep your hand on the plow,
Hold on!

The stubborn earth made the going rough. Hard times in the field and hard times in the old farmer's house. Perhaps he said to himself: "What's the use?" The mule was hardheaded, like some people I know. The plow jerked and revolted. The old farmer sweated and tugged. Then the old farmer's Soul said to his Body: "Keep your hand on the plow. Hold on!"

Tolson then regretted that neither Edwin Markham nor Jean François Millet saw that old black farmer in Missouri. "He was worthy of both a picture and a poem."[10]

From Slater the Tolson family moved to Oskaloosa, Iowa, where Tolson's first poem was published. According to Tolson this was at the age of twelve, but since the subject of the poem is the sinking of the *Titanic* and that occurred on 14 April 1912, he must have been at least fourteen. In "The Odyssey of a Manuscript" Tolson gave a vividly self-mocking description of his adolescent preoccupation with poetry, a description that strongly echoes the familiar hyperbole of Mark Twain: "I scorned the prosaic Jewish and Italian and Polish boys, wore a Windsor tie, and affected the mannerisms of the poets we studied." He then described how, "rocketed into a Parnassian frenzy," he composed his twenty-five-stanza ballad commemorating "The Wreck of the *Titanic*":

The God-driven iceberg in the ballad struck when the drunken revelry was wildest. Glowing stanzas haloed the death of the missionary on his way to Darkest Africa. He was on his knees smiling angelically, hands clasped piously on his breast, deep set eyes fixed on the New Jerusalem, as the ship plunged into the watery caverns. Then my poet's candid camera focused on an infidel, his face ravaged with vices, blanched with fear, as he implored the unanswering heavens to save him from the wrath of an angry God! Taking a cue from William Cullen Bryant, I closed with a climactic apostrophe to the Deity. I was now ready for the Hall of Fame, if not for Westminster Abbey. Several elderly ladies sent in letters burning with religious praise. A white Baptist preacher made the poem the basis for his Sunday sermon. There was some sniveling in the congregation. Tearfully, he concluded: "And a little child shall lead them."

Tolson followed this with a deflating paragraph of oblique social realism:

One afternoon I encountered the Local Socialist on the courthouse square. He was a notorious infidel who went about chuckling that the worst enemies of Jesus were the Christians. He said that if Jesus came to our town saying, "Take what thou hast and give it to the poor," Jesus would catch hell from the Christians! You see what kind of rascal he was. He stopped me and asked with a satanic smile if I had read *Bunk Shooters of Our Time*. I told him I hadn't. He chuckled: "I thought so. Read it before you ruin your next poem." I asked my English teacher about the book and she told me indignantly that the old man was crazy![11]

Joy Flasch wrote that Tolson "learned all he knew" about public speaking from his eighth-grade teacher after the family moved from Oskaloosa to Mason City. "The Odyssey of a Manuscript" places what seems to be the same teacher in Oskaloosa:

> The good woman consumed long hours perfecting my platform manner. She was amply rewarded. No swarthy organ-grinder was ever prouder of a trick-performing monkey. The principal called a special meeting in the school auditorium so that the teachers and students might hear that which was destined for the eyes and ears of posterity! My maiden teacher led me in triumph before the audiences in neighboring towns. On such pilgrimages she warned me against bad little girls who steal the virtue of poets. She pictured their blandishments, quoting the *Proverbs*. As I went along dark streets I had a fearful yearning to meet a strange woman "with the attire of a harlot, and subtle of heart." The good woman called me "the Negro Longfellow," and on the playground a roguish Irish lad changed this to "the nigger Shortfeller." On being reported, he had to remain after school hours and copy Milton's *The Doctrine and Discipline of Divorce Restored to the Good of Both Sexes*. The Saturday after we received our diplomas the Irish boy ambushed me, called me a name that Ernest Hemingway wouldn't write or Sinclair Lewis speak, and made my eye a shade darker. I solaced myself with the thought that poets have always been the victims of man's inhumanity to man. Thus I jockeyed down the years on Pegasus.[12]

Whether Tolson learned the art of public speaking in Oskaloosa or in Mason City, it remained keenly important to him throughout his life. He was a notable performer as speaker, debater, reader, and actor. He became an extraordinarily successful debate coach and a more than competent collegiate dramatic director. The skills of public speaking worked their way into his poetry explicitly in frequent dramatic roles and implicitly in the emphasis he placed on experimenting with sound patterns.

However, the first money he received from writing a poem came in surprising fashion. Tolson related the story in *Caviar and Cabbage*:

> Thanksgiving Day: Mason City, Iowa, 1917. It was a blustery afternoon. The barber shop where I shined shoes was closed. It was located on Main Street and catered to whites. My father was the pastor of the only Negro church in Mason City. The white "Christians" had built the church so that they wouldn't have to worship with their dark brothers and sisters!
>
> I was sitting at a small table in the barber shop, writing a poem for the Sunday edition of the white daily. I heard a sudden noise. I looked up and saw a blonde woman in a fur coat enter and slam the door.
>
> "Don't tell him I'm here," she said breathlessly, and ran into the small room at the rear.

About two or three minutes later a white man rushed in, hatless and excited. Curses against the woman roared from his lips. I saw the revolver in his hand.

"Did you see her?" he yelled. "Did she come in here?"

"All of our customers are men," I said.

He cursed again, hesitated a moment, and stormed out into the blustery street. In about ten minutes the woman reappeared.

"Kid," she said, "you saved my hide."

She pulled her fur coat together at the throat and walked to the table where I sat. She tossed a crumpled bill upon the sheet containing my poem. It was a five-spot. And the first money I ever received from writing.[13]

Tolson's memory for dates is once more mistaken. On Thanksgiving Day 1917 the Tolson family was living in Independence, Missouri, and that year Tolson was attending Lincoln High School in Kansas City. However, the Tolson family did live in Mason City from late 1914 or early in 1915 until 1916. By this time he had begun working at a variety of part-time jobs to supplement the family income. In *Caviar and Cabbage* he told another story set in Iowa from which he drew a disillusioning lesson in race and economics:

As a boy in a small Iowa town my dearest friend was a Jewish boy. I used to hear his mother and father talk about the rich Jews who would have nothing to do with the poor Jews. As a young man, I was a shipping clerk in a Jewish fashion store that employed sixty-two persons. Only three Jews worked in that store. I wondered why. I asked the sophisticated Jewish manager. He liked me because I liked books.

As I was putting the price tag on a gorgeous dress, Mr. X said: "My customers object to Jewish saleswomen."

I made the silly comment, "But you are a Jew."

Mr. X. laughed and said: "MB, some day you'll discover that the dollar is more important than race."

We learn slowly. The best of us.[14]

Tolson wrote of his young friend on another occasion:

Out there on the upheaved flats of Iowa, when I was a boy, the first pal I ever had was a Jew. Little Joe, I called him. We played together, ate together, slept together. A hooked nose, a black skin. It didn't matter. Side by side, Little Joe and I fought off black boys or white. It didn't matter. But the world which the mouth-Christians and the one-hundred-per-cent Americans have made is a hard world, a cruel world. Joe was to learn the dishonor in the word *nigger*. (I hope the editor doesn't delete the word.) I want you to get the full impact of its infamy. I want it to slap you in the face as it has slapped me in the face. As *kike* has slammed little Joe on the chin.[15]

Later, in the proletarian politics of the thirties, Tolson learned how to make the ugly ethnic slurs of American prejudice into verbal weapons for rallying class pride. In "The Underdogs," the closing poem of A *Gallery of Harlem Portraits*, his first epic attempt to represent modern black America through a particular place and particular community, he wrote:

Sambo, nigger, son of a bitch
I came from the loins
Of the great white masters.

Kikes and bohunks and wops,
Dagos and niggers and crackers . . .
Starved and lousy,
Blind and stinking—
We fought each other,
Killed each other,
Because the great white masters
Played us against each other.

Then a kike said: *Workers of the world, unite!*
And a dago said: *Let us live!*
And a cracker said: *Ours for us!*
And a nigger said: *Walk together, children!*

WE ARE THE UNDERDOGS
ON A HOT TRAIL!

"The Underdogs" was written in the early thirties. Tolson then saw himself as part of a new wave of young black leaders emphasizing class as the key concept for the Negro in his struggle to achieve full freedom of opportunity and participation. By the late thirties, World War II had begun, and the argument over U.S. involvement in the war grew more and more heated until the attack on Pearl Harbor. Uniting ethnic minorities to fight a common class struggle took on increasingly patriotic overtones. Whitman became for Tolson an even more explicit literary model than he had been. America should not simply be lauded; its democratic ideals and promises should be made the standard of its performance. Its eidolons should be proclaimed as a poetic and prophetic force that would shape historical reality. Tolson set about building a better world, a better home.

Thus by the time "Rendezvous with America" was published in 1942 he had found still another poetic use for popular ethnic slurs:

A blind man said,
"Look at the kikes."
And I saw

Melvin B. Tolson

Rosenwald sowing the seeds of culture in the Black Belt,
Michelson measuring the odysseys of invisible worlds,
Brandeis opening the eyes of the blind to the Constitution,
Boas translating the oneness in the Rosetta stone of mankind.

A blind man said,
"Look at the dagos."
And I saw
LaGuardia shaping the cosmos of pyramided Manhattan,
Brumidi verving the Capitol frescoes of *Washington at Yorktown*,
Caruso scaling the Alpine ranges of drama with the staff of song,
Toscanini enchanting earthward the music of the spheres.

A blind man said,
"Look at the chinks."
And I saw
Lin Yutang crying the World Charter in the white man's wilderness,
Dr. Chen charting the voyages of bacteria in the Lily laboratories,
Lu Cong weaving plant-tapestries in the Department of Agriculture,
Madame Chiang Kai-shek interpreting the Orient and the Occident.

A blind man said,
"Look at the bohunks."
And I saw
Sikorsky blue-printing the cabala of the airways,
Stokowski imprisoning the magic of symphonies with a baton,
Zvak erecting St. Patrick's Cathedral in a forest of skyscrapers,
Dvorak enwombing the multiple soul of the New World.

A blind man said,
"Look at the niggers."
And I saw
Black Samson mowing down Hessians with a scythe at Brandywine,
Marian Anderson bewitching continents with the talisman of art,
Fred Douglass hurling from tombstones the philippics of freedom,
Private Brooks dying at the feet of MacArthur in Bataan.

All this was part of a prophetic definition of America as

An international river with a legion of tributaries!
A magnificent cosmorama with myriad patterns and colors!
A giant forest with loin-roots in a hundred lands!
A cosmopolitan orchestra with a thousand instruments playing
America!

In the small midwestern towns of Iowa and Missouri, as well as in the intensely urban world of Harlem, the ethnic underclasses held the key to the full realization of the American dream.

But the two poems and the two stories by Tolson published in his Kansas City high school yearbook, the *Lincolnian*, in 1917 and 1918 are innocent of the national and international themes that marked the early years of his professional publishing career. Tolson's first story, "The Cabin's Victim," indicates clearly that he did indeed have an extraordinarily precocious writing talent. The story begins with a young man "wandering in a distant part of our Southern Paradise," a region remote from the scenes of modern activities: "The cool-breathed wind of the sea was in my nostrils and the incessant booming of the waters among the rocks filled my very soul with a weird feeling of the magnitude of Nature's God and the magniloquence of his speech." But the young man's cosmic tranquillity is interrupted by the unexpected sound of other voices. Instinctively he steps aside. Hidden, he observes two strangers appear single file. And here Tolson demonstrated a very early talent for creating striking images and handling complex syntax: "The foremost was a giant of a man: broad and deep-chested, with a hard weather-beaten face and swaggering gait like a lark under a veering breeze. The other was a short, solid built fellow, unkempt, dirty-visaged, with a lewd repulsive countenance and split upperlip."

The two men sense the narrator's presence and lay a trap for him by deliberately arousing his suspicions in thinly veiled sailors' talk. He unsuccessfully puzzles over the enigma of their words until he comes upon "an ebony-colored shieling situated among a few sage brushes." In the hut he stumbles on a corpse. He is beginning to realize that the two murderers are aware of his presence when he is suddenly thrown with such force that "the world became chaos and I oblivious." The young man awakens to find himself rescued by the "erubescent daughter of an inveterate fisherman" who lived nearby. The story ends with the young man expressing his gratitude and the clear suggestion that his free and lonely wanderings are soon to be channeled into a domestic harbor:

> "Thank you, thank you!—"
> "Baby saved your life," he roared, casting a mischievous glance at his daughter.
> "That's what I hear," and I murmured to myself, "Deo Gratias for such as she."

This story prefigures basic themes that recurred throughout Tolson's career. Implicitly, the values of sensitivity and esoteric learning—the narrator has spent "years of laborious research" in "Egyptology, the mystic hieroglyphics of the Chinese, the organic and philosophic works of Marcus de Deanastus, the Arabic and Moorish symbols and many involved cosmic sciences"—are tested by a confrontation with brutal reality imaged in the violent death of the stranger whose "wild and repulsive physiognomy" was "furrowed by the tribulation and dissipation of years." The narrator is rescued from this confrontation by a woman who seems likely to end his wandering ways and anchor his life in the security of home. The story echoes and reinforces the theme of Tolson's experience with the stranger who stepped off the train in Slater and invited him to Paris to become an artist. Domesticity is the anchor against the powerful and dangerous currents drawing one to exotic adventure.

Less than four years after the publication of this story in *The Lincolnian*, Tolson sat on the beach at Atlantic City with his bride-to-be Ruth Southall and gathered the impressions he later made into a poem, "My Soul and I," dedicated to her. Thus he would live in life what he imagined in fiction. But unquestionably his marriage and the family that followed were to test his commitment in ways he could not yet imagine in fiction.

"Wanderers in the Sierra," published in *The Lincolnian* during Tolson's senior year, is even more melodramatic than "The Cabin's Victim" and even more clearly imitative of Edgar Allan Poe. The story is prefaced with verse:

> My soul is like a stagnant pool
> In a desert bleak and wild,
> Where every wind is dry as dust
> And nature fails to smile.
> Like one forsaken and forlorn,
> On a grey, cloud-shrouded shore,
> I rue the day that I was born
> And weep for Ellanore.

The narrator is a disdainfully effete young man who has tried his fortune in the West but is lamenting that his adventures have caused him to lose contact with Ellanore, the love of his young life. He briefly joins forces with Louis McNaster, a young man of similar tastes and sorrow, and, after unburdening themselves to each other, they go their separate ways seeking their lost loves. With little explanation, Tolson has his young man seek and find his Ellanore in a lonely western desert where he rescues her from a villain who kills her father and threatens her. However, as they embrace, the villain, presumed dead, sustains life just long enough to shoot Ellanore, who dies in the narrator's arms. The narrator closes his story with melancholy stoicism:

> The storm is still raging without, but what care I for what the gods will. I have played my game and lost. Now I only wait for Death and a silent grave. Somewhere, beyond the mystic veil, Ellanore and the old man are waiting. Ah the brumal evening is as cold as my heart. I stare into the Plutonian shadows, silently.

Melvin B. Tolson, as he appeared in the Lincoln High School
yearbook of the class of 1918.

Melvin B. Tolson

The name of the narrator, Marcus DuBois, is noteworthy. Nothing in the story suggests a racial theme. The characters are without racial designations. Ellanore has wavy raven hair and in a moment of terror is pale of face. The narrator is a graduate of Northwestern University. There is little evidence that is any more racially telling. But considering that Marcus Garvey formed his United Negro Improvement Association in 1917 and that W. E. B. DuBois was an early and constant critic of Garvey's plans, the name *Marcus DuBois* has cryptic implications that look forward to the elaborately coded language of *Libretto* and *Harlem Gallery*.

There is no such ambiguity or coyness in Tolson's class poem, "The Past, Present, and Future," in the same yearbook as "Wanderers in the Sierra." It unambiguously attempts to rally a black audience:

> Our hearts beat fast, our eyes flame with desire!
> Our souls long for the battle-smoke of strife!
> These very walls instill the eternal fire
> That make men winners in the race of life.
> The maxims taught will make both mind and bones
> Fit for the mighty trials we all must bear;
> But out of them we'll fashion stepping stones,
> In black misfortunes we shall not despair.

In "Retrospection," the poem published the year before in *The Lincolnian*, Tolson drew an elderly narrator, who dozes and remembers two childhood experiences. The first is a boyhood mock war in which he is so engrossed that he loses a sense of time and stays out too late. His mother punishes him by confining him to a room he remembers in exaggerated terror. The second memory comes after the narrator is roused from his doze by his hand touching a hot stove. As he drifts back to sleep, he remembers a school presided over by a sternly effective master. Here the terror at the prospect of punishment seems infused with respect.

The poem's theme is not explicit. It voices the fear of punishment felt by the narrator as a young man, and it implies with dramatic irony the stern necessity and righteousness of discipline. Tolson's experience of discipline both at home and in school apparently was rigorous without being oppressive. Tolson's few published memories of his father suggest that his father was a very earnest, proud man, who expected much of his children and himself.

The curriculum of Lincoln High School in those days was also demanding, particularly in languages and literature, compared to modern curricula. Although Tolson only attended Lincoln for his junior and senior years, a student in Tolson's class who had spent all four years at Lincoln would have studied four years of Latin and two years of German in addition to a course in English, rhetoric, or English literature for each of eight semesters. Tolson valued the training he received and himself became a demanding, if popular, taskmaster as a teacher. He was frequently mockingly skeptical, if not outright contemptuous, of the substitutions made in more "progressive" courses for strong language training.

Helen attended Lincoln High School for a full four years, and she remembers her brother taking a strongly protective interest in her enrollment and attendance. Attending a completely segregated school was a new experience for her. During this time Alonzo Tolson was assigned a new church position almost every year, two of them at some distance from Independence and Kansas City—Wellington in 1918 and Blackburn Circuit in 1919—but apparently the family continued to live in Independence so that the children could attend high school without interruption, until they moved to 2509 Grove Street, Kansas City, in 1919 or 1920.

Tolson later often spoke of having worked at a great variety of jobs during his youth. Many of these are vividly associated with this period when he was finishing high school. Many years later President Truman's criticism of black students who used passive resistance to attain their civil rights occasioned a memory that is written in the third person among Tolson's unpublished manuscripts.

Langston Hughes has called Tolson a great talker. Well, back there, as a boy unconscious of Race, he argued with the white customers as he shined their shoes: ex-Indian Fighters, friends of Jesse James, Civil War bushwhackers, Ku Kluxers, and politicians. His father, the Reverend Alonzo Tolson, was a fire-brand Republican in the Abe Lincoln tradition.

He remembers that Reverend Tolson once said of Harry S. Truman: "He's a good and brave man in a bad party."

Mayor Tolson remembers that his father said to an interracial audience on our first Armistice Day in Independence: "Democracy means equality. So there are only two kinds: a democracy of nobodies or a democracy of somebodies. Which do you want?"

Mayor Tolson says that once a high church official called Reverend Tolson a liar during a trustee meeting. His Pa collared that gentleman, raised his fist, and declared: "I'll strike you down in the name of God!"

That was the atmosphere of Independence in which both Harry S. Truman and M. B. Tolson came up as boys. Is there any wonder, then, that Tolson is shocked by Truman's statement against student passive resistance for Civil Rights.[16]

Explaining the symbolism of the Big House as it appears in southern culture and particularly in the movie *Gone with the Wind*, Tolson also remembered an illustrative Big House experience from these Kansas City years:

"I used to work in the wealthy country club district of Kansas City, Mo. Many times, as I cleaned the drawing-room, through the open windows came the stench of the packinghouses in the river bottoms."[17] Tolson also worked in those packinghouses, and in another *Caviar and Cabbage* column he described in precise and colorful detail his initiation to the meaning of class:

> Every morning I crossed the river into Kansas, with men of all nationalities and races. Wage slavery makes men hard; so I lost some of the softness of the poet.
>
> First, I was a trucker. I pulled five times my weight. The 200-pounders laughed at me on the loading-dock. But in three weeks I was leading the gang. I'd learned the physics of trucking. We went underground to get boxes of meat, where it was 18 degrees below zero. Then we came up on the docks, where it was hot as a furnace. Some of the truckers died of TB. But I was lucky. I scoffed at the Abe Lincolns in the Labor movement who wanted to set Labor free. I thought the unionists racketeers. It took me years to find out that I was a fool. College economics taught me nothing about every-day economics. Yet the late Justice Brandeis commended me as a college debater. Something was wrong.
>
> I hated the packinghouse world. I intended to escape through my college training. The men called me The Kid. They admired my toughness. The Boss boasted about me. He said The Company liked men like me. I usually ate my supper at midnight. You see, I was so tired when I got home that I went to sleep.
>
> The Boss promoted me. I became a loader of refrigerator cars. I could heave a quarter-beef to a hook. I got time-and-a-half for overtime. I was coming up in The Company. Sometimes, when there was a rush, bosses from the Big Office in long white coats came down to the docks. I was the lightest loader and the fastest. Later, I would overhear the bosses cursing the bigger and older hands. I saw the reason for that ten years later. . . .
>
> We worked under miserable conditions. Men stood in water all day. They were always scared of losing their jobs. Most of them bowed under debts. We had the eight-hour day, but we were killing as many hogs in eight hours as we'd killed in ten. This was the SPEED UP. The men grumbled, cursed.
>
> I was on The Tub. Five men set the pace for ten thousand workers in the packinghouse. First, there was the huge German downstairs who stuck the hogs as they passed on a long chain. In five minutes, he was covered with blood. He drank blood—and said nothing to anybody. Everybody feared him. Some said he'd cut a man's throat as soon as a hog's.
>
> Second, there was the Negro dropper. He stood above The Tub and dropped hogs from a turntable into tons of boiling water. He sang blues as he set the killing pace. One day I tried to do his job. A mammoth hog, in its death agony, almost hurled me into the Tub.
>
> Third, there was Old Man Jeff. Old-timers said he was slipping; yet he

could souse hogs faster than a cat can lick its paw. Fourth, there was the little Mexican who hooked the hogs to the dehairing machine. His hands were faster than Joe Louis's punches. Fifth, there was the big black man who split the hogs. With one mighty blow, he could half a 600-pounder. Stripped to the waist, his huge muscles worked like big ebony snakes.

These five men who set the killing pace received big wages. The dirty radicals told the boys WHY. The Company used these five experts to speed up ten thousand men. So the strike came.

One morning, as I attempted to enter the plant, I discovered pickets outside. I didn't want to quit work. I had to make enough money to get to college. Fights started here and there. The workers argued with the five pacesetters. They didn't want to strike. The workers told them about the bad working conditions, the speed up, the poor wages, the women and kids at home without proper food and clothing. The black hog-splitter and the German sticker started in anyway. The angry crowd beat them up. Negroes beat up Negroes. Mexicans beat up Mexicans. Blacks and whites beat up whites.

I couldn't understand that. Negro misleaders hadn't told me anything about the class struggle. I'd thought that whites were always arrayed against blacks. I didn't know that the struggle between Capital and Labor breaks down racial barriers. Then years later I understood. But I didn't learn the lesson in either college or the university.[18]

Late in the thirties Tolson regretted that at the time he did not recognize the value of such work experiences for an ambitious writer. As a student he was more interested in academic success as an escape from the necessity of such grueling physical labor. His strong proletarian convictions did not develop until the thirties, several years after he had married and begun teaching at Wiley College.

Tolson dated his packinghouse experience during the First World War, the "summer before I enlisted," after three years of training as a cadet officer. The date and location seem to be another Missouri *stretcher*. Tolson never enlisted in the army. He enrolled at Fisk University in Nashville in September 1918, just as World War I was winding down. In an early *Caviar and Cabbage* column, he remembered the first time he heard the voice of Bessie Smith from a victrola, on "an autumn night in 1918, when our company was swinging along a lonesome road in Tennessee."[19] Although the column implies a regular army experience, this incident probably took place on a ROTC march at Fisk.

Tolson moved from Fisk to Lincoln University in Pennsylvania for the fall semester of 1919. The reason for the move may be inferred from a letter that remains in his file at Lincoln from Rev. William H. Thomas of Allen Chapel AME Church in Kansas City to Dr. W. H. Johnson, Dean of Arts and Sciences at Lincoln University:

I am sending you the school record of Melvin Tolson. His father has a very small church and is unable to do anything for the boy. You told me 2 years ago that some allowance would be made for the fare of a very worthy boy. Tolson is that boy.

Both Fisk and Lincoln were prestigious institutions for black students. Tolson's attendance at Lincoln and the associations he made there were both personally and professionally important for the rest of his life. Horace Mann Bond, who in 1946 returned to Lincoln as president of the university, was a classmate. He and Tolson corresponded intermittently throughout their distinguished professional careers and gave each other support. Being an alumnus of Lincoln was important to Tolson's nomination as poet laureate of Liberia and hence to the subsequent writing of *Libretto for the Republic of Liberia*. Lincoln in turn recognized the achievements of its distinguished graduate by twice awarding him honorary degrees, a doctor of letters in 1954 and a doctor of humane letters in 1965.

While waiting for Allen Tate's promised critical response to *Libretto*, Tolson noted with whimsical regret that he attended Fisk University while the Fugitives were arguing out their poetic and cultural credo at Vanderbilt only a short distance away. If he could have participated in those discussions, he often implied, his development as a modernist poet might well have begun years earlier. It is at least as interesting to speculate on what differences it would have made to the program of the Fugitives if Tolson had been a participant.

Because of the color line it did not happen. Tolson's academic training at both Fisk and Lincoln was rigorous and conservative. Later he frequently complained that his English professor at Lincoln reacted with discouraging disdain when Tolson excitedly discovered Sandburg's "Chicago." Victorian tastes, as Tolson remembered, prevailed with inhibiting oppression.

Samuel F. Washington, a classmate of Tolson's at Lincoln, remembers Tolson in terms that strongly hint of the traditions and manners Lincoln fostered:

> When we first entered Lincoln University, Tolson and I lived next door to each other, and I saw and talked with him much more in our earlier years than during our upper class years. He and I took long walks through the countryside as verdant freshmen. He appeared chaste and temperate in thought and action, and a believer in a high degree of morality.
>
> "Cap" had a sense of humor and was quite loquacious. During our days at Lincoln there was a practise known as "rabbling," ordinarily called hazing when applied by sophomores to freshmen, or in other cases "horse play." Tolson was one of the first of our sophomore class to be sent "out into the world" (Lincoln jargon for suspended) for rabbling on freshmen.
>
> "Cap" Tolson enjoyed pitching horse shoes, he also enjoyed his pipe. I

The Avenue of Maples, Lincoln University, as it appeared in 1923.

recall Tolson as one of the outstanding men of his class. He was proficient in the literary, debating, and oratorical areas (science and mathematics were not his forte), winning many prizes in the literary field. He graduated "Cum Laude." His character was exemplary.[20]

A later biographical sketch included in the program celebrating the publication of *Rendezvous with America* at Wiley lists some of Tolson's achievements at Lincoln: He "won such prizes as the Elizabeth Train, Obdyke, Randall, Parmley, and Delta Rho in English and debate." Tolson apparently again stretched the truth when he told Joy Flasch that he was captain of the football team both at Lincoln High School in Kansas City and at Lincoln University. He is not listed on the football team at the high school. He was captain of his class team at the university, and this was the source of the nickname *Cap*, but he did not play varsity football.

Tolson majored in journalism and theology. He was chosen commencement day speaker and won a Junior Oratorical Medal. He also was chosen to teach a freshman English class during his junior year. His own memories plus what substantial facts we have suggest that he was a very verbal and intensely intellectual young man who tended to separate his academic experiences from his practical work experiences. The faculty and curriculum of the university apparently reinforced such a separation. His ambition to write poetry, however, persisted and was well recognized. In the Lincoln yearbook, *The Paw*, there is a "collegiately" humorous note: "Cap arrived on campus with a suitcase and basket in 1920; the basket carried his clothes and the suitcase his poems in manuscript. A country paper once published one of them and that ruined Cap."

During Tolson's sophomore year at Lincoln he attended an Omega Psi Phi fraternity dance in Philadelphia. The dance was also attended by Ruth Southall. A girlfriend of Ruth's had phoned to ask if she could stay with Ruth the night of the dance. Ruth's sister took the call and mistakenly reported it as an invitation for Ruth to go to the dance. The young man Ruth was dating at the time was out of town. So Ruth went to the dance with her friend and her friend's date, feeling like a third wheel.

Melvin was not a graceful dancer. Friends bet him five dollars that he could not persuade Ruth to dance with him. He stepped all over her feet, but he won the five dollars. Unsatisfied, his friends challenged him a second time. The Tolson persistence paid off as Ruth reluctantly accepted his invitation (Melvin told Ruth of these bets only after they became much better acquainted). Later that evening, perhaps in part feeling guilty, but clearly also strongly attracted, he very formally asked if she had an escort to take her home. She replied that she was in the company of two friends. Very politely he insisted that he had meant to ask if she had a male escort and if not would

Melvin B. Tolson, as he appeared in 1923 in the yearbook
of Lincoln University, *The Paw*.

she permit him to escort her home. His mannered earnestness again won consent.

On the way home he much admired a ring that she wore, a ring she valued highly. He playfully asked if he might try it on. She permitted him to do so and in the ensuing conversation forgot it. Before leaving her that evening, he gave her his address. Afterward, she realized that he had her ring and she his address. She felt that this was intentional but wrote him quickly to ask if he intended to return her ring. He returned the ring along with a letter a yard long including a profuse apology.

Thus began their correspondence. For the summer of 1921 Melvin had secured a job waiting tables at The Breakers Hotel in Atlantic City. He later wrote at least two *Caviar and Cabbage* columns about his experiences there and regretted that he had not been more alert to the value of those experiences: "I didn't know, in the Roaring Twenties, that I had a ringside seat from which to view Life and write stories." Ruth also took a summer job in Atlantic City after another, preferred job had fallen through. During that summer their courting took a serious turn, and it was then that Melvin wrote "My Soul and I" for Ruth.

In May 1981 Ruth Tolson revisited Lincoln University with me. While we were looking through memorabilia of the years when Melvin was at Lincoln, she noted a reference to his winning the Obdyke Medal as the best individual debater during the academic year 1921–1922. Ruth remembered that Melvin received a ten-dollar prize with the award, and it was with that money that he bought her wedding ring. She took the ring off to show me that they had had *Obdyke Prize* inscribed inside, but fifty-nine years of wear had erased the inscription, as they had the orange blossoms once etched on the outside.

Melvin Tolson and Ruth Southall were married on 29 January 1922, something over a year after they had first met. Melvin was in his junior year but apparently eager to begin a domestic commitment that would anchor his energies and talent. Ruth went home to Charlottesville, Virginia, while Melvin finished the semester. At the beginning of summer she returned to Philadelphia but contracted what they feared was tuberculosis and returned to Charlottesville. After their fears proved unfounded, she rejoined Melvin in the fall of 1922. She soon became pregnant with their first child. She then returned once more to Charlottesville to await the birth of Melvin B. Tolson, Jr., on 19 June 1923.

The Paw, Tolson's commencement yearbook, published a "Poetic Dialogue Between 'Cap' Tolson and Wife." Its humor suggests with crude accuracy the economic and family responsibilities Tolson would soon have to face:

Cap: "Dear Wife, this poem I wrote today, surpasses all I've done
    before.
Wife: "Don't bring me posies Melvin dear,
    When that darned old wolf is at the door.
Cap: "But listen dear, this poem is swell,
    Come 'ope your wondrous orbs and read.
Wife: "You take your poems and step to Heaven
    It's pork chops that I need."

Tolson graduated from college and became a father in the same month.
His father, Rev. Alonzo Tolson, interceded for his son with his Methodist
bishop, and Melvin was secured a teaching post in the English department
of Wiley College in Marshall, Texas, where he was to live for twenty-four
years rearing a family, establishing an imposing academic career, and finally
winning substantial success as a writer.

II

HARLEM VISITED

About the same time Tolson fell in love with Ruth Southall, Langston Hughes, also Missouri born, but four years younger than Tolson, fell in love with Harlem. Here is Hughes's account of his romance:

> On a bright September morning in 1921, I came up out of the subway at 135th and Lenox into the beginnings of the Negro Renaissance. I headed for the Harlem Y.M.C.A. down the block, where so many new, young, dark, male arrivals in Harlem have spent early days. The next place I headed to that afternoon was the Harlem Branch Library just up the street. . . . That night I went to the Lincoln theatre across Lenox Avenue where maybe one of the Smiths—Bessie, Clara, Trixie, or Mamie—was singing the blues. And as soon as I could, I made a beeline for Shuffle Along, the all-colored hit musical playing on 63rd Street in which Florence Mills came to fame.
>
> I had come to New York to enter Columbia College as a Freshman but *really* why I had come to New York was to see Harlem. I found it hard a week or so later to tear myself away from Harlem when it came time to move up the hill to the dormitory at Columbia. That winter I spent as little time as possible on the campus. Instead, I spent as much time as I could in Harlem, and this I have done ever since. I was in love with Harlem long before I got there, and I still am in love with it. Everybody seemed to make me welcome. The sheer dark size of Harlem intrigued me. And the fact that at that time poets and writers like James Weldon Johnson and Jessie Fauset lived there, and Bert Williams, Duke Ellington, Ethel Waters, and Walter White, too, fascinated me. Had I been a rich young man, I would have bought a house in Harlem and built musical steps up to the front door, and installed chimes that at the press of a button played Ellington tunes.[1]

Hughes's love affair brought him directly into the mainstream of the Harlem Renaissance. He easily sloughed off academic concerns. They were mere distractions. His woman was Harlem. His family was made of the artists and musicians gathering in Harlem to create an exciting cultural epoch. Harlem was later to fascinate Tolson, also, but there is no evidence that in 1923 he even thought of it in competition with the attraction of the woman he married, the challenges and thrills of academic achievement, and the demands of all the traditional responsibilities of becoming a husband and father.

Thus, instead of to Harlem, Tolson traveled to Marshall, Texas, to Wiley College, a relatively young black college established by the Methodist church, a college that aspired to be in the West what Fisk was in the East. Although in 1923 it had a long way to go, Wiley provided much of what Tolson hungered for at this time in his life. He reveled in shaking his students out of complacency and apathy. He was deeply gratified in seeing their aspirations and their confidence grow as he bullied and enticed them into achievements they had not known themselves capable of. And his students loved and respected him. The depth of feeling Tolson had for teaching and the rewards it brought him may be inferred from a sonnet, "The Gallows," in *Rendezvous with America* about the effect of a teacher on the life of a community:

> He was my teacher a continent of years ago;
> Yet bright as blood is the red-letter day he came
> Into the drouth of the class, with his wits aflow,
> To freshen the sesame in each alien name.
>
> Month after month, the plan of his alchemy
> Found nuggets of gold where others found alloy.
> And the miracle of his integrity
> Put bone and blood and soul into girl and boy.
>
> He dumped the debris of customs on the refuse heap,
> He tore down fences propped with a great Amen,
> He set apart the huddling goats and sheep,
> He let the oxygen of the freedoms in.
>
> The lame, the halt, the blind—these struck him down;
> Then the gallows of ignorance hanged the little town.

Tolson also enjoyed his colleagues. A few provided true intellectual fellowship and challenge. Even when academic politics became petty and vicious, he had an extraordinary appetite for the struggle. But above all Wiley provided a reasonably secure and civilized environment in which to raise a family, to encourage his children to believe in humane values and to respect and be curious about the world of ideas and learning.

Tolson arrived in Marshall alone with much to learn. Joy Flasch describes a disconcerting initiation:

> Fresh out of Lincoln University, Tolson was excited at the prospect of being a college teacher. He listened attentively to the speeches during the first faculty meeting at Wiley College and was pleased when at the end of the opening session a chemistry professor, who was also a fraternity brother of his,

called him aside and said, "Tolson, I want to talk to you. You're just getting started. Come over tomorrow, and I'll give you the lowdown." Tolson went to his apartment the next evening but was hardly prepared for the sight that greeted him. In the center of the room was a huge table piled high with books. His friend had a forty-five on the table and was applying vaseline to some of his bullets. He carried a cane loaded with lead and also a razor. This was far from Tolson's concept of a professor's accoutrements, but his colleague stated his case clearly: "There are bad Negroes here and 'badder' white folks." Experience would prove the truth of his friend's statement.[2]

Ruth and their infant son stayed in Charlottesville until November, when Tolson received his first paycheck and could thus afford to pay the rent on a house the college made available to him. Arthur, the Tolsons' second child, was born a year later, on 15 October 1924. During the final portion of her pregnancy, Ruth traveled to Sweet Springs, Missouri, the home of Melvin's parents, whom she had not yet met, so that Arthur would be born in the home of his paternal grandparents. It was a considerate family decision since Melvin, Jr., had been born in the home of Ruth's parents.

Almost immediately after Arthur's birth, on 28 October 1924, Tolson organized the Forensic Society at Wiley College. Thus began a debating tradition that blossomed in the 1930s into adventures that went far beyond the usual experience of academic debating and that made a lasting mark on Tolson's career. Tolson also remembered writing a novel, *Beyond the Zaretto*, in 1924. Writing a novel during his first and second year of teaching, while establishing a home for his growing family and preparing courses as a beginning teacher, suggests a strong sense of purpose. Regrettably the manuscript of that novel is lost. However, a story, "The Tragedy of Yarr Karr," was published in the Wiley *Wild Cat* in 1926, which gives us some evidence of Tolson's talent in these early years. The story suggests that his youthful romantic fantasies were as yet far more compelling than the later sterner disciplines of his imagination.

The story is about a young man "born in Greenwich Village, the Bohemian center of New York City," who travels through a series of exotic and melodramatic adventures. The child of an enigmatic, artistic, but lecherous father and a refined actress from a patrician New England family, the protagonist links his fortune with that of a classmate, Marcus Dewey (a play on names similar to the earlier Marcus Dubois), and "In pursuit of the red grape of existence" they wander over Europe and Asia until one "memorable night in St. Petersburg," just as they "thought that the consummation of months of productive toil" with the radical Nihilists was at hand, the czar's assassins close in and they are forced to flee for their lives. They flee to Liverpool, and Marcus dies there of pneumonia. The narrator, shocked and grieved, joins a British expeditionary force in North Africa. They are ambushed by Arabs. The narrator is captured by the fierce Antar Abrahim and taken care of during his captivity by the beautiful Bellah. When Antar murders Bellah's father, Bellah and the narrator escape. The narrator, who by a possibly significant slip is now referred to as Marcus, overcomes Bellah's despairing submission to fate by proclaiming, "Away with superstitions. . . . Man is the master of his fate!" Theirs is an idyllic love journey through the desert until Bellah dances "the dance of love," takes her usual nocturnal swim in the Yarr Karr, and fails to return. Marcus hears only her screams of terror. His desperate search is useless. He suffers from "soul-shock":

> Years have passed. I have attempted to forget. I am now a mission worker in the slums of an eastern city of my native land. I am ministering to the broken souls of men who, like myself, have suffered from "soul-shock." But ever there flows through the vast expanse of consciousness the yellow waters of the fateful Yarr Karr; and ever, in my dreams, I see the bizarre and lovely figure of Bellah, my Bellah, dancing the "dance of love"—there in the golden moonlight on the sands of Northern Africa.

The story is so full of literary clichés that one would like to believe that it is intentional parody, and it may be, but unfortunately there is not sufficient evidence in the story to be certain. Since the story was published in the college yearbook, it may have been written as some kind of collegiate lark, with something less than full literary seriousness. Yet it seems akin to Tolson's high-school fiction. The vocabulary often seems clumsily pretentious, rather than pointedly parodic. Marcus Dewey is described as "a giant oak, tempest-racked and colossal, towering above minutiose shrubs of less virility." The two men's reversal in St. Petersburg is generalized into "the grim causticity of fate." Although Tolson was rapidly maturing into an effective teacher and public speaker and was settling into his role as husband and father, he probably still had considerable sorting out to do to find his mature style as a writer, even though he was now in his late twenties.

Wiley Wilson, the Tolsons' third child, was born 4 February 1927, and Ruth Marie, the fourth and last, arrived not quite two years later on 10 December 1928. Soon after, Tolson found an opportunity to engage his literary ambitions. For the academic year of 1931–1932, Ruth and all four of the Tolson children went to live with Melvin's parents in Kansas City while Melvin enrolled in a master's program in comparative literature at Columbia University. He was supported during the year by a fellowship and lived near Harlem at 326 W. 118th Street. Tolson probably had been to Harlem before, since Lincoln University was not distant. Yet this year, with its stimulating study of the interrelationships of the world's literatures and the experience of Harlem both from living there and from beginning to realize the value such experience might have as subject and inspiration for a writer, became the key initial period of rapid imaginative and intellectual development in Tolson's writing career.

Harlem had already fascinated and charged the imaginations of a generation of writers, many of whom, like Langston Hughes, were Tolson's contemporaries. Tolson's M.A. thesis, "The Harlem Group of Negro Writers," is his earliest written comment on these writers. He almost certainly was aware of their work prior to this time, but the thesis is a very deliberate effort to identify and summarize the importance of their work as a group, both to fulfill an academic requirement and, more importantly, to examine their usefulness as precursors to his own writing career. It is from this point on that Tolson's own work warrants serious critical attention.

Reflecting the strong influence of Alain Locke, Tolson in his thesis emphasized Harlem's role as a cosmopolitan city within a cosmopolitan city, a city that engendered a "New Negro," a cosmopolitan Negro, different from the antebellum and postbellum stereotypes of the past. The New Negro was becoming a source of study and surprise as he revealed an unpredictable mixture of national and racial customs both old and new, native and foreign:

> Being a city in itself Harlem has all the aspects of a diversified modern civilization, plus those differentiating customs, dialects, and modes of thought that Negro peoples have brought from all parts of the world. Alien ideas and native ideas, alien customs and native customs, sometimes remaining unchanged, but often coalescing and producing startling hybrids—these have colored the literature dealing with Harlem.[3]

Tolson treated the Harlem Renaissance itself as a "phase of the post-war development in American literature." World War I, the cosmopolitanism of New York City, and interest and support of white patrons and writers—and particularly of publishing companies—the exciting and ambitious appearance of *Fire* and *Harlem*, the sustaining support of the NAACP and the Urban League, and the growing research in Negro history are all briefly discussed as important contributing factors to the Renaissance.

Tolson then devoted individual chapters to Countee Cullen, Langston Hughes, Claude McKay, Walter White, Eric Walrond, Rudolph Fisher, Jessie Fauset, George Schuyler, W. E. B. DuBois, James Weldon Johnson, and Wallace Thurman. A revealing grouping, perhaps a little heavy on writer-leaders. Notable omissions are Jean Toomer, Arna Bontemps, and Sterling Brown. Zora Neale Hurston is referred to in the conclusion as one of "the new school" of writers succeeding the Renaissance. Marcus Garvey and his movement are virtually ignored. Alain Locke is quoted frequently as the philosophical spokesman for the Renaissance.

Two of the writers Tolson discussed became significant to his own writing career: George S. Schuyler and Langston Hughes. Tolson's enthusiasm for

Schuyler may be a surprise to those who know Schuyler primarily by his later, militantly conservative writings. That is not the Schuyler who was most visible during the early thirties. Tolson described Schuyler as "the arch foe of class snobbishness and a fearless defender of the underdog." He supported his statement with this biographical observation: "He knows the pang of hunger and the feel of uncompanionable city-streets during the dawn hours. He has dragged his weary feet from Harlem to the Bowery to get a free lunch. He has slept many a night in Central Park with dirty newspapers for a pillow."

For Tolson, Schuyler was a radical, a radical in a sense that even the later Schuyler might have admitted with ironic appreciation:

> Dr. DuBois had been thought radical; but, nevertheless, he did respect the middle-class virtues. Schuyler's radicalism, on the other hand, centered its attack on those mores dear to the soul of dark responsibility. The Negro clergy and the caste-system within the race did not escape venomous assaults. Schuyler sneered at the so-called progress of the race. He ripped open the inhibitions and complexes of "Big Niggers."[4]

Throughout his career Tolson's attacks upon the black middle class were as harsh and scathing as he here represents Schuyler's assault to be. In *Harlem Gallery* it is John Laugart's painting *Black Bourgeoisie* that provides a challenge to the Curator's cultural convictions and social diplomacy since he knows it is both a powerful and authentic painting and at the same time a blatant attack upon such "Bulls of Bashan" as Guy Delaporte III and Shadrach Martial Kilroy, men of money and position upon whom the Curator's gallery is dependent. In retrospect one must wonder if Tolson's reputation has not paid dearly for this persistently harsh attack upon the middle class within the black community.

Tolson ignored Schuyler's anticommunism. He saw him as a powerful iconoclast. He was aware that he was more a journalist than an artist, but, since Tolson was soon to begin writing his own fervidly iconoclastic *Caviar and Cabbage* columns, he was sympathetic with Schuyler's purpose. Of *Black No More* he wrote:

> Perhaps in this book George Schuyler is very much the elephant in the china shop, and goes "bludgeoning his way through it, striking down right and left the strawmen it has set up." Schuyler has the zeal of a crusader as he sallies forth against the exploiters of our most popular prejudice. He lays it on with a trowel, so to speak, and the response calls for a big guffaw.[5]

Sometime during his final years at Wiley, Tolson wrote a dramatic version of *Black No More*, but it was not performed until after he had moved to Langston University.

In a concluding paragraph, Tolson quoted a comment from *America's*

News (28 August 1927) with such approval that one suspects he projected a good deal of himself onto the Schuyler he saw. The comment suggests that one "who has probed beneath the tough surface of the satire" and "who sees into the soul of this black Diogenes" will realize that "Schuyler is an idealistic materialist, a whirlwind in the midst of the muddy world. He is a man alone."[6]

The other writer of the Harlem Renaissance who strongly influenced Tolson's later work was Langston Hughes. Tolson saw Countee Cullen and Langston Hughes as "the antipodes of the Harlem Renaissance. The former is a classicist and conservative; the latter, an experimentalist and radical."[7] Tolson left little doubt as to which of these antipodes he was drawn to. Hughes's life stirred many of those fantasies of freedom and travel so ambivalently revealed in the fiction Tolson wrote for the Lincoln High School and Wiley College yearbooks, and against which his mother's strong reaction to the stranger in Slater, Missouri, provided such a dramatic warning: "With a biography that reads like a page from the *Arabian Nights*, Langston Hughes, the idealistic wanderer and defender of the proletariat, is the most glamorous figure in Negro literature."[8] Hughes's early nomadic and impoverished foreign wanderings suggested that Hughes had already found the proletarian golden fleece that Tolson still sought:

> Genoa is famous for its beach combers: derelicts of all nations are to be discovered among them. Langston Hughes joined these outcasts, eating their figs and black bread. In his quest for beauty, unlike his friend Countee Cullen, Hughes found it among the flotsam and jetsam of life, whether he pilgrimaged in Europe or roamed a "nigger street" in Harlem.[9]

Tolson particularly admired how Hughes in "The Weary Blues" "catches the undercurrent of philosophy that pulses through the soul of the Blues singer and brings the Blues rhythms into American versification." In "a few bold, impressionistic strokes" he portrays "the setting, the theme, the atmosphere, the pathos, the climactic suspense, the Negro character, and the odd denouement of the Blues." Tolson also noted that, when racially authentic, the blues "have all the devices of an O. Henry short story with its surprising crack at the end." After discussing the importance of the concentrated repetition in the blues, Tolson quoted from Hughes's "Po' Boy Blues" and then commented, "Langston Hughes understands the tragedy of the dark masses whose laughter is a dark laughter." The "colored bourgeoisie" criticized Hughes's poems as being "just like the nigger Blues," "unmindful that this is the highest tribute they can pay to these artistic creations."[10]

A dramatic incident in Langston Hughes's career, as well as in Tolson's, is referred to only laconically in Tolson's thesis: "In 1932 he [Hughes] went with a group of Negro actors to Russia to make a Negro picture under a So-

Langston Hughes.

viet director, and while there he wrote the poem "Goodbye Christ," which made the headlines in most of the Negro papers for three or four weeks. The controversy was very violent." Tolson in a footnote then referred to an article titled "Goodbye Christ" he wrote for the *Pittsburgh Courier*, which appeared on 26 January 1933.[11] Hughes's poem originally appeared in a European Communist publication, but it was reprinted in the *Baltimore Afro-American*, 31 December 1932.

By 1940, when Tolson finally submitted his M.A. thesis, the outspoken political radicalism of the early thirties was already becoming an easy and popular target for repression. But, as Tolson noted, the controversy that followed the poem's publication in 1933 was violent. A Reverend Mr. J. Raymond Henderson attacked both the poem and the author in the *Pittsburgh Courier*, and Tolson, fresh from his enthusiastic study of Hughes as a Renaissance writer and increasingly concerned with the relevance of the Christian message as it was being taught in a time of cruel economic hardship, took it upon himself to attack the clerical critic and drive home the social message he saw in Hughes's poem. Tolson thus appeared in print before the public at large for the first time in earnest moral indignation, attacking the blindness of a Christian who had lost the true Christ and defending a radical poet who in his satiric attack upon the irrelevance of a religion that was failing to speak to man's dire economic needs was actually revivifying the message of Christ.

The *Courier* published a picture of Tolson and referred to him as "Professor of English at Wiley College, Marshall, Texas, and Coach of the Negro Intercollegiate Debate Champions. Last year he studied in Columbia University on a Rockefeller Scholarship." Tolson's reply to Reverend Henderson was carried in two weekly installments. Two quotations make Tolson's point vividly clear:

> The world is in a terrible condition today, and, if Christianity does not do something to solve the problems of humanity, it will have hurled at it repeatedly such challenges as "Goodbye Christ," and all the personal vituperations of a Reverend Mr. Henderson will do nothing more than increase the force of that challenge. The disciples of Karl Marx carry his teachings forward with a verve and courage that are admirable; the followers of Christ, on the other hand, enter into bootless denunciations. The leaders of Communism starve for hunger and die to put over the teachings of Marx; the leaders of Christianity live in comfortable homes and ride around in big cars and collect the pennies of washerwomen. Magnificent edifices are erected, while people go hungry and naked and shelterless. Preachers uphold or see not the ravages of "big business." "Goodbye Christ" is the outgrowth of tragic modern conditions.

Some paragraphs later, Tolson concludes:

Men are concerned with present-day Christianity. Christianity must come down from the pulpit and solve the problems of today. Men will no longer listen to the echo of that beautiful, but illogical spiritual of long ago:
"You may have all this world,
        Give me Jesus."
In fact, Jesus Christ would not have sung a song like that. He was a radical, a Socialist, if you will. His guns were turned on Big Business and religionists. He heralded the dawn of a new economic, social and political order. That is the challenge to all.[12]

In the *Courier* article and later in *Caviar and Cabbage,* Tolson described an incident with Hughes that must have occurred in the fall of 1931, although Tolson dated it 1932 in his column. In any case the incident clearly left a telling impression. The story begins in "an elegant parlor on Sugar Hill." Hughes, identified at first only as the Poet, and his hostess are talking about his proposed lecture tour through the South. Suddenly Hughes realizes he is missing a rally to collect money for the Scottsboro boys. His hostess tries to persuade him that it is raining too hard:

> There is a tenseness, an agony in the Poet's face. It seems that his life depends on getting to that meeting in time. We hasten downstairs and catch a taxicab. The rain is now torrential. The Poet leans forward, tells the driver to put on speed. The Poet talks passionately about the Scottsboro boys. They are innocent. They must go free. It'll take money.
> The car stops. It skids. Before us looms the great, aristocratic church. It is dark. In front of the church is a milling multitude. We learn that the church would not let the rally be held in the house of God. People said it was just Communist propaganda. The Poet asks me to come with him. I tell him I have a previous engagement.
> Langston Hughes looks at me with a sad half-smile. He says good night. I see him pushing through the crowd in the rain. His face looks tired and old and pain-ridden. I start to get out. Then I tell the driver to step on the gas. But I'm to feel a hundred times that I double-crossed the Scottsboro boys![13]

In the conclusion of his thesis Tolson credited the Harlem Renaissance with making Negro America "conscious of the inflowing of a powerful verve." The writing of the Renaissance "affected and was affected by the larger culture of the new literature that began with the publication of the first issue of *Poetry,* by Harriet Monroe in 1912." The Harlem Renaissance was not a fad, but it "has been followed by a proletarian literature of Negro life, wider in scope, deeper in significance, and better in stylistic methods." Probably buoyed by Richard Wright's winning of the Federal Writer's Project Contest with *Uncle Tom's Children,* an occasion Tolson celebrated as "The Biggest Event of 1938 in Black America" in *Caviar and Cabbage* (19

March 1938), Tolson observed that the "new school of Negro writers—Zora Hurston, Edward Turpin, Marshall Davis, George Lee, O'Wendell Shaw, and Richard Wright"—offer "a radical change in point of view. Most of the members of the Harlem Renaissance portrayed the sensational features of Negro life, which were exploited for the entertainment of white readers. The literature of today is earthy, unromantic, and sociological; and from it emerges Negro characters that are more graphically individualized."[14]

Ruth Tolson told about the acceptance of her husband's thesis and the awarding of his M.A. degree. M. B. had written the thesis and it was accepted except for minor revisions during the year he spent at Columbia. However, since Tolson never placed much importance upon titles and degrees, he carelessly took no interest in making the revisions and applying for the degree until many years later when the Wiley administration began to be increasingly concerned about the college's accreditation and, as a consequence, the appropriate degrees for its faculty members. Tolson's job was threatened unless he finished his M.A. He wrote to Professor Arthur Christy, his adviser, who fortunately had returned to Columbia after being away for some years, and Professor Christy was happy to accept a revised thesis from a poet who by this time had begun to be published in nationally recognized magazines. At the 1940 annual convocation at Wiley, where the achievements of students and faculty were described and rewarded, the president's presentation was dramatically interrupted by a student delivering a telegram announcing that Columbia University had accepted Tolson's dissertation and was conferring upon him the M.A. degree. President Dogan made the announcement, and Tolson's position was saved to the cheers of the assembled students and faculty.

Internal evidence in the thesis suggests, however, that Tolson actually gathered much of the material in it from interviews and criticism over a period of several years after leaving Columbia, the same years that he was writing and rewriting A Gallery of Harlem Portraits and probably even after he had begun his Caviar and Cabbage column for the Washington Tribune. A footnote in his thesis dates an interview with Harriet Monroe in the spring of 1934. Most of the other interviews referred to are undated. However, an interview with Zona Gale took place in Portage, Wisconsin. It is unlikely that Tolson traveled there during the year he studied at Columbia. In Caviar and Cabbage, 23 December 1940, he refers to a trip to Wisconsin with his debate team on Thanksgiving Day 1932. This seems the likely opportunity for his visit to Gale in Portage. Tolson also often frequently referred in his thesis to Harlan Hatcher's Creating the American Novel, which was not published until 1935. There are references to other material published as late as 1938.

Late in August 1933, a conference sponsored by the NAACP was held on the estate of Joel Spingarn at Amenia, New York. Tolson apparently had no immediate relationship with this conference, but the principal thrust of that conference reveals something of the mix of racial and economic currents in which Tolson's publishing career began. At this time, the severity of the economic depression posed a real question about the adequacy of the NAACP's traditional policy and programs. The ideas and concerns of a new generation of potential leaders, selected with commendable prescience, were sought. Ralph Bunche, E. Franklin Frazier, Sterling Brown, and Abram Harris are representative of this younger generation.

These young men denounced the tactics and ideologies of their elders:

> They charged that the ideas of long-time leaders like W. E. B. DuBois and James Weldon Johnson were irrelevant. They were "race men"—men who looked at all problems and solutions with a racial perspective. In their provincialism, the older men had overlooked the obvious relationships between the Negro's problems and the larger issues confronting the nation. . . . While their elders had generally continued to place their faith in the struggle for civil rights within the capitalistic system, many of the young men, like so many other intellectuals during the 1930's, were convinced that industrial capitalism had failed. Hence, the primary problem for black Americans was not civil rights or even racism, but rather the exploitation of labor by private capital. . . . They thought the older, liberal methods of agitation for civil rights would not bring about such reform. The only viable method was for white and black workers to unite and force the necessary legislation because "the welfare of white and black labor is inseparable." The "problem" for these young radicals, unlike their elders, was essentially class, not race.[15]

In September 1937, Tolson's article "Wanted: A New Negro Leadership" was published in *The Oracle*, the magazine of his national fraternity, Omega Psi Phi. This article probably played an influential role in his being invited to write *Caviar and Cabbage*, which began running in the *Washington Tribune* on 9 October 1937.

Tolson absorbed two important lessons from his study of the writers of the Renaissance, lessons that now may seem obvious but that in the early thirties still often came with a surprising shock of recognition: first, that racial material is not intrinsically an embarrassing or demeaning subject for a black writer to engage, rather it is potentially rich ore for him to mine, and, second, the corollary, that the art forms of black people—spirituals, blues, jazz—pose a challenging and exciting opportunity for poets to adapt them to more self-conscious modes of literary expression. But Tolson learned these lessons at the very time that the leading black intellectuals were making it clear that, to deal with the problems created by a harshly pervasive economic depression, the people had to see their racial experience in terms of the broader class experience in America and the world. Thus, during the thirties Tolson and many of his contemporaries accepted the practical necessity of directing their writing specifically to a black audience on particular occasions. But this was seen as a temporary and restrictive necessity. The dilemmas and paradoxes of the black American experience were a product of an aberration in world history, the worship of the false idol of racism, created and sustained by capitalism to insure a dependable supply of cheap labor. Once racism was exposed in all its repugnant deceit, then the writer would find his true, and ultimate, audience, the peoples of the world.

In 1938 Tolson sent an article, "The Odyssey of a Manuscript," to *Scribner's Monthly Magazine*. It was the story of how he came to write his first book of poems, *A Gallery of Harlem Portraits*, and the story of his failure to find a publisher for it. In "The Odyssey" he tells of the origin of *A Gallery* in an experience during his year at Columbia:

> In 1932 I was a Negro poet writing Anglo-Saxon sonnets as a graduate student in an Eastern university. I moved in a world of twilight haunted by the ghosts of a dead classicism. My best friend there was a German American who'd sold stories to the magazines. We read each other's manuscripts and discussed art, science, and literature instead of cramming for the examinations. My ignorance of contemporary writers was abysmal. One cold wet afternoon the German-American read my sonnet *Harlem*, cleared his throat, and said: "It's good, damned good, but——"
>
> The word "but" suspended me in space. I could hear the clock on the desk; its tick-tock, tick-tock, swelled into the pounding of a sledgehammer on an iron plate. The brutal words knifed into my consciousness: "You're like the professors. You think the only good poet is a *dead* one. Why don't you read Sandburg, Masters, Frost, Robinson? Harlem is too big, too lusty, for a sonnet. Say we've never had a Negro epic in America. Damn it, you ought to stop piddling!"
>
> I placed the sonnet at the beginning of my thesis on the Harlem Renaissance. Under the painstaking supervision of Dr. Arthur Christy I had learned the beauty of the inevitable word.
>
> At the end of four years and 20,000 miles of traveling and the wasting of 5,000 sheets of paper, I had finished the epic *A Gallery of Harlem Portraits*.[16]

In spite of its pervasive acknowledgment of the hard times of the Depression and the age-old blues of black people, *A Gallery of Harlem Portraits* is truly a celebration. It is the celebration of what Tolson remembers as his emergence from "a world of twilight haunted by the ghosts of a dead classicism." It is a celebration of his discovery of Harlem, a community that made the dreams and dilemmas of black Americans vivid. It is a celebration of his discovery of a literary heritage that enabled him to link his strongly felt personal, racial, and social experience to a much more direct, yet subtle and imaginative, literary expression. In short it is the celebration of his beginnings as an authentic poet.

Although Tolson lived in Harlem for only one academic year, he visited Harlem frequently during the remainder of his life, and he always carried Harlem in his imagination as a symbolic, ever-changing community. Italy's march into Ethiopia in 1935 underscored in Tolson's mind DuBois's prophecy that the twentieth century was to place the problem of color center stage in world history. Harlem as the meeting place of races, of national cultures, of the repressed past and the prophetic future, of the emergence of a new man, a New Negro, became a recurring challenge and stimulus to Tolson's imagination. Hobart Jarrett, star debater at Wiley in 1935, who later became a professor of English at the City University of New York, described the meaning Harlem had for Tolson: "He talked of Harlem as though it were the omega, and by omega I mean the ultimate, not death, the ultimate achievement of Negro life. He thrilled to it."[17]

In 1932, when Tolson began writing A *Gallery of Harlem Portraits*, Harlem was an immediately felt experience. Since his experience of the community coincided with extensive study of the writers of the Harlem Renaissance, he unquestionably was heavily influenced by the concepts and perceptions of those writers. But the individual portraits, the quick deft touching of humanity in A *Gallery*, are far more memorable than the poem's epic form. A *Gallery* is only a nascent or loosely conceived epic compared to the much more deservedly famous *Harlem Gallery*, published in 1965.

Edgar Lee Masters's *Spoon River Anthology* served loosely as a prototype for A *Gallery*. Through a series of independent dramatic portraits of the citizens of a community, the nature of the community as a whole is implied. Such a concept provides only a rudimentary principle of organization. The portraits are also divided in sections labeled *Chiaroscuro, Silhouettes, Etchings,* and *Pastels,* but what distinctions these headings imply about the four portrait groupings is not particularly obvious.

There are specific links between groups of poems. The stories of Lady Hope, Black Zuleika, and Babe Quest, for example, are linked by a series of dramatic actions resulting from the attraction high-yellow women have for black men. Isidor Lawson has risen from busboy to owner of the Hotel Harlem. The hotel then becomes a focal point for five poems about him, his employees, and his relatives. Sister Slemp is the protagonist of one poem but reappears as a minor figure in other poems. That happens with others as well. The ironic theme of a May–December marriage in "Daddy Oldfield" is reversed in "Sergeant Tiffin." Thus, there are many narrative devices used to suggest that this is truly a community and not just a collection of disparate individuals.

But the strongest unifying device is Tolson's use of lyrics from blues and spirituals within the poems throughout the book. These lyrics comment on the events of the poem, but from a distant communal perspective. They function in a fashion similar to the choric comments in classical Greek drama. They give a sense of the collective experience, in this case, of the historic folk experience, as it may be brought to bear on the particular occasion. Aunt Tommiezene's need for shoes to protect her from the cold is dramatically poised against offhand acknowledgments that she has given a husband and a son to the making of this coldly unsympathetic American city. A refrain from a well-known spiritual thus becomes ironic in its celebration:

> You got shoes, I got shoes,
> All Gawd's chillun got shoes.
> When I git to hebben
> Gonna put on ma shoes
> An' walk all ovah Gawd's hebben.

The irony becomes even more specific when the same spiritual is echoed much later in the poem about Alexander Calverton, president of the Harlem Savings Bank, who boasts of what he has done for the lowly, although the reader is pointedly informed of those he had *forgot*.

> I got shoes, you got shoes
> All Gawd's chillun got shoes.

The reversal of the pronouns underscores the irony.

The blues are more frequently used than spirituals, but Tolson in his M.A. thesis suggested the two forms are closely correlated: "The Spirituals had a religious origin and the Blues a secular one."[18] "Flora Murdock" opens with pointed blues:

> White Man's proud of bein' white,
> Brags about it in de town.
> White Man's proud of bein' white,
> Brags about it in de town.
> White Man oughta shut his mouth
> Wid yellah bastards walkin' roun'.

Flora was once a cook in North Carolina for Mrs. Ulma Asch, whose son comes home from studying art in Paris and rapes Flora. Flora later studies under Madame Alpha Devine and becomes a famous beauty culturist. She meets Albert Asch at ex-Countess Felicia's studio party:

> Albert entertained Flora
> With bizarre tales of the Latin Quarter,
> And said that she reminded him

Of his mother's high yellow cook
Who was crazy about him down in North Carolina.

"Maizelle Millay" also opens with blues, but the story that follows becomes a universal lament against the inevitable aging of a beautiful woman and perhaps a more subtle symbolic lament for the jazzy heyday of Harlem in the twenties supplanted by what seems the terrible inevitability of the depression years of Harlem in the thirties.

Hey, pretty Baby,
Each day you's gettin' ol'.
Hey, pretty Baby,
You turned me down fer gol'.
When you cain't shake dat thing no mo'.
De men will let you go.
Lawd, Lawd,
De men will let you go.

Three parallel stanzas follow, each of which juxtaposes the pathos of Maizelle's aged condition against the glory of her youthful beauty. Then this final stanza:

Maizelle's body is bent
Like a prairie tree
Under the hurrying feet of the wind.
Lenox Avenue does not remember the far-off years
When her Bayou Passion Dance
Led the revelers captive at the celebrated Plantation Club.

Those blues and spirituals interpolated into the poetic portraits of individual characters are meant to remind us, as noted in the introductory poem, "Harlem," that:

Dusky Bards,
Heirs of eons of Comedy and Tragedy,
Pass along the streets and alleys of Harlem
Singing ballads of the Dark World.

The economic depression of the thirties, along with Tolson's more vividly conscious awareness of the tragic history of racism in this country, caused him to think more and more in terms of the necessity for radical class action. In several poems in *A Gallery* and in many columns of *Caviar and Cabbage*, Tolson insisted upon the necessity of the "little guys" of all races uniting to claim their rightful share of power over their own fates from the "Big Boys" who exercised power only for their personal profit. Blacks were too small a minority with too little power to go it alone. They had to join hands with the dispossessed of the world. To believe that the problems of black Ameri-

45

cans would be resolved by increasing participation in free-enterprise capitalism was a fantasy. The profit motive itself was the root of all evil, including racism. As "Jack Patterson" learned from sailing into ports around the world:

> Big fish eat up little fish,
> An' the color of the fish don't count.

Hard times make people, white and black, consider doing what ordinarily seems unthinkable. "The Stranger," "an apologetic elderly gentleman / With a silken white mustache and a classic goatee," recognizes a reproduction of *The Charlatan* by his countryman, Adriaen Brouwer, while holding up a pawnbroker. He then explains apologetically to his victim:

> "These are the times, Sir,
> That try the souls of men . . .
> And also their pocketbooks.
> *Spes sibi quisque.*"

"Edna Borland," abandoned by the father of her pleadingly hungry twin children, is driven to suicide as a decrepit radio sobs:

> *What can I do when everything goes wrong?*
> *What can I do when everything goes wrong?*
> *Ain't no more good since ma sweet man is gone.*

But Freemon Hawthorne has a moment of ominous recognition as he looks at the men in the park:

> When I was a boy in the Ozarks
> I used to go into grandfather's barn
> To watch old Caesar match his feline cunning
> With the cunning of the rats.
>
> One summer there was a drought,
> And the rats became desperate with hunger
> And withered shadows of themselves.
>
> My grandfather said:
> "Keep old Caesar out of the barn . . .
> For a hungry rat is a sensible rat."
>
> But when I crawled into my trundle bed at night
> Old Caesar would sneak down to the barn.
>
> One morning I found his remains
> In a dark corner,
> His bones clean . . . clean as a toothpick.

Coming through the park today,
I saw in the eyes of hungry men
The same look of desperation
That I used to see
In the eyes of the rats
In my grandfather's barn
In the Ozarks.

Zip Lightner, a sharecropper, tells Black Boy "what brings de Jedgment Day," a lesson that Tolson probably learned and used often while organizing sharecroppers in the late thirties.

De People suffers a long time, Black Boy.
De People gits hongry an' hongry. Den de People wakes up.
De People wants to know
Who in de hell give de Big Bosses de right
To put dey damn foot on de People's neck!
Den de People stands up,
Like Gawd intended from de beginnin' of time,
An de People asks de Big Bosses:

"By Gawd, ain' dis a government of de People,
By de People, an' fer de People?"

The concluding poem, "The Underdog," is even more militantly explicit:

Kikes and bohunks and wops,
Dagos and niggers and crackers . . .
Starved and lousy,
Blind and stinking—
We fought each other,
Killed each other,
Because the great white masters
Played us against each other.

Then a kike said: *Workers of the world, unite!*
And a dago said: *Let us live!*
And a cracker said: *Ours for us!*
And a nigger said: *Walk together, children!*

WE ARE THE UNDERDOGS
ON A HOT TRAIL!

Tolson once promised his father he would be a minister. He didn't keep that promise, but it apparently stayed with him as a responsibility for a long time. This promise may have in part motivated him to encourage his son Melvin, Jr., to enter divinity school, but he also wanted his son protected from the draft and a war that, until Pearl Harbor, he viewed with skeptical hostility. At Wiley College, a Methodist school, and throughout the black American community, the vocation of the minister was commonly treated with respect, for the church has historically been a focus for social organization for a great many purposes beyond what we usually think of as exclusively religious. Thus Tolson's radical political thought was frequently fused with earnest religious passion. One hardly questions the appropriateness of Zip Lightner picturing a class revolution in terms of "de Jedgment Day."

Similarly, the Reverend Isaiah Cloud may be completely innocent of any Marxist political beliefs, but his fundamental religious earnestness upsets the privileged bourgeoisie of his church sufficiently that the *Harlem Advocate* carries the headline, "Aristocratic Church Becomes Communistic!" Cloud's insistence on pinpointing his parishioner's egotisms, leveling the social barriers in the church, and "revealing the cancerous and unseemly" causes Napoleon Hannibal Speare and Knapp Sackville, the power brokers of the church and the forerunners of the "Bulls of Bashan" of the later *Harlem Gallery*, to declare:

> . . . he was a preacher and not a pastor:
> The debt on the church proved that . . .
> So they let him go!

Tolson was able to fit Marxist assumptions about class neatly into his Christian training about the rich and poor. Traditional Christian contempt for the vanity of worldly possessions fitted nicely the Marxist contempt for the bourgeoisie and their concern for personal possessions and profit. Tolson did not become a member of the Communist party. He was far too protective of his freedom to subject himself to the discipline of the party. He also had a far too deep and constant faith in the ability of the prophetic voice of the preacher-poet-scholar to effect revolutionary change to be a very thoroughgoing Marxist. But he did not shy away from forging a conceptual basis for radical action by combining Christian and Marxist beliefs, a concept worked out much more explicitly and implicitly in his *Caviar and Cabbage* columns.

Relative to the later *Harlem Gallery*, the role of the artist, and particularly of the poet, in *A Gallery* is conspicuously modest. Vergil Ragsdale is a dishwasher, a consumptive, and a poet. He writes an epic, *An African Tragedy*, but after his death his landlady orders her husband to burn the manuscript as trash. Jobyna, his fiancée, arrives too late to save the manuscript. After some months Playboy Jeeter relieves Jobyna's mourning, but on her wedding night she cries, not as Jeeter complacently believes out of virginal modesty, but "Because she had not given herself to another." Tolson provided the poet Vergil Ragsdale with a reward of sexual fantasy even more ironically distanced than those of the earlier heroes of his adolescent fiction.

Harlem Visited

In the introductory poem, "Harlem," Ragsdale strikes a stoic pose again reminiscent of Marcus Du Bois and Marcus Dewey, but now with a strong belief in the coming of an apocalyptic class revolution:

> "Harlem, O Harlem
> I shall not see the quiet Dawn
> When the yellow and brown and black proletarians
> Swarm out of stinking dives and fire-trap tenements,
> Pour through canyon streets,
> Climb Strivers' Row and Sugar Hill,
> Erase the liveried flunkies,
> And belly laugh in the rich apartments of the Big Niggers.
>
> .   .   .   .
>
> Harlem, O Harlem
> City of the Big Niggers,
> Graveyard of the Dark Masses,
> Soapbox of the Red Apocalypse . . .
> I shall be forgotten like you
> Beneath the debris of Oblivion."

The Curator, who is the central figure of *Harlem Gallery*, is only briefly mentioned in the introductory "Harlem." He has no poem in *A Gallery* to give him historical and dramatic substance. His development from hinted presence to elaborately conceived protagonist clearly indicates the shift in importance Tolson claimed for the role of art and the artist in his later poetry.

Mariann Russell, in her book-length study of *Harlem Gallery*, described this shift:

> The *Harlem Gallery* shares many of the premises of *Portraits* about the economic foundation of oppression. It also deemphasizes political reality to address itself to the concerns of the black man encompassing biological, sociological, and psychological aspects. There is nothing in any way so explicit as the *Portraits*'s call for the underdogs of the world to unite. Revolutionary energy is displaced from the world of political activity to the world of creative activity. This displacement is explained somewhat by Tolson's discussion of the ape of God, the creator. According to Tolson, an ape of God is an inspired poet, "a creator who apes or imitates his Creator." The ape of God, like the prophet, is ignored or disdained by those who pursue material goods. As a result, both prophets and ape of God are "crucified on a Cross of Gold." Like the prophet, the ape of God has foreknowledge; and, like the prophet, the ape of God is apocalyptic; he senses before others "the odor of rottenness in a society." The ape of God is also freedom-loving and catholic in taste and interest. Since no man is an isolate, the ape of God is the enemy of social and personal evil. It becomes obvious that the burden of protest,

apocalyptic vision, and universality has been shifted from the economic to the artistic plane.[19]

The impact of Harlem—both as a real community in which he had lived and daily observed the vivid hardships of economic depression and as a "prophetic" community that measured striking changes in current assumptions about the nature and function of literature from what he had been taught in his undergraduate experience at Lincoln University—caused Tolson to represent the artist in a rather pathetically melancholy role. But, despite his preoccupation with a new "realism" more directly concerned with the everyday problems of human survival, the significance of art as a measure of a community's achievement is still assumed in the metaphor of the gallery and of the individual poems as portraits. Tolson's strong class message never precluded his assumption that art is ultimately the measure of civilization. Throughout his career he often spoke admiringly of Edgar Allan Poe's reference

> To the glory that was Greece,
> And the grandeur that was Rome.

Grandeur marked the lesser achievement of Rome compared to the *glory* that was Greece. Despite Tolson's class-conscious political convictions, Alain Locke's vision of Harlem was far more compatible than was Marcus Garvey's.

But the years from 1932 to the end of the decade, during which Tolson wrote and rewrote *A Gallery of Harlem Portraits*, were years of rich intellectual and social engagement. He channeled much of his own intense concern through his young avatars on his debate teams. The Wiley debate teams by the midthirties had compiled an awesome record of success. But that success was not just a matter of an incredible string of victories. Being a member of the debate team was an adventure in challenging the racial mores of the South and the racial stereotypes of the nation, an experience that instilled pride and confidence in the debaters and initiated them to rigorous disciplines of rhetoric and research. Hobart Jarrett, who anchored one of the last and most famous teams at Wiley, the team that on 1 April 1935 defeated the national champions from the University of Southern California, summarized what it meant to be on the Wiley debate team in an article published in *Crisis*, August 1935:

> Onward, Mississippi! The debaters of Wiley College en route to an eastern university, stop their steaming car at a general store to get some water. A half-intoxicated upholder of Nordic superiority shoots at them twice with a Winchester. . . .
> Beebee, Arkansas! It is three a.m. The White River has gone mad and

leaped its banks. A mob, with flaming torches is scattered along the road, looking for a Negro tramp. A deputy sheriff has been killed as he got into a box car. Off in the swamps the hounds are baying. The Wiley debaters are on the road and the road leads through the tremendous circle of mobsters. But there is a mulatto in the car. Coach Tolson tells him to take the steering wheel. The darker debaters get down in the car. The night is friendly, protecting. The mulatto salutes nonchalantly the grim-faced members of the mob, allaying their suspicions. And the debaters reach Memphis and read about the mob in the morning newspapers. . . .

A car containing some Wiley debaters runs wild, with a broken brake, in a mountain fog, and misses a downward plunge of two thousand feet by a margin of six inches. . . .

On a debate tour out in West Texas, Coach Tolson and the white mentor sleep and eat together. The white coach is passing for a mulatto and having great fun. Then the colored hostess discovers that he is white and asks coach Tolson if he wants to get all three of them lynched for practicing social equality. . . .

Down the years have come the tales of Wiley debaters. Legends have grown up on the campus. Traditions. They're in the atmosphere. When you join the debate squad you feel that you're in for great adventures. Your colleagues tell you about the forensic giants of other days, and the strategy they use to beat distinguished opponents.[20]

Tolson's debate team broke the color line in several states in the South, Southwest, and Midwest. Tolson drilled candidates for his teams extensively, particularly in recognizing and taking advantage of logical fallacies. The candidates usually debated with their coach for one year before being considered for membership on the team. Much of this training took place at the Tolson home beginning early in the evening and extending late into the night. Melvin, Jr., remembers that it was a youthful dream of his to be a member of his dad's debate team. He often hid behind a partition, when he should have been in bed, listening to his father and the debaters. He also often fell asleep there and had to be carried to bed.

The members of these teams often turned into Tolson's lasting friends. Hobart Jarrett became chairman of the English department at Langston University and was instrumental in arranging for Tolson to move from Wiley to Langston in 1947. Benjamin Bell became an exceptionally close friend, sharing many personal confidences as well as being a companion social activist to Tolson in his speaking and organizing activities in the late thirties. James Farmer, later director of CORE and leader of the Freedom Riders, remembers Tolson being flown up to the ceremonies at Rockefeller Center celebrating Farmer's retirement from CORE. Henry Heights apparently was not very consistent in keeping in touch with his former coach, but the character of Hideho Heights in Tolson's *Harlem Gallery* suggests how

From left to right, Hobart Jarrett, Henry Heights, and James Farmer, three of Tolson's star debaters at Wiley College.

deep and lasting an impression Heights made during his several years at Wiley. These are only a few of the debaters whose future careers touched Tolson's own.

Tolson sometimes remembered experiences with the debate teams in *Caviar and Cabbage*. On 26 March 1938 he noted, "I used to boast of the number of Negro and Caucasian colleges and universities my 'system' defeated. . . . That wise old bird Emerson said there's a crack in everything God made, and I was able to find the crack in the debate systems of other coaches." But "after the great debate with the University of Southern California," he "had become aware that there's more to life than winning personal victories. I was training my boys to go after the ugly truth and let the judges and respectable audiences go hang. That's not so easy as you think. It endangers one's job."[21]

These years as a debate coach made Tolson a public figure. The racial adventures that made such entertaining stories for later telling and retelling must have toughened his soul and left some indelible traces on his sense of pride. These years also brought him in touch on occasion with a world of drawing-room privilege and sophistication. In *Caviar and Cabbage*, he twice wrote about the evening after the debate with the University of Southern California, at the elegantly tasteful home of Loren Miller, a lawyer and editor of the *California Eagle*. Miller was also a member of the Meschrabpom Film project in Russia. "No bridge, no dancing, thank God! Just a little heart-to-heart talk among a few blacks and whites concerning the mess our civilization is in." Tolson ended his description of the evening with a car ride during which a "Madonna-like" mluatto woman turns to "a Negro doctor from the University of London, who'd been born in Central America," and asks, "Doctor, [do] you think judgment day will come in the United States?"

The doctor draws slowly on his cigar before answering: "Are Americans with empty stomachs any different from Spaniards or Frenchmen with empty stomachs? . . . I have operated on men in London and Panama and West Africa; and, madame, I have found no difference. Human beings are fundamentally human beings the world over, whether they are black or white, yellow or brown. Madame, empty stomachs mean judgment day in all ages and in all countries."[22]

The structure of debates must also have appealed to and reinforced certain propensities in Tolson's own imagination. Throughout his life Tolson was known to both family and friends as one who loved an argument. There was a particular spot on the Wiley campus where students would gather around him for spontaneous discussion of current and universal issues. He was molding himself into an assertive, but undogmatic, man. He encouraged the most skeptical possibilities, but he insisted on clear, strong statement.

The truth was a matter to be arrived at by collective argument. One can only speculate on how much the sharp exchanges between the Curator, Nkomo, and all the Zulu Club wits of *Harlem Gallery* owe to such experiences, but they extend a pattern that was an essential part of Tolson's disciplining of eager and keen young minds in the essential democratic spirit as well as in the formal principles of debate.

In the mid or late thirties Tolson also became actively involved in organizing both white and black sharecroppers. He frequently referred to this experience publicly, but without ever giving much specific detail. Benjamin Bell, one of his debaters, remembers three weeks in Arkansas, without bath or shave, with Tolson, speaking to sharecroppers in 1936. According to Bell, it was agreed that Tolson prepared the talks but Bell gave them. This was because Tolson as a faculty member would be more vulnerable to reprisal. Ruth remembers that Melvin would often be gone evenings and late into the night, but he felt strongly that she would be safer not knowing any of the details of what he was doing. She remembers a white man coming to their door threatening Melvin one day when he was not home, but she was not certain that it was related to these activities.

Rendezvous with America includes a poem that Tolson directly attributed to these experiences, "The Ballad of the Rattlesnake." The poem begins with a refrain that is repeated at the end:

> *The Sharecroppers sat*
> *In the Delta night;*
> *Many were black,*
> *And many were white.*
> *And this is the tale*
> *From the bearded mouth*
> *Of the dreamer who saw*
> *Green lands in the South:*

The tale framed by this refrain is of the Apaches staking out a blond prisoner next to a rattlesnake with a rock tied to its tail. The Apaches laugh at their prisoner's pleas, and the red chief taunts his foe:

> *A madness crawls*
> *In the rattler's brain*
> *The naked white thing*
> *Is the cause of its pain.*
> *At every lurch,*
> *The blond man dies.*
> *Eternity ticks*
> *Behind the eyes.*

In the end,

Harlem Visited

The desert holds
In its frying-pan
The bones of a snake
And the bones of a man.
And many a thing
With a rock on its tail
Kills the nearest thing
And dies by the trail.

The "dreamer who saw / Green lands in the South" had a double message for his audience of black and white sharecroppers. By giving the thoughts of the rattlesnake and suggesting how it is made to believe the blond man is the cause of its pain and thus becomes the agent of the blond man's death, even while dying itself, the poet comments on the way white and black sharecroppers may be manipulated by racial feeling to their own mutual destruction. But there is also the overriding, dramatically powerful suggestion that the blond man has invaded the territory of a people who are far more hostile to his ambitions and who are far more knowledgeable of the nature of the territory than he anticipated. He is the prisoner and the victim. No mercy is shown, and, given the time and place of the tale, the audience probably is expected to feel none. The days of the Apaches as a threat to the invading whites are gone. But the implacable resistance of the Indians suggests that both the white and black sharecroppers must be just as implacable in dealing with the aggressive landowners before the dreams of "Green land in the South" will be realized.

Tolson wrote two other poems principally concerned with sharecropping: "Zip Lightner" and "Uncle Gropper," both in A *Gallery of Harlem Portraits*, and both probably written earlier than "The Ballad of the Rattlesnake." Zip Lightner remembers when black and white sharecroppers met in the Marked Free Baptist Church "Jest like dey was enterin' de Promised Land." The "ridin' bosses" burned down the church, and the Union brought Zip to New York to tell his story and hasten the coming of "de Jedgment Day." Uncle Gropper is dead, worn out from unrewarded toil on Colonel Midas Hooker's plantation. But, on his deathbed, "the black Socrates of Yazoo Countee" called for the narrator of the poem, and the narrator with ominous resentment is going down to Mississippi to attend the florid funeral that Colonel Hooker is providing. Neither of these poems is as dramatically penetrating as "The Ballad of the Rattlesnake," but they add two other perspectives on a social theme about which Tolson felt strongly.

In the fall of 1938, a new Ph.D. from the University of Chicago joined the sociology department at Wiley College. Tolson took him under his wing, and the two became friends and professional supporters for the rest of their lives. Oliver Cromwell Cox's first major book, *Caste, Class and Race*, was published ten years later, in 1948, but much of the matter of that book was the subject of extensive discussion between Cox, Tolson, and three other Wiley colleagues during Cox's six-year stay. In his preface Cox thanked Melvin B. Tolson, Andrew P. Watson, V. E. Daniel, and Alonzo J. Davis for "face-to-face discussion and criticism of the substance of his book."

Cox challenged the assumptions many contemporary sociologists that racial distinctions are comparable to caste distinctions. He argued that *caste* is characteristic of an ancient and special culture, while *race*, as it is known in the modern world, grows out of the capitalistic need for designating a large group of people as a cheap supply of labor and hence is of relatively modern origin. He saw "the capitalist alliance" of World War II as "interested in destroying the fascists as competitors for world markets and natural resources but [also] in saving them as bulwarks against the proletariat."[23] Like Tolson he saw modern democracy, "still in its fetal stage," struggling to be born in the conflagration.

Cox intended his study as a direct challenge to Gunnar Myrdal's *An American Dilemma*, a study received by white America with suspicious respect, and Cox was particularly critical of many of his most distinguished black colleagues for participating in Myrdal's study. Like Tolson, Cox frequently used Marxist assumptions, but he insisted on his independence from Marxism. He shared with Tolson a passionate egalitarian dream and a critical antipathy to capitalism. Cox was an avid devotee of classical music and a talented painter. He too saw no disparity between elite taste and proletarian convictions. Although they frequently argued vigorously, Tolson and Cox clearly shared many strong beliefs.

During the late thirties, Tolson was also diligently seeking a publisher for his writings. "The Odyssey of a Manuscript" tells of Tolson's self-conscious and ineffectual efforts to enlist the interest and support of H. L. Mencken, Mark Van Doren, Carl Sandburg, Edwin Markham, and Langston Hughes, in that order, in finding a publisher for his first book of poems. He tells of meeting Hughes in Los Angeles after Tolson had been named by James V. Allred, the governor of Texas, as a state representative to the San Diego International Exhibit. He also mentions having just finished "a big chicken dinner with Mae West's butler and maid." This meeting with Hughes and the dinner with Mae West's butler and maid probably also coincided with Wiley's debate with the University of Southern California on 1 April 1935, although "The Odyssey" does not mention the debate. In April 1935, Hughes also addressed the First American Writers' Congress in New York. What he said to that audience gives an indication of what he might have said when he talked to Tolson in Los Angeles:

> There are certain practical things American Negro Writers can do through their work.

We can reveal to the Negro masses from which we come, our potential power to transform the now ugly face of the Southland into a region of peace and plenty.

We can reveal to the white masses those Negro qualities which go beyond the mere ability to laugh and sing and dance and make music, and which are a part of the useful heritage that we place at the disposal of a future free America.

Negro writers can seek to unite blacks and whites in our country, not on the nebulous basis of an interracial meeting, or the shifting sands of religious brotherhood, but on the *solid* ground of the daily working-class struggle to wipe out, now and forever, all the old inequalities of the past . . .

We can expose, too, the sick-sweet smile of organized religion—which lies about what it doesn't know, and about what it *does* know. And the half-voodoo, half-clown, face of revivalism, dulling the mind with the clap of its empty hands.[24]

Since the San Diego International Exhibit took place in 1935, this date suggests that Tolson had finished at least a first draft of A *Gallery* in less than the four years he says it took in the beginning of "The Odyssey." Benjamin Bell, however, remembers him still rewriting the poems of A *Gallery* as late as 1939.

At any rate, these overtures to prominent men of letters were all ineffectual, and Tolson, according to "The Odyssey," sent the manuscript to Macmillan. His hopes were raised when a wire from Lois Dwight Cole indicated that the editors were in disagreement and would require two additional weeks to decide. Unfortunately, the decision was negative. Letters from Bennett Cerf and Maxwell Perkins indicate that Tolson tried Random House and Scribner's with like success. Perkins's letter suggests that Tolson's manuscript, even as many of the characters pictured in the manuscript, was a victim of hard times: "I know that it is bitterly discouraging to try to find a publisher for anything much out of the ordinary, and for poetry of any kind perhaps. I wish we could have done the Portraits, but anybody who was in a publishing house and remembered the efforts that had been made in past years with poetical writings of talents and the very large lack of success, would understand also the publisher's difficulty."[25]

Eventually, Tolson did find a man of literary prominence who praised his poetry, supported his efforts to publish, and became a warm personal friend—V. F. Calverton. Tolson frequently referred to Calverton's *Anthology of American Negro Literature* in his M.A. thesis. Apparently, while he was seeking book publication for A *Gallery*, he sent Calverton some of the poems for *Modern Monthly*. "Hamuel Gutterman" appeared in April 1937. "Jacob Nollen" and "Dr. Harvey Whyte" appeared in May and August. Although a version of "Harlem," the prefatory poem of A *Gallery*, had appeared in the first issue of *Arts Quarterly*, produced at Dillard University early in 1937, these publications in *Modern Monthly* were Tolson's first acceptance from a well-recognized literary journal.

In 1938, Beatrice M. Murphy included three Tolson poems, "Roland Hayes," "The Auction," and "The Wine of Ecstasy," in *Negro Voices: An Anthology of Contemporary Verse*. In her preface, Murphy described the discouraging prospects an unpublished Negro writer faced:

> The role of the Negro writer is a difficult one. Only in exceptional cases does he become the protégé of someone who is "made," or find a guiding hand to help him reach the heights. For the most part his literary efforts are met by a callous indifference, and not until he has carved a place for himself and by himself, through sheer perseverance and determination, are his talents recognized. Nothing could be more fatal to ambition and spontaneous literary production than the "silent treatment" which the young Negro writer encounters. The mediums for publication within his own group are almost nil, and when he approaches the larger white publications, he is perfectly cognizant of the fact that his color might be a determinant factor, were it known.[26]

Calverton, comparatively, had it "made." He was enthusiastic and influential. He was also an extraordinarily flamboyant man whose death in 1940 was a very real loss to Tolson. Calverton was a prolific writer and speaker. The Saturday night gatherings at his Baltimore apartment were famous. Friends and acquaintances from the literary world would gather and drink. Someone would propose a topic for Calverton to discuss. He would retire for a brief period to gather his thoughts, return, and deliver an extempore lecture that usually set off lively discussion and argument. Tolson almost certainly enjoyed such gatherings intensely on eastern visits during 1938 and 1939. Tolson was well known for his gregariousness and extempore speaking ability at Wiley and on a rapidly expanding lecture circuit, and he and Calverton established an immediate rapport and mutual admiration. Calverton already owned keys to many of the doors Tolson wanted to enter, and he did what he could to provide entreé for his new-found friend.

Calverton wrote a regular column, "The Cultural Barometer," for *Current History*. In February 1938, he introduced Tolson and *A Gallery of Harlem Portraits* to his readers—referring to Tolson's book, either by editorial choice or through lapse of memory, as *Harlem Gallery*, the title Tolson used for his later epic:

> One of the most interesting Negro poets of today is M. B. Tolson, who in his *Harlem Gallery* is trying to do for the Negro what Edgar Lee Masters did for the middlewest white folk over two decades ago. Mr. Tolson is a bright, vivid writer who attains his best effects by understatment rather than overstatement, and who catches in a line or a stanza what most of his contempo-

raries have failed to capture in pages and volumes. The Negro he describes in his poems comes to life, candidly, unforgettably.[27]

Calverton then reprinted "Dr. Harvey Whyte," one of the poems from *A Gallery* that had appeared in *Modern Monthly*. Tolson later reciprocated the boost Calverton gave him by recommending Calverton, his magazine, and his books to the readers of *Caviar and Cabbage*. In a letter from Calverton to Tolson dated 23 November 1937 there is an indication of another genial quid pro quo in their relationship: "Now as to lecturing, I do hope you will be able to get some lectures for me in Texas through your various and numerous contacts in various fields." Calverton did visit Wiley College, a visit that offers some humorous insight into Tolson's efforts to serve both his academic and his professional writing interests.

James Farmer was a member of Tolson's debate teams from 1935 to 1938, the last two years becoming a "pivot" man, the key debater charged with picking up any possible arguments the team had not been diligently coached to answer. But Farmer was also interested in dramatics and chaired a student dramatic association. Tolson at this time was beginning to shift his attention to the theater. He founded The Log Cabin Players. He was soliciting funds and material to build a theater on campus. He was instrumental in organizing the Southern Association of Dramatic and Speech Arts. He had written at least one play and probably two by this time.

In 1938, he planned a week-long intercollege dramatic competition at Wiley; in discussions with Farmer and other student representatives, it was agreed that they would seek a judge for this competition of the most exacting standards, preferably a critic with experience evaluating professional theater on Broadway. V. F. Calverton's name was proposed. Farmer remembers writing the letter requesting Calverton to accept the judging task. And Farmer, as he told this story to me, was certain that Tolson had never met Calverton until Calverton arrived on campus. Calverton's 23 November 1937 letter quoted above begins, "It was damn swell meeting you the other day and I do hope your conference with Cerf was inspiring." This strongly suggests that Tolson allowed Farmer and probably others to believe that the selection of Calverton as a judge was far more disinterested on Tolson's part than in fact it was.

Arriving at the Methodist school with a chauffeur and a woman companion who also served as a secretary, Calverton descended on the Wiley campus with a flourish. Arrangements had been made for him to stay in the home of a widowed music teacher who kept a spotless house. Calverton had strenuously objected to staying at a hotel off campus. Prim and proper Wiley reeled at this encounter with the Bohemian East. Calverton was an enthusiastic drinker and womanizer. He loved cigars, boisterous talk, and irregular hours. The music teacher's home, or at least the rooms Calverton stayed in, was soon a shambles. But things got worse when the companion-secretary became resentfully jealous of Calverton's aggressive interest in the Wiley coeds and retaliated by carrying on with the astonished, but curious, males on campus. Through all this hubbub the competition proceeded according to schedule. Since Wiley had no theater, the plays were performed in the chapel. President Dogan scowled ferociously on his occasional visits in barely repressed rage and resentment at Calverton puffing away on his cigar in the audience. Nevertheless, as a judge, Calverton was discriminating, exacting, and fair. In a tribute to Calverton written for the Calverton memorial issue of *Modern Quarterly*, Tolson listed particular benefits that followed from Calverton's visit to Wiley, although he deliberately generalized the time and place. After noting that the Southern Association of Dramatic and Speech Arts paid Calverton for one lecture, "and made him deliver a dozen," and "He came for a day, and stayed a week," Tolson wrote:

> He was an inspiration of Negro youth. There was the case of Clara, a tall brown-skinned girl from a family of oil barons. She was a gay, carefree co-ed flashing along highways in her car. She heard Calverton lecture, and now she is in a Midwestern city writing a monumental work on Negro prostitution. Calverton saw Virgil Richardson in a share-cropper play written and staged by the students in a small Southern college. Perhaps you saw Virgil in *Big White Fog*, called by Langston Hughes "the most significant play yet produced, dealing with Negro life." [James] Leonard Farmer, another boy inspired by Calverton, is today the outstanding youth leader of his people. Benjamin Bell graduates this spring with honors from the Atlanta School of Social Work, and is our most brilliant Marxist student. Hamilton Boswell, the big mulatto from Los Angeles, who followed Calverton around with complete devotion, is now the most radical young clergyman in the race.[28]

Calverton was particularly impressed with Farmer. He told him that he would never be an actor, although he was a young man of sensitivity and intelligence, and he invited him to visit his home in New York City. Since Farmer's father accepted a post at Howard University the following year, Farmer remembered Calverton's invitation and quickly became an enthusiastic friend. Thus Farmer was witness to the close friendship that developed between Calverton and Tolson, both of whom he very much admired.

When Tolson received a telegram in Marshall announcing Calverton's death, the only way he could attend the funeral was to fly east, but as a Negro he was Jim Crowed from flying. He wrote his tribute instead for the Calverton memorial issue of *Modern Quarterly*. He wrote for himself and for his people when he warmly described his friend:

> We've had white patrons who accepted individual Negroes in their closed little worlds. V. F. Calverton was one of us. . . . I've seen him with his coat

off, laughing and shouting across tables that groaned under platters of golden brown chicken, country ham, steaming vegetables, rich pastries, and strong liquors. Yes, he was at home with John Dewey or a Pullman porter, Goethe or a Dallas cook, Jesus or a Beale Street crap-shooter, Tchaikovsky or an ebony co-ed, Langston Hughes or a Yazoo cottonpicker. He received letters from Negro intellectuals and washer-women, preachers and bootblacks. He was George and VF and Calverton to hundreds of Negroes. The elders often referred to him as the *white* white man. I think he liked that better than any of his books![29]

It was in comparison to Calverton's career that Tolson became disdainfully critical of the Gertrude Stein circle of expatriate writers: "Racial prejudice did not cause him to retire to the ivory tower, like many of his contemporaries. During the Jazz Age, when these spiritual nudists made their hegira to Gertrude Stein, at 27 Rue de Fleurus, V. F. Calverton was a voice crying in the American Wilderness for the rights of black men."[30]

Tolson reserved a more personal tribute to his friend for his poem named after Calverton's novel, "The Man Inside":

> They told me—the voices of hates in the land—
> They told me that White is White and Black is Black;
> That the children of Africa are scarred with a brand
> Ineradicable as the spots on the leopard's back.
>
> They told me that gulfs unbridgeable lie
> In the no man's seascapes of unlike hues,
> As wide as the vertical of earth and sky,
> As ancient as the grief in the seagull's mews.
> They told me that Black is an isle with a ban
> Beyond the pilgrims' Continent of Man.
>
> I yearned for the mainland where my brothers live.
> The cancerous isolation behind, I swam
> Into the deeps, a naked fugitive,
> Defying tribal fetishes that maim and damn.
>
> And when the typhoon of jeers smote me and hope
> Died like a burnt-out world and on the shore
> The hates beat savage breasts, you threw the rope
> And drew me into the catholic Evermore.
> We stood on common ground, in transfiguring light,
> Where the man inside is neither Black nor White.

Tolson was making his way into history, and this man, whose "life was an everlasting battle against the idols of the tribe," and who so warmly embraced Tolson in true fellowship, opened many doors and helped to illuminate the way.

III

RECOGNITION AND

WORLD WAR II

Melvin B. Tolson had an extraordinary capacity to absorb frustration and defeat and come out fighting. Joy Flasch wrote that Tolson's reaction to the rejection of *A Gallery of Harlem Portraits* "was to put his 'man-wrecked' manuscript in a trunk and not to write for several years." This is almost certainly what Tolson himself said to Flasch and is even possibly what he remembered having done. But the works published during this period and supplemental evidence from letters make any claim of his ceasing to write, particularly for a period of years, impossible to believe. The late thirties and early forties, the years during and immediately following publishers' rejections of *A Gallery*, were in fact particularly productive years in Tolson's career.

By the summer of 1937 he had written two plays, *Moses of Beale Street* and *Southern Front*, both now lost. On 10 November 1937 he signed an agreement with the William Morris Agency to represent him in all motion picture and stage rights to his plays. He left *Southern Front* in the hands of the agency. In September 1937 his article "Wanted: A New Negro Leadership" appeared in *The Oracle. Caviar and Cabbage* began appearing in the *Washington Tribune* on 9 October 1937 and continued to appear regularly until 24 June 1944. Tolson had become managing editor of *The Oracle* by 1938, and at least three articles by Tolson appeared in *The Oracle* in 1937–1938.

Beatrice M. Murphy published the three poems by Tolson referred to above, and which were not part of *A Gallery*, sometime in 1938. A letter from Maxwell Perkins dated 28 November 1938 refers to the completed "Odyssey of a Manuscript," Tolson's humorously self-mocking effort to make literary capital out of the rejections of *A Gallery*. A 16 September 1938 letter from Perkins also expresses an interest in seeing chapters from Tolson's novel. Perkins advised that "Troubled in Mind" was "a good title."

Among the surviving manuscripts in the Tolson collection at the Library of Congress there are an uncompleted novel, entitled *Dark Symphony*, and a relatively complete novel, *All Aboard*. "Troubled in Mind" was apparently at one time a title for one of these. It is not clear which.

In February 1938, some months prior to Perkins's letter referring to Tolson's novel, V. F. Calverton wrote of Tolson in his column, "The Cultural Barometer," in *Current History*: "At the present time Mr. Tolson is also working on a novel *Dark Symphony* which will *do* for Harlem in prose what his present volume does in verse." Sometime late in 1939 or early 1940, Tolson decided to use the title *Dark Symphony* for a prize-winning poem, which will be discussed more fully later. On 31 August 1939, Tolson's sprightly analysis of the social implications of Max Schmeling's defeat of Joe Louis was published in the Washington, D.C., newspicture magazine *Flash*. Two anthologies, *Sonnets* and *Eros*, included two Tolson poems, "The Breadline" and "The Note," respectively, in 1939. Also in 1939 Tolson was awarded the first Omega Psi Phi fellowship of five hundred dollars, then a relatively princely sum, for creative writing.

A year later he reported what he had been able to achieve with the financial help of the fellowship:

> Without this Omega Fellowship in Creative Literature, I am sure that I could not have completed two distinct works and made singular progress on the third. . . .
> In the first place, I finished the lengthy poem, "Dark Symphony," which won the National Poetry Contest sponsored by the American Negro Exposition in Chicago. The poetry committee was composed of outstanding American writers and critics, and "Dark Symphony," which was selected from among 300 other poems, was exhibited in the Hall of Literature.
> Second, the fellowship enabled me to complete the first epic poem of the race, "A Gallery of Harlem Portraits," which is now in the hands of a publisher, who has gone so far as to make estimates on this 300 page production. . . .
> In the third place, I have made considerable progress on the novel, "Troubled in Mind." With the remainder of my scholarship I plan to take the summer off from my teaching to put on the finishing touches. I have given a full report on the novel to our Scholarship Commission. (Details of plot, Ed.) I am working on the novel daily.[1]

Apparently the final rejection for *A Gallery*, the rejection that supposedly caused Tolson to cease working on the manuscript, did not come until 1940. Benjamin Bell remembers Tolson working on the poems of *A Gallery* at least until 1939, which fits with Tolson's own report above.

Thus far, it would seem likely that "Troubled in Mind" was a title Tolson used for the fragmentary novel *Dark Symphony*. However, an undated letter

Melvin B. Tolson

Tolson wrote to Calverton soon after receiving the Omega fellowship, hence presumably in 1939, but certainly prior to Calverton's death in 1940, indicates that the novel Tolson was working on at the time was *All Aboard*. In the letter, Tolson describes weaving "a lot of good dope on the Pullman Porter's Union" about the story of Duke Hands, who is the protagonist of *All Aboard*. Slim Walpole is the protagonist of *Dark Symphony*. It is possible that Tolson thought of *All Aboard* as in some sense growing out of *Dark Symphony*, although the central character is different in more than name. At any rate he continued working on *All Aboard* throughout the forties and even into the fifties.

However, it was "Dark Symphony," the poem, that proved the key to the publication of Tolson's first book. Frank Marshall Davis, who chaired a committee of judges including Langston Hughes and Arna Bontemps for the National Poetry Contest sponsored by the American Negro Exposition in Chicago in 1940, invited Tolson to enter the contest. Tolson submitted "Dark Symphony" and won first prize. The poem was then exhibited in the Hall of Literature at the Exposition. But that did not end the attention the poem was to bring its author. On 2 June 1941, Edward Weeks, editor of the *Atlantic Monthly*, wrote Tolson: "It gives me great pleasure to accept for the *Atlantic Monthly* your uncommonly fine poem, 'Dark Symphony.' I am very much impressed by the skill with which you have varied your metre, suiting each passage to the mood and tempo of what you have to say, and, unless I am very much mistaken, your lines will find an immediate response from our readers." The poem appeared in the September 1941 issue of *Atlantic*.

At this time, a woman named Mary Lou Chamberlain served on the editorial staff of the *Atlantic*. Sometime later she left the *Atlantic* for an editorial position with Dodd, Mead and Company. Thus it was through correspondence with Mary Lou Chamberlain that Tolson was encouraged to submit a manuscript for publication by Dodd, Mead. The letter announcing Dodd, Mead's acceptance of *Rendezvous with America* came to the Tolson home a few days before Christmas 1943.

On 8 July 1943, the *Atlantic* sent Tolson a check accepting his poem "Babylon," apparently not subsequently published. Meanwhile, the poem "Rendezvous with America" and four additional poems collectively titled "Woodcuts for Americana" were published in *Common Ground* in summer 1942 and spring 1943. In addition to the two novels mentioned above, Tolson worked on another novel, *The Lion and the Jackal*, according to Joy Flasch, through 1939.

In short, considering that Tolson was carrying a very heavy extracurricular load as a debate coach, director of drama, junior varsity football coach, and popular speaker through many of these years, the amount of writing that he

Melvin B. Tolson in 1941 in a picture used to publicize "Dark Symphony."

managed was most impressive. It seems most unlikely that he ever sulked at his failure to find a publisher for *A Gallery*. On the contrary, he was energetically establishing a network of literary friends and colleagues, creating an audience for his words and ideas, and trying an ambitious array of literary forms to embody his beliefs and experiences. And his efforts were winning accumulatingly impressive recognition.

For many years after his poetry began to win critical acclaim, Tolson still did not think of himself as exclusively a poet. Sometime after completing at least the initial version of *Libretto for the Republic of Liberia*, probably late in 1947, Tolson wrote a "Statement of Plan of Work." A stamped note on the page indicates this was probably part of a fellowship application to the Rosenwald Foundation. It begins, "I seem to get the best results when I'm writing both prose and poetry—that is, going from one to the other, one stimulating the other, one recuperating me for the other. . . . So, while working on the novel *All Aboard*, I completed the long poem for the Republic of Liberia and finished the dramatization of George Schuyler's *Black No More*." His writing plans for the period of the fellowship were "to finish *All Aboard* and the epic *A Gallery of Harlem Portraits* and begin the tetralogy covering four generations of Negroes in Africa and the New World."[2] Tolson's major writing achievements were long in germination and characteristically the product of much revision. In an interview apparently given between the publication of "Rendezvous with America" in *Common Ground* in the summer of 1942 and the publication of *Rendezvous with America* in 1944, Tolson was asked what type of writing he found the hardest. He replied: "Poetry. Prose is Gethsemane. Poetry is Golgotha. I don't like to do either. But it's a thing one can't help."[3]

Tolson's poem "The Poet," published as part of "Woodcuts for Americana" in *Rendezvous*, gives a revealing projection of his ideals and expectations as a poet at this stage of his writing career. The first three stanzas almost too emphatically declare that the poet neither needs nor seeks praise or flattery: "The poet cheats us with humility." His rewards are intrinsic in his work: "He shapes and polishes chaos without a fee." Being without vanity, he does not need the "caviar of smile and phrase." This leads to a pointed pun:

> He comes of nobler strain,
> Is marrowed with *racier* ways.

In the third stanza this lack of concern for such vanities becomes proud scorn, a predilection that sometimes seems at odds with Tolson's populist claims for the poet:

> He stands before the bar of pride,
> Gives not a tinker's dam

For those who flatter or deride
His epic or epigram
The potboy, not the connoisseur, toadies for a dram.

The fourth stanza is transitional. The narrator invites the reader to peep through the poet's judas-hole—the peephole in a cell—to see "the dogma of self at work." A paradox is implicit in the setting. Though apparently working in imprisoned isolation, the poet is referred to as "sky-born," and the reader is assured his "eagle's heart abides not in the mole."

The fifth stanza begins the positive assertions of the poet's role:

A freebooter of lands and seas,
He plunders the dialects of the marketplace,
Thieves lexicons of Crown jewel discoveries,
Pillages the symbols and meccas of the race:
Of thefts the poet's magic leaves no trace.

A pirate adventurer, he feels free to steal words, symbols, and ideas from all mankind, but his thefts cause no painful losses. As Tolson's career developed, this predisposition became a hallmark of his style. Both in *Libretto* and in *Harlem Gallery* his eclectic use of African, European, and Asiatic languages and cultural references marks him as one of the more extraordinary pillagers of modern literature.

The sixth through eighth stanzas suggest strong romantic roots as they identify the poet, respectively, as Ishmaelite, anchoret, and champion of the people. As an Ishmaelite, the poet is a challenging presence who "breaks the icons of the Old and New." He exposes the skeletons in the closets of both the Many and the Few. As an anchoret, "He feeds on the raven's bread." This not only suggests that he needs little sustenance, it also implies, in a literary pun, that he feeds on the challenge "Nevermore!" He "Candles worlds whose suns have set" and experiences nature in ways that lesser mortals will never know. His words have magical power. He "unlocks the wilderness with an epithet." The "only martyrdom" of this "champion of the People versus Kings" is poetry. "Freedom's need is his necessity." He blueprints "A bright new world where he alone will know work's menacings."

This poet is both champion and martyr, but his martyrdom is not always clear. His indifference to praise and other vain needs hardly seems martyrdom. Poetry itself is claimed as his only martyrdom. This echoes Tolson's comment quoted above: "Poetry is Golgotha." In the bright new world the poet announces that he "will know work's menacings." Tolson tended to load on the poet enormous responsibility, more perhaps than he was able to particularize in this poem. The poems of *Rendezvous* make it clear, however, that the poet is a prophetic seer. The poet conceives the revolution that makes a new world possible. Like Abba Micah Soudani, the bard of Addis Ababa, he must "Cry the heroes to wake up the dead."

But the poet must also struggle with the historical reality of the world within which he lives. For Tolson, in midlife, but at the beginning of his publishing career, the despair and hunger of economic depression, the apocalyptic carnage of World War II, and the harrowing and enervating persistence of racism made the poet's task to blueprint the bright new world in the dusk of dawn a truly heavy one.

> It was Tuesday on the morning of October 1, in the year 1935. The deep red explosion of the tropic sunrise had purpled the peeks of the hinterland beyond the blue-green tiers of the eucalyptus forest and burst in savage splendor upon the port of Djibouti, the front door of Ethiopia.
>
> Along the sprawl of quay, built of native wood and rock, helmeted Europeans and bushy-haired Somalis had already begun the grind of day. Against a background of monoliths of salt evaporated from the blue Gulf of Aden, the toilers of empire fell into the rhythm of loading and unloading inboard cargo.

The cargo is the material and supplies the Italians need for the invasion of Ethiopia, for Tolson the beginning of World War II, the beginning of a cataclysm in which European civilization, confused by its own capitalistic and imperialistic greed, is rendered suicidal.

Thus Tolson began *The Lion and the Jackal*, a ninety-six-page transcript of prose, which is not truly a novel or even a story. The action is so inconclusive that it seems relatively plotless. It begins in Djibouti a few months after the Wal-Wal incident that sparked the Italian invasion of Ethiopia and Ethiopia's appeals to the League of Nations in Geneva. It moves quickly from the impersonal view of wharf activity to a grimy café run by a seedy Milanese, Dibo, who is entertaining an international adventurer, Colonel Jacques, who is selling arms to the highest bidder. Both are deeply involved in sinister intrigue. Then we hear of the mission of the heroic Abba Micah Soudani, who has failed in his attempt to persuade the governor of French Somaliland that the Italian threat to Ethiopia is equally a threat to his country. Colonel Jacques watches and approaches Soudani carefully, but his efforts are interrupted by the appearance of Lidj Senabai, an old friend of Soudani's and a Danakil. Danakils are fierce and traditional enemies of the Amharis—Soudani's tribe—but the two have transcended such tribal differences in a common national interest.

Lidj later appears at the café and menacingly accuses Dibo of complicity in a plot to steal important Ethiopian military information. He administers frontier justice with his bullwhip, but the information has already been passed on, and he ends up in jail. Then the action shifts to a train en route to Addis Ababa carrying Soudani, Jacques, and others. War is announced by the native drums. The train is abruptly stopped by an old man who deliberately drives his camel on the tracks. A bridge ahead is mined. Soudani learns that the military officer who ordered the old man's action is his son. We join the military group as they march their Italian prisoners, taken at the mined bridge, triumphantly into Addis Ababa. Lieutenant Soudani there meets the father of a comrade in arms who has died heroically at the bridge. He tells the father the tragic story. Afterward, Soudani is convinced that Ethiopia must fight a guerrilla war against the overwhelming technological and numerical superiority of the Italian forces.

The action of the story is primarily an excuse to display a series of characters who reflect the significance of this important world event. Abba Micah Soudani is the most important and most interesting. This "bard of the little people" wears a native *shamma*, has a "magnificent busby of lion mane," was a classmate of Haile Selassie's, and has won respect across all tribal lines for his simple life and his impassioned songs and oratory. He is a national patriot and author of a ballad that has become for all practical purposes a national anthem. He also wears a Chinese dirk and an English pistol, utilitarian and symbolic gifts for his past deeds.

Tolson made this same figure the subject of his poem "The Bard of Addis Ababa," published in *Rendezvous with America*:

> A blooded Amharic scholar
> With the lore of six thousand years
> Yet he wears a sackcloth *shamma*
> From the looms of Tafwaiperes.
> A Chinese dagger in his girdle
> Ranks a pistol of English peers.
>
> His name is an emblem of justice,
> Greater than *lumot* or priest,
> And outdoor courts invoke him
> To sentence man or beast,
> And debtors chained to their masters
> Appeal to the Bard for release.
>
> The battle-cry of his ballads,
> The meters' blood-spurring pace,
> The star-reach of his spearing forefinger,
> The eloquence of his face,
> The seven-league boots of his images
> Stir the palace and marketplace.

Section 2 of this poem uses the refrain from Soudani's patriotic ballad to frame what is represented in the prose story as a prophetic utterance of how the land will suck in the fascists to their doom while native patriots will survive to realize a new dignity. Section 3 pictures a scene from the novel, the return of the triumphant Ethiopian soldiers from the bridge at Takkaze with their Italian captives.

As Tolson grew more aware of the injustice and irrationality of racial experience in world history, his strongly religious and moralistic background frequently caused him to see world events in terms of an apocalyptic vision. God may be stern, but he is just. Righteousness will eventually prevail. The meek and the lowly, the people, shall inherit the earth, although, Tolson frequently added with secular skepticism, only if they work at it. The economic depression of the early thirties was a terrible hardship on the poor, but in the midst of hardship Tolson saw a gleam of hope. He earnestly argued that the depression caused the poor, both white and black, to bury their racial differences, to recognize their common goals, and to organize effectively to achieve them. World War II amplified this same lesson to the international scene. The "superior" European civilizations in World War II and the events leading up to the war were making a mockery of the very civilization European nations pretended to represent. Their downfall seemed imminent. The neglected and misused nations would hold the key to the future.

On May 28, 1938, Tolson began his *Caviar and Cabbage* column:

> Drama: "The Tragedy of Ethiopia." Setting: Geneva. Characters: Representatives of the League of Nations. Time: The year of our Lord, 1938. Author: $$$$$$

The plot and major characters of the drama are clear:

> Capitalism must have profits. It sucks profits from the people at home; then it reaches into foreign countries and wraps its tentacles about China and Ethiopia sucking profits!
>
> Ethiopia was the victim of capitalism in the form of imperialism; Mussolini was put in power by the financiers of Italy. He sold out the Italian people. Today they groan under financial and psychical burdens.
>
> The Unholy Three, England and France and Italy, sold out the League of Nations for thirty pieces of silver. This caused the breakdown of international law that required centuries and centuries to build.
>
> The world cried out in disgust and anger when Germany made a scrap of paper out of the neutrality of Belgium. Of course, people forgot that little Belgium had cut off the hands of black natives in the Congo because they could not bring enough rubber for the white capitalists. My mother used to sing after father had preached in his little church on Sunday morning: "You will reap just what you sow."
>
> England and France and Italy now exploit 500,000,000 colored peoples. For what? For dollars. For profits in gold and oil and rubber and agricultural

products. But at home the masses of the population in these countries tear out their lives against economic injustices. That's the cancer that will eat away these dishonorable governments.

White civilization is sliding downhill. International law today is a scrap of paper. Therefore, Mexico slaps England in the face and gives a belly laugh. The Japanese take a shot at the British ambassador.

Perhaps René Maran, winner of the Goncourt Prize, was right when he declared, in his introduction to the novel *Batouala*, that civilization was a scourge, a conflagration. The white man—I mean the big white man—has messed up the world. He's had two thousand years to make good. He's had the best soil of the earth at his command. Nature and fortune have smiled upon him. But he started out wrong. Because he started out to exploit. He has always believed that might made right. For a while, he walked the earth like a god.[4]

In *Caviar and Cabbage* on 25 May 1940 Tolson reminded his readers of Haile Selassie's ominous warning: "The conquest of Ethiopia means the conquest of Europe." And in that same column he sardonically observed:

The white man is a Frankenstein who created the monster, POWER. This monster was made out of dollars and francs and guineas. That monster has devoured the darker races all over the world. Today that monster has turned upon his creator in a Second World War.[5]

By late 1942, the entry of the United States had changed the prospects of the war. It was becoming clear that the United States would play a leading role in shaping the political future of the world that would emerge from World War II. Tolson wrote strongly in favor of making the end of World War II the end of colonialism:

Mr. Churchill said: "The Allied nations have no wish but to see France free and strong."

We Negroes have no wish but to see Africa free and strong. Too long has Africa been the football of Europeans. I hope the United Nations take the Four Freedoms to the peace table. We have the Atlantic Charter. The Chinese are asking for a Pacific Charter. But I never hear any of the white mouth-Christians talking about the Africa Charter.

I once heard Dr. Aggrey, the black South African, call Africa the question mark of the centuries. This bloody question mark has faced every civilized nation. No white nation has been moral enough to answer the Africans with justice and democracy.

Tolson concluded his column with a strong and pointed reaction to Churchill's beleaguered boast, "I have not become the King's first minister to preside over the liquidation of the British Empire":

I am sorry Mr. Churchill lost his head and uttered those words. Vice-President Wallace has told us that this is the Century of the Common Man.

Mr. Roosevelt has told us we are fighting for the Four Freedoms of Mankind. Now Mr. Churchill tells us we are fighting to preserve the British Empire. That's exactly what the millions of India have been saying. How will those unfortunate words of Mr. Churchill affect the smaller members of the United Nations?

Every nation should rule itself. As old Abe Lincoln said: "No man is good enough to be the master of another."

We want an Africa Charter. I see now that the Atlantic Charter doesn't cover everything. I see why the Chinese and Hindus are doubting Thomases. In this World War II we must clean the Germans and Italians out of Africa. Then at the peace table the English and French must be told to take their little suitcases and leave. We want Africa for the Africans. Come on with the Africa Charter.[6]

The New Negro was a prototype of a new American, and during the twentieth century the "question mark of Africa" was calling for a new man to emerge from the Third World. Abba Micah Soudani, "with the lore of six thousand years" and his Chinese dirk and English pistol, must "cry the heroes to wake up the dead." Africa would swallow the armies of Hitler and Mussolini as it had those of Alexander and Napoleon, but it would take a prophetic poet to shape the redeeming hero who would emerge from the apocalypse. Soudani, while on the train for Addis Ababa, lets his fancy re-create "a Byzantine painting of the Christ, nailed to a cross between thieves, on Golgotha, the Mountain of the Skull. It was a picture done in sombre colors by his young friend, Balachjo, on the wall of a Coptic church at Adowa. The Christ was Black." Adowa was the scene of the famous defeat of the Italian forces in an invasion of Ethiopia prior to World War I. Soudani's role is premonitory of the promise Tolson later represented in Liberia as the "*Mehr-licht* for the Africa-To-Be." He is also a precursor of the penetrating and sophisticated Dr. Obi Nkomo of *Harlem Gallery*.

World War II inevitably had an affect on questions of race. On 22 April 1939, Tolson wrote: "Every intelligent Negro has his eye on Europe and his ear against the United States. Every intelligent Negro is reading some fearless Negro newspaper in order to keep up with the drift of current events. The Atlantic Ocean of Teddy Roosevelt's day no longer exists. Figure it out for yourself. In order for a Negro to interpret the race problem in America, he must know the history of the world, yesterday and today. The race problem in the United States is a pimple on the diseased elephant of civilization."[7] The economic depression of the thirties had caused Tolson and other black artists and thinkers to submerge race into class. World War II caused Tolson to think not merely in terms of the Big Boys of American business but also in terms of the European nations who were the Big Boys of international power and who consequently shaped much of the world's vision of history.

If Tolson's view was to become increasingly global in response to the events of World War II, he nevertheless recognized his obligation, in his newspaper column, *Caviar and Cabbage*, to describe world events in terms that would make their meaning graphically clear to his audience. He drove home the lesson of world events by pointing up the analogies in terms of economic exploitation between the robber barons and the European powers:

> Be not deceived, Black Boy. Sambo steals a chicken, and he goes to jail. A businessman steals bonds, and he goes to Congress. Great Britain steals from 400,000,000 innocent people, and she goes down in history as a "colonizer" and "diplomat."
>
> Your multimillionaire stole when it was "legal and right" to steal. . . .
>
> Hitler and Mussolini came upon the scene late, like John Dillinger and Al Capone. After thieves have fattened themselves, they always say: "Thou shalt not steal." Dollars make conservatives; old age makes profligates gentlemen.
>
> The good old days of capitalism are gone forever. Thank God. . . .
>
> Today millions and millions of people are stoutly opposed to domestic and international robbery. We have a better conception of justice than our forefathers. Hitler and Mussolini are a throwback to the Robber Barons. Hitler and Mussolini want dollars and lands just like the Vanderbilts and Fords and Insulls. Since France and England have gobbled up most of the riches and lands, Hitler and Mussolini have decided to get theirs with bombing planes and machine guns.[8]

Tolson's views are clear and straightforward. His strong Christian background and his traditional literary training blended to create a visionary answer to the problem of war:

> How can we stop wars? How can we blot out the big evil? The Apostle Paul said in a letter to Timothy: "The love of money is the root of all evil." Paul had the lowdown. Take the lousy profits out of war, and there will be no wars! Man's love of money created a Frankenstein named Power. There can be no peace until we get rid of "the root of all evil."
>
> The poet Tennyson dreamed of a Parliament of Man, a Federation of the World. I cast my vote for that. The Big Boys don't want that. They want to pile up "treasures on earth." That means an everlasting series of wars between the Haves and the Have-Nots. In a Parliament of Man, the whites and yellows and blacks should be equal. In a Parliament of Man, a man would be a man for a' that![9]

On Mother's Day 1938, in the Wiley Chapel, Tolson attended a sermon given by Dr. James L. Farmer, the father of James Leonard Farmer, the student debater. He wrote enthusiastically about that sermon a few weeks later. "A sermon is a word-picture painted by an artist-preacher to be hung in the gallery of memories." "I was thrilled by this vivid picture of Jesus the young rebel." Dr. Farmer "emphatically represents modern scholarship in the church, as typified by Dr. Harry Emerson Fosdick and Rabbi Jonah Bondi Wise and Professor William David Schermerhorn."

Dr. Farmer portrayed Jesus as a young man in conflict with his times and his parents, although his mother showed him extraordinary love. "He loved his parents but he loved his duty more. Truth was his polestar. He was a God-man. The greatest God-man working for the ages." The "core of the sermon was the conflict between the hypocrisy of parents and the frankness of youth, the mouth-Christianity of parents and the demands of youth for the everyday practice of the teachings of Jesus." When people find themselves living in a dishonest world, a world in which you can "neither practice what you preach nor preach what you practice," parents are likely to respond, "Take the world as it comes, and make the best of it," while Christian youth says, "Change the world and make it what it ought to be." According to Dr. Farmer, "If ever there was an occasion for radicalism, I declare it is amply provided here. Not an axe to fell the tree, but a spade to undermine its roots, is the urgent need of the times."

When Dr. Farmer pointed out that "Jesus was teaching contrary to the social and religious traditions of his people," Tolson added, "Yes, the Big Boys would be against Him. They would call Him an infidel, an atheist, a radical, a Red." When Dr. Farmer described Jesus' dilemma, "The more popular he became with the masses, the more hostile these leaders became toward Him, and the more determined to destroy Him," Tolson added, "If you become a defender of labor, you become an enemy of capital. If you are a lover of the masses of people, you may expect the Big Boys and their flunkies to get on your trail like a pack of hungry wolves. Jesus found that out."[10]

Tolson saw Marxist ideals and ambitions through the lens of radical Christianity. He frequently characterized himself as "the son of a preacher who was the son of a preacher who was the son of a preacher." That that statement may not be literally true only makes it clear that he very strongly willed such an identification. He also frequently represented himself as "scientific" and "realistic," attacking the dangers of wishfully misrepresenting the world even with well-intentioned idealism. In another *Caviar and Cabbage* column, he explored the implications of Nietzsche's statement, "Morality is the weapon of the weak to curb the power of the strong." Tolson prefaced his examination of Nietzsche's statement with the comment: "I hate the teachings of Nietzsche; but if the Devil tells the truth, I say: 'Amen.'" He then explained that characteristically "only the weak are moral. Strong men and strong races do what they want to do without thought of right or wrong":

> Take the Negro. The Negro is always appealing to the Constitution. Yes, Sambo is always telling the bad white folk about "the brotherhood of man and the fatherhood of God." People wonder why Negroes wear pants ragged at the knees. It's because Negroes stay on their knees begging for Democracy. Negroes sing spirituals to keep white folks from lynching Negroes.
>
> Do you know why Negroes sing "You Shall Reap Just What You Sow"? Well, the Negroes hope this song will scare the white folk. If Negroes had the power to knock the hell out of bad white folk, then the Negroes wouldn't sing "You Shall Reap Just What You Sow." If Negroes had the power to conquer the world they wouldn't sing "You Can Have All This World, Give Me Jesus." If Negroes had a powerful army, they wouldn't sing "Ain't Gonna Study War No More." Since the white man has the army and the navy, there's nothing for the Negro to do but say: "I ain't gonna study war no more."

Of course, Nietzsche's statement applies to other peoples as well, as Tolson's concluding comments make clear:

> Proud England, who walked the earth as conqueror for centuries, exploiting weaker peoples, is today appealing to justice and democracy. We Negroes can understand that. I'm wondering if Englishmen understand the pleas and prayers of black men in Africa and brown men in India.
>
> Belgium cut off the hands of Africans in the Belgian Congo, when the Africans didn't bring in enough rubber. But when the Kaiser's armies overran Belgium in World War I, the Belgians cried for justice and mercy! Today, white Americans are talking frantically about democracy. Why? Because the white folk are scared. For seventy-five years black men begged for democracy, and the majority of whites paid no attention to the appeals of black men.
>
> Maybe that old Negro mammy is wiser than our Big White Folk when she sings in the cotton patch: "You shall reap just what you sow!"[11]

While Tolson would give the devil his due, while he embraced "science" and "realism" as part of a new wave breaking up the crusty mold of conservatism protecting the unjustly privileged positions of the rich and of white folks, he characteristically believed in some fundamental moral law working its way through history. The individual must not be apathetic about demanding justice, he must not use his faith that "you shall reap just what you sow" as an excuse for being passive; however, in the long view of history, Tolson saw substantial wisdom in the old Negro mammy's song—the same song that his mother often sang after his father's sermon on Sunday mornings.

In *Rendezvous with America* Tolson began the section "Of Men and Cities" with "Vesuvius," a symbolic poem that approaches allegory in its explicitness. The "strong men," ironically described as those "who sow not what they reap," decide against the folk wisdom of the shepherd and the counsel of the wise to build the city of Pompeii close to the slumbering, but potentially dangerous volcano, Vesuvius. The shepherd speaks the warning that the reader knows history will confirm. By making an analogy to Rome, however, Tolson suggests that the rumblings of Vesuvius, although described primarily in physical terms, are also in accord with fundamental moral law, that nature cannot stomach the presumption and folly of man. Thus the workings of the volcano become an inevitable judgment. The shepherd speaks:

> Blacksmithing gods live in the cone.
> Sometimes they sleep a century,
> Then rouse and mighty forges roar
> As if they madmen be.
>
> "Is not Vesuvius like your Rome?
> She gorges often and can't digest
> The mass; and so the smithy gods
> Must use the bellows; at their behest
> The bloating lumps are vomited.
> Vesuvius takes her rest.
>
> "Beneath your very feet my lords,
> A city of the dead now lies.
> You cannot change Vesuvius,
> Nor yet the ways of fools and flies.
> Who builds on the volcano's site
> Is strong, nor good, nor wise."

Despite such warnings Pompeii is built and becomes a city of decadent grandeur, but the gulf between master and slave, privileged and poor, carries a clear prophetic message:

> Perfumed eunuchs serve golden plates
> To conquerors of Tyre and Es-Scham.
> The statesmen stroll bronze-lettered flags
> And seal fates with an epigram.
>
> Numidian slaves in the marketplace
> Barter for lords with lordly guile,
> And Roman boys learn at the feet
> Of hoary Greeks who never smile. . . .
>
> The world-wise scribble on frescoed walls
> The scandals of the night before;

The odds and ends of bones and flesh
Shuffle beyond the palace door. . . .

Pompeii's vanities spit contempt
Into the beggars' rags and scars.
Pompeii worships the seven sins
As the seven wise men the seven stars.

The final section of the poem is a description of the eruption of Vesuvius. The closing image suggests that the eruption, although terrible, is a necessary abortive process. Nature cannot abide man's arrogance and folly:

Three days, three ages,
The pumice stones
And jet-black mud
And vestige bones
And entrail lava
Pour from Vesuvius'
Stupendous womb!

When *Rendezvous with America* was published in 1944, World War II was making rubble of the cities of man, the symbols of man's civilized aspirations, long and laboriously built. The arrangement of the poems within the book contains a message aimed at a world at war. The long opening poem, "Rendezvous with America," reminds the reader of the strength America draws from being a nation of peoples from widely different national, social, and racial experiences. "Woodcuts for Americana," a collection of poems, implies a contemporary view of America showing both its warts and roses. "Dark Symphony" celebrates specifically the historic contributions of black Americans and their struggle to gain recognition for their achievements. It ends with a proud and defiant prediction of accomplishment and cultural realization.

The section labeled "A Song for Myself" seems something of a misnomer except for the poem by the same title. But a close reading reveals a theme of survival that strongly links the four seemingly disparate poems of this section. "Sonnets," organized by poetic genre, is an aberration from what seems to be the clear ideological pattern of the titles of other sections. But the sonnets, in keeping with the longer poems that precede and follow, do emphasize the dependence of social well-being on personal integrity and the realization of a democratic ethos. "Of Men and Cities," which begins with "Vesuvius," the poem discussed above, and ends with "Babylon," another long apocalyptic poem, takes an Olympian view of world history as a drama of human aspiration and its many failures. "The Idols of the Tribe" focuses on the corruption of man's dreams by his prejudices, his creation and worship of false gods. And "Tapestries of Time" threads a sturdy faith in human progress through the wreckage of man's history, particularly through the chaos and destruction of World War II. The American attempt to realize one nation of many peoples coalesces with a worldwide attempt to achieve a new democracy of nations, and the success of both efforts ultimately is dependent upon the realization of new possibilities for mankind.

The title poem, "Rendezvous with America," opens with a celebration of the great variety of men and dreams that have come from other lands to make a new nation:

Messiahs from the Sodoms and Gomorrahs of the Old World,
Searchers for Cathay and Cipango and El Dorado,
Mystics from Oubangui Chari and Uppsala,
Serfs from Perugia and Tonle Sap,
Jailbirds from Newgate and Danzig,
Patriots from Yokosuka and Stralsund,
Scholars from Oxford and Leyden,
Beggars from Bagdad and Montmartre,
Traders from Tyrrhenian Sea and Mona Passage
Sailors from the Skagerrak and Bosporus Strait,
Iconoclasts from Buteshire and Zermatt.

These "men of many breeds" make

An international river with a legion of tributaries!
A magnificent cosmorama with myriad patterns and colors!
A giant forest with loin-roots in a hundred lands!
A cosmopolitan orchestra with a thousand instruments playing
    America!

The poem counterpoints specific notable achievements by American Jews, Italians, Chinese, Poles, and blacks against the words of a blind man who says, "Look at the 'kikes,' 'dagos,' 'chinks,' 'bohunks,' and 'niggers.'" America is not always what it should be. "Sometimes Uncle Sam . . . sinks into the nepenthe of slumber."

And the termites of anti-Semitism busy themselves
And the Ku Klux Klan marches with rope and faggot
And the money-changers plunder the Temple of Democracy
And the copperheads start boring from within
And the robber barons pillage the countryside
And the con men try to jimmy the Constitution
And the men of good will are hounded over the Land
And the People groan in the *tribulum* of tyranny.
                    Then
        Comes the roar of cannon at Fort Sumter
        Or the explosion of Teapot Dome

Or the Wall Street Crash of '29
Or the thunderclap of bombs at Pearl Harbor!

World War II seems to sum up all the trials of America, yet Tolson proclaims with Whitman-like serenity and confidence

In these midnight dawns
Of the Gethsemanes and Golgothas of Peoples,
I put my ear to the common ground of America.
From the brows of mountains
And the breasts of rivers
And the flanks of prairies
And the wombs of valleys
Swells the *Victory March* of the Republic,
In the masculine allegro of factories
And the blues rhapsody of express trains,
In the bass crescendo of power dams.
And the nocturne adagio of river boats.

Not only does Tolson hear "the *Victory March* of the Republic" orchestrated in America's technological achievements, but in the concluding stanza America is imaged as a triumphant figure surviving villainous attack:

In these midnight dawns
Of the vulture Philistines of the unquiet skies
And the rattlesnake Attilas of the uptorn seas . . .
America stands
Granite-footed as the Rocky Mountains
Beaten by the whirlpool belts of wet winds,
Deep-chested as the Appalachians
Sunning valleys in the palms of their hands,
Tough-tendoned as the Cumberlands
Shouldering the truck caravans of US 40,
Clean-flanked as the lavender walls of Palo Duro
Washed by the living airs of canyon rivers,
Eagle-hearted as the Pacific redwoods
Uprearing their heads in the dawns and dusks of ages.

"Woodcuts for Americana" is a collection of only loosely related poems, each of which individually suggests some unique aspect of America. "The Mountain Climber" is true to his task, although a series of rhetorical questions vividly points up the painful nature of his imperative climb. The questions also imply his heroic nature. "Old Man Michael" is viewed with condescending humor until he points out that, although farmers blame the failure of their crops on sun, moon, stars, and rain, and although "It's drudgery to weed tares out of wheat,"

"Yet, if the one is many, we shall cheat
The marketplace and lay a harvest by.

"Yes, if the one is many, kinds in kind,
We shall not leave a world of tares behind."

A more ironic proletarian message is suggested in "When Great Dogs Fight." A wretched mongrel intimidated by the size and pedigrees of a bulldog and a mastiff deliberately seizes his opportunity when the other two engage in violent combat:

A sphinx haunts every age and every zone:
When great dogs fight, the small dog gets a bone.

"My Soul and I," the poem Tolson wrote for his wife, Ruth, and "The Man Inside," dedicated to V. F. Calverton, both previously quoted, are also included in this section.

Two other poems, "An Ex-Judge at the Bar" and "The Town Fathers," focus on the ironies of race in the American South. The judge, singing *Dixie* at the bar in Tony's Lady of Romance in celebration of his return from France, becomes an ex-judge when the Goddess Justice, standing on the bar, unbandages her eyes and says:

"To make the world safe for Democracy,
You lost a leg in Flanders fields—oui, oui?
To gain the judge's seat, you twined the noose
That swung the Negro higher than a goose."

The poem concludes in guilty hysterical laughter and drunken fellowship.[12] In "The Town Fathers" it is Fourth of July at the courthouse square when "The Mayor spat / His snuff and said, / 'We need a slogan!' " The Sheriff and Judge, unaware of the irony, applaud the result:

On a neon billboard,
As high as a steeple,
The travelers puzzle
The amazing sequel:
The Blackest Land
And the Whitest People

Three of the last four poems of this section, "The Poet," "Esperanto," and "The Unknown Soldier," comment directly or indirectly on the role of the poet. "The Poet" has been discussed above, but a line from the poem, in which the Poet is described as "A champion of the People versus Kings," serves as an introduction to the subject of "Esperanto." Esperanto is the language of the people, the "catholic tongue of woe," spoken by Chinese, Arab, Jew, Saxon, Eskimo, Latin, Danakil, and Crow. It is from the blood of the people that freedoms are born, and the poem closes with a rallying admonition against the profit motive:

> Now put the freeman's ax
> To the loins of the evil root,
> Now cleave with the freeman's ax
> The charnel-house of loot,
> So that our children wax
> On the freeman's fruit!

The narrator of "The Unknown Soldier" identifies himself with those who fought at Concord Bridge, on Lake Erie, at Stony Ridge, at San Juan Hill and Chateau Thierry, Corregidor and the Arctic Sea. He witnessed "horizontal States grow vertical,"[13]

> These States bred freedom in and in my bone:
> I hymn their virtues and their sins atone.

Thus the narrator identifies himself as the Unknown Soldier whose "faith props the tomorrows," who opens doors "To the Rights of Man," whose

> . . . troubled ghost shall haunt These States, nor cease
> Till the global war becomes a global peace.

The democratic dream must be realized in America and extended to the world.

Tolson made some changes in the text of "Dark Symphony" between its publication in *Atlantic Monthly* in September 1941 and its publication in *Rendezvous with America*. The most important changes are in the opening stanza, but another, minor change is significant thematically. In stanza 4, line 4, as it appears in the book, *his* is underlined: "The New Negro Speaks to *his* America." The effect of much of what Tolson has said about America in the two opening sections of his book, and now in "Dark Symphony," is to stake out a claim by definition. America is a nation of the people, not a nation of the Big Boys. It is a nation of a people who have learned to respect the rights and dignity of other people, not a nation of exploiters, racists, or demagogues. The latter are the true *un*-Americans. Black People share in the authentic American heritage as richly as do any other people.

> Black Crispus Attucks taught
> Us how to die
> Before white Patrick Henry's bugle breath
> Uttered the vertical
> Transmitting cry:
> "Yea, give me liberty or give me death."

The songs of black slaves conjure up "shadow-shapes of ante-bellum years." "One More River to Cross," "Steal Away to Jesus," "The Crucifixion," "Swing Low, Sweet Chariot," and "Go Down, Moses" are provided just enough of a dramatic context to make clear that these songs carried sustaining messages that only the slaves understood. The wrongs that have been suffered must not be forgotten. The New Negro proclaims the accomplishments of his ancestors and boldly shares in the most important cultural activities of today. He is free of the exploitation, profiteering, and fascist subversion that call the Americanness of other Americans into question:

> Thus,
> Out of abysses of Illiteracy,
> Through labyrinths of Lies,
> Across waste lands of Disease . . .
> We advance!
>
> Out of dead-ends of Poverty,
> Through wildernesses of Superstition,
> Across barricades of Jim Crowism . . .
> We advance!
>
> With the Peoples of the World . . .
> We advance!

The democratic promise of America is expanded into a global dream for mankind, and within that dream black America will find challenge, recognition, and support. The rendezvous with America is a rendezvous with self-realization for all the peoples of the world who have been excluded from the full democratic dream by poverty, class, or race.

That the opening sections of *Rendezvous* were strongly influenced by Whitman hardly needs to be said. But that awareness is mildly puzzling when one reads the opening stanza of the title poem of the next section, "A Song for Myself":

> I judge
> My soul
> Eagle
> Nor mole
> A man
> Is what
> He saves
> From rot.

Although the title echoes Whitman, the dimeter lines, the compressed syntax, and the dry understatement suggest a greater debt to Emily Dickinson. If such influences sometimes seem at odds, it apparently did not bother Tolson. He borrowed from each to create his own statement, which implicitly acknowledges and claims *his* American heritage.

The stanzas immediately following make clear that saving oneself from rot is not an easy process. The idols of the tribe everywhere exert their distorting and destructive influence. Unwise prophets divide the earth by class and by birth. There are caesars both without and within who must be conquered. Aggression and self-pity must be resisted. Judgments must be made, not left to God. The true braille of the times must be read amid confusing and ambiguous signals. Acknowledging all these difficulties, the mind is dependent upon the historical moment:

> A sponge,
> The mind
> Soaks in
> The kind
> Of stuff
> That fate's
> Milieu
> Dictates.

But the historical moment is rich in possibilities. Tolson again sounds more like the expansively assertive Whitman, although still in tightly constrained verse form:

> Jesus,
> Mozart,
> Shakespeare,
> Descartes,
> Lenin,
> Chladni,
> Have lodged
> With me.
> I snatch
> From hooks
> The meat
> Of books.
> I seek
> Frontiers,
> Not worlds
> Of biers.

Stoically, however, he accepts the fact that today he can expect only the few to "Yield Poets / Their due." The judgment of the masses must wait for tomorrow.

> I harbor
> One fear

> If death
> Crouch near:
> Does my
> Creed span
> The Gulf
> Of Man?

If Tolson's faith in the power of democracy to make its way toward universal realization is akin to Whitman's, it nevertheless seems much more chancy, much more dependent on the willed actions of humankind to achieve a sense of universal fraternity. The poet must never accede to those forces that would narrow or limit his vision. Yet he thus must announce what few are ready to hear.

"A Song for Myself" introduces a relatively short section of the book, which includes "The Shift of Gears," "The Ballad of the Rattlesnake," and "A Scholar Looks at an Oak." Since "A Song for Myself" is the title of the section as well as the initial poem, the reader is predisposed to read the three additional poems as in some sense expressions of the self, although each of the other poems is written from an impersonal perspective. "The Shift of Gears" is a humorous dialogue between a driver and the mechanic he is consulting to repair his car. The impatient and defensively arrogant driver is indirectly admonished by the mechanic's judgment:

> "A car or a man
> Can outwear the years,
> If horse sense handles
> The shift of gears."

Tolson was a notoriously bad driver. A car was to him a very foreign, if sometimes useful, convenience. And the maintenance of a car frequently was mysteriously frustrating. The driver in the poem is quite probably a mocking self-portrait. However, the mechanic's advice carries more weight than such slight biographical reference warrants. The mechanic is talking about the importance of "horse sense" for the survival of a "car *or a man*" threatened by the aging process. Thus the mechanic's advice humorously amplifies the theme of "A Song for Myself," "A man / Is what / He saves / From rot."

In a much more sinister sense "The Ballad of the Rattlesnake," discussed at some length earlier, is also about survival, or, to be more precise, about its opposite, the failure to survive. The blond man cruelly dies, a victim of his failure to reckon with the hostility of the Apaches. But the refrain of the poem makes it clear that the message of survival is aimed at instilling a sense of common purpose and cooperation among sharecroppers, of whom "Many were black, / And many were white."

"A Scholar Looks at an Oak" is an imagistic poem with the title providing just enough of a dramatic context to point a message. The poem is in three stanzas. The first starkly pictures the hostile environment within which the oak endures:

> Storms slug its head,
> Its shoulders sag,
> Its beard is shorn
> Upon the crag.

The second emphasizes what Tolson meant when he praised something or someone as *vertical*:

> In dawns and dusks
> Its spine alone
> Keeps it erect
> Like Doric stone.

The third stanza compares the brief life of a squash to the long-lived endurance of the oak:

> A squash grows up
> At a summer's stroke;
> An age wears out
> To make an oak.

What the scholar sees looking at the oak is clear. Both the scholar and his people must be firm and upright. They are building for a future firmly rooted against the distractions of petty difficulties. The sturdiness and endurance of the oak tree reflect Tolson's pride in the strength and endurance, or survival, of his people.

There is no such underlying thematic unity to the twelve Shakespearean sonnets in the next section, "Sonnets." Eight of the twelve are about public issues. Four, including "The Gallows," quoted above to illustrate Tolson's commitment to teaching, are about ostensibly personal experiences, although all may well be fictional rather than authentically autobiographical.

"The Gallows" is the most successful of the twelve. The concluding couplet,

> The lame, the halt, the blind—these struck him down;
> Then the gallows of ignorance hanged the little town,

introduces a surprisingly eloquent fablelike argument that is perfectly tailored to the preceding tribute to the teacher. The other sonnets on public issues frequently seem strident. Tolson was probably attempting to use the sonnet form in a manner reminiscent of Claude McKay's "If We Must Die" or "The Lynching," but the dramatic contexts too often result in editorial cartoons rather than carefully wrought metaphors. The ostensibly personal sonnets seem more like literary exercises. The dramatic contexts—a lover speculating on the effect a lie would have on the lovers' relationship, a man unable to relieve a friend's grief, and a suicide witnessed by a friend who felt "a soul compulsion" that was not love—all remain stiffly abstract, insufficiently realized to be effectively moving.

This section of twelve poems is Tolson's only known extended experiment with the sonnet form, and he probably was wise to abandon it. It is the weakest section of *Rendezvous* and serves little purpose in the overall design of the book.

The last three sections of *Rendezvous*, "Of Men and Cities," "The Idols of the Tribe," and "Tapestries of Time," make it clear that the rendezvous with America is a long-prepared-for event that will take place not just in the United States but throughout the world.

"Of Men and Cities" begins with "Vesuvius," which is followed by "The Shipwright," a celebration of the craftsmanship of "The Galahads of the dock" and their product, "an ocean cosmopolite":

> Our matrix shapes our citizen of the world
> To cross the churning mountains of the sea.

In "The Triumph Aster," the flower of that name, growing "Between sky-scrapers of my native street"—presumably in New York City—becomes a symbol of the promise of the triumph of the aspirations of the Chinese people. That the poem is "For Madame Chiang" suggests that Tolson's education in the class struggle was occasionally spotty. "The Bard of Addis Ababa," crying "the heroes to wake up the dead," follows. "Damascus Blade" serenely prophesies the revolution by praising the extraordinary work of "The craftsman of Es-Scham," who

> Has finished his blade
> For the Sunrise Sultan
> Of the Bairam crusade.

"The Street Called Straight" is another oblique attack on the profit motive as the root of all evil. The entrance to "the Street the wise call Straight" in Damascus "hails the sunrise" and celebrates the fact that food and shelter are graciously available without price. The other end of the street, however, poses a rhetorical question with a rather obvious answer:

> But the fishhawk money-changers
> Infest the khans and bazaars;
> And the scented Magdalens beckon,
> Beckon like siren stars.
> As I drain my mug dry in the tavern,

Not far from the Judas gate,
I riddle: "What begets the crooked
In the Street the wise called Straight?"

"Babylon," the last poem in "Of Men and Cities," carries Tolson's apocalyptic warning to a crescendo. This "global city of the golden calves" is a monument to all the sins and vices that grow from worshiping the idols of the tribe. But Daniel has written his message of doom upon the wall of this "Jezebel of the plains," this "Shadow-shape of vanity."

The looter of nations
Shall grovel and pass
Like the lizard's shadow
On the hoar morass.

Like the wandering leper
He shall cry in the night,
And the mockery of tongues
Shall double his plight. . . .

A people divided
Against itself
By the Idols of Race
And Caste and Pelf

Writes its own epitaph
With the fingers of doom:
"Here lies a nation
In a suicide's tomb."

Sir Francis Bacon in the first book of *The New Organon* wrote:

The Idols of the Tribe have their foundation in human nature itself, and in the tribe or race of men. For it is a false assertion that the sense of man is the measure of things. On the contrary, all perceptions as well of the sense as of the mind are according to the measure of the individual and not according to the measure of the universe. And the human understanding is like a false mirror, which, receiving rays irregularly, distorts and discolors the nature of things by mingling its own nature with it.

Fulton H. Anderson has partially explained Bacon's concept as follows:

The human understanding is not a "dry light," but ever "receives an infusion from the will and affections." What a man prefers, that he takes to be true. He shrinks from difficult questions because of his own impatience and their narrowing of his hope. He avoids the deeper problems of nature because of religious superstition; neglects the examination of mean and vulgar things because of pride; and refuses to entertain new opinions from fear of disapproval.[14]

Melvin B. Tolson

Bacon's comments on the idols of the tribe left a deep and lasting impression on Tolson's imagination. He used the phrase repeatedly throughout his writing career. In *Rendezvous* he ironically prefaced his poem "The Idols of the Tribe" with a quotation from Hitler's *Mein Kampf*:

> A state which, in the epoch of race poisoning, dedicates itself to the cherishing of its best racial elements, must some day be master of the world.

The opening section of the poem then describes a primitive community dominated by fear and brutal repression:

> The veldt men pray
> Carved wood and stone
> And tear their flesh
> To vein and love. . . .
>
> Witch doctors whine
> Edicts anew
> And saint their mugs
> Of chloral brew.
>
> Fear grapples fear,
> Crinkles the knife:
> And life is death
> And death is life.

Section 2 illustrates how "The rule-or-ruin class . . . / creates narcissine images of itself," defending "its fetishes from the merest gibe." The "black-veldt god," complacent in the physical advantages his kinked hair, low wide nostrils, and dark skin provide as protection from a harsh climate, "is not aware / of civilizations buried in the jungle's maw." "The yellow god," a vegetarian god, "lulled by the incense wisdom of repose," "turns up his nose / at odors of the carnivorous white." "The Nordic god," "Hairy as the ape, of lip as thin . . . makes a pseudo-science of his skin / And writes his autobiography *Superman*." The race biases produced by worshiping such idols

> . . . sow
> Hemlocks to maim and blind,
> Pile up Sinais of woe,
> Jettison the freedoms of mind,
> Breed the hydras of stealth,
> Set kind razeeing kind,
> Convert to potter's fields the commonwealth.

Section 3 opens by focusing on a Southern town where white genius is wasted keeping blacks down. The "Fuhrer's claws / Dig up dry bones / Of

the gray Lost Cause," and "the ermine class / Throw scraps of hate / To the
starved white mass." Because

> The skull and bones
> Of yesterday
> Haunts those who travel
> The American Way.

The idols of the tribe sow confusion and destruction. They must be de-
stroyed or defied. They inherently invite divine or natural judgment. The
truth will prevail:

> Mein Kampf is lepra
> That whores the soul,
> And the brothels of race
> Nordic bawds control.

> Yet thunderbolt hells
> Of chastening rods
> Smite ever Gomorrahs
> Of Tribal gods!

A letter from Mary Lou Chamberlain to Tolson concerning editorial
changes in *Rendezvous* indicates that as of 4 February 1944 "Idols of the
Tribe" followed "Tapestries of Time" in the manuscript. The argument of
the book, however, strongly insists on the present order. "Tapestries of
Time" is the appropriate climactic conclusion. It begins with a cosmic view
of "a universe / naked of prayer and curse." The odyssey of our world is
viewed by "The hoary druid Time," who

> Sees the *raison d'etre* worming from the slime,
> Discovers the vigils of a soul-rived clod
> In a rendezvous with God.

Implicitly, the rendezvous with America is a step along the path of self-real-
ization that ultimately leads to a rendezvous with God. Time speaks in spite
of "mimic clocks." In the presence of the rape of freedoms and "Pearl Har-
bor's red December," one must "pause to remember / The warp and woof of
the Whole." Attila, Caesar, Alexander, and Napoleon, all such "puny ty-
rants"

> Are scythed like weeds by Prophet Time
> And raked by irony sublime
> Into the mute democracy of death.

Section 3 of "Tapestries of Time" is narrated from the perspective of "the
Undersoul of the quick and dead" and section 4 from the perspective of "the

Oversoul of the brothered dead." In Section 3 man is a "cosmic blunder-head" willing "to die / For truths and freedoms beyond the ear and eye" during golden ages, but blinding himself and others "with the Nietzschean lie" "as his empires climbed on dead men's bones." Science was newborn in the golden ages, when "No *laissez-faire* pimped in the marketplace, / And visions of hell were stumbling blocks to sin." Christ, in a golden age, did all that he could to create a true brotherhood of man, but man failed to heed the meaning of the Cross and instead "soothed his conscience with lotus loves, / And the root of evil became his totem pole."

Hubristically man "leeched the whip that Faith had let alone" in an effort to find "The open sesame of the Master Mind." Man was reduced from the greatness of Shakespeare's time to a mechanism fit for the junkman's dump. "Man's lording freedom of the will" was revealed by the deliberate devastation of Lidice during World War II. Under the sanction of the ancient Nordic myth of Yggdrasill, "He bellied downward to the crawling world."

> The Nazi knave paraded the Quisling clown,
> As quicksands sucked eons of freedoms down.
> Man sits like Rodin's Thinker in the ruins,
> But still he wears the fool's rag-tattered crown.

It is a time of universal consternation.

> When X grinds in its mill Man's golden ware,
> He shakes the very Pleiades with his prayer.

Poets "scurry into the ivory tower" "To escape the wasteland of the Dooms-day Hour." "The ghosts of Milton and Whitman grieve without." Only "The seven-league boots of Revolution" seem capable of effective moral action, while saviors, scholars, public servants, and holy men belie their trust and "Caesar corrals the *hoi polloi*."

> And now about Man magna chartas lie,
> Whose bones the jackals of cynicism licked dry.
> The parliament of ants decrees to live,
> But man can only legislate to die.

But "the Oversoul of the brothered dead" offers a complementary, if contrasting, faith:

> While poets wail jeremiads and forfeit their hair
> And dialecticians syllogize despair
> And diplomats lacerate their covenants,
> Man climbs the cosmic epochs, stair by stair.

Man "is verved with such nobility / His conscience digs a hell to damn itself." He "dovetails yesteryears / With the tomorrows of the hemispheres."

He "understands the tragedy of laughter," "comprehends the comedy of tears," "murals a symphony / As armies grapple in scarlet anarchy," and "sinews a Jesus with immortality."

Man frequently does not perceive the wonders that grow from his accomplishments. The Saxon bard does not dream of the Shakespeare who will follow. The craftsman of Timbuktu hammering iron does not dream of the diesel-powered Zephyr. The doctor of the dark ages does not dream of the "vistas of medicine pinnacled from his view." The Malayan artist, the Angle judge, the Arab sage, the Viking, the Zulu, and the Hellenist all have no means of imagining the wonders to follow their activities. Man must not lose his "mecca of the commonweal" because "the compass fall[s] beneath a Caesar's wheel."

> The daylight ages come, night ages go,
> On sunset hearths, the embers of Waterloos glow;
> And he who tries to stop earth's *Limited*
> Reaps the oblivion that know-nothings sow.

Freedom is earned by rebellion. Man must learn to struggle for his dreams in the bleakest moments of history:

> The valley of dry bones breathes the faith in Man
> And cities gather flesh in the ashes of pyres.

> Stand not like foolish prophets round the biers
> Of worlds embalmed, and grieve away the years.
> Man strides the Atlas of Red-Letter Days
> To hail the Apocalypse of Hemispheres!

Sections 5, 6, 7, and 8 are shorter than 3 and 4 and thus quicken the argument. For Tolson the will to freedom is implicit in the will to live, hence "The will to live dooms tyranny to die." The tyrant's ambition "to change the lunar tide / Of human nature is *ultimately* impossible." In section 6 the narrator assures the reader he has seen death in many fearful and awesome guises, but neither he "nor Prophet Time, shall ever see / The death of Liberty."

Section 7 lists a series of historic occasions when men fought persistently against great odds to retain or to realize their freedom. These occasions are counterpointed by rhetorical, fablelike questions as to whether the cobra, the tiger, or the rats shall control and rule.

The basis for the faith and confidence of the poem's argument having been clearly stated, the concluding stanza opens with a grim picture of the devastation of World War II:

> Cities crunch in the python coil of tanks,
> Stukas grind into bonedust patriot ranks.

Bellies of oceans bloat with men and ships,
Maelstroms redden the Axis apocalypse.

But the narrator quickly reminds us:

In many a midnight Freedom has buckled low
And walked in togaed victory at dawn.

Signs of a happier future are emerging:

Already legends gear the brave and free
From Dunkirk, Sevastopol, and the Coral Sea.

And these signs lead to a vision that provides prophetic strength:

The New World Charter banners the Peoples' fight,
A cloud by day and a pillar of fire by night.

The tapestries of time vindicate the faith of the people:

The Swastika Terror cannot conjure a plan
To stop the calendared March of the Global Man!

In *Rendezvous* Tolson all but completely abandoned the free verse that characterized *A Gallery of Harlem Portraits*. He experimented with many different varieties of rhyme and meter, but his efforts at confining his ambitious prophetic and apocalyptic messages into such tight formal restraints were not always happy. One frequently feels that the form is too mannered for the thought. Rebellion, the quest for freedom, mythic disorder, and rebirth frequently do not fit neatly into quatrains. As an academic, Tolson was almost certainly beginning to feel the influence of the New Critics with their stress on recapturing formal traditions. But Tolson still seemed deeply compelled to speak in a voice that represented the people, whether that of Whitman or that of his father, or perhaps the more compellingly romantic voice of the Amharic bard, Abba Micah Soudani. The result is that *Rendezvous* often seems to look in two directions at the same time. But the impassioned nature of Tolson's vision, no matter how often hobbled by the chosen verse forms, certainly merits far more careful scholarly and critical attention than it has thus far received.

IV

A TIME TO MOVE

There is a man in Texas, Melvin B. Tolson, a professor of English who with a single volume of poetry, "Rendezvous with America," established himself as one of America's important contemporary poets.

When his "Dark Symphony" won the National Poetry contest conducted in connection with the American Negro exposition in Chicago in 1940, he won widespread attention. And Earl Robinson, composer of the well-known "Ballad for Americans," set it to music. The editors of *Common Ground* then asked him to write a poem for their magazine and he wrote, "Rendezvous with America," the title poem of the volume.

Tolson, a man with boundless energy, a gleam in his eye, and a ready sense of humor has been described as "a voice crying in the wilderness." He has been teaching at Wiley College in Marshall, Texas, for 22 years. Most college students in the deep South who do not know him have heard about him. They have heard of his belief in the oneness of little people everywhere no matter what their race. They have heard of his fearlessness before lynch mobs. "One Texan who led a mob against him later gave a piano to his little theatre."

Thus wrote Ramona Lowe in a column for the *Defender's* New York bureau, 24 February 1945. Hers was only one of many published recognitions and reviews of *Rendezvous with America*. Reviews appeared in the *Pittsburgh Courier, Kansas City Star, Los Angeles Times, New York World-Telegram, New York Times, Richmond Times Dispatch*, and *Chicago Sun*. Langston Hughes wrote about *Rendezvous* in his "Here to Yonder" column in the *Chicago Defender*, and Frank Marshall Davis reviewed it for the Associated Negro Press. It was also reviewed in *The Christian Century, Crisis, Negro College Quarterly, New Adventures into Poetry, Phylon*, and the *Saturday Review of Literature*. *Rendezvous* quickly went into a third edition. The publication of Tolson's first book of poems was an important literary event. The enthusiasm and concern of the initial reviews contrast sharply with the present-day scholarly indifference to *Rendezvous*.

All of the reviews were favorable, although a few were restrained, if not

Melvin B. Tolson, June 1945.

grudging. Many were enthusiastic. W. E. Garrison in *The Christian Century* wrote of Tolson: "This Negro poet speaks with one of the clearest, strongest voices now to be heard in verse. . . . Here is vigor of thought with intensity of emotion but without violence; a tragic sense of life redeemed from despair and restrained from bitterness by breadth of sympathy and an unshaken faith in democracy. This is poetry which at once unveils some of the problems of our society and gives magnificent expression to the spirit of America as men of vision dare to hope that it really is."[1]

Margaret Walker, who had won the Yale University Younger Poet's Award in 1942, wrote with enthusiasm and pride, but also noted a problem that was to become more pronounced in Tolson's later poetry, the problem of his poems reaching the audience they deserved: "His is a highly specialized and technical art . . . and his sources run the entire gamut of the civilized history of mankind. What will startle many intellectuals is the wealth of Negro material which provides such a frame of reference. These poems are full of arresting images . . . and he handles difficult forms and metres with comparative ease. No one can say here is another naive Negro poet. He is a poet to be reckoned with by all poets. One hopes and believes that in spite of its almost esoteric nature this book will find a wide mass audience as well as the precience [*precieuse?*]. It deserves a better fate than the precience [*precieuse*] can give it."[2]

Richard Wright, who excited enthusiastic praise from Tolson for *Uncle Tom's Children* and *Native Son*, returned the compliment: "Tolson's poetic lines and images sing, affirm, reject, predict, and judge experience in America, and his poetry is direct and humanistic. All history, from Genesis to Munich, is his domain. The strong men keep coming and Tolson is one of them."[3]

Arthur E. Burke compared Tolson to previous poets of the Renaissance: "Melvin Tolson's *Rendezvous with America* . . . carries one back to Cullen's *Color* and Hughes' *Fine Clothes to the Jew*. No Negro poet save Sterling Brown, in his *Southern Road*, has published in one volume so much that is remarkable for its freshness, its poetic imagination, and above all, its reflection of American life as it affects Negroes. The reader will not find here the same sort of color consciousness found in Cullen, the same rawness of life in Hughes, or the same satirical humor in Brown. All these elements are here, but in a mood peculiar to Tolson. Tolson exhibits a vigorous Americanism, a fine catholicity, a generous humility seldom met with."[4]

Tolson's technical virtuosity provoked a range of reactions. Robert Hilyer mixed critical sarcasm with strong praise. He described Tolson as "a good poet, and a good craftsman. . . . His versification is unusually deft, especially in his handling of the short line. . . . On the whole *Rendezvous with America* is an admirable collection." But he inserted in his brief remarks a

95

complaint, "But no skill can redeem the incorrigible one-stress line" of "A Song for Myself," and a suggestion that the reader pass over the "somewhat gaseous evocations" of the title poem.[5]

William Rose Benet found Tolson's book remarkable and Tolson "a poet of powerful rhythm and original language," but "sometimes Mr. Tolson uses words more for the love of their sound than for their aptitude." He then recommended that Tolson "needs to be more his own editor, but his work is exciting and he has the insurrection in him of the real poet." Benet added some gratuitous racial generalizations that, while clearly intended as praise, are suspiciously patronizing in the vague stereotype they evoke: "I have long thought that the Negro has a special delight in the sound, shape, and color of words that most people lack. In the past their caress upon language, whose meaning was only partially understood, may have been food for humor. There is a great deal more to it than that. They furbish and freshen words, the best of them, whether artlessly or, as here, with art; they polish them till the poetry glows from them."[6]

Nathaniel Tillman noted the appropriateness of Dodd, Mead and Company, who had published Paul Laurence Dunbar's poetry forty years previously, publishing *Rendezvous with America*: "Dunbar was the poet-interpreter of a people still somewhat primitive but struggling to throw off the thwarting effects of years of slavery. Tolson is the full-throated voice of a folk that feels its power surging up and that has come to demand its place in a country it helps to make great and free. Much of the promise indicated in the best of the formal English poems of Dunbar reaches its fulfillment in the poetry of Professor Tolson." Tillman praised the sonnets and especially admired the concluding couplet of "The Gallows": "To me Professor Tolson seems to show a finer mastery of traditional poetic form than most of the recent Negro poets. He handles the quatrain, long or short line, with virtuosity. And he exhibits excellent technique in the twelve Shakespearean sonnets which comprise a section of the volume. Particularly effective are his cryptic final couplets. I liked especially the handling of the delicate personal experience in 'A Hamlet Rives Us' and the ironic note in 'The Blindness of Scorn' ['The Gallows']."[7]

Arthur E. Burke, in *The Crisis* review quoted above, also commented on Tolson's experiments with form, but he found the sonnets disappointing: "One of the most intriguing interests of *Rendezvous with America* is the variety of verse forms. 'Rendezvous with America' and 'Dark Symphony' are especially notable for their variations in rhythm, meter, tone color, and harmony. The one section which may disappoint is 'Sonnets'. Here Tolson does not achieve sufficient flexibility in the Shakespearean form to produce a truly lyrical quality. In form he is mechanical; in matter graphically succinct and never obscure. This suggests that his genius lies in the dramatic and lyrical veins, rather than in the delicately lyrical."

Frank Marshall Davis, whom Tolson at the conclusion of his master's thesis identified as a significant member of the new wave of proletarian writers of the thirties and who was one of the judges of the National Poetry Contest in which "Dark Symphony" won first prize, was terse and staunch in his praise, although he, like Walker, feared that Tolson's poetry would not reach the audience it deserved: "His first volume reveals strength, maturity, and mastery of technique. Most of his poetry is in rhyme, but it is a rhyme as modern as tomorrow. He also has a remarkable gift for epigram. Mr. Tolson lives in no ivory tower. . . . Unfortunately, he is yet too complex for the masses."[8]

How did all this public recognition affect Tolson's position at Wiley College? The answers must be inferred from sparse information. Wiley College arranged a formal program on 29 May 1945 to celebrate the publication and success of *Rendezvous with America*. P. L. Prattis, the executive editor of the *Pittsburgh Courier*, was the featured speaker. The list of honorary patrons included many distinguished names: the editors of *Atlantic*, *Common Ground*, *Life*, *Christian Advocate*, and *Phylon* (none other than W. E. B. Du Bois at the time); the editors of the major black newspapers, the *Chicago Defender*, *Kansas City Call*, *Afro-American*, and *Black Dispatch*; the well-known writers Archibald MacLeish, Theodore Dreiser, Arna Bontemps, Nina Melville, Langston Hughes, and Jack Conroy; and such other notables as Walter White, NAACP secretary; Lawrence Reddick, curator of the Schomburg Collection; Orson Welles, actor and director; and Tolson's father. Few, if any, of these patrons were present at the ceremony, but the listing indicates something of the spread of Tolson's reputation.

However, the fact that Tolson soon afterward accepted an invitation from Langston University to join the faculty of its English department suggests that there was a growing awareness in the poet that his long tenure at Wiley College might well be coming to a conclusion. Surviving members of the Tolson family have expressed mixed feelings about Wiley College and the place it held in Tolson's life. They have many warm and vivid personal memories but also a strong and readily expressed feeling that the administration of Wiley College never adequately appreciated the talent and contribution of Tolson as poet and teacher.

His salary remained meager. For years he sought financial support from both within and without the college to build a theater to provide his students a more suitable arena for performance than the college chapel. What support he received came principally from outside the college. At the close of World War II the administration got into a tense confrontation with returning veterans over housing problems. Because Tolson did not bite his tongue, students trusted and respected him. Such a position caused jealousy and suspicion in an administration bent on maintaining its authority against increasingly challenging students. Tolson's notable success as a writer and speaker only seemed to increase that jealousy and suspicion, although there is no evidence that Tolson was directly involved in these particular student challenges to the administration.

Hobart Jarrett, one of Tolson's star debaters in the midthirties, was now chairman of the English department at Langston. He worked eagerly and effectively to encourage the administration there to make Tolson an offer, and his efforts were joined to those of several others. The decisive factor, however, for the family, was an ordinary, but important consideration, the lack of retirement benefits at Wiley. Langston promised a substantial, though by no means extravagant, raise in pay and greater financial security for the poet and his wife. He had reached a climactic moment in a varied and fruitful academic career. It was a time to reap the benefits and move on to new and different challenges. In age he was late in middle life, but his publishing career was still in its early stages, and the future seemed excitingly open-ended.

Still, Tolson was reluctant to move. His family had to persuade him. The Wiley experience for all of them had been richly rewarding, even though it was now ending with mixed feelings of pride and resentment. It was in Marshall that all the children had grown from infancy to maturity. By the summer of 1947 when the Tolsons left Wiley for Langston, Melvin, Jr., was twenty-four. Arthur was soon to be twenty-three, Wiley Wilson was twenty, and Ruth Marie was eighteen. Only Ruth Marie remained with her mother and father, although the young men kept in close touch with the family.

The family breakfasts and dinners, when "meal time was talk time," when Tolson would try out his poems and his children, testing simultaneously his written words and his family's wit, were becoming infrequent experiences. But there would remain a host of memories kept alive by many enthusiastic retellings, with variations, of experiences at Wiley. One story involved the time when Dad took the kids for a drive to Longview. For some reason Mom was away. They were on their way back home. It was night. They stopped for a red light in Hallsville. The truck in front of them didn't move when the light turned green. Dad pulled around it and went through the intersection. Soon they heard a siren. The truck they had passed had a siren on it, and it was driven by the deputy marshall. For no apparent reason he was irate. He searched the car, probably looking for bootleg liquor, since Marshall was dry and Hallsville wet. He ordered Dad into the truck and took him to jail. The children were left alone in a car in a strange town, not knowing what they had done, nor what would happen to them.

The campus of Wiley College, Marshall, Texas, in 1948.

Melvin and Ruth Tolson at home in Marshall, Texas, 1946.

But Dad came back. He told them that the marshall he encountered at the jail was an older man. While the younger man, the deputy, made false accusations and became increasingly threatening, Dad deliberately spoke only to the older man. An alliance of age against youth was created across racial lines. The marshall finally told his deputy to shut up, and Dad was returned to the car. Tolson's ability to talk himself out of the stickiest and most dangerous situations was always both awesome and reassuring to his children.

Wiley remembers the time when he was in his dad's class at the college and his dad interrupted his lecture to point out with lighthearted sarcasm that Wiley was wearing one of his dad's ties. A few minutes later, after the blush caused by being made the center of class attention had passed, Wiley raised his hand, made a few comments on the academic topic of discussion, then dryly pointed out that the professor was wearing *his* shirt. While Wiley felt free to banter with his father, his older brothers were more intimidated. Because Mel, Jr., and Arthur had gone first, tested the waters, so to speak, the boundaries and rules of male competitiveness were more clearly established and feelings were more lighthearted between Tolson and Wiley.

Mel, Jr., remembers an event that seems to bear this out. His dad had invited him to sit in on his class prior to enrolling in it for credit, but Mel was reluctant to waste his time that way and was confident of his abilities. When he enrolled in the class in question, his father soon confronted him with a question he could not answer. Then his father announced to the class with fairly heavy sarcasm that this was the young man who had such a good foundation that he had no need to audit the course before enrolling for credit. Mel was the oldest son, and Tolson took care to protect his paternal authority from his challenge. Even later in life, Tolson, proud of his sons' academic achievements, would still boast that no matter how many Ph.D.'s they got, they would never catch him. They had started too late. Ordinarily the competition Tolson provoked was stimulating and friendly, but the prickly wit and gamesmanship must have sometimes made it difficult for his sons to share more private weaknesses and doubts.

Tolson's energy was legendary, and it did not let up within the family circle. The talk at mealtime was full of good-humored games and contests. Tolson encouraged a great range of inquiry among all members of his family as well as among his students, and he reveled in intellectual controversy, but he enjoyed the contest of wit and skill almost as much as the satisfaction of intellectual curiosity. Mel remembers him using all the rhetorical tricks he could think of in the arguments that went on at the dinner table. Tolson's extraordinary success as a debate coach, the challenging family discussions at mealtime, the frequent pairing of friendly antagonists in the later poems, and particularly the zestful exchanges of the Zulu Club Wits in *Harlem*

Gallery are all of one piece. Mel also remembers his father years later some-
times pursuing discussions late into the night and into his bedroom even
when Mel, weary, could think only of sleep. Tolson's need for an audience
was earnest and relentless.

Tolson frequently told a story about a neighbor woman in Marshall who
remembered the sound of his typing into the early hours of the morning as if
it were part of the natural noises of the neighborhood. Later the same story
was told about a neighbor in Langston. The story was told with good-
humored appreciation of the woman's tolerance of the writer's queer habits,
but unspoken was also the strong and clear implication that the woman had
little or no curiosity about what the writer was typing.

There were two black colleges in Marshall, Wiley and Bishop, Methodist
and Baptist, rivals on the sporting fields, but allies within the white-con-
trolled community. The tradition of a college or university serving in loco
parentis was certainly strong at both Wiley and Bishop as a consequence.
And if Tolson's family grew up feeling an intimate part of the college com-
munity, Tolson made sure that the college and his students were part of his
family life as well. Many of Tolson's students speak of him as a strong father
figure, and he treated them often as if they were family. His courses were
seldom confined to narrow professional topics. He scolded and cajoled his
students about their manners and attitudes, their ambitions, and particu-
larly their self-perceptions.

As a teacher Tolson characteristically created a bond of concern and trust
with his students sufficient for him to be demanding, even at times insulting,
in order to challenge his students to independent thought and study. He
might ask, "Do you know the difference between a gum-chewing girl and a
cud-chewing cow?" He would then answer his own question without looking
at the offender, "It's the intelligent look on the face of the cow." He had a
famous list of forty uses for the noun. He was a stickler for his classes start-
ing on time. He locked the door, and late students were not admitted. But if
time was important, dress was not. His own was notoriously careless.

He created a dramatic monologue that became a popular feature at pep
rallies. It was about Father Time spreading stars across the heavens while an
awed observer would ask in wonder, "Oh, Father Time, what star is that?"
The stars were named for the schools in the conference, but never was there
a star to equal the great star of Wiley. Jim Farmer remembers that his fra-
ternity, Omega Psi Phi, once asked Tolson to give this presentation on a
formal occasion in the chapel. Tolson was late, and the audience grew res-
tive. A student was sent to his home and found him still dressing. Finally
Tolson arrived and hurried onto the platform to give his presentation. Just as
he was about to begin, a startled look crossed his face, he looked down, raised
both pant legs, and, in mock consternation, bellowed, "Oh my God, I for-

got my shoes!" He constantly ridiculed conventions, but he believed strongly in civilization.

Jim Farmer also remembers Tolson organizing a boycott of Marshall merchants to obtain fairer treatment for black consumers and employees. That may have been the occasion when President Dogan interceded with some understanding whites in authority to quell talk of lynching Tolson. Another experience shared by Benjamin Bell has become an often repeated story among Tolson's friends and relatives. Tolson was invited to speak during the high school commencement exercises at Rustin, Louisiana, in 1938. Four black Americans were lynched nearby the day previous to the ceremonies. Mel, Jr., had planned to drive to Rustin with his dad, but Ruth would not let him go and also tried to persuade her husband not to go. But Tolson was insistent upon keeping his word, so Benjamin Bell strapped two .38s inside his coat and drove to Rustin with the professor.

The sheriff, chief of police, and president of the school board were all there, sitting in the privileged seats reserved for white VIPs. Tolson gave an excoriating speech on the meaning of the previous day's lynching. Directly challenging his audience, he asked, "Where were you good folks when these men were lynched?" The principal of the high school, a Wiley alumnus, died a thousand deaths as Tolson spoke. At the end of his talk there was a loud and ominous silence, followed by suddenly thunderous applause that ceased almost as abruptly as it began. As the audience made its way out of the auditorium, white looked at black and vice versa. Tolson deliberately stepped up to both the sheriff and the president of the school board and spoke affably with them.

The local black residents insisted that Tolson and Bell leave as quickly as possible for their own safety by a back road. With Tolson driving, they threaded their way over treacherous country roads in the night. When Bell questioned Tolson's ability to see the wheel tracks of the road, he responded with exaggerated indignation, "My Gawd Nigguh—the Professor is driving!" They then ran into a tree. Fortunately neither car nor passengers were seriously injured. So they backed off, resumed their journey, and made it safely back to Marshall.

Bell tells another story in which Tolson played a more peripheral, but still important, role. There was an outstanding twenty-one-piece dance band at Wiley, of which Bell was a member. One night on the way back from playing at Longview they came across a car almost completely submerged in water with three men and a woman stark naked inside. They rescued them, only to hear later on the radio a news flash that a band of blacks had run a car with four white people in it off the road and into the river nearly drowning the four whites. Bell and others were arrested. When Tolson heard of the arrest he raised hell until he got President Dogan to get the students out of jail. He later asked an assembly of the college whether "We should continue to let our students play for the debauched whites, if they are unwilling to protect our young people."

Sometimes Tolson's speeches were reported in the newspapers. Arthur Tolson kept a copy of an Associated Negro Press article that describes Tolson's appearance at the University of Texas in Austin in 1946:

> Standing in a packed auditorium, on the campus of Texas University, from which President Homer Rainey had been fired for his liberal policies, Melvin B. Tolson, Professor of English at Wiley College, blasted the myths of race and class superiority. For two hours his pointed epigrams evoked thought, while his eloquence and mastery of facts held the audience.
>
> The Daily Texan, official organ of the University, carried quotations and a summary of the speech on the front page. It was the most dynamic speech ever made here in the struggle for minority rights. . . .
>
> Speaking of his friend Dr. Frank Dobie, visiting professor at Cambridge University, England, who had just been attacked by Governor Coke Stevenson, Tolson said: "During great crises and struggles for human rights, many intellectuals get cold feet, and to warm them they climb into an ivory tower, like T. S. Eliot and Claude McKay. They became 'spiritual'. They talk about 'spiritual' values. That's a form of hypocrisy that keeps them from fighting these dirty battles, these bloody struggles, for racial justice and social democracy."

The Wiley years stayed strong in Tolson's memory and sometimes worked their way in ironic fashion into his later work. R. Henri Heights III, one of Tolson's most brilliant debaters, whose erratic career at Wiley spanned many more years than usual because of discipline problems, wrote Tolson a letter still preserved among the Tolson papers. Heights informed his former professor that he was now a theology student at the University of California, and he described his triumphant initial speech to an assembly of fellow students. Then he closed his letter with these words, which represent the élan that Tolson instilled in his students and that almost certainly stirred a warm response in his own blood:

> Now for the fireworks, I have gone through my copy of "Rendezvous" many times and my conclusion is this: "As a Negro poet you are tops. But you are too big to be a Negro poet. Take up the cause of humanity and become a world poet."

In *Harlem Gallery*, Tolson's last major poem, one of the major characters is named Hideho Heights. He is both the public "bard of Lenox Avenue" and the private author of "E. & O. E.," a poem for which Tolson had many years earlier been awarded *Poetry*'s Bess Hokim prize, but which beyond that had received very little recognition. Joy Flasch made a note from a conversation with Tolson indicating that Heights once also picked Tolson up and carried him through a mob.

Tolson himself wrote a comic nostalgic note about the Wiley faculty member, Simbini M. Nkomo, whose name he later used for Dr. Obi Nkomo in *Harlem Gallery:*

> As an agnostic alien professor, he almost wrecked Wiley College, proudly Methodist, "and the oldest Negro college west of the Father of Waters," whose bourgeois students, out of Christian charity, during the Christmas holidays, included even the poor white trash and the heirs of black slaves as persons to be saved from the wrath of the Angry God. Jonathan Edwards' god. The college turned out, in spite of Nkomo and me, Colored ladies and gentlemen who did not split infinitives. So, Nkomo, African and Africanist, is buried in the Black Belt of East Texas, where the Lady Bird of the White House and the Tittle (Y. A.) of the N. Y. Giants came from. This is my feeble attempt in the remembrance of things past.[9]

But Professor Nkomo was by no means the only Wiley faculty member who shared Tolson's antipathy to bourgeois values. The agony of the depression years had convinced many persons of sensitivity and intelligence of the incompatibility of capitalism with any sense of social justice. Tolson's *Caviar and Cabbage* columns previously quoted indicate the respect and admiration he felt for Dr. James Farmer, the first black Ph.D. in Texas. The deep social concern and hostility to deadening conformity of Farmer's Christianity caused Tolson to see him as a believer in an authentic Christ; not a Christ of showy Christmastime charity, but a revolutionary Christ who insisted on the brotherhood of man being translated into real economic terms. When the Farmer family moved from Wiley College to Howard University in 1938, the Tolsons fell heir to much of their furniture, including a piano on which Mel, Jr., learned to play with considerable skill. It was his music teacher who, to her later regret, offered to house V. F. Calverton on his vividly remembered visit to Wiley.

Tolson found other kindred spirits on the Wiley faculty, men of considerable intellectual curiosity, substantial professional training, and strong social commitment. I have previously quoted Oliver Cromwell Cox's tribute to his colleagues, Tolson, Andrew P. Watson, V. E. Daniel, and Alonzo P. Davis, for their support and challenge while he wrote *Caste, Class and Race.* Cox was Tolson's intellectual peer, and they strongly reinforced each other's social beliefs. Andrew P. Watson was a close personal friend, and the Watson family remained close friends of the Tolsons long after the move to Langston. V. E. Daniel was the dean of the college, and his wife, Maggie, was a student of Tolson's and later a colleague.

After the publication of *Rendezvous with America* Langston Hughes took the occasion to return some of the professional and personal compliments Tolson had previously paid him. On 15 December 1945, in "Here to Yonder" in the *Chicago Defender*, Hughes eloquently recognized the reputation Tolson had built in his long career at Wiley as a teacher and as a poet:

> That Texas is some State! I was down there once or twice myself. And I have found some very amazing things—including Melvin Tolson.
> Melvin Tolson is the most famous Negro professor in the Southwest. Students all over that part of the world speak of him, revere him, remember him, and love him. He is a character. He once turned out a debate team that beat Oxford, England. He is a great talker himself. He teaches English at Wiley College, Marshall, Texas, but he is known far and wide. He is a poet of no mean ability, and his book of poems, "Rendezvous With America," is a recent fine contribution to American literature. The title poem appeared in that most literate of literary of publications, the ATLANTIC MONTHLY.
> But Melvin Tolson is no highbrow. Kids from the cottonfields like him. Cowpunchers understand him. He is a great teacher of the kind of which any college might be proud. It is not just English he teaches, but character, and manhood, and womanhood, and love, and courage, and pride. And the likes of him is found no where else but in the great State of Texas—because there is only one Tolson!

Hughes and Tolson were both Lincoln men, and another former Lincoln classmate also touched Tolson's life significantly in 1945. Horace Mann Bond, Tolson's fellow debater from Lincoln University, was named president of Lincoln. Bond was previously president of Fort Valley State College and in that position had been invited on 11 September 1944 to become one of two representatives of the state of Georgia to the Liberian Centennial Commission. Bond and Tolson had crossed paths during the years since their graduation from Lincoln. On 1 April 1929, "Klops" Bond sent a memo to all the Lincoln University and Wiley College men at Meharry Medical Center announcing that "The Great 'Cap' Tolson, Captain of the Freshman Football Team of the Class of 1923 . . . is bringing a team to Fisk for a debate" on 5 April. A get-together for the Lincoln and Wiley men "featured by a minimum of eats and a maximum of that good old spirit" was scheduled immediately following the debate. The next year Bond was carrying on a research project in the South under a grant from the Rosenwald Foundation. He visited Marshall and took a memorable photo of the Tolson family next to his auto. The photo was later reproduced in a brochure celebrating the twentieth anniversary of the Lincoln graduating class of 1923.

Thus, on 5 January 1946, Tolson wrote Bond congratulating him on being named president of Lincoln. The letter was couched in the accepted, mockingly stilted phrasing of Lincoln rhetoric, and it also included a calculated offer:

The Tolson family in 1930, in a photograph taken by Horace Mann Bond.
The children, from left to right, are Arthur, Ruth Marie,
Wiley Wilson, and Melvin, Jr.

As you know I'm a poor writer, reaping often what I have not sown. Nevertheless, I want to offer my sincere congratulations on your mounting the throne of our beloved Alma Mater. As the years roll by, I feel closer and closer to the days of Auld Lang Syne.

At the outset, I want to say that you must feel free to call upon me at any time when you need me. My pen and my tongue are at your service, and whatever I may have of public or private influence. I heard from Jackson and he says they want me to help on the alumni drive. Okay. If at any time you want to send me on a mission of confidence I'll gladly go. Or pull some strings—since my writings have put me in a position to do so.

Lincoln University was originally named Ashmun Institute after Jehudi Ashmun, who played a heroic role in the creation of the modern nation of Liberia. The American Colonization Society, which sponsored the Liberian venture, established Ashmun Institute with the professed goal of educating laymen for leadership in Africa. Bond's appointment as president of Lincoln University unquestionably enhanced his position as a member of the Liberian Centennial Commission. It seems reasonable to assume that he thus played a key role in the appointment of Tolson as the "Poet Laureate of the Liberian Centennial and Peace Exposition," a title that later came to be generalized as "Poet Laureate of Liberia." Chicago Congressman William Dawson presented this commission to Tolson in a ceremony at the Liberian embassy in Washington, D.C., in July 1947, the very summer Tolson moved from Wiley College to Langston University.

While Bond almost certainly played an instrumental role in this appointment, it was clearly the critical and popular success of *Rendezvous with America* that made Tolson's nomination possible. Two aspects of *Rendezvous* probably appealed to those making the decision. The first is the strong assertion that Tolson makes for black Americans being a part of the national American identity from its beginning, and the second is his view of America, particularly as a result of the events of World War II, playing a part in a worldwide movement toward democratic self-realization, a movement of particular concern for the nations of Africa chafing under colonial rule. Tolson was a striking new presence on the American literary scene. He spoke forcefully and eloquently of international democratic aspirations. His associations with Lincoln linked him to the interests and aspirations of Liberia. Thus his appointment as poet laureate was fitting, although at the time few seemed certain of the implications such an appointment carried.

At any rate, this honor served to underscore the importance of Tolson's move from Wiley to Langston. It became not just a move from one school to another, but a passage from one stage of his career to another. Not that he made any abrupt changes of commitment or belief, but the resolution of World War II, the publication of his first book and the praise it received, and the completion of the most difficult years as a parent now made Tolson and the world he faced markedly different. He was recruited as a significant addition to a faculty. His salary was still only enough to provide modest security, but he had rank and status in addition to the confidence and pride of achievement. He was known in the literary world, and he had friends he could count on for support. In Langston he would be recognized, after seven years of residence, by being elected mayor of the city.

In 1893, Edwin P. McCabe, the founding father of Langston and several other black towns and communities in Oklahoma, advertised in the *Langston City Herald*:

> Langston City is newly settled and is better adapted to the progress of the Negro race than any other city or place in the United States.
>
> Langston City restores to the Negro his rights and privileges as an American citizen and offers protection to themselves, families and home.
>
> Langston City is the Negro's refuge from lynching, burning at the stake and other lawlessness and turns the Negro's sorrow into happiness.[10]

By 1947 this roseate promise had worn more than a little thin. Langston was a relatively small community with unpaved, poorly lighted roads, dependent principally upon the nearby university for employment and trade. In 1952, two years before Tolson became mayor, Langston had a population of 685, approximately the same as in 1893.

But the promise and challenge of such a community clearly appealed to Tolson. At least the oppressive control of the white community was more distant and abstract. The community probably also reminded Tolson at some level of the frontier world in Missouri and Iowa that he knew as a youth. "McCabe's basic philosophy was that Negroes' opportunities lay on the frontier. He was convinced that whites in the West had fewer rigid social ideas and that economic development would be unhampered."[11] At any rate, Tolson would not be confined by the provinciality of this world. He already had clearly established his residency in a larger world as well.

Support for Langston University came principally from the state government, while Wiley College received its support from the Methodist Church. That made a significant difference in the nature of the institutions. Langston by its public nature was more frankly plebeian, less concerned with genteel pretensions. When Tolson arrived at Langston in 1947, it was undergoing something of a postwar boom. The enrollment, swelled by returning veterans, peaked that year at 402. President G. Lamar Harrison, who had been in office since 1940 and was to continue until 1960, an unusually long tenure for Langston presidents, had an ambitious building plan underway. In 1948 Langston became a member of the Association of American Colleges, and within Harrison's tenure it also became a member of the North

Melvin B. Tolson

Melvin B. Tolson in front of his Langston home, 1965.

Central Association of Colleges and Secondary Schools and the American Association of Colleges for Teacher Education.

The problems of a state-supported institution centered in political corruption and bureaucratic inefficiency rather than in the double-talk of moral piety that plagued a church-supported institution. For example, Langston University owned large tracts of land in far-western Oklahoma, for which it received scandalously low rental income for many years. One person in Cimarron County leased a total of 16,800 acres for only $16,300 annual rent. But with the growth of federal support for higher education, the financial condition of Langston was nevertheless much more secure during Tolson's employment there than that of Wiley College had been.

The students at Langston responded to Tolson in much the same manner as had those at Wiley. He was respected, feared, and loved. At both schools it quickly became a tradition that one's education was incomplete without a course from Tolson. The debate tradition had ended at Wiley, and Tolson had developed a strong interest in the theater. That interest was continued and expanded at Langston. He was a demanding and energetic director of drama, just as he had been a demanding and energetic coach of the debate team. Gladys R. Johnson, a Langston student who later did much of the typing for Tolson's manuscripts, remembers the great satisfaction felt when an actress did her part well and Tolson would exclaim, "Didn't she die!" A sterner and more often repeated warning of Tolson's also still echoes vividly in her mind, "Stay on your lines!"

While Tolson willingly assumed the responsibilities of being a teacher at Langston University and a citizen and eventually mayor of Langston City, he increasingly saw himself writing poetry for a future rather than an immediate audience. He did not close himself off to the immediate world, however. As a teacher and drama director he was as popular and effective as ever. The fact that he was elected mayor four times and had to be persuaded by his family not to run for a fifth term is substantial evidence of his continued social concern. But more and more he became preoccupied with shaping his message in a form that would last. Using hints and insights from his extensive reading of other authors, complemented by a rich store of impassioned living experiences marked by strong moral and social concerns, he created poems intended to speak to the needs of the emerging man of the future.

In 1958, John Ciardi wrote an essay, "Dialogue with an Audience," that in effect spoke to the dilemma of poets with populist convictions writing apparently esoteric and elitist poetry. Ciardi's statement did not break new ground in 1958 but rather summarized assumptions that had already become principles as the New Criticism spread its influence. Certainly Tolson was groping toward such ideas of audience in the late forties and early fifties. By

Melvin B. Tolson

1958 Ciardi had become a significant professional friend and supporter of Tolson. In later years Tolson would often reiterate the distinction Ciardi here makes between "horizontal" and "vertical" audiences. Ciardi's statement was couched in the form of a dialogue between Poet and Citizen, although in fact it often seems more like a dialogue between an instructor and a student in an introductory literature class assigned to read Wallace Stevens. It concludes with the Poet giving a short sermon in response to the Citizen's question, "Who *are* you modern poets for? Is there no such thing as an audience?"

"What is the idea of 'the audience'? Is it enough to argue 'I have bought this book of poems and therefore I have certain audience-rights'? I think, first, one must distinguish between two ideas of 'the audience.'

"One idea may be called the horizontal audience and the other the vertical audience. The horizontal audience consists of everybody who is alive at this moment. The vertical audience consists of everyone, vertically through time, who will ever read a given poem.

"Isn't it immediately obvious that Stevens can only 'be for' a tiny percentage of the horizontal audience? Even Frost, who is the most seemingly-clear and the most widely loved of our good poets, certainly does not reach more than a small percentage of the total population, or even that part of the population that thinks of itself as literate—as at least literate enough to buy a best-seller. The fact is that no horizontal audience since the age of folk-poetry has been much interested in good poetry. And you may be sure that a few spokesmen sounding off in the name of that horizontal audience are not going to persuade the poets.

"All good poets write for the vertical audience. The vertical audience for Dante, for example, is now six centuries old. And it is growing. If the human race has any luck at all, part of Dante's audience is still thousands of years short of being born. . . .

"The point is that the horizontal audience always outnumbers the vertical at any one moment, but that the vertical audience for good poetry always outnumbers the horizontal in time-enough. And not only for the greatest poets. Andrew Marvell is certainly a minor poet, but given time enough, more people certainly will have read 'To His Coy Mistress' than will ever have subscribed to *Time*, *Life*, and *Fortune*. Compared to what a good poem can do, Luce is a piker at getting circulation."

"Impressive, if true," says the Citizen, "but how does any given poet get his divine sense of this vertical audience?"

"By his own ideal projection of his own best sense of himself. It's as simple as that," says the Poet. "He may be wrong, but he has nothing else to go by. And there is one thing more—all good poets are difficult when their work is new. And their work always becomes less difficult as their total shape becomes more and more visible. As that shape impresses itself upon time, one begins to know how to relate the parts to their total. Even Keats and

Shelley confounded their contemporary critics as 'too difficult' and 'not for me'."

The Citizen throws his hands up, "All right, all right: I've been out-talked. But who *does* write for me? I'm willing to give it a try."

The Poet shrugs. "The sort of try you gave Stevens? But no matter. The point is why *should* I write for you?—you're going to be dead the next time anyone looks. We all are for that matter. But not the poem. Not if it's made right. If I make it for you I have to take the chance that it will die with you. I'm not sure you're that good an investment. Besides which, I have to invest in myself. If we happen to share some of the same sense of poetry, it may work out that I do happen to write for you. But that would be a happy bonus at best. I still cannot think of you as a main investment—not till you show a better 'vertical sense'."

"We who are about to die," says the Citizen, "salute the poems we cannot grasp. Is that it?"

"Like nothing else in Tennessee," says the Poet bowing.[12]

V

NOVELS AND PLAYS

Melvin Tolson felt strongly that the world should be different from what it was, radically different. He said so frequently from the lecture platform. He said so frequently in his *Caviar and Cabbage* column. But he also wanted to say so in some form that would provide a broader and deeper public response than his talks or his journalism could promise. While in the late forties his success in publishing his poetry consistently moved him toward addressing the vertical audience, he still had high hopes for more immediate and more spectacular success in the novel or the drama.

None of Tolson's novels or plays were published during his lifetime, although some of his plays were performed. The manuscripts that remain of his efforts in both genres are substantial, though fragmentary. Nothing remains of his first novel, *Beyond the Zaretto*. The ninety-six-page typescript of *The Lion and the Jackal* has been discussed in Chapter III. Another ninety-six-page typescript, with gaps, remains of *Dark Symphony*. *All Aboard*, which apparently Tolson labored over for many years, survives as a typescript of 409 pages. It ends inconclusively, but with what probably was intended as the final episode. Two full-length dramas, *The Moses of Beale Street* and *Southern Front*, plus two one-act plays, *The House by the Side of the Tracks* and *The ABC Cafe on Deep Eighteenth*, all written in Marshall, are lost. A biographical note on Tolson that appeared in *The Negro Caravan* in 1941 briefly indicates the subjects of the two full-length dramas: "*Southern Front*, which deals with the unionizing of Arkansas sharecroppers, and *The Moses of Beale Street* (in collaboration with Edward Boatner), a Negro miracle play."[1] *Black No More*, Tolson's dramatization of George S. Schuyler's novel, is complete except for a few missing pages. It apparently was written during the last years at Wiley but was not performed until 1952 at Langston. Most of the first two acts of *Fire in the Flint*, Tolson's dramatization of Walter White's novel, plus three one-act plays that make up a work titled *Upper Boulders in the Sun*, all written at Langston in the fifties, remain. The significance of these manuscripts to Tolson's career is worth considering.

Of the two novel manuscripts yet to be discussed, *Dark Symphony* precedes *All Aboard*. The hero of *Dark Symphony*, Slim Walpole, is a fugitive from Kansas City, where he killed a man. He comes to Harlem as a city of refuge, but he is afraid. He carries a fiddle and plays music ranging from the blues to the classics. Apparently unknown to him, a thief, known as The Fiddling Burglar, has been practicing his trade with notorious success. So Slim, feeling guilty and fearful and carrying a violin case, attracts suspicion. His first night in Harlem, the streetcar he is riding in has a wreck. He is not seriously hurt, and all he can think of is getting away without attracting attention.

A sharpster representing the streetcar company easily persuades him to sign a release. Slim is then followed by Runty Otto Spender, who berates him for missing his chance to make some easy money. Runty persuades Slim to see Runty's employer-lawyer, Ulysses S. Lightner, the next morning. Runty goes to Lightner's basement office that evening, and the two speculate on the value of their prospective client. Meanwhile, Slim enters a mission, where a sternly earnest white preacher is trying to infuse a bored and hungry audience with a sense of cultural pride and moral indignation. He introduces a black friend, Professor Solomon Enoch Capers, who is writing a six-volume history of *The Negro in Western Civilization*, to deliver a lecture. Runty comes looking for Slim but misses him and discovers instead an old girlfriend. Slim next enters a basement dive, where he is challenged by the nattily dressed Yellow Boy, who is presiding over a card game. Slim parries the man's verbal attacks with ready, insulting wit, but he does not enter the card game. He is persuaded to play his violin, as he had been persuaded at the mission. He plays and sings a blues song about a New Orleans Creole woman. Kiffie, Yellow Boy's girl, comes in with fire in her eye and a razor in her hand. Slim then watches a striking scene of sexual violence. Kiffie humiliates Yellow Boy by forcing him to strip off all his fancy clothes, while he pleads his love for her. He is persuasive but succeeds only in heightening her intense emotional ambivalence. As they embrace and kiss, her teeth clamp his tongue and her razor shreds his buttocks. The watching men are sickened by the spectacle, but they are restrained from interfering by a sense of rough justice. Slim stumbles out of the mission into an all-night café, where he strikes up a promising relationship with the waitress, Ruby Ritter, who is tough, perceptive, and sympathetic. There the manuscript ends.

At two points Tolson wove suggestively autobiographical material into Slim Walpole's story. The first is as Professor Capers begins his lecture in the mission:

"When I was a lad in Iowa," said Professor Capers, "I suffered from a racial inferiority complex. In our small school were boys of many nationalities and races. The Italian boys were familiar with the lives and works of Leonardo Da Vinci, Galileo, Dante, and Michael Angelo. So was I. The German boys knew the glories of Schiller, Kant, Frederick the Great, and Goethe. So did I. The Jewish boys reveled in the achievements of Moses, Solomon and David. So did I. But herein lies the tragedy, Gentlemen: I, a Negro boy, knew nothing about Negro history. When I heard the ignorant say, 'A nigger ain't nothing', I bowed my head in shame. A black wall of prejudice had shut out from me the shining names of Antar, Pushkin, Dumas, Cuffe, Nat Turner, Gabriel, Henrique Dias, Frederick Douglass, Crispus Attucks, Phillis Wheatley, and other notables of African descent!"

Slim thrills to Professor Capers's renaissance of racial pride, but Capers is a lonely and somewhat pathetic figure unlikely to find a large or responsive audience for his message. Reverend Benjamin Mott apologetically asks his derelict audience for contributions to support Capers's work.

Like Capers, Tolson, too, grew up in Iowa among a variety of ethnic whites. He consistently argued that black Americans must revise the history commonly taught them in American culture to recognize the significant role of African culture and the achievements of men and women of African descent. He would frequently quote Gertrude Stein's laconic comment that the Negro suffers from nothingness as a base point from which to argue. Late in his own career he planned an epic poem of five volumes detailing the history of black Americans beginning with their African origins. *Harlem Gallery: Book One, The Curator* was to be the first volume.

But, if Capers is a projection of Tolson, the dramatic context also reveals that Tolson, very much aware of the pathos of Capers's position, was by no means resigned to being a lonely academic voice crying in a modern urban wilderness. He understood that the men in Capers's audience had more immediate and intense needs that would have to be met before Capers's legitimate cultural message could reach its mark. This was a major motivation for writing a novel rather than giving a lecture. Tolson was trying to reach his audience by more subtle and penetrating means.

The second, more personal, autobiographical note in the narrative occurs as Slim settles into a seat in the mission and hears the men singing, "*You shall reap just what you sow.*" He remembers

the little African Methodist Church at Moberly, Missouri. In the place of the seedy, pathetic, white mission worker stood his dark-brown father, angular, dynamic, eloquent, picturing like a great actor the glories of God and the wiles of the Devil.

There in the front pew sat his brooding little mother, fixed eyes following the drama of his father, emaciated hands folded on the thin lap that had rocked him to sleep as a boy. Slim remembered that his father was never at his best in the pulpit when the brooding little woman was absent. His enemies in the membership accused him of preaching for his wife instead of the Lord God Almighty!

The scene shifted suddenly and, for some reason inexplicable to Slim, he saw his mother reposing in her black coffin below the pulpit. The loving hands of those whose quick lips had reviled her had piled the casket and altar high with lovely flowers. He remembered the tearing sobs of his father as self-important persons dressed and rehearsed for the occasion pronounced innumerable obituaries. That was the last funeral he ever attended. The scornful comments of some sisters on how "easy" he'd taken the death of his mother made the boy vomit and cry hysterically on the church steps.

In the valley, on the mountain,
You shall reap just what you sow.

Slim then associates the corpse of his mother with that of the man he had killed on New Year's Eve in Kansas City.

When Tolson remembered his own father's preaching, he often commented on his mother's presence as well. He probably did not actually remember the church in Moberly, since the family moved from there when he was only three months old, but the churches in Slater, De Soto, or New Franklin could do as well. "The Odyssey of a Manuscript" makes clear that Tolson's mother, as well as his father, served as an inspiring sympathetic audience. She is pictured as sharing his literary hopes and ambitions, as understanding the fascination and power of story and song. In "The Odyssey" he says that he assumed the responsibilities of a writing career to realize her ambitions, which were thwarted finally by death.

Lera Hurt Tolson died on 1 April 1934. Notice of her death appeared in the *Kansas City Call* on 6 April. Coincidentally, Tolson's debate team was to meet the debate team from the University of Kansas on 20 April in Kansas City. The same issue of the *Call* announced that the debate was to be sponsored by a woman's organization, whose president was Helen Wilson, Tolson's sister. One could easily imagine under those circumstances that Melvin drew some of the same misunderstanding remarks about taking his mother's death "easy" that Slim remembers with such bitterness. But there is no question that Tolson was in truth very deeply moved by his mother's death. The fact that her death reappears here in fictional form is evidence of that.

But the use of this experience in fiction is more important for the hint it provides us about Tolson's own writing ambitions. Sometime in the late thirties he apparently abandoned the story of Slim Walpole and began writing the story of Duke Hands, the protagonist of *All Aboard*. The differences between these two protagonists are notable, although there are certainly other reasons evident in the manuscripts to suggest why Tolson abandoned the former for the latter. *Dark Symphony* is principally concerned with Slim Walpole's initiation to Harlem as a city of refuge, a theme common among the Renaissance writers whom Tolson studied for his master's thesis. *All Aboard*, on the other hand, is the story of what happens during twenty-four hours on a Pullman car, seen from the point of view of a quick-witted, capable, and ambitious porter. Tolson gave *All Aboard* dramatic and historical concentration by setting it on the eve of prohibition and weaving in a plot in which Duke is recruited by a well-known mobster to head up a network of Pullman porters to serve in the supply and sale of bootleg liquor.

Clearly the latter story has more exciting possibilities than the former. But the shift from Slim Walpole to Duke Hands also seems to have been liberating to Tolson's imagination. Slim, while a man of wit and pride, is burdened by the murder he has committed, a murder he associates with the death of his mother. He comes to Harlem wounded, hoping to find a new life. Duke Hands is also young and capable. His life, as Slim's, is yet to be determined. However, while he has had many experiences, some of which he would rather forget, he does not carry the heavy psychic burden that Slim does. He is on the road looking for possibilities, and people respond to his easy self-confidence.

The differences in the two protagonists reflect what was happening in Tolson's career. Tolson apparently stopped writing *Dark Symphony* and began *All Aboard* at about the time he achieved substantial success in getting his writing published. When Tolson wrote of the death of his own mother in "The Odyssey of a Manuscript," he gave her dying words the power of a commandment for him to succeed as a writer. However, by 1939, his long apprenticeship, when he must have carried doubts about his career as a serious literary artist, even as Slim Walpole carried the burden of that only dimly characterized murder in Kansas City, was coming to an end. His mother as audience was now replaced by a more satisfying public audience. When Slim sings *Sometimes I feel like a motherless child*, the reader feels it as an unwitting summary of his life. Duke Hands, on the other hand, exuberantly remembers his mother singing a different kind of song:

> The fare is cheap and all can go,
> The rich an' poor are there;
> No second class on board this train,
> No difference in the fare.
>
> Get on board, little children,
> Get on board, little children,
> Get on board, little children,
> There's room for many more!

The manuscript of *All Aboard* indicates that there was merit to many of Tolson's ambitious hopes for it, even though it has serious flaws. The story of Duke Hands, who is working on the Pullman coach The Grand Saline on the crack Chicago Limited bound from New York to Chicago on 16 January 1920, the evening before Prohibition is to go into effect, has extraordinary possibilities. In addition to being challenged by the last-night games and parties of passengers, whom he is expected both to serve and to control, Duke is also the object of a plot conceived by Cesare Baroni, notorious racketeer, and Lady George Dumas, a beautiful and experienced Creole opportunist. They plan to make Duke the key figure in their effort to organize the Pullman porters into a profitable bootleg network. Duke is drawn to Baroni, or Scar Lip, as Duke more frequently refers to him, because the racketeer takes no guff from anyone and coolly penetrates the pretentious righteousness of many who oppose him. Baroni also recognizes Duke's abilities and respects him as a man. Duke is attracted to Lady George for her luxuriant sexual beauty as well as for her obvious sophistication and social prowess. She in turn finds him attractive from more than a professional point of view. He is held back from Scar Lip's offer by his fundamental repugnance at deliberately hurting others and the dread of the lonely and violent end that a life of crime promises. He is held back from Lady George's charms by a vague distrust of her motives, but more effectively by the memory of another romance that had blossomed quickly just before the train pulled out. This romance was with Hilda, a West Indian cleaning woman, who has her mind set on moving up in the world à la Madame C. J. Walker. Despite Hilda's West Indian background, which sometimes causes antagonizing confusion between her and Duke, they share strong common class experiences and hopes, although Duke is more than a little skeptical of Hilda's blunt enthusiasm for becoming a part of dicty, or black bourgeois, success.

The principal weaknesses of the novel are, one, that the central action is often suspended while we learn about the background of many of the individual characters, and, two, that these episodic stories sometimes reduce to heavy-handed social melodrama and the characters consequently reduce to predictable caricatures. The novel, for example, is at its worst in the story of John Merritt, a sympathetic white inspector who interrupts Duke and Hilda's lovemaking before the Chicago Limited starts its journey. Merritt is a former professor from a university in the Ozarks who becomes a political victim because of his liberal racial views. He wrote a book, *The Negro: A Man*, in answer to another scurrilously racist book, *The Negro: A Beast*, by Dr. Osbert Demmer Pew. Merritt confronts Demmer at a lecture given by the latter. During the question-and-answer period, Merritt creates suspense by observing, "One thing puzzles me, Dr. Demmer." He then pauses until Demmer is forced to ask weakly, "What is that, my dear Doctor?"

" 'Just this,' said John Merritt, hunching up his shoulders and leaning forward in his old classroom manner. 'By what miracle of a recipe did you concoct the drivel you've just spewed up?' " Merritt's sarcasm is described as having the effect of a bomb, and "the meeting collapsed like the caving in of a fire-gutted roof." Such an extravagant authorial claim is not dramatically credible. For a reader such easy sarcasm is more likely to prove disappointing.

The rest of Merritt's story is also melodramatically facile. Merritt grew up as part of the privileged class of the South. John Crowe Wolf, his boyhood companion, was poor white. Wolf diligently worked his way through law school and into politics, losing out to Merritt in their courtship of the same girl. Wolf has stored up resentment against Merritt for the privileges of his social position and for his romantic loss. Faced with a difficult election, he sees the opportunity to exploit the popular racist reaction to Merritt's book. He becomes a successfully poisonous demagogue, who is ultimately murdered by his own brother, who in turn resented Wolf's success and his callous indifference to the poverty of their parents. But the damage to Merritt's career is done. He is blacklisted from any academic post and becomes a philosophic inspector on the railroad. Duke Hands befriends him and introduces him to the sublime pleasure of Mammy Hagar's fried chicken. It is on this visit to Mammy Hagar's restaurant two days before the New York to Chicago run that Duke first runs into Cesare Baroni, and Baroni is sufficiently impressed with Duke to set in motion his plan for using Duke in his bootlegging organization.

All the passengers who board The Grand Saline contribute to "the follies of this human comedy on wheels." They include Lt. O'Connell, preoccupied by a severe leg wound from World War I but moved to speak fervently about the courage of black soldiers from his experience as an officer of the Black Watch; Herron Stafen, an officer-artist who deserted the German army during the war; Lola Jane Tudor, a flapper poet from Arkansas by way of Greenwich Village who is living off an increasingly resentful middle-aged businessman; Judge Jim Eddy, who vigorously and drunkenly protests prohibition as an invasion of civil liberties and has to be put to bed by a solicitous wife with Duke's help; Ophelia Angoff, a desiccated Virginia lady who insults and threatens Duke out of sexual and racial frustration; and Mrs. Gladstone, a cheap blonde who leaves her husband in New York to make a play for Baroni.

The passengers of The Grand Saline are broadly drawn caricatures, but their stories and their actions are characteristically more compellingly and vividly biting than the story of John Merritt. There is, for example, an effective episode when Ophelia Angoff insists that Duke interrupt Baroni's scandalous visit to Mrs. Gladstone's berth. Duke does so with considerable misgivings, and Baroni leaves the berth with cool sarcasm. A short time later Mrs. Gladstone misses her diamond ring. For a moment it looks like Duke will be the scapegoat. Then Ophelia Angoff bitchily suggests that the thief could have been Mrs. Gladstone's visitor. Mrs. Gladstone is first caught off-guard and embarrassed by the suggestion, but then recognizes its probability. In anger she demands that Baroni be summoned. Duke brings him. Baroni handles her charges with easy contempt and quickly cows her by suggesting that her husband be telegraphed to meet the train in Chicago. He then disdainfully peels off two thousand dollars, more than the price of the ring, from a roll of bills that he carries and suggests the whole matter be forgotten. Duke later finds the ring in a broom handle as a gift from Baroni, an inducement for him to join his big-bucks scheme.

The collection of people, the trip from New York to Chicago, and the deliberate choice of 16 January 1920, the eve of prohibition, are all meant to provide a cross-section of America at a significant historical moment as seen from the point of view of a young black porter who provides the service that allows the passengers, away from the ordinary restraints of job and home, to express themselves with unflattering self-indulgence. The spectacle causes Duke to question how he is, or wants to be, related to the social world these people represent.

Hilda poses the question first. She is naively but determinedly on her way up. She offers Duke a role at her side. Her frankness, her simple acceptance of the task of realizing the American dream of material success with its glamorous rewards of money, clothes, and social power regardless of the costs, appeals to him. It is like her sturdy healthy sexuality. Yet he pulls up short. He is not yet ready to make a commitment. He wants to retain the freedom and the possibilities of a traveling man.

Hilda's offer is quickly challenged by a second, that of Cesare Baroni. Baroni's offer is also backed up by the seductive charms of Lady George, although Duke does not yet realize that the two are partners. The Amercian dream is now gilded, offering an even quicker rise to success, money, clothes, and social power with the added factor of great risk—and excitement. Baroni mocks the law, but within the historical setting of the novel the law is represented by prohibition, a law for the reader already discredited and repealed. The law is also that made by racist politicians like John Crowe Wolf, and it is the force by which decent men like John Merritt lose their proper positions in society. Tolson suggested in *Caviar and Cabbage* that modern-day racketeers were direct descendants of the nineteenth-century robber barons of capitalism. Baroni's and Hilda's ambitions are indeed fueled by the same crude American drama. Baroni is, however, more ruthlessly and nakedly efficient in the quest. Hilda's more modest charms seem dim and commonplace by comparison to those of Lady George.

Nevertheless there *is* still a higher law. Tolson's strong Christian upbringing asserts itself. Such a twisted view of the future of man in society must somehow intrinsically fail. The Chicago Limited crashes. Ophelia Angoff, Southern racist bitch, clings desperately to the despised nigger porter, and he saves her. Duke becomes a hero. Baroni dances Mrs. Gladstone around Chicago, while Mr. Gladstone pathetically tries to find his wife. Duke, on his way to an appointment with Lady George, meets a scavenger-pusher whom he sternly warns against preying on the innocence of the young son of the family Duke lives with. And there, unfortunately, the extant manuscript ends.

Two contrasting characters serve as occasional mentors for Duke. The Professor opens Duke's eyes to liberal ideas about class and race, and Sloe Gin, another porter, is invoked as the shrewd folk figure who has learned to use white folk's stereotypes to his own advantage. Sloe Gin teaches, "You kin ketch mo' flies wid molasses dan you kin wid vinegah." The roles of the Professor and Sloe Gin balance each other and suggest Duke's effort to find a role for himself that recognizes the strength and experiences woven into rituals of black survival and yet is not racially provincial.

An early episode makes clear a different and more positive relation between Duke and the American dream than that suggested by the offers of Hilda and Baroni. It comes in the novel just before the passengers board the Chicago Limited. The Professor has used Duke's surname, *Hands*, to point out the fallacy of Duke's unwitting reference to "a self-made man." The Professor's remarks are then woven into Duke's reflections as he composes and sings a ballad about Uncle George (Pullman), who dreamed and created that palace of pleasure, the Pullman car. Duke, for the moment feeling happy and contented with himself, identifies with Uncle George and his dream:

> *Uncle George he had a dream,*
> *Tossing on his bed one night:*
> *"Gonna build a palace car*
> *So a man can sleep all right."*
> *Help 'im, Lord, oh, help 'im, Lord,*
> *So a man can sleep all night!*

Uncle George calls the carpenters and mechanics together, "bottles of rye on their lips, pipes in their mouths, wads of tobacco like plums in their jaws." He leads them to "an old shed, broken-down like a giant with bugs in his lungs. . . . Their spirits caved in like empty sacks."

"Uncle George thought of a manger in Nazareth and cried, 'Can anything good come out of this shed?' " Uncle George then tells the boys what he wants, "lower berths on seats, upper berths dropping from the roof, woodwork of black walnut, gold trimmings, velvet carpets—a car wider and higher than any other car the world has ever seen!"

> Uncle George called out the boys,
> Eyed 'em whole, then eye for eye;
> Said, "We gonna build something big,
> Something wide and something high,
> Something man nor beast nor bird
> Ever saw with the naked eye!

> "Something for the Glory Road,
> Rolling, Rolling, 'cross the Land.
> Mirrors, carpets, cushion seats,
> Walnut woodwork, spick and span,
> Hanging beds all trimmed with gold,
> Rolling, Rolling, 'cross the Land."

As Duke grins at his inward vision of Uncle George and his boys, "the Midwestern giant with great horny hands all around him—hands ready to build a miracle of civilization," he remembers the Professor's explanation of the probable origin of his own name and the tribute it implies to the work of his ancestor-craftsman:

> The horny hands set to work, as hands work when the heart is in the work. Muscles strained without knowing the strain. Furrows of dirt and sweat came into faces—black and white. A mighty symphony surged up and out. It rocked the old shed from center to post, poured into the big city, challenging the high hats, the low hats. Horny hands building a new job— a job for ten thousand black men in white jackets and blue coats. Horny hands building a new job for steel workers, wood workers, white collar workers, swivel-chair magnates. Horny hands bring to unborn millions palaces and hotels on wheels.
> As Duke dreamed, the horny hands with upraised hammers and saws shut out the picture of Uncle George. The guitar wailed like a lost soul at the mourners' bench and the agony of the blues of a people came into the ballad of Labor:
> > Hear, Lord, hear them hammers ring
> > Down in that shed by the C & A;
> > Hear them saws, Lord, hear them saws
> > Buzzing, buzzing, night and day;
> > Help them hands, Lord, help them hands
> > Down in the shed by the C & A!

This celebration of the accomplishment of workers hardly seems relevant to the events that follow. But it suggests why Duke feels uneasy at Hilda's invitation to imagine himself in formal dress at the ceremony celebrating the opening of Madame Hilda's Beauty College, and why the reader feels a sense of regret and loss as Duke seems to succumb to Lady George's charms. Tolson worked on *All Aboard* through the forties and probably into the fifties. The dream of a social order controlled by labor, where meaningful work, particularly craftsmanship, was greatly valued, was rapidly becoming only a nostalgic memory. Duke's lyrical tribute to the Pullman car anticipates the Futurafrique celebrated at the end of *Libretto for the Republic of Liberia*. It also indicates why Tolson once considered coupling *Libretto* with a poem about John Henry to make it of sufficient length to be published as a book. In retrospect it is most regrettable that Tolson did not find the editorial understanding and criticism he needed to make *All Aboard* into the impressive novel it had the potential of becoming.

Of the plays that Tolson wrote while teaching at Wiley, only *Black No More* survives. There are frequent references to two one-act plays written during the thirties, *The House by the Side of the Tracks* and *The ABC Cafe on Deep Eighteenth*. Little is known about either. *Southern Front*, a full-length drama, was also written during the thirties, and Tolson had substantial hopes for its success. In the playbill of *Fire in the Flint*, produced in 1952, *Southern Front* is noted as scheduled for publication in an anthology of Negro drama. As far as I can determine, it never appeared, and the manuscript apparently is now lost.

Tolson also collaborated with a colleague at Wiley, Edward Boatner, a professor of music, on a musical, *The Moses of Beale Street*. Boatner and Tolson made the rounds of agents and producers trying to place their production one summer in New York, probably the summer of 1937. Boatner remained in New York, giving up his post at Wiley, but Tolson returned to job and family. Boatner now remembers writing two plays with Tolson and leaving both of them with an agent. However, he cannot remember the names of either the plays or the agent. There is a persistent belief within the Tolson family that *The Moses of Beale Street* was later transformed into *Cabin in the Sky* without appropriate acknowledgment, although no reference to this appears in Tolson's manuscripts or letters. Professor Boatner's comment on this belief is that the agent to whom he gave the two plays "could have had the nerve to give the play a new title and allowed some one else to produce it." However, Professor Boatner, eighty-three years old when queried, insisted that his memory of this matter is very faint.[2]

The surviving dramatic manuscripts, with the exception of *Black No More*, are all plays Tolson wrote after he moved to Langston in 1947. Both *Black No More* and *Fire in the Flint* were dramatic adaptations of books by the same titles. Both were produced in 1952. "Transfiguration Springs," "The Fence War," and "Bivouac by the Santa Fe" are one-act plays intended as parts of a collection to be presented for the golden anniversary of Oklahoma, under the title *Upper Boulders in the Sun*. I can find no record that *Upper Boulders* was ever performed, although "Transfiguration Springs" was included in a Dust Bowl Players production, *Episodes in Negro Drama*, 22 May 1959. The other episodes in that production were "Scene One" from *The Emperor Jones* and "Judgment Day" from *God's Trombones*.

A first page of a lengthy letter dated 21 March 1947 from someone at the New York office of Paramount Pictures to Tolson concerning *Black No More* survives among the Tolson manuscripts. It offers a revealing comment upon the perceived public sensitivity to the racial subject of the drama and a brief, but telling, critique of the manuscript. It serves as well as implicit evidence of the substantial hopes Tolson had for his dramatic efforts:

> Dear Professor Tolson:
>
> Knowing the limited time you have at your disposal in New York, I am hastening to get the script of BLACK NO MORE back to you.
>
> I enjoyed reading it and do feel the satirical idea behind it is amusing but I am still pretty sure it is a subject the studio would have qualms about handling on the screen. I may be wrong but I suspect, too, that the dramatization does not make all its points as well as it should. The script is over-long, inclined to seem a bit jumpy because of the numerous scene breaks, and in some cases dialogue is substituted at too great length for action—as where one character phones in an account of a street accident and the audience is told about something instead of seeing it. This sort of thing, of course, is always one of the main problems encountered in turning the book into a play.
>
> While my opinion is that BLACK NO MORE isn't quite ready for Broadway in its present shape I hope you can manage, during your stay in New York, to get in touch with people who may be able to help prepare it for some future production. I still think you might do well to contact the American Negro Theatre.

In Tolson's master's thesis he gave the writings of George S. Schuyler considerable attention. V. F. Calverton had praised Schuyler's work enthusiastically in his *Anthology of American Negro Literature*. Schuyler, in turn, in the preface to *Black No More*, expressed his "thanks and appreciation to Mr. V. F. Calverton for his keen interest and friendly encouragement." The caustic, iconoclastic wit that caused Schuyler frequently to be referred to as "the black Mencken" clearly appealed to Tolson. Yet Tolson's dramatic adaptation of Schuyler's *Black No More* is as interesting for its clear differentiation between the two writers' social attitudes as it is for their strongly shared zest for the clash of wit and ideas.

The difference between the novel and the play is most apparent in the

Melvin B. Tolson

treatment of the doctor who invents the process of transforming blacks to whites. In Schuyler's novel he is named Dr. Junius Crookman. His role is important, but secondary to that of the protagonist, Max Disher, whose opportunistic adventures and misadventures preoccupy the reader's attention. Tolson changed Crookman's name to *Crogman* and gave him a more prominent share of the viewer's attention. Crogman is the focal point of act 2 of Tolson's three-act drama. In Schuyler's novel Crookman

> saw in his great discovery the solution to the most annoying problem in American life. Obviously, he reasoned, if there were no Negroes, there would be no Negro problem, Americans could concentrate their attention on something constructive. Through his efforts and the activities of Black-No-More, Incorporated, it would be possible to do what agitation, education and legislation had failed to do. He was naively surprised that there should be opposition to his work. Like most men with a vision, a plan, a program or a remedy, he fondly imagined people to be intelligent enough to accept a good thing when it was offered to them, which was conclusive evidence that he knew little about the human race.[3]

Schuyler hardly took the doctor's idealism seriously, and by naming him *Crookman* he implied ridicule, if not culpability, although Schuyler's story leaves Crookman's motives more vague than vicious.

Schuyler's novel was published in 1931, but his story is set in 1933–1940. Tolson wrote his drama in the aftermath of World War II, when the Nazi persecution of the Jews was publicly recognized. Thus, Dr. Crogman, studying in Germany, as did Dr. Crookman, has a motivating experience that gives added social seriousness to his experiment. "I was in Europe five years. I saw the rise of Nazism. I saw how a dictator, with a bogy of an ism for the upper classes and the bogy of race for the masses, could wipe out the freedom of a great people and strangle to death a culture." Crogman's idealism, like Crookman's, may appear naive, but his idealism is not simply ridiculed. Saving black Americans from the fate of the Jews in Germany is far too serious a matter for that.

Crogman makes the above statement in an interview with a reporter, Ethel Burgess. He then adds a statement that seems to voice Tolson's own beliefs: "As a scientist I believe the truth will make you free. But truth is a universal discovered through the painful process of inductive reasoning; no it is like a star that cannot be seen by the naked eye." This poetic definition of truth causes Ethel to ask, "Do you mean that truth is beyond the comprehension of the average mind?" Crogman's response reinforces the impression that Crogman is here speaking for Tolson himself:

> I can only say that dominant ideas seem to come from above. The people accept what is said *loud* enough and *long* enough. It's a matter of time and

place. A slave may proclaim the virtues of slavery, and a capitalist-without-capital may proclaim the virtues of capitalism.

Ethel then asks sharply, "Does this make you pessimistic?" Crogman half-laughs and replies, "Only when I forget you can't fool all the people all the time! At first, I was naively surprised by human inertia."

By the late forties Tolson, too, had had to admit to himself that human inertia was greater than he believed. The revolutionary changes he had hoped for and predicted in the thirties and early forties were not completely foreclosed, but they certainly seemed much further off and more unpredictable than he had expected. The masses once more seemed far more interested in competing for a share of the capitalistic pie than in joining together to reshape a society on the basis of cooperation and a sense of universal brotherhood. World War II had ended and the Third World was emerging from colonial rule, but it was far from becoming a triumphant force in world politics.

Crogman's belief in the ultimate power and value of the truth to make men free coupled with his elitist belief that "ideas seem to come from above" is one of the first explicit statements of a position that was increasingly characterizing Tolson's writing.

But to return to the contrasts between Crookman and Crogman. Max Disher, in Schuyler's story, after going through the Black No More treatment, heads for Atlanta to find the beautiful white woman who snubbed his black self in the Honky Tonk Club on New Year's Eve. Disher works his way to prominence and wealth by infiltrating The Knights of Nardica, a fictional version of the Ku Klux Klan. Schuyler's story, for the most part, follows Disher's experiences. Crookman consequently serves as a distant foil. Tolson changed the story to have Max Disher become the president of Black No More. He is still an opportunistic entrepreneur, and he is, temporarily at least, carried away by his fascination with the beauty of the white Helen Givens. Two buddies of his are also in top administrative positions in Black No More, and all try to control and contain Crogman's idealism to their own social and economic advantage. Crogman, by contrast, appears as the idealistic scientist whose work has extraordinary social promise. Ethel, the objective reporter, says, "his discovery means the defeat of fascism in the United States." But Crogman's work is constantly threatened with compromise and dissipation by the selfish hunger for power and money of those around him.

Crogman idealistically insists, against the protestations of his business advisers, "As we grow bigger, we must grow smaller." He insists on passing on the savings made possible by growth to the consumer least able to pay for the service: "You see, it's the common laborer who suffers most from race prejudice—the loss of job, the underpay, the daily and hourly insults. The white collar worker can escape into his closed little world. So we mustn't forget that Black No More is primarily for the man farthest down. His reach, therefore, must not exceed his grasp."

Tolson, however, also gave Max Disher's double-dealing a more sympathetic interpretation. In Schuyler's story, Max goes for the ultimate prize, control of the White House, until an investigation into the assumed racial purity of white Americans reveals that the candidate he is backing had Negro ancestors. In Tolson's story, act 1 outlines Max's desertion of both Minnie and Sadie, yellow and brown women with whose affections he has been toying. He heads for the same dumb, but beautiful, white cracker whom he prizes in Schuyler's novel. But the early part of act 3 is given over to Minnie's revenge, aided by Sadie. Then Max reveals that his dealings with the Knights of Nardica have ultimately been in the interest of Black No More. Max confronts Givens, the Grand Giraw of the Knights and father of his fiancée, with the truth about Max's own racial identity and the threat of using the embarrassing information he has gathered. Thus Max redeems his racial pride and his manhood at the end of the play.

Tolson added another personal comment to the play by having Max assume the name *Wiley Bishop* in his role as president of Black No More. The reference to the two black colleges in Marshall, Texas, considering the play was originally intended for performance at Wiley, apparently was directed at the two schools' commonly acknowledged aim of preparing students for entrée into the racially imitative black bourgeoisie. Max's redemptive turnabout at the end of the play suggests, however, that there is always hope for authentic racial self-assertion.

In short, Tolson, while maintaining much of the comic tone of Schuyler's story, gave it a more explicitly earnest social message. Rather than sustaining the apparently disinterested and sweeping farcical laughter of Schuyler, he pointed the comedy more directly at the racism that is the American form of fascism and at the socially shortsighted competitive striving for selfish personal ambitions. Dr. Crogman's unselfish dedication to the benefit of his fellows through his scientific achievements separates him from the more vulgar concerns of those immediately about him, but there is a strong underlying assumption that the truth he is seeking to manifest, regardless of the rightness or wrongness of his personal efforts, will ultimately prevail.

Fire in the Flint, Tolson's dramatization of Walter White's novel, was written to be performed for the national convention of the NAACP in Oklahoma City on 28 June 1952. It was performed in the Municipal Auditorium before an audience estimated at five thousand. A photograph shows an urbanely gracious Walter White, dressed impeccably, congratulating an obviously pleased Tolson, in short sleeves, before the cast gathered for a curtain

Melvin B. Tolson is congratulated by Walter White after a performance of *Fire in the Flint* by the Dust Bowl Players in Oklahoma City on 28 June 1952.

call. Unfortunately, the surviving manuscript ends with act 2, scene 2, but even the incomplete manuscript makes clear some of the changes Tolson made in White's story to make it more suitable for dramatic production.

The most conspicuous change is the introduction of a new character, a nurse-secretary for Dr. Kenneth Harper, named Yutha. Since Yutha is the name of Tolson's sister, who, like his mother, died of cancer, this change probably was intended as a memorial to his sister as well as a means of staking out a personal claim on the story. It was, in any case, a dramatically effective change. Yutha and Bob, Kenneth's younger brother, are paired off romantically, and their relationship counterpoints Kenneth's courtship of Jane Philips, which is taken from the novel. Since Yutha, like Bob, is challenging and direct, and as an outsider in the family is thus even freer than he is to speak her piece, they also effectively point up the generational changes in expectations in the South.

Another related change is the way in which Joe Harper, Kenneth and Bob's father, is remembered. In White's novel, the father protected his family and collected an impressive legacy of property and money by publicly and sometimes even ostentatiously accepting the demeaning role that whites in Central City, Georgia, prescribed for Negroes. Tolson gave the father more pride and made him an advocate of staying as far away from whites as possible. It is a minor change, but it prepares for the eventual militancy of Bob and Kenneth.

The most interesting shift, however, is in Kenneth's literary interest. This young man, who has studied in the American East and in Europe and deliberately returned to his hometown in the South to make his excellent medical training of service to his community and of profit to himself, in White's novel brings back with him an impressive taste for a wide range of writers, Rolland, Dreiser, Shaw, Willa Cather, D. H. Lawrence, Knut Hamsun, Conrad, and especially Du Bois. In place of such a broad range of literary reference, in Tolson's play Mamie, Kenneth's sister, catches him reading Ibsen's *Ghosts*. Then the dialogue develops an analogy between the ghosts that haunt the Alvings and the ghosts that haunt the idealistic hopes and ambitions of young black people in the South. Again it is an effective change.

Since the surviving manuscript is incomplete, any critical observations must be qualified. The changes discussed above suggest that Tolson had a clear sense of dramatic purpose and formal design. The first two acts involve Dr. Harper in two testing cases, Emma Bradley's emergency appendectomy and the murder of Bud Ware. Tolson used these two events almost exactly as they appeared in White's story, but he changed the characters and literary allusions to make the significance of these cases more pointed and more resonant.

Tolson's appetite for argument and for conversational games must, however, be counted as a mixed blessing. The dialogue is often crisp and entertaining, but occasionally the flair for loaded sarcasm makes the characters seem only devices for verbal display. Tolson found it hard to resist the bright remark, the cascading of dialogue to a surprising twist. Occasionally the role of the character speaking seems only incidental. Nevertheless, one cannot help regret that this play remains incomplete and relatively unavailable.

Tolson wrote a letter to his wife, Ruth, from Detroit dated 1958, although internal evidence suggests that the letter was written in June 1957. Tolson wrote that in four weeks he had completed writing four episodes, "Transfiguration Springs," "The Fence War," "Beyond Round Mountain," and "The Underground Railroad Station." Two one-act plays by the first two titles survive in the Library of Congress manuscript collection along with another not mentioned in Tolson's letter, "Bivouac by the Santa Fe." Neither "Beyond Round Mountain" nor "The Underground Railroad Station" seem likely to have been earlier titles for "Bivouac by the Santa Fe," so I assume they were two separate episodes, written and then discarded or lost.

These dramatic episodes were written to be performed as part of the public celebration of Oklahoma's golden anniversary. The reason for their not being part of that celebration is not clearly known. The only record of performance of any of these episodes is that mentioned previously from a stage bill dated 22 May 1959, which indicates that "Transfiguration Springs" was performed along with scene 1 from O'Neill's *The Emperor Jones* and "Judgment Day" from James Weldon Johnson's *God's Trombones*. The episodes dramatize the role of black Americans in the settling of Oklahoma and apparently were intended for a broadly diverse audience. They carry a strong claim for racial recognition coupled with a long-suffering but determinedly persistent message of racial goodwill from the black community to the general public.

"Bivouac by the Santa Fe" concerns several black soldiers who are part of an inadequate federal force trying to protect Indian Territory in Oklahoma from illegal landgrabbers. Sergeant Pierson, the ranking noncommissioned officer of the group, constantly reminds the men of their soldierly duty as they gripe about Texas badmen, Indians, and the natural dangers and hardships of the territory. Private Dix complains: "I didn't bargain for this godforsaken country with its rattlesnakes and coyotes and tornadoes. And what do we get outa it, Sergeant? The Civil War is over. We're free—free to go and build something for ourselves."

Sergeant Pierson responds: "By God, you're building something for yourself! You're building the greatest country in history. A country free and united now and forever!"

But the events that follow challenge Pierson's assertion. Chief White

Horse enters with a sample poster that is clear evidence that white landgrab-
bers are encouraging a wholesale violation of the Indians' territorial rights.
The soldiers acknowledge the problem. They even acknowledge that black
Americans led by members of Pierson's family are participating in the viola-
tion, but they jokingly insist that it's different for the blacks. "They were
getting the hell outa Texas" to set up Negro towns. "Do you blame 'em? If
I owned Texas and Hell, I'd rent out Texas and live in Hell! Black men have
been running to the Indians in Oklahoma for salvation since I don't know
when." Tolson must have inwardly smiled at this as a caricature of his own
move from Marshall, Texas, to Langston, Oklahoma.

The black soldiers' efforts to uphold the law are seriously complicated by
the racial hatred resulting from the savage frontier warfare between whites
and Indians as the land-hungry whites move in on Indian land. Sergeant
Pierson and his men already have in custody an Indian, Flat Top, whose
family has been slaughtered by whites and who consequently undertakes to
scalp as many whites as he can in retribution. Then Tex Cunard, a white
man who has also lost his family and has a notorious history of scalping In-
dians for retribution, is captured. Pierson, with a grim sense of justice remi-
niscent of Tolson's "Ballad of the Rattlesnake," orders Flat Top and Cun-
ard to dig a grave to serve as an arena in which they are to face each other
with bowie knives with only the survivor able to climb out.

But White Horse has earlier warned of the approach of a tornado. Flat
Top, sensing the danger of the wind, tries to flee but is restrained. Then
Cunard, while digging, has a heart attack. Pierson points up the irony of this
heartless man suffering a heart attack and on first impulse is ready to leave
Cunard in the grave. The Indian, too, "starts off, then turns back as if drawn
by some irrepressible force outside himself."

> "We pick 'im up, Sergeant?"
> "Yes, Flat Top, we pick 'im up. After all, we're human."
> (As the lightning darts across the sky which is now turning black and,
> with a deafening roar mounting momentarily, Pierson and Flat Top carry
> Tex toward the stockade.)

During the bus boycott in Montgomery, Alabama, in 1955 and 1956, Mar-
tin Luther King wrote of the philosophy that governed the tactics of the
participants:

> We have discovered a new and powerful weapon—non-violent resistance.
> Although law is an important factor in bringing about social change, there
> are certain conditions in which the very effort to adhere to new legal deci-
> sions creates tension and provokes violence. We had hoped to see demon-
> strated a method that would enable us to continue our struggle while cop-
> ing with the violence it aroused. Now we see the answer: face violence if

necessary, but refuse to return violence. If we respect those who oppose us, they may achieve a new understanding of the human relations involved.[4]

Neither Sergeant Pierson nor Melvin B. Tolson was fully committed to non-violence, but in the late fifties Martin Luther King and his philosophy were winning a very large and enthusiastic share of public attention. The procedure of first challenging racial injustice then responding to the racial aggression inherent in that injustice with understanding and compassion was demonstrably producing social change. Tolson's three dramatic episodes are infused with the values of King's principles for social action and change, but the ending of "Bivouac by the Santa Fe" labors this message crudely.

On 27 February 1954, John Ciardi, following the publication of Tolson's *Libretto for the Republic of Liberia*, wrote to Richard L. Brown, assistant director of the Bread Loaf Writers Conference: "I do indeed have a nomination for a Bread Loaf Fellowship and an enthusiastic one. Undoubtedly the most rocket-driven poet we have published is M. B. Tolson." Tolson became a permanent Bread Loaf Fellow in poetry and drama and thus began a much prized association with Robert Frost. The influence of two of Frost's poems, "Mending Wall" and "West-Running Brook," are indirect but very strong in the two remaining dramatic episodes, "The Fence War" and "Transfiguration Springs."

"The Fence War" is set in 1883. The big ranchers who can afford the cost are fencing in their open range. Bill Farmer, who cannot afford the fence and whose son-in-law has been shot, is awaiting a band of men from Robbers' Roost whom he has hired to tear down the fences Old Man Stiggers has put up. Farmer also believes Old Man Stiggers is responsible for the shooting of his son-in-law. Four men from Robbers' Roost arrive, an Indian, a Negro, a Mexican, and a Southern white, and they are boastfully democratic:

Cracker Boy: Yes we're all democrats—with a small "d." We don't have no fences in Robbers' Roost. We give everybody a chance, Indians, Nigras, Whites, Mexies, Southerners, Yankees—just every damn body. Now, you said you're in a Fence War out here. You don't want the fences these big ranchers are putting up; so you're just like us, and we're willing to work with you, because both of us believe in the same thing: no walls, no boulders, no fences between men. After all, out in Robbers' Roost, we believe in Jeffersonian democracy.

Bert (Farmer's right-hand man, shocked): Ain't that something—you scalawags talking about Jeffersonian democracy?

Mexie (with a threatening gesture): I wouldn't say that, if I was you, Senor. We . . . men. We . . . no scalawags. We believe in Tom Jefferson. We believe in Benito Juarez. We . . . men!

Then begins an intense discussion about the pay the men are to get for the job. The men demand white man's pay of eight hundred dollars, since they take considerable risk and believe in and promise *efficiency*. Farmer tells of his grudge against Stiggers because of the shooting of his son-in-law, and that makes the men back off since they do not assume any obligation for intentional killing. At this point their bargaining is interrupted by Dead-shot Pierson, U.S. marshal, who holds them all at gunpoint until he identifies Bert Adler, Farmer's right-hand man. He accuses Bert of shooting Farmer's son-in-law. Bert acknowledges the shooting, bitterly regretting that he only wounded his victim. He had given the son-in-law a letter introducing him to his family in Independence, and the son-in-law had taken sexual advantage of Bert's younger sister, Hilda. The sudden twist of events causes Farmer to call off his bargain: "Cracker Boy, the deal is off . . . the fence is down—the fence of hate that I built in my own mind against Old Man Stiggers. (They watch the grim spectre of Bill Farmer fade against the horizon.)"

In Tolson's letter from Detroit to Ruth he also wrote: "Each episode has a dramatic surprise ending that ought to get the audience. I want a good play, keen drama, as well as history." In this instance his desire "to get the audience" with a surprise ending led him astray. The conflict between the ranchers who can afford to fence in the open grange and those who cannot is in no way resolved by the information about who shot Farmer's son-in-law. Farmer's summary message, "the fence is down," thus seems hollow and pious, an effort to appeal to the predisposition of the audience rather than a serious examination of a historical conflict. Tolson also often referred to Frost's poem "Mending Wall" with a surprising failure to register the ironic ambiguity over whether fences do indeed make good neighbors or not.

"Transfiguration Springs" is more of one piece. John and Bonita Pierson traveled from Virginia ten years ago. They reached a fork in the Santa Fe trail and had to decide whether to stay and settle in Indian Territory or to continue westward seeking gold in California. The following dialogue, with its strong echoes of Frost's "West-Running Brook," tells how they made their decision:

John: There we were a green bridegroom and a greener bride, just out of Slavery in Virginia. Then you saw that beautiful spring, with its sparkling fresh water; and you said, right out of the clear blue—I remember your exact words—"John, this is our Garden of Eden. So we'll settle right here." Then you said, "John, what day of the month is this?" And I said, "August 6." And you clapped your hands and said, "Transfiguration Day! Good Luck!"

Bonita: Then *I* said something which *you* said *you'd* always remember.

John: I don't remember what *you* said, but I do remember that I took my pick-ax and cut *Transfiguration Springs* on the upper boulder in the sun. It's still there!

John and Bonita, like Fred and his wife in Frost's poem, have a strong, deep marital bond. The action of the play takes place precisely ten years from the day of their naming Transfiguration Springs. The country is in the midst of a drought. Cattle and crops are dying. The Piersons' spring is a saving resource for them and their neighbors, but Ernest Jenson—later his Christian name is given as Saul—a proud white Southerner, will not ask for help from a black man. Sarah, his wife, worried and apologetic, calls on the Piersons. Ernest then bursts in angrily. John Pierson confronts Ernest with evidence that he had been visiting the spring secretly at night. Jenson begins to deny the evidence when another white neighbor, Logan, calls to invite the Piersons to a square dance on this anniversary date and to give John a handkerchief Logan has picked up by the spring. The handkerchief makes the case against Jenson irrefutable. While he struggles with his pride, Sarah, his wife, tells a story about the loss of Bessie, the cow she raised from a pet calf. Logan fills out Sarah's story by explaining how John Pierson saved Sarah's life when she tried to rescue Bessie. Sarah was unconscious before and after the rescue, so neither of the Jensons had known of John's act. Jenson manfully swallows his pride and his racial hatred. Although sixty years old, he acknowledges, "we live to learn, and learn to live." He tells of his grandfather, a member of one of the first families of Virginia, christening him Saul:

Bonita: And, just as ancient Saul was hard on Christians—
Jenson: I was hard on niggers. Mrs. Pierson, why don't you go on with the parallel. On the road to Damascus, Saul got the hell knocked outa him. So tonight Saul Jenson got the hell knocked outa him! I guess now everybody is satisfied.
Bonita: Except for one thing.
Jenson: What's that, Mrs.—er—(He almost chokes.)
Sarah (laughing): Saul, does it choke you to call a Negro woman "Mrs."?
Jenson (Bowing theatrically): Mrs. Pierson, you are about to ask the noblest Virginian of them all a question.
Bonita: The square dance is tonight. I like that name "square dance." Square—a square deal for all of us. We'd like to have you and Mrs. Jenson go with us.

One can imagine this being an effective conclusion to a large public celebration of Oklahoma's golden anniversary. The challenge is clothed with carefully measured sentiment. The story moves smoothly and relentlessly toward its celebration of integration dependent upon the transfiguration of Saul Jenson. Unfortunately "Transfiguration Springs" was never performed for its intended audience, and its dream of interracial brotherhood seems nobler for its aspiration than for its historical realism.

VI

PUBLISHING *LIBRETTO*

In 1947, when the Tolson family moved to Langston, Melvin Tolson was forty-nine years old. However, he represented his age as forty-seven, the same age as the twentieth century. And he may have believed it. DuBois, in *Souls of Black Folk*, proclaimed the twentieth century as the century of the color line, and Tolson often repeated DuBois's proclamation. He had a strong sense of living in a fateful moment of history and of this moment carrying a weighty challenge as well as an extraordinary opportunity. It was not as fashionable in the late forties as it is now to speak of midlife crises or passages, but clearly Tolson was going through a rather remarkable passage in his professional career. He was soon to write a major poem celebrating a new world of man to emerge after colonialism was dismantled and a new democracy of nations to be realized. And before that poem was published in toto he was to write and publish another, "E. & O. E.," in which the narrator-poet laments the paralyzing weight of historical awareness:

> 'Sdeath!
> The toil
> of doomsday struck
> *I-ness* in me
> between parentheses
> of my eternity.

The editors of *Poetry* indicated their esteem for this poem by awarding it the annual Bess Hokim prize. In keeping with the theme of the poem, Tolson once indicated his bleakest feelings about this midlife passage by this ironic entry in his journal:

(1) In 1 A.D. – Brother Tolson
(2) In 1775 – Citizen Tolson
(3) In 1917 – Comrade Tolson
(4) In 1950 – Not a damn thing!

This entry, however, is balanced by a draft of a poem, "The Woman 1950," that includes this stanza:

> The woman 1950 is too old
> to be with child,
> Job's comforters surmise:
> yet a mother's build
> and a baby's size
> set travail's horizon—
> not the mother's age;
> as the Globe's stage
> wombed Hamlet's word and guise.

After living through the ordeal of the economic depression of the thirties, Tolson never again was free of the expected threat that it would recur. He felt that he could not be free of that fear unless there was some fundamental change in the American economic system. World War II, succeeding the depression, was seen by Tolson as an international apocalyptic conflagration, a true crisis of western civilization. Yet the world and its history continued, and Tolson characteristically insisted that the seeds of promise were always contained in such social catastrophes. Nevertheless, midpoint, the eye of the storm, is often the scariest moment of all. The base has been laid. The sense of promise and possibility is ripe, but the promise and possibility always seem to appear in forms surprisingly different than anticipated. The goal becomes veiled by a number of crucial choices, and one senses the enormous and perilous responsibility of choosing wrongly.

As a writer Tolson was still experimenting with fiction and drama as well as with poetry. He always enjoyed strong, direct, and immediate contact with an audience. He was a practiced and enthusiastic speaker. He observed the powerfully broad public impact of such books as *Native Son* and *Grapes of Wrath* with respect and admiration. A poet could rarely hope for such an impact. But, even in the novel, postwar literary fashion demanded change. "Artfulness" was increasingly in style, an "artfulness" that served a variety of functions, including, on occasion, the masking of unpopular, or even dangerous, political or cultural statements. The contrasts in style between *Native Son* and *Invisible Man* indicate the dramatic changes that were taking place. The changes were a consequence of a variety of cultural factors, but the cold war between Russia and the United States accompanied by a repressive political climate was certainly one of the more obvious. Academic fashions were heavily influenced by the political climate. The New Criticism had emerged triumphant. The published utterances of Eliot and the Southern Agrarians carried an authority often far beyond, and different from, their intentions. The original classical agrarian dream took on increasing overtones of conservative authority. While Tolson was by no means ready to give up his ambitions as a dramatist and novelist, clearly he was gaining success as a poet. He had been named poet laureate of Liberia, and, while the obligations and significance of such an appointment were somewhat vague, he characteristically set about making them meaningful by his own industry and initiative.

He wrote a poem commemorating the centennial of the founding of Liberia. He sent this poem to both *Poetry* and *Atlantic*, who rejected it. George Dillon's letter of rejection from *Poetry* (27 September 1948) survives. Edward Weeks's from *Atlantic* does not, although Tolson refers to it in a letter to James Decker of the Decker Press (17 February 1949). Dillon explained that because *Poetry* was "so heavily overstocked" any poem needed to have the unanimous vote of all three of its editors. "In such circumstances a long poem such as this one is ruled out almost automatically." He did have generous critical praise for the poem, however:

> We all thought the "Libretto" a very good performance, much stronger than we would expect such an occasional poem to be. Our youngest (and most severely critical) editor commends its "new imagery and its nice sense of disciplined rhythm, especially in some of the shorter sections in the middle." I agree with that, and it seems to me, too, that the historical allusions are well managed, vivid, and interesting.

Dillon added "two minor criticisms": "the last stanza of the first section and the entire last section do not seem to us good enough for the rest." The concluding section would continue to draw criticism even after the poem had been much revised.

In his letter to James Decker, Tolson wrote that Dr. Horace Mann Bond "had suggested that I bring out the poem, 'Libretto for the Republic of Liberia', in a book by itself, with an Introduction and a Critique." Tolson's letter summarizes how he came to write the poem, pointing out the special relation between Lincoln University and Liberia. It also holds out to Decker the reassuring incentive: "Dr. Bond informs me that he will co-operate financially, to a modest degree."

On 19 February 1949, Tolson wrote to Allen Tate asking him to write a preface for *Libretto*. He began his letter by reminding Tate that, when editor of *Sewanee Review*, Tate had returned Tolson's poem "The Horns of the Bull" because Tate's "desk was crowded," asking Tolson to return it later. Unfortunately, Tate left the editorship before Tolson could do so. In reviewing how he had come to write the *Libretto*, Tolson modestly explained, "It seems that belatedly I have initiated the modern movement among Negro poets."

On 8 March, apparently having received a favorable reply from Decker,

Tolson wrote him again enthusiastically planning the format and promotion of the book. He announced, *Libretto* "is now with a critic friend." The next day he wrote to Bond:

> Well the *Libretto for Liberia* is to be published! *And we won't have to do it!* It has been taken over by the Decker Press, of Belles Lettres, and will be brought out de luxe. The publisher is very enthusiastic, and plans several big occasions in connection with the coming-out. He says it's a natural for critics and the metropolitan press and wire services. Now, while Decker has taken over officially, it is my desire that you squeeze the orange for all it's worth from the point of view of Lincoln University. *Poetry* carried the announcement that "Cap" is the only American who has even been appointed to a laureateship. I hadn't thought of that!
> Were you able to put *that* through your Board?

That refers to an honorary doctorate for Tolson not awarded until 1954.

In this same letter Tolson told his former classmate, "*Collier's* magazine is interested in a series of poems I am doing on the life of Abe Lincoln. This is secret, of course."[1] Besides revising *Libretto*, Tolson continued to write new poems and apparently to do some revisions of *A Gallery of Harlem Portraits*. "The Negro Scholar" appeared in the *Midwest Journal* in 1948. "African China," a combination and revision of two poems from *A Gallery of Harlem Portraits*, appeared in the "Negro Poets Issue" of *Voices*, edited by Langston Hughes in the winter of 1950. These poems will be discussed in greater detail later along with "E. & O. E.," "A Long Head to a Round Head," and "The Man from Halicarnassus," all of which appeared in print before *Libretto* eventually was published, late in 1953.

A 9 May 1949, letter of Tolson's to Tate indicates that he had heard from Tate about *Libretto* and that Tate had agreed to write the preface, although he had some questions about what ought to be in it. It is significant to a critical controversy that developed after the publication of *Harlem Gallery* to note here that since this letter refers to Tolson's letter to Tate of 19 February as if there were no other letters between them during that time, and since there is a lapse of less than three months between Tolson's initial request to Tate and this reference to Tate's acceptance of the task, that in fact Tate did not refuse to write a preface for *Libretto* as Dudley Randall many years later reported that Tolson told him. That story is not compatible with the evidence in the surviving Tate–Tolson correspondence. On the contrary, Tolson indicated in this letter that he had made significant changes in his manuscript on his own initiative since sending Tate the earlier draft. Tolson began his letter: "I shall not try to say how much I appreciate your appreciation of the poem and 'the official necessities of the occasion.' " Tolson assured Tate that, although he understood his "anxiety about *how* to write the Preface," he had no qualms about Tate's doing so since, "as a critic you have no precedent." He suggested a 1 August deadline and then added: "I have added to the poem, since I wrote you, and polished it. I feel it's much improved in totality of effect—also in its scope and depth. I'm re-typing it now and will send the new copy next week."

Tolson apparently was not satisfied with the revisions he had made by 9 May. He wrote Tate again on 1 June explaining that new revisions had caused delay in sending Tate the poem and detailing the changes he had made in lines 155–57 of the poem as finally published.[2] As an example of the thorough combing he was giving the text, he made this comment about the formal structure of *Libretto*:

> Of course this world of the poem, in harmony with the dictates of the theme and occasion, had to be far-flung and various in space and time, techniques and ideas, persons and symbols. I can only hope that the diatonic structure supports the conception. I may say that each word, foreign or archaic, was selected for its particular effect in the unity underlying the diversity of the scheme.

Tolson added a p.s. to his letter reemphasizing his conception of the importance of *Libretto* in the history of black American writing, a contention Tate eventually incorporated into his preface: "I forgot to mention, Mr. Tate, that I believe the *Libretto* marks a 'fork in the road', a change in direction, for what is called Negro Poetry. Between me and you, it's long overdue."

On 4 January 1950, Tolson wrote again to Bond explaining that he was still "waiting on the critic who is writing the introduction for the *Libretto*." Apparently Tolson guarded the identity of this critic closely until he had the preface in hand. Along with matters concerning Lincoln University, its alumni, and a prodding reminder to Bond about the proposed honorary doctor of literature degree, Tolson mused with some satisfaction over the success of "Dark Symphony," which "has been published in Germany, broadcast in Paris during the holidays, lectured on at London University by Dr. Poole of Amsterdam University, and now set to music. Funny how little things get puffed up making the rounds!"

Tate's eagerly anticipated preface apparently arrived by 4 March 1950. On that date Tolson began a letter to Tate acknowledging receipt of the preface; however, that letter was not sent. A revised letter was sent to Tate dated 15 March. It is a carefully composed letter, as if Tolson now assumed that his letter might well become a matter of literary history. Tolson began with a matter of personal health. He was relieved to report that the doctors examining him had not discovered a malignancy. He was free of cancer. The examination may well have occurred on a visit to his sister Helen Tolson Wilson in Detroit, for he next described an anecdote set in Detroit, which apparently Tate enjoyed, and which Tolson referred to again in later correspondence, correspondence that Tolson apparently planned with Tate's support to submit to *Sewanee Review* for publication.

> I have read the Preface and also during my absence *On the Limits of Poetry*. In Detroit's library on Cadillac Square I came across your *Collected Poems* in the reading room. The book was shabby; and on many of the poems horny hands had left grease spots in their textual analysis. When I put it up it was picked up by an Uncle Remus (I imagine from Paradise Valley); and when I left an hour later he was sitting in a corner with tighter wrinkles in his face. I casually passed him and he was tracing the lines of the *Ode*. I thought about that a long time, coming back on the train. By the way the most meaningful artistic problem in the *Ode* I have not seen discussed in the journals.

Tolson referred to Tate's "Ode to the Confederate Dead" and the critical problem of to whom the "Ode" is addressed.

As for Tate's preface to the *Libretto*, Tolson wrote that he had "studied it carefully in relation to the various schools. It is an atom bomb dropped on two worlds." The preface takes on a significant biographical interest when one notes Tolson's reactions to it. Tate began by sketching the cultural irony of the *Libretto* being written for an official occasion:

> One can imagine, in Washington, during the New Deal, a patriotic poem being read by the late Stephen Vincent Benet; but not, I assume, by the late Hart Crane. That may be one difference between the literary culture of official Washington and that of Liberia: Mr. Tolson is in direct succession from Crane. Here is something marvelous indeed. A small African republic founded by liberated slaves celebrates its centenary by getting an American Negro poet to write what, in the end, is an English Pindaric ode in a style derived from—but by no means imitative of—one of the most difficult modern poets.

Tate then offered high and enthusiastic praise, "there is a great gift for language, a profound historical sense, and a first-rate intelligence at work in this poem from first to last." He suggested that, even acknowledging the notable achievements of Langston Hughes and Gwendolyn Brooks, Tolson's achievement in *Libretto* marks "the first time, it seems to me, a Negro poet has assimilated completely the full poetic language of his time, and, by implication, the language of the Anglo-American tradition." This is, of course, the point Tolson had been prompting him to in his early letters.

Tate then concluded:

> It seems to me only common sense to assume that the main thing is the poetry, if one is a poet, whatever one's color may be. I think that Mr. Tolson has assumed this; and the assumption, I gather, has made him not less but

more intensely *Negro* in his apprehension of the world than any of his con-
temporaries, or any that I have read. But by becoming more intensely *Negro*
he seems to me to dismiss the entire problem so far as poetry is concerned,
by putting it in its properly subordinate place. In the end I found that I was
reading *Libretto for the Liberian Republic* not because Mr. Tolson is a
Negro but because he is a poet, not because the poem has a "Negro subject"
but because it is about the world of men. And this subject is not merely as-
serted; it is embodied in a rich and complex language, and realized in terms
of the poetic imagination.

Tate's attempt to subsume the "Negro" characteristics of the poet and
the poem under a high compliment to their art represents the blandly pa-
tronizing tone of white critics that many black writers and critics during the
fifties resented and rebelled against with increasing racial assertiveness. Yet
it also includes a warranted high compliment. Tolson was, indeed, aiming
for a universal audience willing to slough off the myths of race that so char-
acterized European and white American historical perspectives. But to win
through to such universality he assumed one first had to revise the naively
arrogant Western racial perspective by recognizing with respect the past
and potential cultural achievements of non-Western and, particularly for
Tolson's poem, African, cultures.

Tolson approved the emphasis Tate placed on artistry, on form, but he
did so in such a manner as not to demean the significance of content, "Ne-
gro" content. In his letter he wrote:

> The core of your thesis is sound. The poet is first the maker. To emphasis
> [*sic*] Form in a period of bad taste is not to de-emphasize Content. To say
> that a chef must know the culinary art is not to say that he is to use poor in-
> gredients. However, if he has the best ingredients and turns out a bad meal,
> he is a poor cook. So the hotel gets rid of him. Because I want a good carpen-
> ter, it doesn't follow that I want termite-eaten boards in my house. The
> milieu gives the poet his clay; he is only the potter. Kaolin tells the connois-
> seur about the superior whiteness and hardness and sonority of the material
> with which the potter had to work in his milieu, but the shape that he gives
> the porcelain determines his artistry. Is not that the reason the figurines of
> ancient Benin influence the moderns?

Tolson continued to stress the importance of social environment for the art-
ist as he tried to find accommodation with the man whose support prom-
ised to open doors to critical recognition previously closed to black American
writers.

But Tolson was not just making a deal. He was also beginning an impor-
tant new commitment. In the early thirties V. F. Calverton's *Modern Quar-
terly*, the man and magazine so important to Tolson's early career, emanated
strong social criticism of T. S. Eliot, who was increasingly becoming the

poet-hero of the New Critics. Ernest Sutherland Bates wrote an article for *Modern Quarterly*, published in 1933, the title of which clearly indicates the substance of his argument, "T. S. Eliot: Leisure Class Laureate."[3] Calverton himself followed this in 1934 with a review of Eliot's *After Strange Gods* entitled, "T. S. Eliot—An Inverted Marxian."[4] Tolson, some years later in his poem "Tapestries of Time," echoed the *Modern Quarterly* position:

> To escape the waste land of the Doomsday hour,
> His poets scurry into the ivory tower.
> The ghosts of Milton and Whitman grieve without,
> While the moderns sonnetize a hothouse flower.

Tolson's revisions of *Libretto* and his persuasion of Tate to write the preface began a conversion in his attitude toward modernism in poetry that marks 1948, the year he probably began the revision, as as significant in the development of his writing career as 1932 had previously been. In 1932 he laid "the ghosts of a dead classicism." In retrospect he felt betrayed by his academic training at Lincoln University, which had kept him insulated from the significance of modern realistic writers such as Sandburg and the writers of the Harlem Renaissance whom he came to study belatedly. By 1948 he apparently had become convinced that the modernist revolution in art was more pervasively triumphant than he and his mentors from the *Modern Quarterly* realized.

In the winter 1950 issue of *Voices*, Tolson reviewed John C. Neihardt's *A Cycle of the West*. He wrote feelingly of Neihardt's background and concerns: "He has had a vivid career as farm hand, book-keeper, beet-weeder, marble-polisher, Indian agent, school teacher, newspaperman, researcher in the legends of trapper and trader. Beneath the diversity of these phenomena is an underlying unity, a hidden premise that his poems bring into daylight. One sees it in the 'Cry of the People'. Edith Sitwell, for example, would never have thought of such a subject. Not so with Elizabeth Barrett Browning. Or Whitman, perhaps."

Yet ultimately Neihardt, as all poets, must be measured, according to Tolson, by the test John Peale Bishop proposes in "Speaking of Poetry":

> *The Ceremony must be found*
> *That will wed Desdemona to the huge Moor.*

Here, of course, Desdemona is form and the Moor is content. Neihardt's material comes from the rawness of frontier life. It is the Moor of content in his crudest state. Form is stylistic, cultivated, traditional. In this instance it is formidably difficult to find a ceremony to wed Desdemona and the Moor. Thus Neihardt mixes, as one critic has pointed out, his prairies and trappers with terms like Ilion, Iseult, Clotho, and Styx, to produce the bizarre and incongruous. . . . What one remembers about the *Cycle* is the bulk of incident and character—not the brilliance of craftsmanship, not the photo-vivid focus of discovery. Desdemona and the Moor meet at dead of night in small inns, but the marriage of form and content does not come off. I think the fault lies in the idiom. It is not modern. It is Victorian. To be specific, it is Tennysonian. It's all right for the Lady of Shalott, Sir Galahad, and Lancelot; ill-fitting for Hugh Glass and Jamie and Jed. It is again nineteenth century manners for twentieth century man.[5]

By 1955 Tolson was even more certain about the historical inevitability of modernism. In a review of Jacques and Raissa Maritain's *The Situation of Poetry*, he wrote: "When T. S. Eliot published *The Waste Land* in 1922, it sounded the death knell of Victorianism, Romanticism, and Didacticism. When Eliot was awarded the Nobel Prize in Literature, the victory of the moderns was complete. Poetry will never be the same. The modern idiom is here to stay—like modern physics."[6]

These later comments underscore the change in Tolson's views implicit in his initial response to Tate's preface, in which he noted, "The emphasis on Form and Content shifts from age to age, as it should. Nature and nurture try to establish an equilibrium. Integrity produces balance in an artist. It is the compass in the storm. It is the shell between what's inside a man and out. So an artist buys the truth and sells it not. I am not talking about the charlatans, of course. They are in Art as well as in the Capitol and the Cathedral and the Marketplace."

These observations led Tolson to comment to Tate on the special problem of audience for the Negro poet: "I sometimes think a minority group is the best laboratory in which to study social phenomena. The contradictions of the society are sharper here, because of the pressure from above and below. If the vanguard White poet is isolated, his Negro fellow is annihilated between the walls of bi-racialism. I like your term 'provincial mediocrity'. It has already started across Negro America." Tolson scorned the *embourgeoisement* of Negro America throughout his life. He read and quoted E. Franklin Frazier's *Black Bourgeoisie* with avid ironic pleasure. A black middle class growing in numbers and riches was no source of satisfaction to Tolson. It only made his audience seem more remote. Capitalism, black or white, was doomed by its inherent faults. Throughout the thirties and forties Tolson had been outspoken in calling for radical social change. Art was to awaken people to the need for a truly just and democratic society. Those artists who retreated from the confusions and compromises of immediate social commitment were consistently scorned for their cowardice. By the late forties and early fifties national and academic politics made such views increasingly unpopular, if not dangerous. Thus Tolson began to look toward a future audience. Lincoln High School in Kansas City and Lincoln University in Pennsylvania had strongly imbued Tolson with a pride in academic achievement that almost inevitably carried some elitist assumptions along with it. Thus even in Tolson's most outspoken period of radical populist beliefs one can discover some surprising elitist positions. Now, however, the elitism of the modernist literary movement provided a convenient rationale for his growing belief that *his* audience, like that of many an artist with integrity and vision, lay primarily in the distant future. He was beginning to posit the same audience that John Ciardi in 1958 would label "the vertical audience."

In an undated entry in his journal, Tolson wrote:

> The size of an audience that understands a work of art at the time of its first appearance is no argument against the merit of the work of art. Cultural and civilizational changes produce new ideas and new forms of art. The idiom of old works of art may be esoteric at the farthest remove; and the idiom of a new art may be esoteric at the closest remove.

Ultimately, however, a poem must reach a popular audience. The artist must not divorce himself from the concerns of the people. The indictment of the artist who retreats to the ivory tower, which Tolson made in "Tapestries of Time," is reasserted in "Ti" of *Libretto* by the judgment that the divorce of art from the concerns of the common man is a symptom of a culture suffering from the false worship of the idols of the tribe, hence, a culture on the descending cycle of the Ferris wheel of historical change.

Late in 1961 Tolson wrote to his former Wiley student and still close personal friend Benjamin Bell and his wife, Kate. His informal comments reveal his eventual resolution of the conflict between his elitist and proletarian assumptions. In response to Bell's praise for those portions of *Harlem Gallery* that had just been published in *Prairie Schooner*, he wrote:

> A puzzle to me: Shapiro and T. S. Eliot are in a knockout struggle over Esoterism and Obscurity in modern poetry and criticism, from the NY *Times* through the *Saturday Review*, etc. (Even the Venerable Frost has been dragged into the arena; but I can see him grinning and winking in damned Yankee style, in the unaccustomed limelight. A sense of humor is manna in the wilderness of Capitalism. The Irish and Jews and Sambos discovered that.) My work is certainly difficult in metaphors, symbols and juxtaposed ideas. There the similarity between me and Eliot separates. That is only technique, and any artist must use the technique of his time. Otherwise, we'd have the death of Art. However, when you look at my ideas and Eliot's, we're as far apart as hell and heaven. I guess Shapiro, a Jew of the Jews, sees that and takes me under his wing. I guess I'm the only Marxist poet Here and Now.
>
> Now, about the little people. Remember "ideas come from above." If you went into the street and said to a ditchdigger in Chi, "Who is Shakespeare?" he'd say, "The greatest writer that ever lived." Now, he wouldn't know a

damned thing about *Hamlet* but he might quote some of THE Bard's sayings that he picked up from the boys in the ditch. Ideas sift down. Marx and Lenin and Castro were not *of* the masses but *for* the masses. What does a Cuban peon know about *Das Kapital?* If you gave him a copy, he'd wipe his behind with it! Well, a peon has to use *some* kind of paper. What's better than that you can't read?

But in 1950, if the vanguard white poet was isolated and his Negro fellow threatened with annihilation, then Tolson greeted Tate's preface with a critical hyperbole undoubtedly occasioned in part by the high compliment that Tate had paid Tolson and by his anticipation of the literary dividends that would flow from it. Thus Tolson closed his letter to Tate: "I am trying to say that, as I look back along the trail of Negro poetry for 250 years, I see the Preface as our literary Emancipation Proclamation. I also believe that the introduction and the *Libretto* ought to go far in re-enforcing your premise in Art. And I shall be delighted to have it appear in *Poetry.*"

A few days later, on 27 March, Tolson wrote to Bond with a triumphant flourish naming the critic who had written the introduction:

At last the great Allen Tate has sent in the Preface. It took him almost ten months to the day. As you know, he is the toughest of the New School of Criticism.

He says: "For the first time, it seems to me, a Negro poet has assimilated completely the full poetic language of his time and, by implication, the language of the Anglo-American poetic tradition."

At long last, it seems, a black man has broken into the rank of T. S. Eliot and Tate! We have been completely ignored heretofore. In my *Notes* to the poem (it requires them) I am seeing that Lincoln University shall come to the attention of these superintellectuals of the English-speaking worlds. Tate is bringing out the Preface in *Poetry* before the book!

Apparently in 1950 there was sufficient professional respect between Karl Shapiro, then editor of *Poetry*, and Allen Tate that Shapiro was happy to publish Tate's preface, although, fifteen years later in an introduction to Tolson's *Harlem Gallery*, Shapiro would take strong issue with it. On 14 August 1950, Tolson wrote to Tate that he liked "the idea of having Mr. Karl Shapiro run the Preface as a sort of advance notice." He also announced that he had decided for "moral reasons" to stick with Decker Press. Tate apparently had offered to recommend the poem to a larger publisher. Tolson indicated that Dodd, Mead, his previous publisher, thought the poem, then only fourteen pages, too small for a book. He then indicated that two public occasions were planned to launch the book, one in Monrovia and the other in Washington, D.C. He did not know what to expect in Monrovia, but he savored the prospect of the event in Washington, "since the one in Washington is headed by Dr. Mary McLeod-Bethune (you doubtless know of Mrs. Roosevelt's chum and the octogenarian 'First Lady of Negro America'), you can well imagine the social and diplomatic fanfare." Tolson dedicated the *Libretto* to Mary McLeod Bethune.

On 7 April, a week earlier, Dr. Bethune had written her gratitude for the dedication and promised that she would do all that she could in setting up the premiere. But a good part of her letter also expressed her grief at the recent passing of Dr. Carter Woodson. By 5 May, Dr. Bethune seemed even more intensely preoccupied with Woodson's death and her recent participation in a ceremony memorializing him, and she begged off from assuming leading responsibility for the Washington occasion: "Please, Tolson, do not put on me the responsibility of any direct setting up for the presentation of your book."

In July 1950, *Poetry* published Tate's preface and an early version of "Ti" from *Libretto*. It was this publication that William Carlos Williams celebrated as of historical significance in the evolution of America in book 4 of *Paterson*:

> —and to Tolson and to his ode
> and to Liberia and to Allen Tate
> (Give him credit)
> and to the South generally
> *Selah!*

> —and to 100 years of it—splits
> off the radium, the Gamma rays
> will eat their bastard bones out who
> are opposed.
> *Selah!*

But Mary McLeod Bethune's backing off from a leading role in the Washington celebration was only a harbinger of a more serious setback in Tolson's publication plans for *Libretto*. On 25 October he wrote to Tate, "Mr. Tax of the Decker Press was killed in an auto accident and the company has gone under. I got the letter from the lawyer for the estate just an hour after I mailed the final draft of *Libretto*." The *Libretto* manuscript was at this point in the hands of Mr. Giroux of Harcourt, Brace & Co., and Tolson was adding notes to the poem at the suggestion of Karl Shapiro. Tolson professed to Tate,

> To say that the preface has caused a revolution in Negro letters is a very mild understatement. I see that Langston Hughes in a long poem at the anniversary of the Schomburg Collection in New York City came out in new habiliment. The dress was a trifle ill-fitting, but it was good for my old eyes.

Among the Tolson manuscripts in the Library of Congress there is an incomplete three-page letter to Tate that apparently was not sent. There also is an incomplete ten-page manuscript titled "Excerpt from a Letter to Allen Tate." And in addition there is an untitled manuscript that is apparently another version of "Excerpt from a Letter to Allen Tate." These manuscripts are what survive of Tolson's efforts to prepare an article for *Sewanee Review* representing his correspondence with Tate. The correspondence is described as growing out of Tolson's telling Tate about the incident of the Uncle Remus in the public library just off Cadillac Square in Detroit. Tolson now added some background to the incident. A strike was going on, and Tolson observed the "venerable colored man absorbedly reading a book of modern poetry" among "a number of dull-eyed workingmen."

Tate is represented as having written of this anecdote to Tolson: "I have told several times to friends your story of the Uncle Remus in the library in Detroit reading my 'Ode to the Confederate Dead'—always with great effect. One solemn sociologist, on one occasion, asked: 'Shouldn't he have been informed that the heroes honored in that poem were anxious to keep his people in slavery?' I leave the answer to you." While the correspondence is principally preoccupied with the techniques and traditions of the Pindaric ode, and even more particularly with the preposition *to*, usually found or implied in the titles of odes, it is also readily apparent that Tolson wanted very much to clarify the sociocultural significance of the man he observed reading Tate's poem in the library.

In his 15 November letter Tolson had had second thoughts about having referred to the man in the library as "Uncle Remus," but he then developed the cultural ironies of such a figure in a modern, American city:

> We are forced to look more closely at the nature of Uncle Remus and the nature of the poem—the intellectual geography of Uncle Remus and the imaginative geography of the ode. . . . In our Uncle Remus we face a unique character: a post-bellum figure we cannot pigeonhole culturally and historically. Who is Uncle Remus? Perhaps in giving him this name I myself have become a stereotyper. And I should know better. Once in 1919, I sat in a great audience. A score of dignitaries were on the platform. A Demosthenes got up to award the Spingarn Medal. In the sea of applause an ancient plantation-looking figure arose. Three thousand people got up with him. Below this timid, forlorn Uncle Remus in a sawed-off salt and pepper coat and Charlie Chaplin trousers ranged 100 products made from the peanut. I've been told that Henry Ford wanted to buy his mind at $10,000 a year; but the sage of Tuskegee didn't have sense enough to sell it. I'm thinking too of an Uncle Remus at a little Negro school across the tracks in Huntsville, Texas. I was told by a local Babbitt that this venerable scholar was always tying up the local Solons with Greek and Latin and Hebrew quotations. In fact, he had on the wall of his tiny office: "Small minds are interested in persons, average minds in events, great minds in ideas." So perhaps our Uncle Remus is a disinherited post-bellum scholar from the South,

marooned among the unparadised in Paradise Valley, by one of the "artis-
tries of Circumstance."

In the "Excerpt" Tolson agrees with Tate's scorn for the "solemn sociolo-
gist's irrelevant question." However, in addition to the textual argument
that the sociologist "didn't read the poem, but read *into* the poem his read-
ing of a non-poem," Tolson points out that the sociologist patronizingly
implies "Uncle Remus" is more simpleminded than the observable facts
suggest:

> First, our Uncle Remus doesn't need the information of your solemn sociol-
> ogist: (a) he was born in a family of ex-slaves; (b) an ancient man who has
> intelligence enough to read modern poetry would certainly see a fact big
> enough to hide modern poetry from your scholar.

> Second, the fact that our Uncle Remus knows about the slavery of his people
> both from experience and history should set his sensibility against the very
> title of the *Ode*. Since this does not occur, we are forced to examine the na-
> ture of our Uncle Remus and the imaginative geography of the poem.

Tolson probably hoped that, if these remarks were published in the *Sewanee
Review*, readers might be induced to transfer the invitation to examine the
nature of Uncle Remus and the imaginative geography of Tate's poem to
himself and "the imaginative geography" of *Libretto*.

On 28 November 1950 Tolson typed a draft of a letter to Tate that said
in part: "I'm glad you liked my comment on the lines from the Ode. I want
to revamp them before sending them to *The Sewanee Review*. As a veteran
of many campaigns, I find it best to leave the cons without a leg to stand on
before the moment of decision." A later, unfinished paragraph in this draft
letter makes it clear that Tolson found Tate's "Ode" subversive of tradi-
tional antebellum Southern assumptions: "If I were the Chairman of the
un-Southern Activities Committee, I would most certainly prosecute you
as a Fifth Columnist. The Ode is a flagrant deviation from the ante-bellum
Party Line! More than that, it is defeatist. You tell our Youth in Gray that
even if they have the demonic courage of Stonewall's legions in charging the
barricades of the damned Yankees—'they will not last'. Socrates was sent to
the worms for less than that!" This final comment was not part of the letter
Tolson actually sent to Tate on 29 November.

Both the draft and finished letter began with Tolson saying that he was
sending *The Libretto* manuscript to Mr. Wheelock at Scribner's. The 29
November letter also included, as did the draft letter, an indication that
Tate had seen comments from Tolson on Tate's "Ode." Tolson said he was
revising these comments and would send the revisions to Tate, since Tate
and Mr. Palmer were friends. Then he asked Tate's advice: "I've been a lit-

tle puzzled just how to prefix the note on Uncle Remus. Should it be an editor's note? Should I include in the 'Letter' my three-fold comment on Uncle Remus and the two examples I gave of Uncle Remuses I have known? What is the deadline?" Tolson added one more comment that indicates his unhappiness with the national political environment at the time: "I'm a little blue: I'd give anything if my fellow-townsman, Mr. Truman, had a knowledge of history and a modicum of imagination."

John Hall Wheelock rejected the *Libretto* manuscript on 4 January 1951. Tolson wrote to Tate on 28 February asking for another suggestion for a publisher. He included a copy of a letter he had received from Alain Locke and quoted from a letter that Theodore Roethke had written: "I thought the excerpt in *Poetry* was very exciting, and was astonished it wasn't given one of the prizes."

This is the latest letter that I have been able to locate from Tolson to Tate. Clearly the Tolson manuscripts in the Library of Congress and the Tate papers at Princeton University do not fully represent the correspondence. But what does exist indicates a relationship more complicated than, and different from, that described by Dudley Randall in 1966 after an interview with Tolson, which was later accepted and repeated by Joy Flasch.[7] Tolson never embraced Tate as a warm personal friend as he did V. F. Calverton, Robert Frost, and Karl Shapiro. Tate's conservative social views were too distant from Tolson's convictions for there to be much more than professional respect between the two. However, the letters indicate that Tate was generous in his efforts to promote and find a publisher for *Libretto*. It is also no small surprise that Tate would cooperate with Tolson so supportively in the latter's effort to publish a representation of their correspondence in *Sewanee Review*.

Allen Tate may have needed a great deal of instruction in the probable or possible history of the Uncle Remus that Tolson observed reading Tate's poem in a Detroit library, but, through Tate's discerning critical appreciation for authentic poetic talent, he had been brought to acknowledge the "great gift for language," the "profound historical sense," and the "first-rate intelligence at work in this poem [the *Libretto*] from first to last." Thus the former Fugitive had testified that, through the alchemy of art, Tolson's preoccupation with poetry as "the main thing," although making him "not less but more intensely *Negro* in his apprehension of the world," had enabled him to write a poem "about the world of all men." Tate's response suggested that as a black poet Tolson did not have to close out the white world. Art could be the bridge to a new universal understanding in which black people and black culture would flourish. Uncle Remus, as Tolson well knew, may have seemed simple and artless to the parents who watched him telling tales to their children, but through him and a countless number of deceptively ingenious artists like him, black culture had thoroughly infused American culture, whether white America recognized it or not. Tolson, however, was looking beyond white America to a world audience waiting somewhere in the future, and Tate's recognition of his poetic artistry was a potentially important milestone in his quest.

Following the letter to Tate on 28 February 1951 there is a gap of many months in Tolson's correspondence referring to the *Libretto*. More than twenty months later, on 4 December 1952, he wrote to Ruth, who was teaching in Perry, Oklahoma, earning the family a second income, that he had just heard from Jacob Steinberg of Twayne Publishers, who wanted him to come to New York before Christmas:

> He says I have a book that ought to benefit or "make money for both the publisher and the author," which poetry seldom does. But he also says no poet goes thru Gethsemane to make money; that the Negro people should support me, "because you are the most precious thing the Negro has in America!" Ain't that something!
>
> Ciardi of Harvard gave me a big send-off. I want to bring the book out in the summer, but he tells me I don't have much "time for production, design, and announcements." Meantime I have planned a production for Langston in May, which will out-Flint the "Fire in the Flint." The campus—even Harrison—is excited.

Jacob Steinberg became Tolson's publisher and a warm personal friend.

A year later, on 18 December 1953, Horace Mann Bond wrote to Tolson that he had just received two copies of *Libretto*. Bond had returned from an African trip that he described with proud gusto. He enclosed a check for five dollars and asked Tolson to inscribe two copies of *Libretto*, one for Dr. Nnamdi Azikiwe and the other for The Right Honorable Kwame Nkrumah, prime minister of Ghana, both Lincoln alumni. After many delays and many revisions, Tolson's *Libretto* was finally before the public. The extent of its audience and its impact on that audience would now begin to be tested.

VII

WRITING FOR THE

VERTICAL AUDIENCE

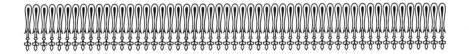

In his preface to *Libretto for the Republic of Liberia*, Allen Tate described the image that caught and focused his attention on first reading Tolson's poem: "On the first page I received a shock, in that region where bored scepticism awaits the new manuscript from a poet not clearly identified, when I saw Liberia invoked as

> . . . the quicksilver sparrow that slips
> The Eagle's claw!"

It is appropriate to begin an explication of *Libretto* with this startling image. In its context in the poem it answers a question of the meaning of *Liberia* and implies how Tolson was intent on using history as prophecy. Liberia was, of course, an offshoot of American history, an effort by Americans, white and black, to establish a new nation, by sailing east instead of west, on a continent of ancient human habitation—perhaps the most ancient in the world. Tolson developed many of these particular historical ironies later in the poem. But beyond these historical facts, he saw Liberia, as its name implies, as the offshoot of a dream of democratic freedom, the *"Mehr licht* for the Africa-To-Be," which itself is a part of an emerging universal brotherhood that makes a mockery of the divisive idols of the tribe of race, caste, and class. The quicksilver sparrow eventually extends the flight of the eagle. In a letter to his publisher accompanying a final draft of the notes to his text, Tolson suggested how far he intended to extend historical fact into prophetic possibility:

> In the seventh section, I use a telescope to see [that] the Africa of yesterday and of today is ancient history. First I see a streamlined express volting across the continent from Capetown to Cairo, past modernistic cities such as our time never saw! Second, I see the new Africa from the deck of a magnificent steamship gliding thru the moonlight up the Congo. Third, I see

the new Africa from the prow of a gigantic airliner on its way from Monrovia to Jerusalem—the really New Jerusalem. Fourth, I find myself in the great hall of the United Nations of Africa, when they're drawing up the African Charter!

In the eighth section, I return to my salutation of Liberia, with the theme a world at peace. I use the Ferris Wheel of Tyranny and the Merry-go-round of democracy as my symbols, one for the past, the other for the future.[1]

Thus Liberia is announced in the opening section, "Do," as a product of an idea born in history with the implicit potential as a nation of becoming an important part of the transition to a future universal democracy.

In "Re," the second section, Tolson invokes an African Whitman, "The Good Gray Bard in Timbuktu," to remind the world of the cultural greatness of Songhai, the African kingdom that preceded the advent of the Europeans. Under the wise and solicitous rule of Black Askia, learning was respected,

> The law of empathy set the market price,
> Scaled the word and deed: the gravel-blind saw
> Deserts give up the ghost to green pastures!

The University of Sankore attracted scholars, regardless of skin color, from Europe and Asia. But the golden age of Songhai passed. The narrator describes the historical devastation, blending the metaphors of the African griots, or wisemen, and the sophistication of a universal scholar:

> *Lia! Lia!* The river Wagadu, the river Bagana,
> Became dusty metaphors where white ants ate canoes,
> And the locust Portuguese raped the maiden crops,
> And the sirocco Spaniard razed the city-states,
> And the leopard Saracen bolted his scimitar into
> The jugular vein of Timbuktu. *Dieu seul est grand!*
>
> And now the hyenas whine among the barren bones
> of the seventeen sun sultans of Songhai,
> And hooded cobras, headless mambas, hiss
> In the golden caverns of Falémé and Bambuk,
> And puff adders, hook scorpions, whisper
> In the weedy corridors of Sankoré. *Lia! Lia!*

"Mi," the third section, briefly caricatures the key figures and circumstances of the origin of the Liberian venture in America. Immediately after observing the ill fate of the original voyage of "black Pilgrim Fathers to Cape Mesurado," one could hardly have foreseen the role Liberia was to play in World War II as a source of rubber to the free world and as a base for Allied bombers, which

Melvin B. Tolson

Let loose the winging grapes of wrath upon
The Desert Fox's cocained nietzscheans
A goosestep from the Gateway of the East!

"Fa" presents three portentous images, a gorged boa, an assassin eagle, and a tawny tiger with a human skull between its forepaws. Each image is followed by the repeated line, *"in the interlude of peace."* Midlife, midcentury, midepoch, the dangers of war and exploitation, for the moment resolved, remain ominously threatening. Tolson was particularly proud of the image he created of the tiger:

> The tawny typhoon striped with black
> torpors in grasses tan:
> a doomsday paw is flung across
> the leveled skull of man   . . .
>
> *in the interlude of peace.*

He commented on this passage: "The warmongers will have a chance to gnaw on that a while! Here is portent, prophecy, the dynamite of implication; and, personally, I wonder if I ever did anything better."

"Sol" begins with the voyage of Elijah Johnson, who retraverses the Middle Passage in an effort to find the redemptive seed in the bitter ashes of an earlier cultural crime and to find the bright promise of the future by reversing the compulsively western trek of Western civilization. He makes his way eastward to Africa through memories of those black brothers and sisters sacrificed to the greed of the slave trade,

> He hears the skulls plowed under cry:
> *"Griots,* the quick owe the quick and dead
> A man owes man to man!"

There follows a series of insightful and ironic sayings of the griots that give the lie to Guernier, whose words are pointedly mouthed by parrots, *"Seule de tous les continents, l'Afrique n'a pas d'historie!"* "Sol" closes with Elijah Johnson brooding over the catastrophes that have challenged the Liberian venture, but with an enduring sense of ultimate vindication:

> And every ark awaits its raven,
> Its vesper dove with an olive-leaf,
> Its rainbow over Ararat.

"La" recounts the glacial changes that caused many animals to move southward to sub-Saharan Africa while "Northmen brandished paws / And shambled Europe-ward, / Gnashing Cerberean jaws." Later in history Jehudi Ashmun, "spined with dreams," appeared "to cudgel parrot scholars / and slay philistine schemes." After his wife's death Ashmun dedicated himself to realizing the dream of Liberia. His words close the section and again effectively counter a division of black and white, Europe and Africa, that stems from an ancient geological event:

> He said: "My Negro kinsmen,
> America is my mother,
> Liberia is my wife,
> And Africa my brother."

The final two stanzas of *Libretto*, "Ti" and "Do," are the most complex and demanding, yet they center on very straightforward themes that have been stated in simpler terms many times in Tolson's work. "Ti" opens with a reminder of the centennial celebration of Liberia's existence and a rhetorical plea that the mistakes of man not destroy the promise that runs through the history of Liberia as well as the history of mankind in Africa:

> . . . let no Miserere
> venom the spinal cord of Afric earth!
> *Selah!*

This reminds the reader of the importance of *Liberia* as announced in the opening "Do":

> The rope across the abyss
> *Mehr licht* for the Africa-To-Be!

Pilate's words, "*Ecce homo*," set the irony of Liberia's birth. A new man, a new salvation, is to emerge, just as the world seems most unwilling to recognize it. World War II with its massive disruption of European colonial rule has signaled the vulnerability of the dominance of the white world:

> O Great White World, thou boy of tears, omega hounds
> lap up the alpha laugh and *du-haut-en-bas* curse.

The narrator wonders rhetorically how Africa, Mother of Science, has endured man's arrogance and misuse:

> What dread *elboga* shoved your soul
> into the *tribulum* of retardation?

The pretensions of man's cultures, "Rome's casketing herself in Homeric hymns," are set against the geographical oneness of the world:

> The Jordan flows into the Tiber,
> the Yangtze into the Thames,
> the Ganges into the Mississippi, the Niger
> into the Seine

It is the arrogance and error of man's cultures that

enmesh in ethos, in *masôreth* the poet's flesh,
intone the Mass of the class as the requiem of the mass,
serve *adola mentis* till the crack of will
castle divorcée Art in a blue-blood moat . . .
write Culture's epitaph in *Notes* upstairs.

And it is against such a lamentable cultural condition that the narrator invokes *"Cordon Sanitaire,"* a more universal synonym for "the spinal cord of Africa," in a rather tortured metaphor, to "extract, the eyeball's mote!"
The State "from slave, feudal, bourgeois or soviet grout, / has hung its curtain," and "he who doubts the white book's colophon / is Truth's" has found himself "Behind the curtain" and doomed to the fate of Laocoön. Before the recent challenges to the unity of the free world posed by Nazi Germany and Soviet Communism there was the more fundamental division of "the Many, the Few." Tolson sketched an impressionistic image of the decadence of such a cultural condition:

Like some gray ghoul from Alcatraz,
old Profit, the bald rake *paseq,* wipes the bar,
polishes the goblet vanity,
leers at the tigress Avarice
as
she harlots roués from afar:
swallowtails unsaved by loincloths,
famed enterprises prophesying war,
hearts of rage (*Hanorish tharah sharinas*) souls of chalk,
laureates with sugary grace in zinc buckets of verse
myths rattled by the blueprint's talk,
ists potted and pitted by a feast,
Red Ruin's skeleton horsemen, four abreast
. . . galloping . . .
Marx, the exalter, would not know his East
. . . galloping . . .
nor Christ, the reveler, His West.
Selah!

By 1950 Tolson was distinguishing Marx from Soviet communism as markedly as he distinguished Christ from the Christian churches of America.
A few lines later Tolson characterized the age by the linguistic symbol *pesiq,* which he noted means "divided." He added with a mockingly poetic semblance of logic: "It seems to me that this linguistic symbol gives us a concrete example of the teleological—perhaps the only one. By an accident of *a priori* probability, the sign in itself indicates both cause and effect, and the index of the relationship is served synchronously by either *paseq* or *pasiq.* Of course the protagonist of the poem uses them for his own purpose on

another level." Division creates a dilemma that causes the narrator to sum-
mon the "Peoples of the Brinks"—I suspect that *Brinks* refers to the brink-
manship of Cold War foreign policy as well as to the Brinks Company noted
for its safe transportation of large sums of money—to

> come with the hawk's resolve
> the skeptic's optic nerve, the prophet's *tele* verve
> and Oedipus' guess to solve
>   the riddle of
> the Red Enigma and the White Sphinx.

The Gordian knot of world intellectual and power conflict is suggested by
Tolson's use of the nicknames for Nietzsche and Trotsky, *il santo* and *pero:*

> while *il santo* and *pero* hone phillipics [*sic*],
> *Realpolitik* explodes the hand grenades
>   *faits accomplis*
> in the peace of parades.

But there is a promise of rebirth, though painful, in the midst of this global
confusion:

> Esperanto trips the heels of Greek;
> in brain-sick lands, the pearls too rich for swine
> the claws of the anonymous seek;
> the case Caesarean, Lethean brew
> nor instruments obstetrical at hand,
> the midwife of the old disenwombs the new.

The next four stanzas of "Ti" begin with references to the utopian vision
of the world's peoples, "The *Höhere* of Gaea's children," "The Höhere of
God's stepchildren," "The *Höhere* of X's children," "The *Höhere* of one's
pores, *En Masse*." The concluding stanza then recounts the shift from a
time marked by "the ferris wheel / of race, of caste, of class" to a time in
which the masses, known now by a variety of scornful epithets, nevertheless
ultimately ride the democratic merry-go-round. On 19 October 1940, in a
Caviar and Cabbage column, Tolson wrote:

> The history of man heretofore has been the history of the rise and fall of
> nations. I presume to call this the Ferris Wheel Theory of History. . . .
> The vanity that makes a people think itself superior to another people is
> the vanity that leads to its defeat. Pride goeth before a great fall! A ruling
> class never learns anything from the downfall of other ruling classes. . . .
> There can be no democracy without economic equality. Thomas Jefferson
> said that when he wrote the Declaration of Independence. There can be no
> brotherhood of man without a brotherhood of dollars. I have another theory.
> It is based on economic and racial brotherhood. I presume to call this the

Merry-Go-Round of History. On the merry-go-round all seats are on the same level. Nobody goes up; therefore, nobody has to come down. That is democracy, as I see it. In a brotherhood, all the members are equal.

Racial superiority and class superiority produced the hellish contraption called the Ferris Wheel of History. Democracy will produce the Merry-Go-Round of History.[2]

In the last four stanzas of "Ti," Tolson insisted on the inevitability of the democratic Merry-Go-Round of History with an eloquence engendered by a dramatic incredulity that the peoples of the world once awakened and enlightened would tolerate the exploitation that accompanies belief in the idols of the tribe. It is a deliberately naive belief, a Whitmanian belief founded in a faith in the power and righteousness of innocence. Greed and power are the corrupting agents. Shared wealth and power would destroy such divisive concepts as caste, class, and race. The oneness of the world's peoples would become manifest.

Oliver Cromwell Cox's impressive *Caste, Class and Race*, mentioned earlier, was published in 1948. In it, Cox attacks the assumption of many contemporary sociologists that racial distinctions are comparable to caste distinctions and hence are equally ancient in origin. Cox insists upon their radical difference and argues that race as it is known in the modern world grows out of the capitalistic need for designating a large group of people as a cheap supply of labor and hence is of relatively modern origin. Cox's argument coincides with what Tolson persistently said in *Caviar and Cabbage*: "The Jew and the Negro and justice have been crucified on a cross of gold in a dollar civilization. *A priori*, the profit system is the cause; racial prejudice is the result. They are Siamese twins. When you kill one, the other will die. And not before."[3] It is from such a belief that "old Profit, the bald rake *paseq*" emerges.

In his book Cox also makes an earnest statement of faith in the power of democracy, a democracy distinct from the individualism prized and fostered by capitalism. Although Cox's statement is muted by sociological terminology, one can sense the passion that lies behind his words. It was a passion for democracy that Tolson shared:

> Sometimes it is estimated that capitalism is basically interested in "the fundamental value and dignity" of the individual. This conclusion is seldom, if ever, demonstrated but it is ordinarily associated with individualism. As a matter of fact, however, democracy is the supreme champion of individual worth and personal value because it reaches down irresistibly and facilitates the political upthrust of that major group of persons known as the masses; it concerns itself with the personalization of the least privileged individuals. Democracy tends to confer upon every individual a priceless sense of wantedness in the society—a sense of being a recognized part of a supremely vital

organization. By this means alone the individual is able to form a positive conception of himself as a responsible social object. On the other hand, individualism champions the cause of the successful few and of the ablest, it despises the weak and jealously withholds its privileges and recognition from the common people.[4]

Nnamdi Azikiwe, who was to become president of Nigeria and was one of Lincoln University's most notable graduates, is quoted by Tolson as an African authority in *Libretto*. In 1937 Azikiwe's *Renascent Africa* was published, a book Tolson almost certainly was familiar with, although he does not refer to it specifically in the notes of *Libretto*. In his preface Azikiwe lists five bases necessary for the emergence of the New Africa. Explaining 4 and 5, he wrote:

> The Renascent African cannot create a new social order without an economic foundation. No longer must wealth be concentrated in the hands of the few. No longer must the profit motive guide and control the aims in life of the African. No longer must the wage-earners be told of a dignity that does not seem to exist in labour.
>
> Let the Renascent African make tomorrow secure for posterity, and a milestone is reached toward African economic interdependence with the rest of the world. . . .
>
> 5. *National Risorgimento* is inevitable. When the Renascent African has cultivated spiritual balance, regenerated his society, planned his society economically, and has experienced mental emancipation, his political status cannot be in doubt. It is from within that the element of national greatness springs.
>
> Let Renascent Africans usher in a New Africa, and Africans of tomorrow need not continue to be in political servitude. The forces of nationalism are automatic, especially when factors leading to them are intelligently directed. The right of self-determination is a phenomenon which defies human ingenuity.
>
> Forces which were responsible for the birth, growth, and decay of Ethiopia, Egypt, Babylo-Assyria, Phoenicia, Greece, and Rome will determine the fate of the West, the East, and Africa.
>
> "For all I know," said George Bernard Shaw, "the next great civilization may come from the Negro race."
>
> This prophecy is enough for me, unless one cares to read Oswald Spengler's *The Decline of the West*.[5]

Tolson's dream of a new international democracy emerging from the ashes of capitalism and the subsequent realization of the injustice of colonial exploitation was shared by many and appeared in many shapes.

The final "Do" of *Libretto* begins in heavy irony, characterizing the present as a hag grubbing in the garbage of morbidity and decay:

Melvin B. Tolson

a *pelageya* in *as seccas* the old she-fox today
eyes dead letters mouth a hole in a privy
    taschunt a corpse's in a mud-walled Troy of *jagunços*.

The ancient biblical injunction of money as the root of all evil is reaffirmed in contemporary and international references:

below the triumvirate flag & tongue & mammon
while *blut und boden* play the anthem *iron masters gold*
    rubble shilling frank yen lira baht and dime
    brass-knuckled (*la légalité nous tue*) and iron-toed
    wage armageddon in the temple of *dieu et l'état*
    o earl of queensbury o last christian on the cross

But Tolson then counterpoints the destructiveness of man's past errors with evidence of his faith in man, an absurdist fool, but a visionary, "a pataphysicist in a cloaca of error." The historic significance of Lincoln's response to moral imperatives with an oblique reference to Whitman's prophetic celebration is linked to Third World national independence movements and then ironically countered by blunt reassertions of imperialist power and the Japanese code words that preceded the ruthless attack on Pearl Harbor:

lincoln walks the midnight epoch of the ant-hill
and barbaric yawps shatter the shoulder-knots of white peace
    jai hind (dawn comes up like thunder) *pakistan zindabad*
    britannia rules the waves *my pokazhem meeru*
    the world is my parish *muhammed rasulu 'llah*
    - *hara ga hette iru* oh yeah *higashi no kazeame*

The struggle between good and evil is characterized in an image that suggests the reason for Tolson's dividing his ode into sections titled with the notes of the diatonic scale:

naifs pray for a guido's scale of good and evil to match
worldmusic's sol-fa syllables (*o do de do de do de*)

But a world language, a world recognition, is emerging:

worldmathematics' arabic and roman figures
worldscience's greek and latin symbols
    the letter killeth five hundred global tongues
    before esperanto garrotes voläpuk *vanitas vanitatum*

Yet such signs of hope and promise are literally deluged by man's destructiveness. The American use of atomic bombs bring the walls "tumblin' down," but the peace that follows is a stunned peace:

and no mourners go crying *dam-bid-dam*
about the ex-streets of scarlet letters

only the souls of hyenas whining *teneo te africa*
only the blind men gibbering *mboagan* in greek
  against sodom's pillars of salt
  below the mountain of rodinsmashedstatues *aleppe*

Following such a bleak report of the present is one transitional stanza of lines centered on the page that asks rhetorically about similar bleak moments of the past that were the consequence of greed and its spawn of conflicts frequently cast in racial terms. The rhetorical question implies that such moments have been subsumed, even as this moment will probably be, in a historical pattern obscured at the time. The final line of the stanza contains a dramatically understated and coded answer: "*Ppt. knows.*" Tolson's note refers the reader to Swift's *Journal to Stella. Ppt.,* an abbreviation for Poppet or Poor Pretty Thing, is a reference to Stella, or Esther Johnson, the woman with whom Swift shared his most intimate thoughts. Swift's letter entry for 15 March 1712 refers to the Queen's intention to visit "Parliament on Tuesday, if the Houses meet, which is not yet certain; neither, indeed, can the Ministers themselves tell; for it depends on winds and weather, and circumstances of negotiation. However, we go on as if it was certainly to meet; and I am to be at Lord Treasurer's to-morrow, upon that supposition, to settle some things relating that way. Ppt may understand me."

The need to act with faith in the midst of uncertainty, the importance of sharing hopes and expectations even though elaborately guarded and coded, suggests the significance of the relation between Swift and Stella for Tolson. That Jonathan Swift, noted for the strength and sensitivity of his moral indignation to man's depravity, could communicate his inmost thoughts to the understanding but elaborately sheltered Stella suggests that even Tolson's seemingly overwhelming questions concerning man's grotesque aggressions in the name of race may be capable of being communicated and answered. "*Ppt. knows.*"

Tolson believed in the power of knowledge, the power of truth, as radically as Henry David Thoreau. No matter how private, how buried, the truth will make itself known. This was his faith in writing for a future audience. It was for him axiomatic that the idols of the tribe, no matter how pervasive their destruction, will themselves eventually crumble. They are false gods. "*Ppt. knows*" asserts that the truth, though guarded, is known; thus it expresses a quietly wistful assurance of the future. This wistful assertion, however, is only a prelude to a full-blown celebration of Africa and the world as they are to become. It is a matter of faith that the rope across the abyss to the future has held.

I have quoted above Tolson's letter to his publisher indicating his plans for what eventually became part of the eighth and final section of *Libretto,* although at the time he apparently intended to conclude with the stanza in which the Merry-Go-Round of Democracy replaces the Ferris Wheel of Tyranny. As finally revised and printed in "Do," the journey is more ambitiously surreal, and an auto is added to the train, steamship, and airplane mentioned in his letter. The mythical journey begins with the auto, the Futurafrique, "the *chef d'oeuvre* of Liberian Motors." After slipping through the traffic of Monrovia, the Futurafrique "skis toward the Goodlowe Straightaway, whose coloratura sunset is the alpenglow of cultures in the Shovelhead Era of the common man." It outraces the Momolu Bukere Black-Hound, which is winging its way toward Khopiru, which Tolson defines in a note as " 'To Be'. The concept embraces the Eternity of Thence which, free from blind necessity, contains the good life." Racing sportively with the Oriens and the Europa, the Futurafrique "eclipses the Silver Age Gibbet of *Shikata-gai-nai*." Tolson explains that *Shikata-gai-nai* means "it cannot be helped" and expresses

the stoicism with which Japanese villagers meet the earth convulsions of sacred Fujiyama. In other lands it is fate, kismet, predestination, artistries of circumstance, economic determinism. . . . Sometimes it takes the form of the sophistry, *human nature does not change*. As a hidden premise it blocks the kinetic; it confuses the feral with the societal and leads to *petitio principii*. . . . In the poem, however, the flux of men and things is set forth in symbols whose motions are vertical-circular, horizontal-circular, and rectilinear. In spite of the diversity of the phenomena the underlying unity of the past is represented by the ferris wheel; the present by the merry-go-round; and the future by the automobile, the train, the ship, and the aeroplane. I placed the ship image in the middle of the images of swifter vehicles to indicate the contradiction in the essence of things, the struggle of opposites, which mankind will face even in Khopiru and Höhere. By the Law of Relativity, history will always have its silver age as well as its golden, and each age will contain some of the other's metal. Because of these upward and onward lags and leaps, it is not an accident that Liberia reaches her destination, the Parliament of African Peoples, after the aerial symbol.

After eclipsing the Silver Age Gibbet of Shikata-gai-nai, the Futurafrique joins the Oriens, the Auster, the Americus, and the Europa, and glissades "into the cosmopolis of Höhere," which once was the "habitat of mumbo jumbo and blue tongue, of sasswood-bark jury and tsetse fly, aeons and aeons before the Unhappy Wight of the Question Mark crossed the Al Sirat." The latter reference is to Africa, whose geographical shape suggests the question mark, crossing by means of the bridge, or the right way of religion, over infernal fire into a promised paradise.

The voyages of the train, the ship, and the airplane are briefer than that of the auto. The United Nations Limited "telescopes the polygenetic metropolises polychromatic between Casablanco [*sic*] and Mafeking, Freetown and Addis Ababa." The swan-sleek Bula Matadi "skirrs up the Niger" with a cargo collected from "Tel Aviv, Hiroshima, Peiping, San Salvador, Monrovia, and Picayune." Tolson's experience of living in the American South is facetiously but deliberately intruded with the latter reference. Then *Le Premier des Noirs* of Pan-African Airways takes off among "the glass skyscrapers of Cape Mesurado, meteors beyond the Great White Way of Kpandemai, aglitter with the ebony beau monde," and ultimately "eagles its steeple-nosed prow toward the Very Black and the iron curtainless Kremlin!" Thus, as Tolson explains in his letter to his publisher, "Liberia reaches her destination, the Parliament of African Peoples."

These voyages represent a celebration of modern technology, placing the ancient in contact with the future and promising an enlightened global oneness not just of international geography but of time as well. Frequent references to Whitman suggest his "Passage to India" as the prototype for this section of the poem. The section on the Parliament of African Peoples that follows is Tolson's variation of Tennyson's "Parliament of Men."

The opening stanza of this section reminds the reader that, although the quicksilver sparrow eventually *slips* the eagle's claw, there are several implicit acknowledgments of the importance to Liberia of the American eagle's flight:

> The Parliament of African Peoples plants the winged
> *lex scripta* of its New Order on
> Roberts Avenue, in Bunker Hill
> Liberia . . .

The New Order, however, ultimately is a product of "alpha ray ideas" that transcend national origins. These ideas project, of course, Tolson's own priorities. The "scales of Head and Hand" are poised, acknowledging the value of labor.[6] At the beginning of its voyage the Futurafrique "slithers past the golden statues of the half-brothers as brothers, with *cest prace*." Tolson's note translates the final phrase as "all honor to labor." Another alpha ray idea is "Science has dominion over Why" and "Art over How." The prophetic role of scientist and artist is emphasized as the Parliament

> bids Man cross
> the bridge of Bifrost and drink
> draughts of roses from verved
> and loined apes of God with
> leaves of grass and great audi-
> ences.

Tolson insists on retaining the role he persistently prized of the Socratic gadfly. As he suggests in his note on *Shikata-gai-nai*, even the golden age will not be ideally pure and static:

The Parliament
  pedestals a new
golden calendar of Höhere and
quickens the death-in-life of the
unparadised with the olive al-
penstocks of the Violent Men.

"The Violent Men" refers to "the stigmatized advocates of the Declaration
of Independence in the First and Second Continental Congresses." The
"Iscariot cuckolded Four Freedoms" are given new life, and the axiom
unto each according as any one has need is brought out of storage and made
ready for use. "Cicerones of the witch-hunt" are banished, and "Pros and
Cons Incorruptible" are encouraged to have at it freely.

This Parliament of searching and open inquiry, protected from biased
political opportunism and economic needs, still must ultimately also free
itself from the cultural warping that has been an insidious by-product of the
inequitable distribution of the world's political and economic power. The
economic and cultural dominance of Europe ultimately gives way to a liber-
ated and fruitfully peaceful universal order of mankind. Man's imagination
is freed from the self-inhibiting restrictions with which past generations have
shackled it:

The Parliament of African Peoples signets forever
  the *Recessional* of Europe and
  trumpets the abolition of itself:
  and no nation used *Felis leo* or
  Aquila heliaca as the emblem of
  blut und boden; and the hyenas
  whine no more among the bar-
  ren bones of the seventeen sun-
  set sultans of Songhai; and the
  deserts that gave up the ghost
  to green pastures chant in the
  ears and teeth of the Dog, in
  the Rosh Hashana of the Afric
  calends: "*Honi soit qui mal y
  pense!*"

Libretto opens with a question, "*Liberia?*" The answer is that it is more
than a place or a nation. It is an aspiration toward freedom, a means of em-
bodying the vision of a man who saw himself speaking particularly for those
peoples of the world suffering the injustices of race and caste, but ultimately
for all the peoples of the world. Just as Harlem, for Tolson, was always a
dream and aspiration as well as a real geographical city, so he developed

Liberia into an extraordinarily ambitious symbol of worldwide aspiration toward freedom and democracy. Tolson deliberately chose to look at the hopes and promises inherent in Liberia's past and its key position on a continent of nations emerging from European colonial rule. He deliberately looked past many well-known social problems of contemporary Liberia: the troublesome social division between the descendants of American settlers and the native African peoples and the dangers of the extraordinary power of American corporations and the autocratic rule of the national government. He clearly was aware of such problems. Some years earlier he had recommended to the readers of *Caviar and Cabbage* George Schuyler's harshly critical report on Liberia, *Slaves Today*. However, once he had accepted the designation *poet laureate of Liberia*, it would hardly have been appropriate for him to criticize the country honoring him. Instead he chose to celebrate the democratic aspirations inherent in its founding ideals and its potential role in a brotherhood of nations seeking to realize a universal democratic dream.

Clearly Tolson had created a poem that was startling in its mix of mode and ambition to the critics of its time. There were some early favorable reviews in key publications. Selden Rodman both praised and damned the poem without shedding much light on it in the *New York Times Book Review*. After some rather gratuitous reflections on race and literature, Rodman concluded: "It is not only by all odds the most considerable poem so far written by an American Negro, but a work of poetic synthesis in the symbolic vein altogether worthy to be discussed in the company of such poems as 'The Waste-Land,' 'The Bridge,' and 'Paterson.'" Following up on these suggested comparisons, Rodman found "The felicities of language, when they occur, are not as with Crane inspired by a Dionysiac frenzy, but as with Eliot intellectually contrived. . . . By the same token Tolson's weaknesses are the weaknesses one encounters in 'The Waste-Land.'" Then quoting a few lines from "Ti" concerning "The Höhere of Gaea's children," Rodman struggled to cover territory on both sides of the fence:

> This kind of writing becomes at its best academic and at its worst intellectual exhibitionism, throwing at the reader undigested scraps of everything from Bantu to Esperanto in unrelaxed cacophony. Eliot's taste was equal to giving the results of such a method dignity; Tolson's taste is much more uneven. And when it errs, no one is reminded of Picasso's dictum: "To search means nothing; to find is everything."
>
> At his best, Tolson finds a great deal. His poem opens vistas undreamt of by the English-speaking poets of his race and by few poets of other races.[7]

John Ciardi wrote a terser but more informed review for *The Nation*. Referring to "a number of books of poets not generally represented in anthologies," he singled out Tolson's *Libretto* as "certainly the most ambitious and in some ways the most compelling." This is the heart of his review:

> With a prodigious eclecticism, and with a percussion as has not been heard since Hart Crane's "The Bridge," Tolson constructs a vision of Africa, past, present, and future, the whirlwind center of half the world's imperial greed and passion, and—as Tolson sees it—the last new continent and future of the world, "Futurafrique." There are times when Tolson's heaping on of image after image and of phrases from German, Spanish, French, and from African languages as well, leaves the reader knocked out: too much is happening too fast, and the result seems to be not exaltation, but dizziness. When Tolson succeeds, however, one feels a force of language and of rhythm as breathtaking as anything in the range of American poetry.
>
> This is obviously a book to return to. The blast of language and vision is simply too overwhelming for first judgments. It seems a reasonable guess, however, that Tolson has established a new dimension for American Negro poetry.[8]

Tolson seldom responded in writing to criticism. But J. Saunders Redding's review in the *Afro-American* provided a notable exception. Carl Murphy, president of the *Afro-American*, sent Tolson a copy of the review, and Tolson responded with a letter to Murphy challenging Redding's judgment. Redding noted that, as a critic, he had "a fundamental objection to poetry which the author must himself interpret for his readers in an addendum of notes. At best, such notes indicate one of two things, and at worst, both things: that the poet found his talents unequal to the full requirements of the particular necessary communication; or that he was deliberately uncommunicative and obscure—in which case his notes are a patronizing gesture to minds the poet assumes to be less recondite or subtle or appreciative than his own." Redding also derided Tate's claim that the "poet has assimilated completely the full poetic language of his time," finding such a statement "nonsense on its face." "But having disposed of these irritating thorns, there is balm in *Libretto for the Republic of Liberia* to soothe the pricks. It is in the poem's virtuosity; in its often brilliant 'poetics'; and in those frequent lines that scintillate like jewels in the sun. Commonly, the scintillating lines are the simplest lines, and the simplest lines are those that comprise the section titled 'Ti', the 'Selah' passages, which, Mr. Tate notwithstanding, find their inspiration in DuBois rather than in Hart Crane."[9]

In his reply to Redding, Tolson quoted from Tate's preface to set the issue: "What influence this work will have upon Negro poetry in the United States one awaits with curiosity." To this Tolson added, "Today we know what effect the poem had on a topnotch Negro critic." Then, acknowledging his own involvement, Tolson tried to eliminate questions of primarily personal concern:

For the Vertical Audience

It is difficult for me to write this letter, because I am involved. For the sake of the Race, I wish I were not. I have faced mobs for the rights of my people in the Deep South; so I do not have to protest my love. As to my standing among the major poets of England and America, one can easily discover my status. I would not hit one key on this typewriter to try to prove myself a poet. The critics of the New York *Times, Poetry, Kenyon Review, Accent, etc.*, will have to determine that; and there's nothing—absolutely nothing—that M. B. Tolson can do about that. The "Libretto" is in the lap of the Gods—as we used to say at Lincoln.

Now, Mr. Redding did not review the book: he reviewed his prejudices against modern poetry. Let us look at some of them. He is against "an addendum of notes." This bias started in 1800, when William Wordsworth published the Preface to "Lyrical Ballads." For two hundred years poets have given prefaces or notes to readers. T. S. Eliot, the *only* American poet to win the Nobel Prize in Literature, the Master of the super-intellectuals, added notes to his epic, "The Waste Land." David Jones, in that English masterpiece, "The Anabasis," uses notes. Furthermore, those distinguished poets have had their works explained by the best critics in all the little magazines and countless books of criticism. Critics like Empson, the greatest critical reader in the British Empire, and Blackmur, the greatest critical reader in the United States, have not been insulted by the "addendum of notes"; these critics found neither a failure to communicate nor a patronizing gesture—to quote Mr. Redding—in the poets I have cited.

Every art and every science have reached an amazing state of complexity today. When Socrates said, "Know thyself," he did not know how deep was this aphorism. . . .

As Heraclitus said, "Everything is in a state of change and the only thing that does not change is the law that everything changes." This is the dialectic of history. Picasso does not paint like Michael Angelo. Neither does T. S. Eliot write like Milton or Spenser or Longfellow. I'm looking now at Oscar Williams' celebrated "A Little Treasury of American Poetry"; it's nothing like the anthologies I used at Lincoln. Newton's physics has given way to Einstein's.

A modern playwright has a different technique and language from those of Shakespeare. Nobody can change that fact.

Now, if one wants to be a modern poet, one must study modern poets—and the greatest—Stevens, Rimbaud, Blok, Eliot, Pound, et al. I have done this for twenty years. Whether I have succeeded or failed, you will have to ask contemporary *major* poets and critics. . . .

Mr. Redding has a fetishism for "simple lines." He says that my section "Ti" has simple lines! My God, that section covers a hundred different books of the ages and two dozen languages! The allusions are imbedded; it is, in some places, a surface simplicity only!

Away with the simple Negro! This is a book to be chewed and digested. If Negro scholars don't get busy on it, white scholars will.[10]

Redding's review had hit a nerve. Tolson's letter ostensibly makes modernism the issue, but lurking close to the surface is a fear black writers must frequently contend with in one form or another: the fear of being accused of cultural passing, of entering the mainstream at the expense of abandoning the race. Tolson clearly saw himself in the vanguard of an army of black cultural soldiers who would make the African past a centerpiece of the world's future, not by re-creating the flip side of white racism, but by realizing a more racially enlightened democratic dream. Yet here was J. Saunders Redding, by education and experience a man whom Tolson would expect to be most sympathetic with his ambition, cutting him down as if he had wandered from that long and lonesome road that was the only true racial path.

It did not help that the book drew only two other reviews in journals particularly concerned with the black experience. Howard R. Fussiner wrote a short, unenthusiastic review for *Phylon*. He described Tolson as "an intellectual poet of evident intelligence. Not especially original, he has been subject to fashion." Fussiner concluded his review with weak me-tooism:

> I feel (as does Mr. Rodman) that the work is not helped by his emphasis on esoteric virtuosity, but essentially Mr. Tolson does credit to his epic subject, the birth and growth of a modern Negro state.
> Allen Tate's preface inquires where American Negro poetry, hitherto parochial, will go from here. *Libretto* offers a new challenge.[11]

Arthur P. Davis, writing for the *Midwest Journal*, was impressed with the praise given *Libretto* by Tate, "one of America's outstanding critics." He quoted Tate, but then added more assertively:

> This is indeed high praise, perhaps the highest that any Negro poet has received from an American critic of Allen Tate's rank. In the face of such a statement, I hesitate to say what I must in all honesty say, which is simply this: for me *Libretto* is not a completely successful work; in spite of its astonishing word-magic and its undaunted power, it doesn't quite come off as a poem.

When he first read the poem Davis "was convinced that it was sheer nonsense." "After three more readings and a close study of the footnotes . . . the poem began to take on meaning and significance. Far from being nonsense, the work began to assume impressive proportions." Noting that Tolson's characteristic mood "tends to suggest oratory rather than normal conversational speech," Davis described the effect of Tolson's style:

> The energy of his writing shocks you. He flings huge chunks of history, literature, myth, legend, proverb, and prophecy at you; and he does it in African dialect, Arabic, Greek, Russian, Latin, Japanese and several other

languages. He overwhelms you with the violence of his imagery and his startling verbal pyrotechnics. In short, you leave the poem amazed at the writer's wide range of knowledge and his incredible energy and versatility. You leave with the feeling that you have witnessed a great performance; you are not convinced that you have read a successful poem (at least that was my feeling).

Davis insisted that *Libretto* is not an integrated whole, but his argument carried him nevertheless to a grudging respect:

> Failing to fuse his material into a single whole, he has given us a series of spectacular segments, not a convincing integrated poem.
>
> With this shortcoming and with others that one could mention, *Libretto for the Republic of Liberia* is still an impressive and significant work. Because of its word-magic, because of its astounding versatility and energy, and because of its endorsement by Allen Tate, it will become a landmark in Negro literature.[12]

Lorenzo D. Turner, reviewing *Libretto* for *Poetry*, accurately summarized Tolson's racial message:

> It is in Section VII, however, that the wider and more significant implications become evident. Africa's isolation and retardation are here attributed to the color prejudice and racist theories of peoples of certain foreign governments, "blind men," who have been concerned primarily with exploiting Africa and have remained indifferent and hostile to the preservation of its culture. Italy's rape of Ethiopia, South Africa's *apartheid*, German fascism—all forms of imperialism and totalitarianism, ancient or modern—fall within the range of the poet's impassioned attack.

Turner also approvingly noted Tolson's sophisticated development of his poetic legacy from Whitman:

> In the earlier parts of this concluding section, as in the first seven divisions of the poem, the poet gets many interesting effects by the skillful use of novel stanzaic patterns and by variations in the length and arrangement of the lines. The very end of this section is clearly reminiscent in style of much of Whitman's poetry but far more erudite. Here are frequent repetitions, inventory passages, and masses of details, all of which contribute to the total imagery of the poem as well as reveal the robust optimism of the poet.

Turner concluded his review with unstinting praise:

> *Libretto for the Republic of Liberia* is not merely an occasional poem. In its breadth, in the subtlety and richness of its allusions, and in the force and suggestiveness of its language, it is a triumph of poetry on the grand scale.[13]

With the exception of Turner, the black critics were skeptical. The white critics were more enthusiastic, but they were few, and their welcoming of

Tolson into the literary mainstream where his poem would be compared with such poems as *The Bridge, Paterson,* and *The Waste Land* apparently evoked very mixed feelings in the black community. There are later, significant critical responses to *Libretto* to be noted, but these immediate reviews with their hesitancies and uncertainties, sometimes racial, sometimes not, must have disappointed Tolson. Allen Tate's praise, which seemed initially such a prize, rather than proving a stimulus to a more probing critical reading and explication seemed to function instead as a kind of scarlet merit badge provoking attention to itself rather than to the deed it represented.

Several years later, in *Harlem Gallery,* section 4 of "Chi," Tolson would ironically point to the racial dilemma of the black artist as a product of white racism ably assisted by the prejudices of the black bourgeoisie:

> Poor Boy Blue,
> the Great White World
> and the Black Bourgeoisie
> have shoved the Negro artist into
> the white and not-white dichotomy,
> the Afro-American dilemma in the Arts—
> the dialectic of
> to be or not to be
> a Negro.

Later, in "Psi," the Curator addresses Black Boy and poses this dilemma in even more poignant terms:

> Black Boy,
> in this race, at this time, in this place,
> to be a Negro artist is to be
> a flower of the Gods, whose growth
> is dwarfed at an early stage
> a Brazilian owl moth,
> a giant among his own in an acreage
> dark with the darkman's designs,
> where the milieu moves back downward like the sloth.

Tolson's journal notes are undated and helter-skelter on the page, but some of them seem pertinent here. One was quoted earlier, but its application to the argument makes it worthy of repetition:

> The size of an audience that understands a work of art at the time of its first appearance is no argument against the merit of the work of art. Cultural and civilizational changes produce new ideas and new forms of art. The idiom of old works of art may be esoteric at the farthest remove; and the idiom of a new art may be esoteric at the closest remove.

Tolson's sense of humor, however, remained intact:

For the Vertical Audience

A little of the *Libretto* is a dangerous thing.
Drink deep or touch not the Liberian spring.

Another note in the journal gives a specific and suggestive clue to what Tolson himself saw as the relation between *Libretto* and other poems to which it has frequently been compared: " 'The Bridge' is a way out of the pessimism of 'The Waste Land'; the 'Libretto' is a vista out of the mysticism of 'The Four Quartets.' " Another comment on Crane suggests how Tolson saw his own efforts relative to Crane's: "I believe Crane lacked a perspective of himself against the backdrop of history." And two comments on the moment in history give insight into how Tolson intended *Libretto* to relate to its historical time: "The most violent revolution in the world is taking place—not in Russia, not in China, but in American poetry." "First time in history the white man ever stood before an international jury of nations with a black jury. Hitherto all white."

The critical response to the *Libretto* did not end with the immediate reviews. Tolson was surprised and pleased when Stanley Edgar Hyman in 1958 in a *Partisan Review* article accepted Tate's assertion that *Libretto* was "in the direct succession" from Crane's *The Bridge* and also accepted other critics' identification of its techniques with Eliot's *The Waste Land* or Pound's *Cantos*, but then added: "Reinforcing rather than denying these analogies, I would insist on its kinship to the associative organization of the blues."[14] In a later interview Tolson commented on Hyman's claim: "That acute observation surprised me, for, in the *Libretto*, to which it referred, there was no surface sign of the blues; however, I do write jazz ballads, but the *Libretto* is very literary, to say the least."[15] For Tolson the blues were an umbilical cord to the black experience. While he might cover it with fancy or formal clothes, he was always proud to acknowledge the strength of the tie.

When Karl Shapiro wrote his introduction for Tolson's *Harlem Gallery* in 1965, his claim for Tolson as a great poet "who speaks in Negro" reminded critics and readers of the claims Tate had previously made for Tolson in his preface to *Libretto*. Shapiro, by this time clearly no critical friend of Tate's, tried to distinguish between his own claims for Tolson and those of Tate in an article published later in 1965 in the *Wilson Library Bulletin*:

> Mr. Tate is a confederate of the old school who has no use for Negroes but who will salute an exception to the race. He sees Tolson as an exception because "For the first time . . . a Negro poet has assimilated completely the poetic language of his time and, by implication, the language of the Anglo-American tradition." Mr. Tate invites Mr. Tolson to join his country club. But the crux of the matter is that Tate says: "the distinguishing Negro quality is not in the language but in the subject matter . . ." for subject

matter can only deal with one's suffering and contaminate the beauty of poetry.

I have tried to correct this statement in my own introduction to Tolson's recently published *Harlem Gallery*. Tate considers that the use of Negro subject-matter in poetry . . . limits the Negro poet to a "provincial mediocrity." I will not trouble you with my opinion of the modern classicism which Mr. Tate represents . . . except to point out that this powerful critic does not consider the theme of Negro suffering good enough for the art of poetry, just as though the theme of America was not good enough a theme for the poet Hart Crane. But in trying to assert that Tolson has been assimilated by the Anglo-American tradition, he puts Tolson in quarantine and destroys the value of the poem—possibly this critic's conscious intention. . . .

The refusal to see that Tolson's significance lies in his language, Negro, and that only that language can express the poetic sensibility of the Negro at the door of freedom, is a final desperate maneuver to contain the Negro within the traditional culture. And for that it is too late. The tradition is already ante bellum.[16]

This struggle between the conservative Tate and the liberal Shapiro, both white, for the prize of exhibiting the black poet Tolson as a member of his camp reminds one of an African proverb Tolson used in *Libretto:* "It is the grass that suffers when two elephants fight." Tolson received some real benefits from the praise and support of both these sincere, if opposed, white critics; however, their attempts to generalize their response to his poetry into commandments on race and literature were clumsy and became distracting points of controversy for later black critics. Since much of this controversy also refers to the later *Harlem Gallery*, it is better to defer the remainder of the discussion of it until after full consideration of the later poem. It is necessary to note here, however, that the argument began with the publication of *Libretto*.

Two later critical responses to *Libretto* call for discussion.[17] In 1965 Dan McCall came to Langston University to teach for the summer. By then McCall probably had begun work on his critical study published in 1969, *The Example of Richard Wright*, but he apparently met Tolson for the first time that summer. Tolson's personality, his talk, and his poetry all made a very strong impression on McCall. McCall's first novel, *The Man Says Yes*, which was also published in 1969 and contains a fictional representation of Tolson, will be discussed later. However, McCall also wrote a brief, but impressively perceptive note on *Libretto* for *American Quarterly*, a year after his Langston teaching experience. It is noteworthy that at a time when *Harlem Gallery* was winning Tolson gratifying critical recognition from several quarters, McCall, with the sound instincts of a responsible academician, chose to look back at *Libretto*.

McCall tried to explain why "Tolson's great poem has not yet gathered

the audience it deserves." Admitting that the poem is inherently difficult
with its multilingual references and its dramatically shifting ironies, McCall
focused upon a principal problem in Tolson's relation to the modern American poetic tradition:

> While the verse seems to be that of Pound in the *Cantos* or Eliot in *The
> Waste Land,* Tolson does not really belong in the modern American tradition of poetry. His main difference stems, first of all, from his refusal to accept a primary assumption of those who have shaped the tradition: poetry
> is an art of privacy. Tolson restores to the poet his function of singing to the
> community. There is a profoundly personal voice in his poetry, but it is not
> a private one: in the *Libretto* he addresses himself to the Republic. That
> poetry of such difficulty should be intended for a wide audience indicates
> that Tolson conceives of his poem as a kind of master singing-book for the
> country, a storehouse of education for the Futurafrique. His achievement is
> that he can write about it without becoming hollowly official.

McCall contrasted *The Waste Land* with *Libretto*: "Eliot describes a
failure of civilization; the poem establishes a sense of terrible loss. Grace has
been withdrawn from the society of Western man. . . . But in reading the
Libretto one feels a certain 'pell-mell joy,' " resulting from a revolutionary
sense of the high comedy of history. McCall quoted Sartre's "Black Orpheus":

> It is when he [the African poet] seems suffocated by the serpents of our culture that he shows himself the most revolutionary, for he then undertakes
> to ruin systematically the European acquisition, and that demolition in spirit
> symbolizes the great, future taking-up of arms by which the Negroes will
> break their chains.

McCall then commented:

> Tolson breaks his chains with bolts of laughter. There is in the *Libretto* an
> exuberant spirit proper to the occasion of mastering the white man's power
> and turning it back on him: see how I master the master. At times Tolson
> seems to be running wild in the white castle of learning. You have made me,
> he is saying, a black thief in the night; I am a Negro and have made my
> meals on what I hooked from your white kitchens and now that I have made
> my way into your study—see here—I walk off with your library. The result is
> high comedy.

McCall concluded by explaining Tolson's use of multiple voices in terms
of the ambitiousness of his purpose:

> Tolson's poetic integrity would not allow him to retreat into the folksiness
> of Langston Hughes—making things "simple"—nor would it allow him to
> lose his own voice in mere imitation. He gives us folk-wisdom and out-

pounds Pound to show what is involved in a country which is profoundly both African and American; these modes of poetic intelligence are symbolic of stages in the development of the Liberian mentality. . . .

Liberia is America in its past, African in its future; the poem incarnates this doubleness of the Liberian experience. The *Libretto* is both "talki-talki" and "deepi-talki." Tolson explains, in Note 163: "Cf. La Varre: 'My black companions had two languages: deepi-talki, a secret language no white man understands; and talki-talki, a concoction of many languages and idioms which I understood." Tolson delights in his ironic capacity to embrace a nation; he tries out a variety of voices adequate to sing for the country whose national poet he is. The *Libretto for the Republic of Liberia* deserves our attention not only as a poem of virtuoso splendor but also as a book-length celebration of the Afro-American experience.[18]

The second later critical response to *Libretto* is Jon Stanton Woodson's doctoral dissertation, "A Critical Analysis of the Poetry of Melvin B. Tolson," featuring an eighty-four-page chapter on *Libretto*. It is Woodson's thesis that "the *Libretto* was written to serve as both a parody of *The Waste Land* and as a corrective to the admitted incompleteness of Eliot's methodology and the disorderliness of the historical form of the poem that Tolson perceived within *The Waste Land*."[19] According to Woodson, by 1947 "Tolson had abandoned his interest in Marxism and Social Realist poetry." Taking his cue from Eliot, Tolson studied the Tarot and "found a symbology that allowed him to poetically express his own theories concerning world history, while, at the same time, acquiring a systematic substitute for purely Marxian historical analysis."[20] While noting that Eliot's use of the Tarot was deliberately inexpert, Woodson asserted, "Tolson learned the proper constitution of not only the Tarot pack but of the esoteric symbology that stands behind the cards." Because of Tolson's formal emphasis on the number *eight*, Woodson suggests that Tolson used a blend of Gnostic and Tarotic symbologies.[21]

Woodson's thesis begins with an explication of Tolson's "The Man from Halicarnassus," seen as a key into the cryptography of *Libretto*:

The first stanza of "The Man from Halicarnassus" makes it evident that Tolson wrote the *Libretto* in such a way as to please and flatter both the Establishment (and Allen Tate in particular) by use of Marxist complexity, while flattering the Liberians, for whom he served as Poet-Laureate. While accomplishing both of these tasks, Tolson also secreted within the verbal difficulty and misleading notes the ironic doctrine that those who say "Yeas" to life do not realize that they exist along a periodic continuum—"change / that changes not" ("The Man from Halicarnassus," ll 57–58) and will eventually pass from the historical scene. Though Tolson invoked the formation of a "Parliament of African Peoples" in *Libretto* (pp. 52–55), a political dream analogous to Herodotus' "idea of a great union of Greece for aggression against Persia" (Wells, p. 321), he does this so that it will form a veil of esoteric meaning over the underlying meaning of the poem, detectable only to initiates. These initiates will then be able to learn, though presumably they will already know, that divisiveness is futility, that the only meaningfulness in history is the appearance of the fully formed human type, whether he is called "a free individual(s)" (Wells, p. 232), "The Man to be" (as Tolson calls him in "The Man from Halicarnassus"), the Superman (Nietzsche), or the "World-Historical-Individual" (Hegel) (pp. 28–29).

Thus Woodson constructed an explication of *Libretto* that makes it seem even more cryptic than it is. While he has done a creditable scholarly service in tracking down and evaluating a host of the literary references and allusions in Tolson's poem, his statements about Tolson's beliefs are contradicted by much biographical evidence. As I suggested at the beginning of this chapter, the period in which Tolson wrote *Libretto* was undoubtedly one of important changes in the direction of his professional writing career, but he did not suddenly convert to a whole new system of beliefs. To see him as a student of the esoteric Christianity of Gurdjieff, à la Jean Toomer, does not fit the known facts of his life. As late as 1961, writing to former student Benjamin Bell and his wife, in the letter quoted above, he whimsically lamented, "I guess I'm the only Marxist poet Here and Now." He then chuckled at the shrewdness of Old Man Du Bois, the greatest "strategist on the Left." My preceding discussion of *Libretto* also points to several instances in which Tolson developed and repeated ideas that were previously well established in his writing.

While Tolson may well have familiarized himself with the symbolism of the Tarot and may well have alluded to it in *Libretto*, the meaning of *Libretto* is not dependent on such esoteric information. Ultimately, however, after discounting the role of the Tarot, my major disagreement with Woodson's interpretation of *Libretto* comes in his discussion of the final section, "Do." Woodson's insistence on Tolson's obscurity leads him to believe that Tolson is ironically mocking the golden age sketched at the end of the poem:

So committed is Tolson to hermetic obscurant devices, that this much-desired politically harmonious state is mocked in note 619: "By the Law of Relativity, history will always have its silver age as well as its golden, and each age will contain one of the other's metal." It is evident that the self-assured optimism of ". . . it is not an accident that Liberia reaches her destination, the Parliament of African Peoples, after the ariel symbol . . ." is mere bravado: the thesis of the poem is that this only happens by means of a nuclear conflagration, and that it holds the future decline of Africa as its inevitable outcome.[22]

Woodson suggests that "Do" shares the eschatological pessimism of Rimbaud's *Illuminations,* and he then discusses the conclusion of the poem as a paradoxical problem: "For Tolson, as for Rimbaud, the difficulty of the operations of poetry was that the poem must in some way create the reality of the Golden Age at the end of cyclical time."[23]

In my view Woodson's interpretation is oversubtle and makes Tolson appear more cynical and pessimistic than in fact he was. I believe that Tolson himself was a yea-sayer, that despite a keen awareness of how man has often made his culture into an engine of cruel and irrational destruction, Tolson believed that man was working his way toward a universal culture in which he would be freer than ever before to realize his human potential.

Yet on a quite different level Woodson's dissertation is a most welcome sign that the young scholars of today and tomorrow may yet be willing to accept the critical challenge Tolson posed in the *Libretto.* Woodson's dissertation is critically bold and impressively broad-ranging in its scholarly references. Tolson wrote the *Libretto* when an enormous amount of critical effort was being expended in interpreting such hallmarks of modern literature as *The Waste Land, The Bridge, The Cantos,* and *Ulysses.* He clearly planned and hoped for a similar effort to be expended on his own poem. Whether the compelling power of his vision and the magic of his words will yet draw such critical attention remains in doubt, but Woodson's effort makes the likelihood of such critical attention seem more credible and more possible.

VIII

BRIDGING THE PEAKS

The *Libretto for the Republic of Liberia* was Tolson's major preoccupation during the years immediately following his move to Langston, but it was not the only poem he worked on during this period. Five shorter poems were published between 1948 and 1952, and all add something to our understanding of the changes *Libretto* signaled in the direction of Tolson's professional ambition. The poems and their years of publication are "The Negro Scholar" (1948), "African China" (1950), "E. & O. E." (1951), "A Long Head to a Round Head" (1952), and "The Man from Halicarnassus" (1952). A sixth poem was apparently written during this period, although it was not published until many years later. In a letter to Horace Mann Bond on 9 March 1949, Tolson wrote: "It seems that *Collier's* magazine is interested in a series of poems I am doing on the life of Abe Lincoln. This is secret, of course." *Collier's* for some reason lost interest; however, "Abraham Lincoln of Rock Spring Farm," published in 1963 as part of Herbert Hill's anthology *Soon, One Morning*, is probably either the series of poems referred to or at least one of them.

"The Negro Scholar" appeared in the first issue of *Midwest Journal*, published at Lincoln University in Jefferson City, Missouri. Of the six poems it is the most traditional in form, comprising twenty-four quatrains of blank verse. The responsibilities Tolson ascribes to the Negro scholar bear upon some of the major concerns of *Libretto*, thus suggesting that the poem, despite its variance in style from the densely referential *Libretto*, was probably written during the gestation period of the latter.

The Negro scholar serves his people by providing them with the awareness of their past necessary to a sense of pride and identity:

A race that has no culture is a bastard
Among the arrogant of blood and lucre;
Thus, thus the Negro scholar in our day
Is born to be a genealogist . . .

To me, to you, his lineage is a chain
Of syllogisms flung to bridge the peaks
Of moments of the conscience of mankind.
And though the X of destiny has gulped

A linking premise, here and yonder, let
No cynic write the epitaph of doom.
The ground the Negro scholar stands upon
Is fecund with the challenge and tradition

That Ghana knew, and Melle, and Ethiopia,
And Songhai; civilizations black men built
Before the Cambridge wits, the Oxford dons
Gave to the Renaissance a diadem.

Behold the University of Sankore
In Timbuctoo, a summit of the mind!
Behold, behold Black Askia the Great,
The patron-king of scholars, black and white.

While Tolson frequently lauded the value of science, he was fundamentally a humanist. The scholar

     . . . must seek
The bedrock facts, but never worship them:
The goal is Man, not objectivity.

However, keeping his eye clear for the great questions, he scorns

The idols of a class, a caste, a race,
And tilts with giants of the pros and cons.

Nevertheless, the scholar is not cloistered from the world. He is actively engaged, and his people benefit directly from his potency:

The Negro scholar must uproot the lies
Of ermine classes, puncture sophistries,
Break through dilemmas, rip the fallacies
Between his people and the Bill of Rights.

The Negro scholar is a prophecy,
A cloud by day, a pillar of fire by night,
Seen by black slaves upon the auction block,
Seen by black rebels with the grapes of wrath.

Tolson consistently believed in the power of words infused with imagination to change the world. Thus he characteristically assumed that the scholar and the poet shared a common prophetic ground. What he wrote of the scholar often seems as applicable to the poet. The *Libretto* is, of course, a scholarly poem. Its elaborate scholarship is the principle source of the criticism directed against it. But its scholarship was clearly meant to be

> a chain
> Of syllogisms flung to bridge the peaks
> Of moments of the conscience of mankind.

"African China" is one of Tolson's most frequently anthologized poems. It first appeared in a special "Negro Poets Issue" of *Voices*, edited by Langston Hughes in the winter of 1950. It was subsequently reprinted in *Lincoln University Poets: Centennial Anthology, 1854–1954*, edited by Waring Cuney, Langston Hughes, and Bruce McM. Wright. In 1967 Robert Hayden chose this poem and a selection from *Harlem Gallery* to represent Tolson's work in the anthology *Kaleidoscope*. And in 1971 Ruth Miller chose "African China," "Dark Symphony," and "Lambda" (from *Harlem Gallery*) to represent Tolson in *Blackamerican Literature, 1760–Present*.

"African China" is of special interest partly because it is a link between Tolson's earliest poems about Harlem and his latest. It is a combination of two poems that were written as part of *A Gallery of Harlem Portraits*, "African China" and "Wu Shang."[1] "Wu Shang" is the source of stanzas 1-4 of the later version of "African China," and the earlier "African China" is the source of stanzas 5 and 6. The combined narratives are rewritten in a more modern poetic idiom. A "Statement of Plan of Work," which Tolson apparently prepared for a fellowship application to the Rosenwald Foundation, indicates that, as early as 1947, Tolson thought of *Harlem Gallery: Book One, The Curator* as the first book of a tetralogy. In later years he frequently spoke of *Harlem Gallery* as a revision of the much earlier *A Gallery of Harlem Portraits*, even though there are only vestiges of the latter visible in the final poem. "African China" thus probably represents an effort to rework portions of the early manuscripts into a more modern poetic representation of Harlem, although the revised poem does not itself appear in any form in the final *Harlem Gallery*.

In the original poems Lou Sing's marriage is unrelated to Wu Shang's extraordinary ability to minister to his Harlem customers' distress with magical words. Combining Lou Sing and Wu Shang into one character and having the marriage follow three examples of Wu Shang's verbal facility gives much greater dramatic significance to Wu Shang's story. It, in effect, suggests that Wu Shang by his effective empathy has earned the right to marry Dixie Dixon, that he has earned a place in the Harlem community. By giving Wu Shang the knowledge of "the diademed word" as a "masterkey to Harlem pocketbooks," Tolson made him into something of a poet-philosopher. This is dramatically emphasized when the "connoisseur of pearl / necklace phrases" encounters Big John, a tragic blues figure:

Sometimes the living dead
stalk in and sue for grace,
the tragic uncommon
in the comic commonplace,
the evil that the good
begets in love's embrace,
a Harlem melodrama
like that in Big John's face.

That Wu Shang can sense the nature of Big John's hurt and find the appropriate words to bring Big John a vital and sustaining recognition suggests that Wu Shang's oriental wisdom has proved to be a cultural asset, and he is initiated and accepted into the Harlem community. He brings Big John to recognize that,

The bigger thing, as always, goes unsaid:
the look behind the door of Big John's eyes,
awareness of the steps of Is,
the freedom of the wise.

Wu Shang's wit and wisdom thus prepare the reader for the serene answer to the skepticism of "The unperfumed": "Good Gawd, / China and Africa gits wed!" For Wu Shang, Dixie "is a dusky passion flower / unsoiled by envious years." For Dixie, Wu Shang is "her very own oasis in / the desert / of Harlem men." But Wu Shang and Dixie have a child. Although Wu Shang and Dixie "walk / the gauntlet, Lenox Avenue," in dignity, their son becomes the butt of other children's racial aggression and displaced fear. It is unclear whether the boy is intended to signal that the idols of the tribe are in fact crumbling or that the idols are still so strong that they have infected even the victims of racial bias to such an extent that this child of a biracial, bicultural marriage will not have a chance to flourish:

The dusky children roll
their oyster eyes
at Wu Shang, Junior, flash
a premature surmise,
as if afraid:
in accents Carolina
on the streets they never made,
the dusky children tease,
"African China!"

The story of African China apparently attracted Tolson as a dramatic illustration of what he had observed many years earlier in his master's thesis, "Harlem is the unique product of New York City as the meeting-place of races and cultures in the Western Hemisphere." Set against the historical view of the *Libretto*, it contains only a wistful, bittersweet hope of that universal, multiethnic democracy where the idols of race, caste, and class have been effectively obliterated.

The increase in dramatic complexity and intensity from *A Gallery of Harlem Portraits* to "African China" is coupled with some significant changes in style. *A Gallery* was modeled after Edgar Lee Master's *Spoon River Anthology*. Like the latter it created an easy familiarity between its readers and its characters. It risked being prosaic in exchange for easy immediate communication. "Wu Shang," for example, begins:

> Wu Shang, lover of elegant phrases
> Hated the laundry work
> To which the kismet had chained him;
> But his trade grew steadily,
> Despite his shortcomings,
> For his sunny spirit and jeweled philosophy
> Charmed dusky customers.

Tolson reworked this passage to open the later poem:

> A connoisseur of pearl
> necklace phrases,
> Wu Shang disdains
> his laundry, lazes
> among his bric-a-brac
> metaphysical;
> and yet dark customers,
> on Harlem's rack
> quizzical,
> sweat and pack
> the forked caldera of
> his Stygian shop:
> some worship God,
> and some Be-Bop.

The language is more challenging. It displays a more boldly self-conscious pleasure in the play of sounds and the ironic wit of its references. The stereotype of the Chinese laundryman is intellectually tougher. The reader is further distanced from the character. He is made aware that he is in the presence of a work of art, not just sharing everyday experiences among friends. Just as modern poets had followed modern painters in renouncing the limitations of realistic representation, so Tolson was belatedly beginning to feel his way into a modern idiom that confessed its literary nature more openly and tried to make a virtue of it. Wu Shang lazing "among his bric-a-brac / metaphysical" may at first seem almost too close a parallel to Wallace Stevens's foppishly elegant philosophers, but Tolson's protagonist also proves ultimately to be a very sturdy streetwise shopkeeper. The polished comic gloss provides prismed reflections absent from the earlier, more deliberately prosaic poem.

Tolson also experimented with syntax. For example, he increasingly used nouns as verbs. Two examples in a short span of the revised poem indicate the status and intent of his experiment:

> When Dixie Dixon breaks a leg
> on Arctic Lenox Avenue,
> and Wu Shang *homes* her, pays her fees,
> old Kismet knots the two
> unraveled destinies.
> The unperfumed
> wag foot, forefinger, head;
> and belly laughter *waifs* ghost rats
> foxed by the smells of meat and bread;
> and blank walls blab, "Good Gawd,
> China and Africa gits wed!" (Italics added)

The first example, "and Wu Shang *homes* her," works immediately and effectively. The explicit meaning of taking Dixie into his home is clear, and appropriate sexual suggestions play effectively around the phrase. The second example, "and belly laughter *waifs* ghost rats," is far more questionable. The explicit meaning is not so apparent. It seems intended to suggest that the hearty laughter of "the unperfumed" is their means of denying the pangs of hunger. These hunger pangs are projected as those of "ghost rats foxed by the smells of meat and bread," and the belly laughter makes these ghost rats into waifs, or homeless children. But to get to this meaning one must pause and self-consciously reconstruct a series of verbal equations. Tolson increasingly risked such confusion or ambiguity as he tried for syntactic concentration.

Combining two poems from *A Gallery* to create a more complex dramatic situation and then reworking the style of the dramatic narrative to make it more intellectually demanding and more explicitly artful clearly foretell the direction of Tolson's ambition and talent as he was thinking of how he was to revise his early epic effort *A Gallery of Harlem Portraits* into what eventually became *Harlem Gallery: Book One, The Curator*.

"E. & O. E." appeared in *Poetry* in September 1951 and won for its author *Poetry*'s Bess Hokim award for the year. It too has an important link to Tolson's final epic effort. In "Chi" of *Harlem Gallery*, the Curator brings a deaddrunk Hideho Heights home and puts him to bed on the sofa. Then he chances upon a poem called "E. & O. E." According to the Curator:

here was the eyesight proof
that the Color Line, as well as the Party Line,
splits an artist's identity
like the vertical which
Omar's *Is* and *Is-not* cannot define

Examining the manuscript, the Curator focuses on a key question in the poem:

"Why place an empty pail
before a well
of dry bones?
Why go to Ninevah to tell
The ailing that they ail?
Why lose a golden fleece
to gain a holy grail?"

This question causes the Curator to speculate on why should Hideho Heights, "the *Coeur de Lion* of the Negro mass,"

in an age of anesthesiology
seek relief
in the bark of a toothache tree?

The Curator is surprised that the Hideho Heights whose style is so confident and recognizable on public occasions should have in this poem "aped the dubiety / of a wet cake of soap." The Curator notes:

The poet's mind kept shuttling between
the sphinx of Yesterday and the enigma of Today,
like the scepter of Amphion in Thebes
'twixt fragments of requiems and stones of decay.

The Curator then makes a distinction between the concerns of everyday mortals and those of the poet, again suggesting that Tolson was increasingly writing for a future audience, an audience beyond the most immediate interests of his time:

Time!
Time?
The poet's *bete noire*, I thought.
We everyday mortals
wrought
on the cis-threshold of the sublime
are concerned with *timing*
not with *time*.

The Curator closes his comments on Heights's manuscript by quoting with surprise a passage from the beginning of section 8 that reveals Heights as steeped in the post–World War I, Parisian experience of American expatriates and then following that with the final section 12, which essentially denies any ambitious claims of the poet to affect the world. In the complete "E. & O. E." as published in *Poetry*, the negative statement of section 12 is qualified by the modest, but assured, claim that concludes section 11:

> I sought
> in a Tarshish nook
> neither the Golden Fleece
> nor the Holy Grail
> but a pruning-hook.

By omitting this qualification, Tolson made Hideho Heights's personal statement in the poem discovered by the Curator seem even more dramatically pathetic than Tolson's statement about himself in the original poem.

The Curator's discovery of "E. & O. E." and what it reveals about Henry Heights is probably a caricature of what Tolson thought "E. & O. E." actually revealed about his own role as a poet. "E. & O. E." is the other side of the coin from *Libretto*. As *Libretto* is a grand, confident, public document— although its confident utopianism is admittedly often played against a historical awareness that threatens the realization of its dream—so "E. & O. E." is a personal statement of doubt and a self-consciously deliberate scaling down of poetic ambition. It is not personal in the sense that the *I* closes off all matters social and historical, describing only a physical or psychological awareness. Tolson is almost never personal in that sense. By this time his assumption of the tri-dimensionality of the self—the self as a product of biology, sociology, and psychology—had become so ingrained that he could not image a private ahistorical self. "E. & O. E." looks at a *historical* dilemma from the personal perspective of a poet. Where *Libretto* prophesies a collective human realization, "E. & O. E." dramatizes the dilemma of a particular black American poet given a Jonah-like commandment to deliver God's message to Ninevah in an apocalyptic moment of history.

The poem begins with a mocking logic representing *to be or not to be* as the horns of an as yet unidentified dilemma, although the dilemma apparently is that of a poet rather than of the narrator. Section 2 also clearly identifies the dilemma as racial. The irony is that the narrator's resolution of the racial dilemma is in effect no resolution at all. The power of determining his identity is not in his own hands:

> Though
> I dot my *i* in this
> and rend the horns
> of tribal ecbasis,
> the Great White World's

uncrossed *t*
pockets the skeleton key
to doors beyond
black chrysalis.

The conflict between his self-determined identity and his publicly determined identity produces the traditional black American double vision that Tolson then caricatures mockingly. There is no question of his contempt for the process by which society determines his identity.

In defense
of Madame de Civilis,
a zombi slut who came to preen
in Fornix Square,
I toppled the guillotine
into the moat
dug by the *adola mentis.*

Yet the clock of fate or time ticks on relentlessly, and there are portents of an apocalyptic change—whether for better or for worse is by no means clear. The narrator speculates on a number possibilities and begins ominously:

O sight-
less listeners on
Abraxa's storm
cellar stair,
is it
Everyman
from the no man's land
of Everywhere?

But by the middle of section 5, the narrator is speculating on happier purgative consequences:

is it, is it,
the whited sepulcher's
dike capsizing
in the dolor
of the rising
tide of color?

Whatever time or fate brings, the narrator readies himself for the consequence:

Open, locks,
whoever knocks!

But the "Tartufean shill" poses a temptingly cynical question, the same question that the Curator finds in Heights's manuscript:

> "Why place
> an empty pail
> before a well
> of dry bones?
> Why go to Ninevah to tell
> the ailing that they ail?
> Why lose the Golden Fleece
> to gain the Holy Grail?"

The power of the world to blind and confuse the sight of the most piercing seer is represented eloquently:

> I have seen
> the unlaid ghosts
> of twenty sex-o-clock cities along
> the White Whale's Acheron
> freeze the dog
> days, make
> the crow's nest hog
> like the spine of a dated truth:
> hawk eyes
> unspectacled by ruth
> are not hawk-eyed enough
> to pierce the winding sheet of fog
> that turns hawk into quail . . .
> to pierce the seascape's brambly night,
> lopped rough,
> sheared white,
> by arc blades of the gale.

Section 7 begins with a climactic confession of near spiritual paralysis occasioned by an awareness of the apocalyptic nature of the historical moment:

> 'Sdeath!
> The toil
> of doomsday struck
> *I-ness* in me
> between parentheses
> of my eternity.

Death, however, is not as fearful as dying, which the narrator defines in terms of a debilitating threat to identity:

Dying
is the ogress
lying
in penumbra
wrying
identity to the dregs
with tentacles of
the seven plagues.

The narrator in section 8 assesses his past, but he does so chiefly in negatives. He begins with the passage the Curator quotes from Hideho Heights's manuscript, which describes his participation in the post–World War I Parisian world of fervid experimentation in modernism:

yet out of square,
I have not said,
"Hippoclides doesn't care."

This qualification is important. It is a reminder of Tolson's earlier criticism of the modernists who seemed deliberately to dissociate themselves from social concerns.

The narrator follows with a phrase implying that he sees that the black American brings to modern poetry a healthy iconoclastic imperative:

Until
my skin
was blister copper,
I have not stood within
the free-soil gate,
pole in hand,
to knock off monkey hats
exported to the hinterland.

In the notes to the poem Tolson indicated that he was referring to Ataturk's effort to proscribe the fez as a means of ridding Turkey of debilitating religious power and thus making it more free, modern, and secular. The implied analogy is to the artist who was not prompted to similar action against the idols of the tribe until his skin "was blister copper."

The artist throughout sections 8 and 9 is represented as caught in the flow of history, unable to control or affect events, even unable to envision a better world:

. . . I
have glimpsed no Sea
of Marmara between
illusion and reality;

between *finesse* and *geometrie*
no green
green desert where
years come to me.

The artist's identity, or for that matter any person's, is strongly dependent upon his relation to the culture within which he lives. The artist's, and one might infer particularly the black American artist's, sense of the tenuousness of his relation to his culture is then acknowledged in section 9:

I, from Dan
to Beersheba,
have been a stone
skipping over water;
to atone,
my solar plexus sought the navel cord
in vain. I have grown
as empty as a cenotaph set
among deaf-mutes without
a one-hand alphabet.

Section 10 finds the artist, like Jonah, or like Paterson, overwhelmed by the responsibility of his mission, trying desperately to reduce or even evade it: "Let this cup pass from me!" But there is no escape. His fate is relentless and inevitable. There is no course other than through the Adamic fall to the promise of rebirth, although the conditions of that rebirth remain in doubt:

. . . then *le mal du siècle* plummeted
me, like the ignis fatuus
of a bedeviled thunderhead
over and over and over
the tissue cataracts of Widows' Tears
and across the plateaus of fishes dead . . .
eternities later, by Fear set free of fears,
though churned by entrail-dooms volcanic,
the *Weltschmerz* twisted me like the neck of a torticollis
in enzymatic juices oceanic,
and swirled me down and down and down
the fabulous fathomless fatty-tumorous canyon of the whale
with the grind and the drag
of the millstone
sphinx of Why
on my wry
head and neck . . . alone . . . alone . . .
        to die
    gyrating into the wide, wide privacy

of the Valley of Hinnom's By-and-Bye . . .
      down
      down
      down
untouched by the witches' Sabbath of any wall
until the maelstrom womb of the underworld swallowed my
      Adamic fall!

Section 11 announces the resurrection, not of a glorious redemptive Christ, but of a diminished Jonah,

a jonah shrunk
by a paraclete
Malebolgean.

But this Jonah-artist is allowed to speak in his own voice with a quiet assertive dignity:

I sought
in a Tarshish nook
neither the Golden Fleece
nor the Holy Grail
but a pruning hook.

The quiet assertion, like the understated *"Ppt. knows"* in the *Libretto*, is then set against the closing section 12, which, however, when quoted by the Curator in *Harlem Gallery*, seems unrelievedly negative in its disclaiming:

Beneath
the albatross
the skull-and-bones,
the Skull and Cross,
the Seven Sins Dialectical,
      I do not shake
      the Wailing Wall
            of Earth
      nor quake
      the Gethsemane
            of Sea,
      nor tear
      the Big Top
            of Sky
with Lear's prayer,
      or Barabas' curse,
      or Job's cry!

Libretto for the Republic of Liberia treats the realization of a multicultural world order as fated once it can be imagined, even though there is ample awareness of man's proclivity to frustrate such idealism by his worship of false gods. "E. & O. E." looks at the imagining of the new order from the point of view of a poet-prophet who has been singled out for a key role in voicing those powerful truths that will effect this remarkable social realization. He works his way through fear to a more reassuring humble acceptance of his responsibility following the paradigm of Jonah.

When Tolson first wrote to Allen Tate about writing a preface for the *Libretto*, he mentioned having previously sent a poem, "The Horns of the Bull," to *Sewanee Review* while Tate was editor. Since no manuscript of a poem with that title survives, it is tempting to speculate that the title may have been a punning reference to the horns of the dilemma that the poet-narrator faces in "E. & O. E." It would have been like Tolson to send an editor a poem complementary to one he had previously rejected.

"A Long Head to a Round Head" is a relatively short but intensely concentrated poem built on several esoteric, ambiguous references. The key challenge is the title and what it indicates about who is speaking to whom. To be longheaded implies taking a wise, long-range view of events, but the phrase *round head* ordinarily brings to mind the Puritans opposed to the Cavaliers in the reign of Charles I. The Cavaliers, on the other hand, were not particularly known as long heads. So the title seems to mix apples and oranges, just as the text of the poem reveals contesting views of history. The speaker is mocking the shortsightedness of the exclusive, narcissistic, aristocratic views of the person he is addressing, presumably a round head. I strongly suspect that Tolson intended this poem as a cryptic message distinguishing his own view of history (the long head's) from that of T. S. Eliot (the round head). Eliot may well have seen himself as more closely associated with the Cavalier than the Puritan tradition, but Tolson, grounded in the bohemian leftist politics of the twenties and thirties, would be more likely to caricature him as a Puritan, or perhaps even more to the point to see him revealed in the inhibited confusion of his character J. Alfred Prufrock. There is a specific reference to Prufrock at the end of section 2:

> None calls the folds of Caesar's toga back:
> before your vanity
> westers to the maggot's feast,
> your izzard thought shall be
> of trousers creased.

Of course, if Tolson and Eliot are the long and round heads, they are only broadly representative of contending views of history. Tolson seems to be working out a problem that was faced by many a poet at this time, a problem of which his notes in his journals and his comments in letters and speeches suggest that he was keenly aware. How could one acknowledge the technical literary achievement of Eliot, whose stature loomed so large, particularly in the American academic world in the late forties and early fifties, and still declare one's independence from Eliot's social and political views? The argument of Tolson's poem is that the round head is too timorous to take the long view of history. He feeds the narcissistic vanity of those who identify with the traditions of the aristocratic power of the past. Inhibited by the repugnance he feels toward the vulgar modern world, he treats the frequent symptoms of the decay and death of the privileged world with which he identifies as historical aberrations rather than as inevitable prophecy. The round head is represented by Alcuin, who warned Charles the Great that he should not heed those who are accustomed to say *"vox populi, vox Dei,"* the voice of the people is the voice of God, for the ragings of the mob are always near to madness.

The long head's, and Tolson's own, contrasting democratic view of history is made unmistakably clear in the concluding stanzas:

> Salons may cheep
> *Odi profanum vulgus et arceo,*
> remembering not
> anonymous thumbs and index fingers keep
> the candelabra of the ermined aglow,
> remembering not
> the nameless tier
> the ultimate Thule of a name,
> just as a hundred thousand hands
> pyramided Cheops' fame.
>
> A despot is to the people as
> a dangling participle to a noun:
> a sceptre's seal is an iota's scribble
> upon the testament of a crown.

For Tolson power inevitably flows from the people, and truth must ultimately be consecrated by the people's understanding. Historical forces may create a gulf of understanding between the leader and the masses, but for a leader to scorn the people, and particularly the results of their labor, is to commit suicide. A culture, and ultimately all mankind, is an organism so interdependent that ideas of privilege and exclusiveness are poisonous and must be rejected.

The title of Tolson's poem "The Man from Halicarnassus" is followed by an epigraph from H. G. Wells: "The poet in Herodotus takes possession of the historian." The poem is a dramatic monologue delivered on the occasion of the historian's being awarded ten talents by the Athenians for *his-story.* Herodotus had left his native Halicarnassus because his work had not received the favor there that it deserved. Herodotus thus makes a dramatically ironic public statement of some of the same issues that are treated introspectively by the narrator-poet of "E. & O. E."

Herodotus's opening comment to the Athenians suggests, however, that he assumes a sophisticated and understanding audience. The action takes place on Ares Hill, the same Areopagus where, as Tolson was well aware, Saint Paul years later addressed a different audience of Athenians. Herodotus refers to his listeners as "Togas of the Yeas," who for the sake of Clio, the muse of history, have awarded him the ten talents in spite of the fact that he is from another land. He ironically acknowledges the danger of rewarding a historian with money by noting that this award also teaches him "the ways, in Typhon's shop, by which the shekel / decores the vase to dull the Juts's surmise." Nevertheless, he reassures his audience by two references to his own *History*. In book 2 Herodotus, describing the habits and nature of the crocodile, remarks on the wondrous accommodation that this huge and dangerous beast has achieved with the trochilus, a slight, defenseless bird who enters the crocodile's mouth when he is resting on land and cleans it by devouring the leeches accumulated there during the crocodile's foraging in the water. Herodotus's statement, "the trochilus is safe / in crocodile jaws," is thus meant to assure his Athenian audience that the contract between the muckraking historian and his Athenian audience is well understood on both sides. It is the security of this contract, dependent on the historian's imperviousness to the temptation of monetary rewards, and the community's recognition of the value of the cleansing function of historical truth, which leads Herodotus to assure the Athenians that they have no need to conjure him up as a Hippias of the Scroll, Hippias being a tyrant who once ruled Athens and later threatened it with the aid of an armed force of barbarians.

He then boasts of his professional integrity by making an impossible supposition that would, if possible, be followed by shameful consequences:

> . . . When gnomon fails
> its shadow, my integrity shall be a beggar's cup
> outside the banking-house of Egibi
> or, Cheops-like, send Clio to the stew.

In his *History* Herodotus pointedly told the story of how Cheops's lust for memorializing his life by a magnificent pyramid led him to raise funds even by sending his own daughter to the stew. However, the truth of history is ultimately not dependent on the personal integrity of Herodotus or any other individual or even on the preservation of the language of any particular culture. The impersonal and inevitable "Tomorrow's tomorrows" will reveal the historical truth even as Herodotus has revealed the truth of "yesterdays in Cabiri."

Herodotus then invites his audience to look across the Aegean at Halicarnassus, which Darius treated shamefully as a mistress and which, more shamefully, because of the "ciphers in her womb," disdains Herodotus's *History* "as Heliopolitan spit." His estrangement from his native place makes him seem as "soul split / from body" and raises questions about the nature of his consequent identity: "is it *i* or *you* or it?" The possible analogies between the dilemma of Herodotus and that of Tolson in particular and the black American writer in general are open and inviting.

In the *Libretto* Tolson acknowledges a strong debt to W. E. B. DuBois's *Dusk of Dawn*. DuBois in turn quoted Herodotus extensively to illustrate the interpenetration of African and Mediterranean cultures. Thus the image Herodotus next invokes is charged with meaning. In his *History* Herodotus told the story of the Egyptian king Psammetichus who created a test designed to discover which people surpass all others in antiquity. He gave a herdsman two children to bring up. They were to be kept from any contact with language except with each other: "His object herein was to know, after the indistinct babblings of infancy were over, what word they would first articulate." The herdsman obeyed orders carefully for two years. Then the children both spoke their first distinctive word, *Becos*. *Becos* is the Phrygian word for *bread*. Thus Psammetichus acknowledged the Phrygians to be of greater antiquity than the Egyptians. In his poem Tolson has Herodotus remember an Ethiopian eunuch symbolically crying this Phrygian word as he stretches his hand toward Athens. The image implies man from his first intelligence reaching toward the cultivated wisdom of the democratic city state of Athens to complete himself, to become a full man in history. Herodotus identifies with this man: "I was as he, an iota of the Man to be, and he as I, / lonely as the only / peak's disintegrated rock." Tolson, too, felt the lonely pathos of playing a role in the early stage of a culture's self-realization. He too identified with the Ethiopian eunuch in his sense of being only "an iota of the Man to be" and of longingly wondering how different he would be if he had lived amidst the mature culture of a sophisticated city.

Herodotus insists that he is not merely reacting to either a personal or a professional hurt, "I am no pigeon homing from a dialectic shock"; nor is he a professional drudge impervious to human needs and aspirations, an "oxhoof treading ugh upon a scroll." In the classroom and from the podium Tolson frequently insisted upon man's tridimensionality, his biological, sociological, and psychological nature. It is this tridimensionality that Tolson has Herodotus request the Sons of Athens to recognize both for him and for Man by writing in stone, "The soul of Tresas equals Tresas' sole." This tridimensionality underscores the question that Herodotus previously raised about the split in his identity stemming from his alienation from his native Halicarnassus.

The importance of place, both geographical and social, to personal development is then reinforced by quotes from two historic antagonists of Athens: Cyrus and Hippocrates. Cyrus, who brought the Persian empire to Lydia, speaks with a stern eye to the strengths necessary for military conquest, "Soft lands give birth / to soft men." Herodotus suggests that this dogma should be studded with the tyrant Hippocrates's aphorism, "Race is geography."

But if this truth is acknowledged, what is to be made of the restless surge of peoples back and forth from Asia to Europe to Africa that Herodotus records in his *History?* A culture, a polis, a city, comes into being and is invaded and desecrated by barbaric strength. The words, the artifacts, produced, become mockeries of pretension as the persistent pattern of conquest and reconquest empties them of relevant meaning. Yet they continue to give one eloquent persistent message:

> . . . these are the soul's upsurge to fetter change
> that changes not . . . to smash the vial
> of Tartarean hemlock that Time, the while he gloats,
> pours down the throats
> of the triumvirs, Mineral and Vegetable and Animal.

Herodotus then makes a heartfelt plea with an implied warning that grows from the observations of his *History,* and his plea is clearly meant to be heard in the midtwentieth century as relevant to another poet-historian as well:

> Oh, that we had a Petala to link the lands
> Of Sunrise and Sunset! World feuds ferment like yeast
> in Parthian malts and rob the senses. I
> fear the thunder in the West, and the lightning in the East.

The poem closes with the oracular musings of a "trireme sage" from Egyptian Heliopolis, who, by way of the Ethiopian city of Meroe, is sanding scrolls for the island city Elephantine:

> "A people can be bat serpents flying
> black abises dying,
> or gods outwearing
> Calpe and Abila tearing
> *Ne plus ultra* asunder!"

Herodotus confronts his audience with a challenging choice between oblivion and new, triumphant possibilities of social order. The people will and must decide. While Herodotus does not prophesy the new world order seen in *Libretto,* he makes clear its possibility.

"Abraham Lincoln of Rock Spring Farm" is also concerned with a fateful moment of history experienced by individuals inadequately prepared to understand even their own roles in the extraordinary changes portended. The occasion is the birth of Abraham Lincoln, viewed principally through the experiences of Tom and Nancy Lincoln, Abe's parents. However, Tolson also employs the full eloquence of the poet-historian to contrast ironically with the troubled perspectives of his more time-bound characters. Thus the opening two stanzas set the stage with a richly suggestive sense of the historical drama about to be played:

Along the Wilderness Road, through Cumberland Gap,
The black ox hours limped toward Sunday's sun
Across a bluff clay belt with scrawls of stone,
Where bird and beast quailed in the bosom brush
From February's fang and claw; the stars
Blue white, like sheer icicles, spired aglow
As if the three wise men barged in the East
Or priests in sackcloth balked the Scourge of God.

Foursquare by the rite of arm and heart and law,
The scrubby log cabin dared the compass points
Of Rock Spring farm, man's world, God's universe,
The babel of the circumstance and era.
The frozen socket of its window stared
Beyond the sprayed crabapple trees, to where
The skulls of hills, the skeletons of barrens,
Lay quiet as time without the watch's tick.

Then with a line that echoes the extraordinary range of human possibilities with which Herodotus confronts the Athenians, Tolson, the poet-historian, introduces the father of Abraham Lincoln:

Not knowing muck and star would vie for him,
The man Tom sank upon an ax-split stool.

Aunt Peggy, the experienced and knowing midwife, with "her keyhole look," sees in Tom Lincoln something of the lonely pathos of the Ethiopian eunuch in "The Man from Halicarnassus" and the narrator-poet of "E. & O. E." She explored

Beneath the patched homespun, the hue and cry
Of malice, until she touched his loneliness,
The taproot that his fiber gave no tongue.

Nancy, the mother-to-be, has puzzled over the meager information that her mother, Lucy Hanks, gave her about the circumstances of her birth:

Year in, year out, the daughter tinkered with
The riddle of her birth; the mother chided
The woman Nancy as she had the child,

"Hush thee, hush thee, thy father's a gentleman."
The butt of bawd, grand jury, Sunday bonnet,
Lucy, driven, taught her daughter the Word,
And Nancy, driven, taught her son the Word,
And Abraham, driven, taught his people the Word!

The comic irony of Lucy's effort to put the best face possible on the questionable circumstances of Nancy's birth becoming the controlling *Word* handed from mother to daughter to son and finally becoming the prophetic liberating *Word* of Abraham Lincoln to his people is clearly fully savored and intended by Tolson. Since he too was born in February in a frontier midwestern community and probably also puzzled over the deliberately repressed circumstances of the birth of one of his parents, the passage almost certainly also carried a charge of personal feeling.

But Tom is unaware of the historical drama in the making. Feeling defeated by the harsh challenge of the frontier he asks Aunt Peggy, "Now that our Nancy's time is come, I'm haunted / By my own nothingness. Why breed nobodies?" Aunt Peggy answers:

"It's true, down in the barnyard, blood speaks loud
Among the hogs, the chickens, the cows, the horses;
But, when it comes to Man, who knows, who knows
What greatness feeds down in the lowliest mother?"

Aunt Peggy reminds Tom of the strengths of his father who "Conquered a land with gun and ax and plow, / Baptized it in his blood!" Then she generalizes:

"What's in a baby is God Almighty's business;
How the elders wring it out is worry enough!
The best, the worst—it's all, all human nature."

Her remark causes Tom to remember an encounter with an Oxford don, a clubfoot scholar of fervent democratic idealism, in a frontier tavern on the previous New Year's Eve. Tom then raised the question, What is human nature? The scholar respected the question and answered:

"My new idea fed to his new baby
Would fetch the New World and the New Year peace!
The sum of anything unriddles the riddle:
The child whose wet nurse is the mother-of-all
Grows like a pine unmarked by rock or wind.

"To make a New World and a New Year, Plato
And Jesus begged the boon of little children!

Now Citizen Lincoln asks, 'What's human Nature?'
It's what we elders have: no baby has it.

It's what our good and bad graft on the neutral.
It's what our rulers feed the boy and girl.
It's what society garbs nature in.
It's a misnomer: call it *human nurture!*"

This improbable scholar echoes what Tolson frequently said on other occasions. Man is born a tabula rasa. His cultural environment enables or restricts him from realizing the potentialities of his nature. History reveals the extraordinary promise of human cultivation as well as man's almost incredible capability for barbarous destructiveness. Thus the challenge is to identify and enhance the power of the Word, which will enable man to create the institutions within which he can realize his full potential. While man is a product of human nature, each new birth holds the seed of radical change. Running through what is admittedly an anarchic history of ups and downs of human civilization, Tolson professed to see a thread of democratic realization. At times he spoke of it as if it were inevitable, yet he also persistently insisted that it must be willed and worked for by man to be achieved and sustained.

Aunt Peggy abandons Tom to his doubts and questionings when she hears Nancy's sounds of muffled pain. Tom's visions of what his life should be, compared to the grub living it is, gnawed at him and "wrung the soul of joy and beauty dry." As "The black ox hours limped by, and day crawled in," the baby, Abraham, is Sabbath-born:

Like ax and helve, like scythe and snath, the bond
Held Tom and Nancy: she smiled at his halt smile,
His titan's muss in picking up the baby.
Tom frowned and spat, then gulped, "He's legs! All legs!"
Aunt Peggy beamed, "Long legs can eat up miles."
Tom gleamed, "The hands—look at the axman's hands!"
And Nancy mused, "The Hankses' dream, the Lincolns',
Needs such a man to hew and blaze the way."

Since this poem was intended for *Collier's,* Tolson probably felt the challenge to make his statement available to a popular audience. He never equaled Robert Frost or Langston Hughes in their ability to blend profound and complex implications imperceptibly into a seemingly innocent story or drama. The folksy characters of this poem sometimes raise self-consciously philosophical questions with more convenience to the author's statement than credible similitude to their own dramatic situation. However, for the later student of Tolson this at least has the advantage of laying bare the framework of many of his beliefs and assumptions, which are more obscure and ambiguous in his more esoterically phrased poems of this same time. This poem is similar to *Rendezvous with America* in both style and thought, but it implies rather strongly that as late as 1949 Tolson felt no need to change his beliefs in any substantial manner, even though he was experimenting at the same time in other poems with marked changes in style.

IX

LANGSTON—THE HUB OF

A UNIVERSE

In "Bivouac by the Santa Fe," two black soldiers talk over the problems of keeping order among the land-hungry people moving into Oklahoma territory. One notes that the whites are pouring in and taking over. The other counters that a whole trainload of Negroes has also arrived. But the first insists that that is different: "I had two uncles and three cousins in that bunch. They were getting the hell outa Texas. Do you blame 'em? If I owned Texas and Hell, I'd rent out Texas and live in Hell! Black men been running to the Indians in Oklahoma for salvation since I don't know when."

In 1947 the Tolson family did not run to the Indians for refuge when they arrived in Oklahoma, but they did choose to live in Langston, one of several communities originally intended to attract blacks by giving them a sense of security and racial identity through the opportunity of living in an all-black community. Langston dated from the same landgrabbing days as "Bivouac by the Santa Fe." Tolson and his wife bought a home in Langston in 1950. At that time the university owned bungalows, duplexes, and World War II barracks in Langston, and most of the faculty lived in them.

The Tolson home was modest, on an unpaved street just off State Highway 33, an easy walk to the campus. With the boys off on their own and Ruth Marie away at college, there was no need for a large house, and Tolson's fear of an approaching depression conditioned him to be cautious about assuming any large mortgage. On 13 May 1953 Tolson wrote with satisfaction and relief to Ruth, who was then teaching in Perry, Oklahoma, in her first full-time, paying job since their marriage: "and TODAY paid out the $700.00 (includes interest, taxes, and insurance) on the house. At last we got a home all paid for. Not a debt on it! The bank values the property at $9,000—without furniture. Carlotta thinks I need more insurance—tornadoes, etc." Tolson probably sat in the Zulu Club, a recreation room finished off in the basement, as he drank to paying off the mortgage. The serious

Melvin B. Tolson

The Tolson home in Langston, Oklahoma.

drinking and even more serious argumentation that went on in this room over the Langston years became the model for the meetings of the Zulu Club Wits in *Harlem Gallery.*

But if the house was all paid for, money was still a problem. In the same letter to Ruth, Tolson indicated he was sending Wiley one hundred dollars for his wedding and suggested that Ruth send him fifty dollars for the honeymoon, but he announced that he could not send the money and attend the wedding too. He expressed a weary sympathy for Wiley's concern with money matters: "Well, he's just getting started on that. God knows I understand, for I had them 30 years. But, of course, his wife can help and expects to. I didn't know until this year what it means to have a wife making her own money!" One item on the list of expenses that kept him from his son's wedding attests to the difficulties and risks a poet had in reaching an audience: $650 for publication of *Libretto.*

In the same year the Tolsons moved into their Langston home, Ruth had an operation on her left shoulder, which continued to be somewhat restricted in use for the rest of her life, although it did not stop her from buying a bicycle when she neared her sixtieth birthday years later. Ruth also had a hereditary hearing deficiency that was shared by Arthur and Ruth Marie. Years earlier she had taught part-time at a rural school outside Marshall, Texas, but her full-time teaching job in Perry was a self-conscious and willed statement that she would not let her age, gender, or physical liabilities keep her from active participation in the world's affairs. Later in the fifties she also enrolled at Oklahoma State University and by 1957 had completed an M.A. degree in education and library science.

In June 1952, the NAACP held its forty-third annual convention in Oklahoma City. For many years Tolson had actively supported and participated in NAACP programs in various parts of the country, and he wrote and directed his dramatic version of Walter White's *Fire in the Flint* for this convention. The preamble to the 1952 convention indicates the political concerns of the time:

> The seriousness of this election year exists because there are those who under the guise of securing tideland oil money for the state, or under the masquerade of States Rights, or government economy, or further restriction of collective bargaining rights, would endanger our national security, destroy all of the social gains derived from government in the last two decades by resurrecting an outmoded and much abused political philosophy.

Just a year before, W. E. B. DuBois, for many years editor of the NAACP magazine, *Crisis,* at the age of eighty-three and after a lifetime of extraordinary intellectual and social service, was insultingly indicted as an agent of a foreign power and jailed because of his service on a committee working for nuclear disarmament. On 16 September 1953, Tolson wrote to a friend, Dick Paige, referring to this threat of political repression: "On the national front, of course, I've been deeply disturbed by McCarthyism. But I believe his attack on the Protestant clergy may be his downfall. Americans don't seem to realize how dangerous he is."

Against this background of national concern, the racial repression dramatized in *Fire in the Flint* probably was intended to carry contemporary political overtones. The changes Tolson made in Walter White's story as evidenced by the incomplete manuscript that survives were discussed in Chapter 5. The performance occasioned little notice in print, certainly notably little in relation to the effort Tolson made in writing and directing the play. However, the occasional references in Tolson's later letters to the play register no regrets. He wrote of the performance with pride. Apparently the reaction of the immediate audience, at least, was gratifying.

Three years earlier Tolson's dramatic talents had also earned him surprising consideration for the lead role in a musical version of *Cry the Beloved Country*. On 22 June 1949, Langston Hughes wrote to Arna Bontemps: "Do you know any nice gentle old Negro who could play the lead in *Cry the Beloved Country* which I've been trying to help Maxwell Anderson and Kurt Weill to cast?" Bontemps replied on 26 June:

> A person you should have Mamoulian-Anderson-Weill consider for *Cry the Beloved Country* is none other than M. B. Tolson. His hair is gray, he has the gentleness, etc., and moreover he has been a director of little theatres and debating teams for years. He is at home on a stage. I think he would love it, that he could easily get a leave from Langston U. for this purpose, and that he would be a stomping success. And he is very much the Roland type! Tell Reuben I send this nomination with my warm regards and best wishes for the success of this new production.

Hughes made the suggestion. Weill asked him to phone Tolson, and Tolson was reported to be enthusiastic about the project. A question arose about Tolson's singing voice. Although they were not consulted, those Wiley debaters who were subjected to Tolson's singing while driving across the Southland had no question about his singing voice. At least Hobart Jarrett and Benjamin Bell, many years later, found the prospect of Tolson playing a lead role in a musical uproarious. At any rate, for some reason not clear in the correspondence of Bontemps and Hughes, someone else got the part.[1]

A few months after the performance of *Fire in the Flint*, Tolson joined many of the best-known black writers of the day to celebrate Jackson State College's Diamond Jubilee. In 1965 Tolson gave a talk on "The Foreground of Negro Poetry" as part of a centenary celebration of the Emancipation

Proclamation. The memory of the 1952 meeting was still so vivid thirteen years later that it took up more than a third of his talk. His own words give a sense of the importance of the occasion:

> October 19–24, 1952, President Reddick [*sic*] of Jackson College, in Mississippi, held a Festival of Negro Poets. In 1963, President Kennedy imitated this Negro educator in Washington, D.C. History will record these two events. Think of it! Over 3,500 people gathered in the auditorium to hear the leading Negro poets of America recite their own poems! I believe it was Professor Bachelor who told me that if an atom bomb had been dropped on Jackson College, Negro literature would have been destroyed! The gentleman from Guthrie was right!
>
> Langston Hughes was at Jackson College. . . . When he and I were invited to visit a Negro reformatory school near Jackson, Mississippi, I had the audacity to recite to those unfortunate boys one of Langston's most powerful poems, "Mother to Son". . . .
>
> I looked down into the faces of those Negro boys. They were no longer the faces of juvenile delinquents, from the towns and plantations of darkest Mississippi. I turned to Langston Hughes. I saw in his eyes the same light that I saw in the eyes of those boys. I sat down. Langston grasped my hand— and held it. There was no applause. There was only a deafening silence, an unforgettable silence.
>
> We are back again in the auditorium at Jackson College. People, people, people of every complexion; yet united in oneness of spirit, oneness of destiny, as they listen to the voices of their poets. Sterling Brown, scholar and integrationist, recites "The Strong Men"—the strong black men who, from plantations and slums, keep coming on, keep coming on in spite of poverty and illiteracy and superstition. Robert Hayden, professor and modernist, holds the audience breathless with his lyric, "Homage to the Empress of the Blues." A little dark woman named Margaret Walker, who won the Yale Poetry Prize, delivers in a soulful voice stanzas from her book, *For My People*. Owen Dodson, novelist and dramatist, touches the hearts of the people with his memorable "Epitaph for a Negro Woman." Moses Carl Holman, Rosenwald scholar and teacher, spellbinds us with his "Letter Across Doubt and Distance." M. B. Tolson recites his "Dark Symphony."[2]

The 1952 gathering of writers was also vividly remembered years later by Langston Hughes. In 1965 Hughes introduced Tolson at a poetry reading of the American Society for African Culture in New York. He told of a pointedly humorous adventure that he and Tolson had had in Jackson at the end of the festival. Hughes had heard that the crack Panama Limited, which stopped at Jackson on its way from Chicago to New Orleans, was very reluctant "to haul coal." Even Charles S. Johnson of the Urban League complained he was unable to get a ticket on this train in Chicago. Since Tolson was wiser in the ways of the South, he took the initiative. He and Hughes

Melvin B. Tolson

A distinguished group of poets gathered for the Festival of Negro Poets, 19–24
October 1952, in Jackson, Mississippi: (*back, from left to right*) Arna Bontemps,
Melvin B. Tolson, Jacob Reddix, Owen Dodson, Robert Hayden;
(*front, from left to right*) Sterling Brown, Zora Neale Hurston,
Margaret Walker, Langston Hughes.

bought tickets for New Orleans days in advance, arrived at the depot an hour ahead of schedule, but boarded only at the last minute. The conductor then held up the train while he called down the line of cars searching for an empty drawing room to avoid seating them with the white passengers. They finally ended up riding in the most elegant drawing room on the train, although, after the rigors of the conference and considering the early hour in the morning, they both slept most of the way to New Orleans.[3] This event took place about two years after Tolson had planned to submit his correspondence with Allen Tate to *Sewanee Review*, but it suggests his strategy and motive. As a southern black, he challenged and crossed many color lines that limited his freedom.

The early years of settling in at Langston contained many difficulties and frustrations, and the promise of professional rewards seemed unendingly delayed. But in 1954 the world smiled and embraced M. B. Tolson. *Libretto for the Republic of Liberia* finally was published in December 1953, and it precipitated a wealth of recognition and honors. The critical reception described above was often tentative and grudging, yet the attention given the book was notable. As a consequence Tolson was offered a fellowship in poetry and drama at the Bread Loaf Writers' Conference, Lincoln University came through with the long-anticipated honorary Doctor of Letters degree, and the Liberian government conferred upon Tolson the Order of the Star of Africa. In a very different vein, his fellow citizens of Langston elected him mayor. And Tolson was invited to play a conspicuous role in the state visit of Liberian President William V. S. Tubman to the United States late in the fall. All in all, a very heady year.

Early in 1954, on 11 January, the Liberian embassy honored both the author and his new book with a literary tea attended by academic, literary, and diplomatic dignitaries. Ambassador Clarence L. Simpson was host, and the guests included, besides Tolson and his wife, Presidents Mordecai W. Johnson of Howard University, G. L. Harrison of Langston University, and Jacob L. Reddix of Jackson College in Mississippi. Diplomatic representatives from Canada, Israel, Germany, Finland, and Austria attended. Peter Vierek entertained the guests with a reading. The *Washington Post* noted that the Liberian embassy was the first embassy "to sponsor a literary tea honoring an American poet." It was an auspiciously impressive initial promotion for *Libretto*.

Selden Rodman's review of *Libretto* appeared on 24 January in the *New York Times*, and William Stanley Braithwaite, after reading Rodman's review, wrote a congratulatory letter that same day. Jack Steinberg wrote a letter to Tolson on 29 January assuring him that the book was selling nicely. He also informed Tolson that Constance Curtis of New York was arranging "a party, tea or something for you on behalf of the book," and he helped to arrange for Tolson's expenses to be paid.

On 26 February, Tolson gave a lecture at Fisk University as part of the celebration of Negro History Week. The next day John Ciardi, executive editor at Twayne, wrote to Richard L. Brown nominating Tolson for a fellowship at Bread Loaf: "Undoubtedly the most rocket-driven poet we have published is M. B. Tolson." Ciardi apparently sent Tolson a copy of his letter, and Brown wrote Tolson on 12 March outlining the process for selecting fellows, explaining the terms of the fellowship, and inviting him to submit any additional material for his nomination. The committee later offered Tolson the fellowship, and he happily accepted.

Before Tolson traveled to Bread Loaf, he was knighted by Ambassador Simpson of Liberia. On 6 May, Ambassador Simpson, at the Liberian embassy in Washington, explained the reasons for honoring the poet:

> Liberia as the only Negro Republic in West Africa considers itself indebted to a highly accomplished humanitarian of our race, Dr. M. B. Tolson, who has within our generation and time offered a new phase to the poetic works of Negroes as well as to the world. . . .
>
> By this token, the President of Liberia, who is also Grand Commander of the Star of Africa, has found it timely and appropriate to confer a distinction upon Dr. Tolson, which admits him to the Knighthood of the Order of the Star of Africa.
>
> May I add, that only persons who have made a valuable contribution to the enhancement of the Peoples of Africa and for the betterment of humanity are honoured with a decoration as the one which, on this occasion, is being awarded Dr. Tolson.
>
> I extend him congratulations and best wishes for further service to his proud race and beloved country.

On several ceremonial occasions in the later years of his life, Tolson would wear the emblem of his knighthood, the Star of Africa, prominently hanging from a ribbon around his neck.

Ambassador Simpson's reference to Dr. M. B. Tolson was premature. Tolson was awarded his honorary Doctor of Letters from Lincoln University on 8 June, approximately one month later. Sharing honors with Tolson was Lessing J. Rosenwald of the philanthropic family whose foundation had supported a great many black writers and scholars. This was a proud moment for Tolson, who was first recommended to Lincoln University in 1919 as a "worthy boy" for whose fare allowance should be made.

Later in the summer, but still before going to Bread Loaf, Tolson stopped in Detroit to visit his brother Rubert and his sister Helen and to have a thorough physical examination from a fraternity brother, Dr. Saulsberry.

From Bread Loaf he wrote to Ruth: "I got the report on my throat—strained muscles aggravated by bad teeth, smoking, drinking and lecturing too hard. They are to give me later reports I'm to pick up on my heart and arteries. I'm really glad I had this thing done. For the first time I know cancer symptoms—male and female. All to be watched."

In the same letter he described his first few days at Bread Loaf, "There's nothing like it before in my life." There were one hundred student poets and writers, four fellows, and twelve guest lecturers attending the conference— "I'm the only guest poet fellow. . . . We fellows live in a cottage and are served by maids. Every night at eight we go to a concert or lecture in the Little Colonial Theatre, and then we go to the Cocktail Hour—which may run till three in the morning. Never saw so much good liquor of all kinds in all my life. Great talk!"

On the day Melvin wrote to Ruth, Robert Frost was on a State Department–sponsored trip to Brazil, but he was scheduled to return to Bread Loaf in a few days. Many years later, on the occasion of Frost's death in 1963, Tolson reminisced about his initial meeting and acquaintance with Frost:

> Saturday afternoon, Ripton, Vermont, 1954. The vast velvety lawn was crowded with writers and writers-to-be. [Mrs.] Theodore Morrison, Frost's secretary, said to me: "Robert wants to see you."
>
> Puzzled, I followed her. My mind wandered and wondered. Shaking hands, dropping a word here and there, Robert Frost edged his way toward me. We exchanged greetings, as man to man, as poet to poet.
>
> Thinking of his "Mending Wall," I said: "The stones don't tumble down here. They're cemented."
>
> For the first time I heard him laugh. "Industrialism changed customs," he said. "I wrote 'Mending Wall' 40 years ago."
>
> "If you hadn't," I explained, "I couldn't have lectured on it in the South."
>
> He stared at me soberly: then he chuckled and inquired if I could meet him in Breadloaf at a certain time. I shook his hand with both of mine.
>
> That week hurricane Carol smashed, tangled and flooded New England. She even destroyed the steeple of Boston's famous old North Church. The appointed afternoon came and I knew no one would face that deluge. The phone rang urgently. Mrs. Morrison said, "Robert is waiting for you."
>
> I borrowed a raincoat and umbrella. Conscience-goaded, I hurried to the guest cottage. He sat before the fireplace, his eyes kidding mine. Hour after hour, we talked—about poetry, the race problem, Faulkner's adventures in South America, the two streams of progressivism and ultraconservatism in American history, the artist as a people's eyes and ears, the Cold War, the vogue of the writer-in-residence. He wanted to know what Negro colleges were doing to help Negro writers and artists.
>
> Some days before I had sent him a long ode on Liberia. He now handed

Melvin B. Tolson and Robert Frost.

me two copies of the "Complete Poems of Robert Frost": one autographed for President Tubman of Liberia, the other for me. He had written in mine: "To M. B. Tolson for the pleasure I had in his Libretto. Robert Frost, Ripton Vermont, September 1, 1954." I recalled a little breathless, words from his free-spoken Introduction: "The figure a poem makes. It begins in delight and ends in wisdom."

I've known two venerable poets from the Great White World. Both have now joined the Immortals. What Edwin Markham said in "Lincoln, the Man of the People," the Man with the Hoe could now say of Robert Frost— a lordly cedar goes down on the hills . . . "And leaves a lonesome place against the sky."[4]

Tolson was proud of his acquaintance with Frost and later noted that Frost had promised to appear at Langston for Tolson's retirement in 1965, a promise only his death prevented him from keeping.

Only a few weeks after Bread Loaf, President William V. S. Tubman of Liberia was scheduled to arrive in New York City. The *African Dawn*, the ship carrying the president and his party, arrived in the harbor on the evening of 14 October, but since New York City Mayor Wagner's reception committee was prepared to receive the president on the sixteenth, the ship stayed in the harbor until the scheduled official reception. Gov. Phil M. Donnelly of Missouri wrote to Tolson on 7 October asking him, as poet laureate of Liberia and as a native of Moberly and former resident of Independence and Kansas City, to "represent the state of Missouri upon the occasion of President Tubman's arrival in the United States."

Tolson wrote to Ruth on 17 October describing his part in the welcoming ceremonies:

> Saturday, at ten, we greeted the President at the wharf. A fine brass municipal band, the military, hundreds of flags, dignitaries galore, etc., etc. As they played the Liberian national anthem, the *African Dawn* glided into port. It was a thrilling sight.
>
> Harrison [President G. L. Harrison of Langston University] and Simmons [J. W. Simmons, wealthy friend of Harrison's] were there in their glory. Prexy had a brand-new suit. I had on Rube's light grey topcoat and hat— looking like Bear Brummel himself—and stepped out of a grey Cadillac with Ambassador Dudley and his madame and the founder of the Friends of Liberia, Mrs. Gumps, whose brothers and mother run N. Y. politics. Prexy turned white as dignitaries saluted the Poet Laureate!
>
> Then led by a squadron of cops—N.Y.'s mightiest—the cavalcade sped into N.Y. stopping traffic on Broadway and Fifth Avenue. On to the Waldorf-Astoria, with the Liberian flag atop and white flunkies bowing and scraping! Lord, Lord, I never thought I'd live to see this!

Tolson also described attending a private party given by President Tub-
man, a party, he emphasized to Ruth, that "neither Harrison nor Simmons
knew a damned thing about":

> Here I was stealing the show, sitting on the right hand of the President, with
> *Him* drinking a toast and Ambassador Simpson holding my hand and I'm
> holding a pint glass of *real* Scotch! And the President saying casually: "Dr.
> Tolson, we shall see that you visit our country next year!"

Not all of this letter concerned President Tubman's arrival. Tolson also
mentioned that Carl Cowell had asked to be his literary agent and he had
spoken to Jack Steinberg about Cowell's request: "He [Jack] was hurt. He said
we had got on well and he didn't see the need of an agent. Why cut him in?
I told him nothing nor anybody would come between us. He's afraid some
big company might try to steal me. But you know I never play the *Judas!*"

President Tubman traveled from New York to Washington, D.C., and
from there boarded a private railroad coach to visit several universities in
the South, including Langston. Tolson apparently followed Tubman from
New York to Washington, D.C. There is a program card from the reception
for Tubman at the Mayflower Hotel, 20 October, among Tolson's papers. A
reception was scheduled at Langston for 9 November, but Tubman cut his
tour short and returned to New York City instead to spend his last few days
undergoing a routine physical examination and meeting with businessmen
interested in extending their activities to Liberia. He sailed from New York
City bound for Haiti on 12 November.

In the spring of 1954 Tolson was elected mayor of Langston. He was to be
reelected for three additional two-year terms, thus to serve a total of eight
years. Being a mayor was to prove useful to his writing career. Jack Steinberg
wrote to Tolson on 5 July 1955:

> So you've gone and done it. Become an Honorable. Makes a very interest-
> ing literary item, and I shall see that the news is spread. You're very generous
> in attributing some responsibility to Twayne, and we'll gladly accept.
> I think out of all this a book certainly ought to emerge. Make Langston
> immortal.

In a letter to Ruth marked 1956, but which was probably written late in Au-
gust 1955, Tolson anticipated being received by Mayor Wagner of New
York City, a fellow knight of the Star of Africa. He then added: "Sweet-
heart, this 'Mayor' title is a salestalking thing. Everybody bowing and scrap-
ing at City Hall. Whoever heard of a mayor and poet laureate all wrapped
up in one?"

Just before Tolson's third election, the *Oklahoma Black Dispatch* gave
this assessment of his mayoral career:

The Hub of a Universe

It is not often that a city is fortunate enough to have as its mayor an individual of international importance. Mayor Melvin B. Tolson, author, playwright, and poet laureate of Liberia, is well known on three continents. Last year he was the invited guest of President Tubman and was given acclaim by thousands who visited Monrovia at that time. As author of the "Ode to Liberia" [sic], his name was ringing from the Liberian borders of Sierre Leone on Northward to Dakar in French territory. His work is equally well known on the Old Continent among intellectuals.

In suggesting to the people of the town of Langston that they re-elect Mayor Tolson for another two-year term as their mayor, we are inclined to say that Mayor Tolson honors the town rather than the town honoring Dr. Tolson, whose erudition and learning have been turned during the past two years to sound municipal planning and urban growth. We believe the town has had a more orderly and planned existence. At least, it is the first time a governor of this state has seen fit to visit this municipality.[5]

Langston, Oklahoma's oldest Negro city, had celebrated its sixty-eighth anniversary the Sunday before, and Gov. Raymond Gary gave the major address celebrating the event.

But being mayor was not all ceremony and glory. Langston was a small, relatively poor city. Because of its size, the mayor was all too readily available to its citizens for complaints about poor lighting, the chat covering the dirt streets, or police services. A few entries in Tolson's notebooks refer to his experiences as mayor. Under the caption "Mayor's Sayings" he wrote: "To old Prof. Taylor: 'That petition is toilet paper and you know what to do with it.'" In a better humor he wrote an anecdote about an old man in Langston who, crippled, on relief, and with a wife half his age, persisted in adding to the population every year:

> Finally, under protests of the best ladies, I advised him to use birth control since he had no self-control. He said, "Too late, Mayor, I'm got another coming next month."
> I said, "Do you care if I give him a name?"
> "No, I'd like that!"
> I said, "Name him, Caboose!"

Another entry mixes humor and indignation:

> One good lady said to me: Your enemies have no plan. I asked them for one. You are mistaken, Madame. They do have a plan. They have the same plan for the city treasury that a hog has when he sticks his nose into the trough. They have the same plan that a rattlesnake has when he rattles at a rabbit. They have the same plan that the devil had when God kicked him out of heaven.

By his fourth term Tolson's family was trying to persuade him not to run again. The revision of *Harlem Portraits* had taken much longer than anticipated, and the feeling was growing that he was wasting valuable time on matters of local concern that were trivial in comparison to his literary ambitions. A letter remains among Tolson's papers suggesting that in fact Tolson's mayoral service was becoming mired in petty resentments. It is dated 8 May 1963, after Tolson left office, and it is from the chairman of the Langston City Council:

> The City Council voted unanimous [sic] on not paying you the $434.37 you loaned the city of Langston, Oklahoma. The Council asked for the note. O [sic] course, you know no note was ever drawn up. It was discussed that you were informed if you put your money into a city government there was no way of getting it back. For these two reasons the Council doesn't feel obligated to pay you at all.

But such a churlish note is not the most appropriate conclusion to a discussion of Tolson's experience as mayor. In the privacy of his journal he summarized the value of his experience of living in Langston, which must certainly have included his experience as mayor: "I wouldn't take anything, as a writer, for having lived in an All-Negro town: I now know *what* is human, *what* is American, *what* is Negro."

Nineteen fifty-five was as busy for Tolson as 1954 had been. He wrote a review of Jacques and Raissa Maritain's *The Situation of Poetry*, prepared and directed performances by the Dust Bowl Players of Jean Paul Sartre's *No Exit* and of Langston Hughes's *Simply Heavenly*, proposed making a tour of European capitals as poet laureate representing Liberia, and negotiated for a Lincoln University Press with himself as editor and Twayne doing the publishing and distribution. Late in the year he read portions of the *Libretto* over Voice of America. Shortly afterward President Felton Clark of Southern University attempted to persuade him to move to Southern University. And about this time he was elated to be invited to attend President Tubman's third inauguration in Monrovia during the first week of January 1956 at the Liberian government's expense.

Tolson reviewed the Maritains' *The Situation of Poetry* for the spring 1955 issue of the *Midwest Journal*. Early in this review he emphasized the triumph of literary modernism.

> When T. S. Eliot published *The Waste Land* in 1922, it sounded the death knell of Victorianism, Romanticism and Didacticism. When Eliot was awarded the Nobel Prize in Literature, the victory of the moderns was complete. Poetry will never be the same. The modern idiom is here to stay— like modern physics.

He then noted that the Maritains' title implies a dualism: "(1) the situation of poetry in the human spirit; (2) the situation of poetry in our time." To illustrate the first he summarized:

The business of poetry is not logical sense but poetic sense. The poem must be a poem, a work of art, *first*. . . .

Literature is not *life*; it is an *illusion* of life. It is the reality of the imagination, of the creative process itself. In the 19th century poetry began to become conscious of itself *as poetry*. It was no longer a poeticized sermon or moral. . . . "In poetry," Heidegger explains, "man is concentrated upon the depths of his human reality." And in line with this idea, the authors argue that "the poem is a vehicle of poetic inspiration as the flute is a vehicle of music, the painter's brush a vehicle of vision."

While poets are affected by the "complexity of our age—what W. H. Auden has called *The Age of Anxiety*"—even as are nonpoets, Tolson referred with approval to the Maritains' insistence upon distinguishing poetry from mysticism, magic, and more rational forms of knowledge:

The intuition of the poet differs from that of the mystic, magician and philosopher; the poet's aim is antipodal. Poetic knowledge is "germinative virtuality" and is objectified in the work of Art. A poet is interested neither in the control of a god nor in the revelation of God. He is the Greek *poietes*, the creator; and the effect of the poem is the Aristotelian *catharsis*.

This is a far more discriminating view of the poet's role than Tolson announced in "The Poet" in *Rendezvous with America*. These middle years found Tolson belatedly concentrating and focusing his own writing role. Craft or artistry assumed increasing emphasis. Artistry enables the poet's vision to survive the threatening flood of historic events. Yet the poet has no choice but to swim in the flood. Tolson qualified his approval of the Maritains' assessment of the situation of poetry with this final observation:

Perhaps the chief quarrel I'd have with the Maritains lies in their emphasis on the subjective. The poet does not live in a vacuum. He, like other men, is a tridimensionality: his biology, his sociology, his psychology. As Ben Jonson said of Shakespeare: he is both *born* and *made*. No man escapes his race, his milieu, his class, his moment of history. The reality of his epoch passes through his *chemique* [*chimie*] and shapes his idea and image, his content and form. The creator is created as well as his creation. Great Art does not repeat itself, but, like history, obeys the Heraclitean law of change.[6]

This review may have prompted Oliver Cromwell Cox, who was then teaching at Lincoln University in Jefferson City, where *Midwest Journal* was published, to send Tolson the table of contents to his forthcoming book, *The Foundations of Capitalism*, although, in light of their longstanding friendship, Cox may well have been planning to do so anyway. On 14 May, Tolson wrote a letter to Cox describing the relations he saw between his social convictions and his relatively new but fervent embrace of modernist literary assumptions:

I got the Table of Contents this morning. From what I could glean be-
tween the lines, it's colossal—stupendous. While I'm not a racist, I'm glad
that you of my so-called Race did it! I remember that Calverton said back in
the 30's that the Negro had never produced a profound thinker. He was ve-
hemently attacked, of course, in the dark bourgeois press. Had he lived, he
would have died happy! You are the Negro thinker who has breathed the
concepts of the stratosphere!

I'm not much of a letter writer, you will agree. But one thing is missing
that would add much to the Table—a chapter on Capitalism as reflected in
literature. This *must not* be ignored. It proves the whole theory of capital-
istic specialization, as nothing else I know. . . . You spoke to me about
esoterism in poetry; it's comparable to specialization in industry and com-
merce. In discussing maladjustments the greatest examples are found among
artists, as the most sensitive of subjects. . . . At one time the poet and
priest were one and the same man; now it's different. There's a reason for
that: the division of religion and literature.

Why was Shakespeare supreme in heroic individuality of his heroes? And
the last literary genius to assimilate the conventions of his age—Goethe?
These fit your thesis. The ebb and flow of economic epochs are always seen in
literatures. Surrealism, existentialism—all come within your scope, buttress
your case.

Cox did not heed Tolson's advice. It is hard to see how he could have
treated literature as a special touchstone of the development of capitalism
without seriously altering the rest of his discussion. But Tolson's suggestion
underlines once more how persistently he saw his own role as artist con-
trolled and directed by his sense of what was happening worldwide. The
esoteric nature of modern writing is a by-product of specialization in indus-
try and commerce, and black writers as well as white writers must anticipate
it and represent the dreams and needs of their people within the matrix of
this historic inevitability.

Shortly after writing to Cox on 14 May, Tolson directed and produced
Sartre's *No Exit* with the Dust Bowl Players. He was proud of the produc-
tion and later remembered discussing it with Richard Wright in Paris on his
return trip from Monrovia. *No Exit* was dedicated to Liberian Ambassador
Simpson, who did visit Langston and probably was present for the 27 May
performance of the play. There is a photo of Ambassador Simpson and Lang-
ston Hughes, among others, standing behind Tolson seated at a table with
pen in hand poised over a script. The photo is on a page of the playbill for
the 5 November production of *Simply Heavenly*, but the page is concerned
with the prior production of *No Exit*. If the photo was taken on 27 May, as
seems probable from the group assembled and the context, it is difficult to
explain Hughes's presence when coupled with a letter dated 28 May, the

next day, from Hughes to Tolson sent from New York City about *Simply Heavenly*. The letter's content gives no indication that Hughes and Tolson were together the day before.

Regardless of that minor mystery it is heartening to note that Tolson could turn from shouldering the weight of world history to planning a play about Jesse B. Simple, who looked at the strangely complicated goings on of the modern world through the shrewd, deflating skepticism of a street bar in Harlem. And Tolson respected and appreciated Jesse B. even as he respected and appreciated the genius and scholarship of Oliver Cox. In his letter Hughes informed Tolson that he had arranged to have Dave Martin, composer of the music for *Simply Heavenly*, send copies of the music to Tolson if Martin could find time between his engagements with the Sammy Davis band. Hughes also planned to be on hand for the performance of *Simply Heavenly*. Both Tolson and Hughes clearly understood that much care and craft were necessary to produce the unpretentious simplicity of Jesse B. Simple on stage. In a postscript, Hughes also wrote: "Just mentioned you in my 2nd autobiography." Apparently, however, the mention was later omitted.

On 4 August 1955, Jacob Steinberg wrote Tolson a formal letter that began: "This will confirm our arrangement whereby you are to serve Twayne Publishers as Associate Editor in charge of liaison with Lincoln University Press." A paragraph detailing Tolson's royalty share as compensation for this work followed. On 23 August, Horace Bond wrote Steinberg: "Announcement of the proposed Lincoln University Press would now be premature. I am all for it, and I have not the slightest question that our Board will accept the proposal." Bond explained why August was a bad month in which to get the necessary board approval, but he proposed to send a "round-robin" letter to members of the board after 1 September. He asked Steinberg for supporting information about Twayne Publishers and its first publications. He also suggested that, if Allen & Unwin had not yet found an American publisher for Kwame Nkrumah's autobiography, "this would be a 'natural' for the proposed Lincoln University Press." He then closed: "I can assure you that in my opinion, the acceptance of the idea of a *Lincoln Univeristy Press* by our trustees may almost be taken for granted. But I cannot get formal assent until early in September."

In the letter to Ruth written from New York late in August 1955, previously referred to, Tolson wrote, "I'm on my way to meet Bond at Twayne's, because Steinberg wants me, instead of Ciardi to rewrite Bond's 'History of Lincoln University'—200,000 words have been done on the mss. already." But for some reason the Lincoln University Press as proposed was not established. There is no record that Bond ever proposed it to Lincoln's governing board. A year later, on 25 September 1956, Steinberg complained to Tolson:

I wish you were a little easier to work with since I feel that in a business way we can help each other quite a bit. But what with the time and place barriers none of our discussions seem to get off the ground. For example, the Lincoln University Press business started off so swimmingly and nothing came of it. I should have thought that you would get Bond off his hobby horse and I am sure if you were somewhat nearer we could both of us have done some proselytizing.

Tolson's letter to Ruth from New York in which he mentions the meeting between him, Bond, and Steinberg is also full of other revealing news. Wiley Wilson remembers the events described in the letter vividly. Late in July or early in August 1955, his dad surprised him with a call from Union Station in Washington, D.C., to pick him up just a day after Wiley had arranged for his wife, Deloris, to visit her mother so that Wiley could spend a week in solitary seclusion studying for his comprehensive exams for his Ph.D. "As Dad was a nonstop talker who insisted that you listen so that you could respond, my studying ended. On Wednesday I gave up and called Aunt Pauline in Philadelphia to tell her that dad was coming to visit her."[7] Then Tolson traveled to New York after spending a few days in Philadelphia. His letter to Ruth from New York begins on a note of sentiment: "I guess it was foolish and expensive of me to call you as I did last night; but after 30 years you know how I am. I just wanted suddenly to hear your voice." He then described his meeting with Felton Clark, president of Southern University, over the possibility of moving to Southern:

> We talked and he balked on salary! Of course, his mind was on the Paris trip. However, he's paying expenses for my coming here! He wants me to go to Southern for an interview when he gets back. They want me like hell, but Felton says the legislators would have to be sold on the Litt.D. instead of the Ph.D. I told him my price was the same as theirs. And moreover, I have a name! Well, you told me to do it. He even considered giving me a year to decide and talk things over with you. My being a Mayor knocked him out. He said that title would make me the most unique poet in the world!

Before closing his letter, Tolson admonished, "Don't talk about the Southern Deal." Apparently this was one of several offers he received to move from Langston, but he did not move again until he accepted Tuskegee Institute's offer of the Avalon Chair in Humanities the year following his retirement from Langston.

In addition to describing his meeting with Clark, Tolson also told Ruth of reading *Libretto for the Republic of Liberia* for the Voice of America:

> Well, the poem was a great success! I delivered it over the Voice of

America—to all the continents and the seven seas. *The* Mrs. John Dulles was there, and we became chummy! She knew Harriet Tubman of my "Dark Symphony." We're to exchange ideas and books.

Tolson also wrote that he was "trying to catch Mrs. Walter White," that he had "got to see Langston on the play," that he was "to be received by Mayor Wagner of New York and the City Council in a formal presentation of the 'Libretto', since Tubman gave him [Wagner] also 'the Star of Africa,' " that he was discussing a possible agreement with the *New York Times* to do an article on President Tubman's inauguration, and that he had seen "the Ambassador again to draw up formal plans for a possible tour of European capitals." It is no small wonder that he was also "dead tired." But he did not forget his family concerns: "Tell Arthur not to worry. I'll get him placed. Just get that degree! You, too, this fall." Then with happy pride, "Things never looked brighter for this cynic!"

When Ambassador Simpson visited Langston in May for the performance of *No Exit* dedicated to him, Tolson had broached the possibility of being sent by Liberia on a tour of European capitals as the U.S. State Department had sent Robert Frost to Brazil and other nations. On 25 August, Tolson wrote to Simpson reminding him that Frost's tour of South American cities was evidence "that the cultural plenipotentiary to foreign capitals has become a cardinal feature of international public relations" and suggesting that his recent election as mayor of Langston, his appointment as associate editor of Twayne Publishers—"the only American Negro to occupy such a position"—and his poet laureateship of Liberia should give him "exceptional opportunities to promote the cultural welfare of the Republic through contacts with editors, mayors, professors, writers, and the intelligentsia of foreign countries."

Tolson's proposal was not accepted; however, by 31 November he had received an official invitation to attend President Tubman's third inauguration with all expenses paid. It was on that date that he wrote to the Bureau of Vital Statistics in Moberly, Missouri, for a copy of his birth certificate suggesting that he was born in Moberly, "February 6, 1900—or thereabout." In a letter to Bond on 5 December he indicated that he would be flying from New York City to Monrovia on 27 or 29 December and asked how Bond's manuscript (presumably the history of Lincoln University) was coming on. Bond replied on 19 December, somewhat chagrined that, although he too had received an invitation, "no reference was made to transportation." He added, "I have done nothing with the manuscript since I saw you last August." This probably refers to the meeting between Tolson, Bond, and Steinberg that Tolson had mentioned to Ruth. Bond's reference also probably indicates that at least at this date the Lincoln University Press was still considered a likely means of publishing Bond's history of Lincoln University.

Tolson did not write an article for the *New York Times* on Tubman's third inauguration, nor did he write about his experience of the inauguration in any other context I can find. There are invitations for cocktails, a garden party, and the inaugural ceremonies among Tolson's manuscripts. He apparently was well cared for and feted. He did write a poem for the occasion intended "For His Excellency William Vacanarat Shadrach Tubman, President of the Republic of Liberia." The poem seems hastily composed, and Tolson apparently made no effort to publish it afterward or even to bring it to anyone's attention. Perhaps in the ordinary course of affairs he did not care for the world to see the somewhat extravagant compliments he was willing to pay President Tubman on this special ceremonial occasion. Although crude, measured against his better poems, this poem still reveals his constant desire to outline a dream of international justice and brotherhood that might influence the plans and aspirations of those who directly control political power. "The Black Man's Burden" serves as a corollary to the themes developed in *Libretto for the Republic of Liberia*:

> Your Excellency, no laureate's rhyme
> Can add one jot or tittle to
> The stature of a man; so I
> Evoke the you-ness that makes you You:
> Liberia stretches forth her hand,
> In brotherhood to every land!
>
> We who had eyes to see and ears
> To hear the clock of history
> Prayed for this pillar of fire by night,
> The apocalypse of liberty:
> Liberia stretches forth her hand,
> In brotherhood to every land!
>
> Your master plan for Liberia
> Answers the dolichocephalic lie
> Versed in "The White Man's Burden" when
> He left his Magna Charta to die:
> Liberia stretches forth her hand,
> In brotherhood to every land!
>
> You were the midwife, patient, wise,
> Who helped Liberia give birth
> To miracles of rubber and gold
> Hid in the night-womb of the earth:
> Liberia stretches forth her hand,
> In brotherhood to every land!

You sceptred tribes with ballots, crowned
With suffrage the Afric woman; this boon,
A precedent for a continent,
Shall be waxing sun at noon:
Liberia stretches forth her hand,
In brotherhood to every land!

An Alfred the Great in Africa,
You visioned meccas for the youth,
Where hand and heart and head discover
El Dorados of modern truth:
Liberia stretches forth her hand,
In brotherhood to every land!

No Crusoe on a desert island,
You send your Talented Tenth afar,
To give and take, to unmake and make,
In the blood and sweat of things as they are:
Liberia stretches forth her hand,
In brotherhood to every land!

Like John of Patmos, you ensphered
Argosies across a continent,
Where, through dark ages only the feet
Of man and beast left their imprint:
Liberia stretches forth her hand,
In brotherhood to every land!

Before the United Nation's bar,
In a voice that Justice endowers,
You plead for freedom of thought and speech
For smaller as for bigger powers:
Liberia stretches forth her hand,
In brotherhood, to every land!

The walls of Jericho tumble down,
Two hundred million blacks defy
The White Man's Burden. "Africa
For Africans!" the Africans cry:
Liberia stretches forth her hand,
In brotherhood, to every land!

Perhaps because this single instance of foreign travel came so late in Tolson's life—near his fifty-eighth birthday—or perhaps because his stay in Monrovia was so caught up in official ceremonial gatherings, he made little effort to record his direct observations of Liberia, or for that matter of Paris on his brief stopover on his way back to the United States. This eager and curious traveler within the United States and within the world of books and ideas seemed, judging from the lack of any conspicuous record, curiously inattentive to these initial experiences of different lands and different people. Melvin, Jr., was studying at the Sorbonne at the time, and he remembers that the weather for the day of his father's visit was dismal. They spent much of the morning trying to find a restaurant where his father could have a proper American breakfast of ham and eggs. Then they met Richard Wright, and Wright and the two Tolsons talked for hours in a café. Melvin, Jr., remembers that much of their conversation centered on Wright's mystification at James Baldwin's surprisingly disparaging description of the role of *Native Son* in the history of black American writing in the recent publication of *Notes of a Native Son*.

Some years later Tolson told Joy Flasch that Wright pointed out a café where Jean Paul Sartre hung out, leading Tolson to describe the Dust Bowl Players' production of *No Exit*. Wright, according to Tolson, was incredulous that a Negro college would produce such a play. Tolson responded, "It was staged at Princeton. And if it was good enough for those white students, it's good enough for black students. After all, I went to a Little Ivy college." To Tolson's mention of Sartre's message that "Hell is other people," Wright was reported to have laughed and countered, "Hell is Mississippi." According to Flasch's notes, that led Tolson to observe that both Wright and Faulkner, "the two greatest writers of Whites and Blacks," saw hope on the horizon in spite of "the filth in the South." In support of his point Tolson pointed to the role Faulkner drew for the Negro in *Intruder in the Dust* and the significance of "Bigger's seeing through Max" in *Native Son*.

Following this one-day stopover in Paris, Tolson again stopped in Detroit on his way back to Langston. Arthur Tolson has retained a clipping, probably from the *Michigan Chronicle*, picturing Mayor Albert E. Cobo of Detroit extending a key to the city to Mayor M. B. Tolson of Langston, Oklahoma, who was returning from witnessing the inauguration of President Tubman of Liberia. This was probably the last ceremonial hurrah directly traceable to Tolson's being named poet laureate of Liberia. The laureateship plus his election as mayor in 1954 had been parlayed into a public relations extravaganza that over eight years counterpointed Tolson's embrace of literary modernism as the appropriate and inevitable means of expressing his visionary international populism.

On 25 September 1956 Jack Steinberg wrote to Tolson:

> How goes everything with you? Have you had a chance to put in some licks on *Harlem Portraits*? I look forward to reading this one of these days and I don't mind telling you that I await it with anticipation. *Libretto* sent the shivers up and down my spine but I didn't understand too much of it unless I heard the poet delivering his lines. *Harlem Portraits* I expect to be not only a literary but understandable hit.

Libretto was done. *Harlem Gallery* was to do. Not that *Harlem Gallery* would receive exclusive attention. Tolson's imagination was too restless for that. There would always be other projects as well. Yet *Harlem Gallery* was crafted much more deliberately than anything Tolson had previously written. He prepared pages and pages of metaphors, similies, and esoteric notes. The subject itself had been seeded in his imagination since at least 1932. The particular poems of *A Gallery of Harlem Portraits,* his first epic representation of Harlem life, are nowhere visible in *Harlem Gallery,* but the idea of Harlem as a city, and more particularly of a gallery within that city, being a measure of the civilization, in the fullest sense of the word, that a people had achieved—that idea sent out myriad roots and blossoms in his imagination over the many years since the seed had first been planted. This was not to be a forced flower as was *Libretto,* written in response to an honor that limited and controlled what was appropriate for him to write. Because Harlem was his own turf—commonly so considered by black Americans no matter where they lived—he felt freer to represent its failures and hypocrisies as well as its prophetic aspirations. Finally, *Harlem Gallery* was to be a summary poetic statement of years of self-examination and both intensive and extensive discussions with others on the role of the artist as a citizen of the black American community and the world and the promise of justice and beauty that art could bring to history.

Yet events would intrude upon the poet's task and distract him from his goals. The celebration of the sixty-eighth anniversary of the city of Langston became an important event as Oklahoma Governor Raymond Gary spoke in honor of the occasion. Tolson's pride in Langston and his interest in its history became an important element in his efforts to encourage Arthur, his second son, to continue graduate work and complete his Ph.D. Arthur eventually wrote a doctoral dissertation that evolved into a book published in 1972, *The Black Oklahomans, A History: 1541–1972,* of which the history of Langston is a significant part.

In early summer of 1957 Tolson was in Detroit, staying with Helen, writing the dramatic episodes of *Upper Boulders in the Sun,* to be performed as part of Oklahoma's golden anniversary. He wrote Ruth about how the writing was going:

Now for the play. When I wrote you, I'd started off red hot—that is creatively. Then I bogged down. I spent the time reading until my eyes were sore. Then my imagination started again. People don't know how the imagination works—day and night. I've been clicking ever since. It's hell trying to weave scraps of history into an integrated work of art. It has to be sound historically, yet it must be artistic. A play has to move or it becomes a talkie—especially a racial play. My eyes are opened. Some things are going to shock folk.

Ruth had sent him a copy of Roscoe Dungee's editorial praising his service as mayor and endorsing his candidacy for a third term. She also informed him of Horace Mann Bond's resignation as president of Lincoln University. Tolson was grateful for the editorial and surprised by Bond's resignation. Ruth also wrote him about the celebration of President and Mrs. G. L. Harrison's twenty-fifth wedding anniversary, for he responded to her description of the party with a compliment to her: "Yes, you really look great when you're fixed up—despite Father Time!" He intended to return to Langston for a couple of days around the first of July, "but there's really little business I can do. The play's the thing. So I may wait until I finish the thing." Nevertheless, he reassured her that he would be there for her graduation. Ruth received her M.A. degree from Oklahoma State University in education and library science that summer.

In September, Tolson wrote to Bond, now dean of the School of Education at Atlanta University, welcoming him back to the South, "the battlefield of ideas." Bond apparently had nominated Tolson for membership in the American Society of Africa Culture. Tolson gladly accepted and added:

> I was invited to the Congress, but I was minus the wherewithal. The invitation came from Director Alioune Diop. If Mr. Lehman underwrites another trip, see if you can pull me up the gangplank. I believe that an exegesis of "The Libretto" would reveal what has happened and what is happening and what will happen in the World of Color.

But neither "Mr. Lehman" nor anyone else offered to pay Tolson's way to future meetings of the Congress, and for a time his life settled back into a more regular routine.

In the fall of 1960 Dean Leroy Moore asked Tolson to review *The Purposes of Higher Education* by Huston Smith, apparently for a gathering of faculty. The first nine typewritten pages of the review survive among the Tolson papers and indicate some of his characteristic concerns. Unfortunately the review is not complete. Tolson began by remembering a book he read as a boy in his "clergyman-father's" study. This caused him to think of Aristotle's famous Academy, where the philosopher said to his students: "On the education of the youth depends the safety of the State," a statement Tolson found just as true in October 1960 in "the face of Intercontinental hydrogen bombs and guided missiles." After noting that Smith's book involves a history of human education, he approvingly quoted Robert Penn Warren: "I read history in order to get a perspective of myself." Tolson then added an important distinction between *training* and *education:* "Training enables a man to make a living; education enables a man to make a life. The Great Teacher of Nazareth said: 'I came that ye may have life, and live more abundantly.' "

Tolson suggested that most Americans identify with the Puritan or Victorian worlds of the past, "a world of clear-cut alternatives." He quoted Toynbee to point up his criticism of this predilection: "All America's problems are becoming human problems, of the kind that require patience and compromise, instead of . . . sheer energy and zeal." The American tendency to oversimplification, a tendency to substitute faith for truth, gave him an opening to repeat Francis Bacon's warning against the worship of idols, including the idols of the tribe, after which he added ironically: "Therefore, one should never let his conscience be his guide, according to comparative anthropologists like Franz Boas and Ruth Benedict."

To illustrate Smith's observations in his book about the selective process as a problem in man's efforts at objectivity, Tolson commented: "But to select is to leave out. For example, W. H. Auden, the greatest poet of England, told me that he never read any book reviews of his poetry. Why? Because the critics hampered him with their biases. On the other hand, I get a kick out of literary reviews, pro or con." On the problem of reconciling *objectivity* and *commitment*, Tolson said:

> The most powerful philosophical and literary groups in France today are called the Existentialists, who have been nicknamed the apostles of "Dreadful Freedom." They say that modern man is doomed to negative independence and the consequences are: loneliness, insecurity, insignificance, directionlessness, and meaninglessness. Neurosis and psychosis plague us. It is not an accident that the greatest novelists and dramatists and poets of France, England, and the United States are either pessimists or cynics. . . . The faculties and students in hundreds of American colleges and universities were shocked when Professor Trilling placed the venerable poet Robert Frost with the Eliots and Verlaines, who are prey to doom. The seriousness of this ideological battle was revealed when Pasternak, the greatest poet of Russia, was awarded the Nobel Prize in Literature and pandemonium raged around the civilized world, because of his novel *Doctor Zhivago*.

Tolson then noted, "Professor Smith emphasizes that in trying to escape from Dreadful Freedom one may embrace dictatorship or conformity," a danger Tolson fought most of his life. Some of these themes and references were already worked into the manuscript of *Harlem Gallery* then being prepared.

Sometime in 1960 Ruth suffered a breakdown. She was hospitalized and given shock treatment. Tolson's concern and fears for her can only be inferred. Her illness is not referred to in surviving letters, and apparently she recovered relatively rapidly with no recurrence of the emotional disorder. Ruth referred to this episode in her life in a conversation to me but did not elaborate or give it great significance in her husband's life.

Early in 1961 Tolson received a letter from John Howard Griffin, whose

Melvin B. Tolson

Black Like Me had excited considerable public interest the year before and apparently had moved Tolson to call the author. The letter was sent from Mexico on 24 January 1961:

> I have had a growing sense of guilt about you for some time. You first telephoned me during a time of great confusion; the second time you called I was ill and faced with a stack of work. I should have written you immediately, for you cannot guess how much your encouragement meant to me during that desolating time. Had I written, I should have told you that more than your encouragement was important to me—I was flattered to have such a distinguished colleague come to my side—more than flattered, moved, honored.
>
> Finally, late on a rainy night, high in the Sierra Madres, I put my work aside and write the letter I have long wished to write.
>
> I will be simple and straightforward with you. I feel that if we should meet we would "click." Indeed that we should be friends. There is a sort of unusual warmth in my admiration for you. Perhaps this is because I am not a poet, though I greatly loved French poetry (which is all that I know, all that I am really sensitive to, alas). I have made the attempt, but poetry in English does not reach me. Nevertheless, I can admire the poet, the man. All of this is very clumsily put.
>
> I hope that on my tour in April I will get somewhere in your vicinity and that we can at last meet. Also, if you ever get down into this country, my home is always yours. In the meantime, I hope that from time to time we may correspond.

It would be surprising if Tolson did not respond to this letter, but there is no indication among his surviving papers of further correspondence with Griffin.

In the fall of 1961, the first seven sections of *Harlem Gallery* were printed in *Prairie Schooner*, then edited by Karl Shapiro. A letter Tolson wrote to Ben and Kate Bell, 28 December 1961, indicates that the entire poem was completed by this time and that Shapiro had offered to publish the whole of it, but that Steinberg would not stand for it. "Capitalism again!" concluded Tolson. Much of the rest of the letter provides a striking view of Tolson informally justifying his literary modernism to a close friend and former student who sympathized with his political views:

> A puzzle to me: Shapiro and T. S. Eliot are in a knockout struggle over Esoterism and Obscurity in modern poetry and criticism, from the *N.Y. Times* through *Saturday Review*, etc. (Even the Venerable Frost has been dragged into the arena; but I can see him grinning and winking in damned Yankee style, in the unaccustomed limelight. A sense of humor is manna in the wilderness of Capitalism. The Irish and Jews and Sambos discovered that.) My work is certainly difficult in metaphors, symbols and juxtaposed ideas. There the similarity between me and Eliot separates. That is only

technique, and any artist must use the technique of his time. Otherwise we'd have the death of Art. However, when you look at my ideas and Eliot's, we're as far apart as hell and heaven. I guess Shapiro, a Jew of the Jews, sees that and takes me under his wing. I guess I'm the only Marxist poet Here and Now.

Now, about the little people. Remember "ideas come from above." If you went into the street and said to a ditchdigger in Chi, "Who is Shakespeare?" he'd say, "The greatest writer that ever lived." Now, he wouldn't know a damned thing about *Hamlet* but he might quote some of THE Bard's sayings that he picked up from the boys in the ditch. Ideas sift down. Marx and Lenin and Castro were not *of* the masses but *for* the masses. What does a Cuban peon know about *Das Kapital?* If you give him a copy, he'd wipe his behind with it! Well, a peon has to use *some* kind of paper. What's better than that you can't read.

There is not a greater strategist on the left than Old Man Du Bois. He always catches the Wall Street Boys with their pants down and their backs bent at the proper angle. I admire The Toe Groza of the Cleveland Browns. Who is a better place-kicker? Only Old Man Du Bois. Joined The Party at 93! Now, mind you, he's in Africa writing a Negro encyclopedia! *Jet* says he's the most popular Negro in Africa! Lawd, Lawd, Lawd!

Melvin, Jr., remembers his dad having trouble deciding on an appropriate ending for *Harlem Gallery:* "He stopped work on it, read tons of things, etc. and finally came up with the 'Black Boy, White Boy' sequence, which he found satisfying." Since the book was not published by Twayne until late 1964, Tolson's indication to the Bells that the entire poem was finished when the *Prairie Schooner* published the beginning sections probably needs to be accepted with reservations. There apparently was no shopping around for a publisher as there had been for *Libretto*. Jacob Steinberg was still Tolson's staunch friend as well as publisher, and the manuscript was his to publish. At any rate, by the spring of 1964 Tolson was reading galley proofs. Then came one more challenge, a challenge he was to face courageously and over which for a time he was even to triumph, but one against which ultimately he could only lose.

It began with unexpected stomach pains. Tolson's dread of cancer was based upon tragic family experience. His mother, Lera, his sister Yutha, and his brother Rubert had all previously been its victims. Since 1954 he had had regular examinations to watch for its symptoms. Even so neither his doctor nor he believed the abdominal pain was from anything other than the gallstones his doctor insisted on removing. The fear of cancer was repressed, but the operation revealed the worst—malignant cancer. Tolson's doctor predicted that he had no more than six months to live.

Tolson proved his doctor wrong. He was to live for more than two more years with the aid of modern medical technology, a skilled and dedicated physician, and the sustaining tonic of the extraordinary recognition that the publication of *Harlem Gallery* was to bring. *Harlem Gallery* was a greater triumph than *Libretto,* and the tributes it won were more satisfying. It was not necessary this time around to win the public's attention by playing up Tolson's unusual roles as poet laureate of Liberia or mayor of Langston. The tributes came directly in response to his achievement as a poet.

X

HARLEM GALLERY:

FROM CHATTEL TO ESQUIRE

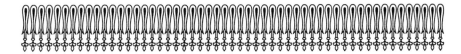

In 1938, when Melvin Tolson was deeply committed to radical proletarian political action, he wrote a *Caviar and Cabbage* column proclaiming that the most important event of the year for black America was Richard Wright's winning of the Federal Writers' Project Contest in New York City with *Uncle Tom's Children.* To be sure Richard Wright was a writer with a strong proletarian political message, and Tolson was as eager to point up the power of this message as he was the author's artistry:

> There's plenty of TNT in that title; and there's genius in the pen of this young storyteller who came out of the Delta bottoms, where Old Man River and the good white folk raise hell, when the Lord God Almighty has His back turned and the big senators are trying to decide if it's constitutional to have human bonfires on the lawn of the Courthouse Square.[1]

Tolson, like Herman Melville, believed that it was a primary task of the artist to expose unpopular truths, but he also believed from his earliest years as a writer that there was significant power in the art of the artist.

Tolson believed the black artist to be doubly burdened in American society by its racism and its corrupting materialism. In the same column he quoted a white editor to point up the significance of Wright's triumph over the handicap of racism:

> Arnold Gingrich, famous editor of *Esquire,* said in an editorial on Simms Campbell, brilliant Negro artist, that the road to success is twice as long, twice as hard, for a Negro genius as it is for a white man. Despite this handicap, Richard Wright defeated 600 white novelists. I take my hat off to him— not because he's a Negro but because he's a genius. Race is a biological myth and racial prejudice a virulent form of insanity.[2]

But in this same column Tolson also turned scornfully on the black press and its preoccupations with the frivolous concerns of its middle-class patrons. He was incredulous at how little attention had been paid to Wright's achievement: "My God! What does a Negro genius have to do to get his picture on the front page of a Negro weekly beside the six-inch-square grin of Madame Alpha Devine, proprietress of the Kitchen Mechanics Beauty Parlor?" Like W. E. B. DuBois, Tolson insisted that the destiny of his race not be corroded by a preoccupation with material success:

> A race is not judged by its dollars. Its skyscrapers. Its big business. Its high-powered cars. If these things measured racial and national greatness, America would lead the world. Wise men judge a race by its geniuses. Its arts and sciences. Its Einsteins and Charles Darwins and Voltaires. In other words, a people is judged by its brains. The Royal Society of Arts of Great Britain will tell you that if you take George Washington Carver out of Alabama you may blot out the whole state and the world wouldn't miss it twenty-four hours later.[3]

More than twenty-five years later, in *Harlem Gallery: Book One, The Curator,* Tolson continued to hold essentially these same positions, yet in his poem he explored and explained their implications with much more deliberate and subtle artistry. *Harlem Gallery* was to be the first volume of a five-volume poetic epic detailing the odyssey of the black American people. He began with the present, midtwentieth century, where his people had arrived. To measure how far they had come, what could be more appropriate than a gallery of their art? A people's place in history is determined in large part by their art, which is why Richard Wright's achievement was so important in 1938. *Harlem Gallery,* however, is narrated not from the perspective of the artist but from that of a gallery curator, a man who knows art and artists, but who also must mediate between the artists and the monied patrons of the gallery, patrons who if left to their own inclinations would destroy the very art they profess to be interested in. Tolson's poem dramatizes in considerable detail the Curator's friendships with artists while only sketchily implying his difficulties with "the bulls of Bashan" who provide the funds necessary for the gallery and his job, but the reader is nevertheless constantly reminded of the compromises demanded of the Curator.

The first artist we meet in the poem, John Laugart, has created a painting titled *Black Bourgeoisie,* which, like Richard Wright's *Uncle Tom's Children,* carries an explosive charge. In addition to John Laugart, the Curator has two other artist-friends who play major roles in the poem. Mister Starks is a pianist, a conductor, a composer, and a poet. Hideho Heights is a "bi-facial" poet, who composes the "racial ballad in the public domain" as well as "the private poem in the modern vein." Together they extend the meaning of art within the poem to encompass music and literature as well as the visual arts. The vivid personal stories of these three dramatize the wasting effects that the pervasive American racism and the unwitting hostility of the black middle class with its debilitating fascination with money and display have on the seriously committed black artists. They also document and inspire the meditations and the discussion of the Curator concerning the cultural significance to be gleaned from observing the symbiotic relation of the artist and his audience.

Tolson added yet one more major character to extend and challenge the Curator's observations, an Africanist and an African, Dr. Obi Nkomo, who "absorbs alien ideas as Urdu/Arabian characters." Nkomo is at home with the most sophisticated Western ideas, yet he retains the wisdom of the tribal traditions of his native Africa. In a limited sense his life telescopes the several centuries of the black American odyssey, but, by eschewing the middle passage, the experience of slavery in America and all of its biological and social consequences, he is also set apart as an objective, albeit intensely interested, outsider. He is ironic and penetrating and often challenges with good reason the Curator's positions. The Curator respects his wit and frequently quotes his wisdom.

Harlem Gallery is divided into sections headed by the twenty-four letters of the Greek alphabet. Hideho Heights upon entering the Harlem Gallery challenges the precedence of the visual arts by ironically reminding his audience of the biblical injunction, "In the beginning was the Word. . . . not the Brush!" The prophetic biblical tradition gives a special resonance to such Greek terms as *logos, alpha,* and *omega,* and the use of the Greek alphabet suggests both the comprehensiveness and the wholeness associated with moving from alpha to omega. Tolson intended a comprehensive epic representation of the event-filled odyssey of Afro-America, yet he also strongly believed that the midtwentieth century was a transition period in world history, which, though turbulent and threatening, nevertheless held promise that the fullest flowering of Afro-American culture and the fullest realization of world citizenship were still in the future.

Tolson chose to use again the odic form he had found congenial in *Libretto;* however, this ode also carries with it the distinguishing traits of the dramatic monologue that shaped many of the poems of *A Gallery of Harlem Portraits.* Because of its structure, the best way to understand the dramatic and argumentative developments of *Harlem Gallery* is to examine it section by section, in the poem's own order.

The first five sections of the poem, "Alpha" through "Epsilon," are an introduction to the Curator and his views on art. More particularly, the Curator explains the meaning that the Gallery has for him and for the historic moment, gives a rather self-deprecating description of his own professional qualifications, makes a testament to the power and authority of art and the artist, and recognizes the forces inimical to both.

Thus the Curator begins by noting that the Harlem Gallery as an "Afric pepper bird" awakens him to "a people's dusk of dawn." In the *Libretto*, Tolson made frequent references to DuBois's *Dusk of Dawn*. Here the Curator echoes the phrase to suggest that the Gallery informs its viewers of both the obscured richness of its people's past and the veiled prophecy of its people's future. In both *Caviar and Cabbage* and *Libretto*, Tolson quoted Dr. James E. Kwegyir Aggrey's description of Africa as "a moral interrogation point that challenges the white world." Since perception of Africa is linked to the perception of Afro-Americans and their history, and since both are matters of contention between those who wish to denigrate Afro-Americans and those who wish to recognize their achievement, the Curator sardonically images the age as "a dog's hind leg," which, like the question mark, is suggestive of the geographic shape of Africa. The image suggests that the age's "moment of truth [is] in pawn," yet to be redeemed and recognized.

The moral drama of this moment in history is then suggested by the anguished response of Beelzebub, the Lord of the House of Flies, to Goya's painting *The Second of May*, picturing the Spanish people's heroic defense against the invasion of Napoleon's force led by Marshall Murat, Napoleon's brother-in-law. Beelzebub's discomfort before the truth of the artist's picture anticipates a later scene when Guy Delaporte III, a patron of the Harlem Gallery, comes face-to-face with John Laugart's *Black Bourgeoisie*. The subject of Goya's painting and its effect on the Lord of the House of Flies also emblemize the reaction of the Great White World to the people's struggles in Africa and Asia. While the Curator is awakened by an Afric pepper bird to a people's dusk of dawn, the Great White World is bedeviled by alarm birds signaling what is happening on the Day of Barricades in Asia and Africa. Like Buridan's ass, the Great White World is immobilized by its ambivalence toward the revolutionary events occurring in Asia and Africa.

From describing the Gallery and its historical significance, the Curator turns with self-conscious mockery to picturing himself. He represents himself as sometimes playing "Roscius as tragedian" and sometimes "Kean as clown." Without the help of the stage mechanism professionally known as "Sir Henry's flap," which would enable him to disappear from this world as he might find it convenient, he sticks his neck out by choosing as a curator the high points of human history on which he and his gallery viewers are to venture. He accepts the risk of representing the truth of history selectively. He is well aware that those who would change man's nature through changing his view of the world are seldom given a friendly reception. More particularly, he knows that those who have attempted to make black America's portion of the American heritage visible have often been treated violently.

The "dry husk-of-locust blues . . . syncopating between / the faggot and the noose" causes him to question whether his task of preparing the rich and telling art of his people for public viewing does not set him up like a Hambletonian sheep for fleecing, if not for slaughter. The pervasive American "myth of the Afroamerican past," like "the lice and maggots of the apples of Cain," creates the terrible price of such fear.

Images of the Southwest movingly suggest Tolson's own empathetic identification with the Curator's bluesy world-weariness:

> Sometimes the spirit wears away
> in the dust bowl of abuse,
> like the candied flesh of the barrel cactus which
> the unpitying pitch
> of a Panhandle wind
> leaves with unpalatable juice.

The Curator concludes his self-portrait by affirming the strength he gains from repeatedly questioning his own identity as a distinct individual, as a human being, and as a Negro. Nevertheless, that questioning goes on amidst the confusing mix of the "clockbird's / jackass laughter," or the noise of those who would confound the truth with their prejudices, and "the pepper bird's reveille," the awakening of a people's dusk of dawn. Thus "the plain is twilled and the twilled is plain."

The Curator begins Beta by asking two basic questions: "*what* is man?" and "what *manner* of man is this?" The first question is rhetorically addressed to Tempora because it seeks to go beyond time, to raise a question about the essential nature of man. But to face such a question is also a humbling experience, since it is next to impossible to find a comprehensive answer. Hence the question's principal value is as a means of pulling down "the ladder of sophistry." But man does live in time and place. So the second question, addressed to Mores, is also relevant, "what *manner* of man is this?" But again the Curator suggests a paradoxical value to the question by his parenthetic comment, "Guy the ologists in effigy!" Tolson frequently mocked the pretentiousness of abstract systems of thought and even more the rigidity of social institutions, such as political parties or churches, that were based on abstract systems that do not adapt to historical change. Isms and ologies, to his mind, were more likely to interfere with accurate perception than to aid it.

The Curator, as his author, also values skepticism. Without the ability to question and reject, one cannot know "the archimidean pit and pith of man." But he does express faith in art and the artist as the most dependable sources of an accurate knowledge of man: "go to Ars by the way of Pisgah" and "to the ape of God, / go!" He does not have much patience with lotus eaters and insists that to explore the "*in* and *out* of man" the nice discrimination suggested by "the clarity / the comma gives the eye" is of much greater use than the clouded distant perspective indicated by "the head of the hawk / swollen with rye."

The Curator renounces any ambitious claims for his personal taste or perceptions. He insists, however, that the false will be distinguished from the true by the inevitable evolutionary process of human life:

> The great god Biosis begets
> the taste that sets apart
> the pearls and olivets.

He modestly acknowledges that again and again he has personally failed to meet the challenge of great minds and great souls who make extraordinary demands on their audience. "In the drama Art," he plays only "a minor vocative part," as "an ex-professor of Art." He emphasizes the *ex*, as he proclaims his freedom from professional vanity or biasing commitment to any particular artistic movement: "not even a godling ism of Art rises up to bow to, / nor a horseshoe bias perches above the door." But while he "was not gilded . . . with the gift of tongues," like "the Young Men labeled by their decades / The Lost, The Bright, The Angry, The Beat," he nevertheless has a quiet trust and pride in his own professional commitment:

> but within the flame is a core
> of gas as yet unburnt
> and undetected like an uninflected spoor.

Thus with ironic detachment he confidently caricatures the movements of the last few decades:

> As a shoemaker
> translates a second-hand boot,
> each decade reshaped the dialectics of
> the owl's host,
> the lamb's bleat,
> the wolf's cry,
> the hyena's laugh.
> As serpents, sly,
> The Lost, The Bright, The Angry, The Beat
> (tongues that tanged bees in the head around the clock)
> did not stoop the neck to die
> like a dunghill cock.

In "Gamma" the Curator makes an eloquent tribute to the magical power of art to give shape and meaning to the ponderous reality of human history. His opening statement recognizes both the redemptive and the confusing aspects of art in a democratic state: "The mecca Art is a babel city in the people's Shinar." Apostates and apostles jostle each other in crude and clamorous righteousness. Experience, unredeemed by art, "downstages Heart and Hand and Soul," creating a midnight show in which "No catharsis homes; / no empathy calls." Enter the artist, in the person of Utrillo, and the "*dis*figured Montmartre street" is *trans*figured "into a thing of beauty, to haunt / the unhaunted and the undaunted."

This magical redemptive power of the artist is linked by the Curator to a memory of the shrewd faith of his "Afroirishjewish" Grandpa who believed that

> *somehow,*
> the Attic salt in man survives the blow
> of Attila, Croesus, Iscariot,
> and the Witches' Sabbath in the Catacombs of Bosic.

This ability of man to survive extraordinary trials by his wit will enable him to cross "the wilderness Now" from "the dread sea Hitherto" to "the promised land Hence." Thus the Curator links the magical wit of the artist with the tough aspiring faith that enables man to believe in a progressive human history while acknowledging at the same time the pervasiveness of barbaric destruction.

"In salon, café, and studio, / from Greenwich Village to Montparnasse," tempered by the chastening blues experience—in *Libretto* Tolson equated black ghetto laughter with the Yiddish *lachen mit vastchekes*, "laughing with needles stuck in you"—the Curator's "eyes and ears have shadowed the pros and cons" "across the dialectic Alps from Do to Do," the high points that art has created out of human experience. The extraordinary range of the Curator's selective imagination, this "magicked pageant," is indicated by two powerful paintings with sharply contrasting effects: Paolo's *Sodom*, which by its terrifying indictment represents the power of art to penetrate gaudy human evasions to reach a cleansing truth, and Tintoretto's *Paradise*, which encourages and enhances human aspirations with its pulsing colors.

In "Delta" the Curator ironically considers the relation of the artist to his age, his heroic persistence when he is at odds with his age, the raison d'être of art, and the magic power art has over its lovers. He begins by asserting that, no matter what the historical condition, the artist's brush is controlled by either God or Caesar. The Curator has little faith, however, in any individual critic's ability to determine which controls any individual brush. A work of art ultimately must be measured by the people it represents:

> the world-self of the make
> believe becomes the swimming pool of a class,
> the balsam apple
> of the soul, and by the soul and for the soul,

Melvin B. Tolson

> or silvered Scarahaeus glass
> in which Necessity's *figuranti* of innocence and guilt
> mirror themselves as they pass.

If a false art, "brass," awakens the trumpet of a time, resulting in a mistone, the pain suffered by the age is only "the ghost of the pain / the artist endures." Like Everyman, the artist collects and endures the pain of his age alone.

But the Curator pays tribute to the strength and endurance of the artist in a series of complimentary metaphors, although the artist may survive his tasks at the cost of becoming a pathetic figure:

> The artist
> is
> a zinnia
> no
> first frost
> blackens with a cloven hoof;
> an eyeglass
> —in the eye of a dusty wind—
> to study the crosses and tangles in warp and woof;
> an evergreen cherry
> parasitic upon a winter sun;
> a paltry thing with varicose veins
> when the twelve fatigues are done.

The élan necessary to the artist may be a delight or a curse as he lives "through golden age and dark." Siva, "the Vedic god of the snaky noose," is invoked to warn the artist stoically to refrain from substituting his personal passion or lust for the failure of prophetic power:

> Let thy blue eyes
> resist white stars of red desire.

The impulse to create art frustrates objective description, but it is recognizable intuitively. It "is a question mark: without the true flight of the bat, / it is a hanker in the dark." Since it is a reflection of what one is capable of seeing, it takes on a variety of colors and shapes and a varying sense of drama:

> "What color can escape
> the fluky flues in the cosmic flux?"
> Perhaps the high-C answer lies
> in the wreck the sea sucks
> back into her bowls. Let
> the *Say* be said:

"In Philae the color is blue;
  in Deir-el-Baheri red;
  in Abydos yellow—
and these are by the ravens fed."

Ultimately art must pass an even stronger test than the taste test to which Elizabethans subjected their wine and meat—it must pass the test of survival, of escaping extinction, which is constantly threatened from many sides.

   Yet if art is inextricably bound by the time and place from which it issues, it nevertheless is capable of arousing a response so passionate that it seems timeless in its intensity. Thus the Curator concludes this section lecturing like a professor, but a professor whose respect for the austere dedication of scholarship can be translated into a moving tribute to the vivid astonishment art is capable of evoking:

Art
is not barrel copper easily separated
        from the matrix;
      it is not fresh tissues
    —for microscopic study—
         one may *fix*;
   unique as the white tiger's
    pink paws and blue eyes,
          Art
   leaves her lover as a Komitas
deciphering intricate Armenian neums,
      with a wild surmise.

"Epsilon" is the conclusion of the Curator's introductory disquisition on art and its relation to milieu and a preparation for the shift to the more dramatic action of the poem, beginning with the Curator's visit to John Laugart's studio in "Zeta," the next stanza. The Curator opens and focuses the section with a scathing reference to the force that has bedeviled all Afro-American history in many pernicious disguises, "the idols of the tribe."

   In 1897, some months before Tolson was born, W. E. B. DuBois, addressing the American Negro Academy, spoke of the "distinct mission" of the Negro race: "It is our duty to conserve our physical powers, our intellectual endowments, our spiritual ideals; as a race we must strive by race organization, by race solidarity, by race unity to the realization of that broader humanity which freely recognizes differences in men, but sternly deprecates inequality in their opportunities of development."[4] A few years later in *Souls of Black Folk*, published when Tolson was five years old, he posed, in foreboding terms, these questions:

What if the Negro people be wooed from a strike for righteousness, from a love of knowing, to regard dollars as the be-all and end-all of life? Whither, then, is the new world quest for goodness and Beauty and Truth gone glimmering? Must this, and that fair flower of freedom which . . . [sprang] from our father's blood, must that too degenerate into a dusky quest of gold?[5]

DuBois's sense of the race's mission was broadly felt and frequently repeated during Tolson's youth. The warning DuBois voiced by identifying the most obvious threat to this sense of mission also became frequently repeated, particularly by ministers, artists, and intellectuals.

In 1957, while Tolson was writing *Harlem Gallery*, E. Franklin Frazier published *Black Bourgeoisie*. Tolson had no trouble accepting the strongest indictment Frazier made of the black middle class. For Tolson, the Lord of the House of Flies, or Beelzebub, is continually working to corrupt or disrupt the progression of human history by encouraging the worship of false idols, the idols of the American tribe. The black bourgeoisie, or the bulls of Bashan, worship the most corrupting idol of all, money, which threatens to co-opt the authentic democratic dream of Americans and of peoples everywhere. The false idol, race, was created to serve capitalistic interests. It divided the world's people and left a bitter but proud cultural legacy for those who were subjected to exploitation through its worship. It is an extraordinary challenge, requiring the toughest wit, the most searching scholarship, and the boldest imagination to embrace and celebrate this cultural legacy without inversely or perversely idolizing race and thus inadvertently worshiping the very idol that has created such havoc in Afro-American history.

Thus the Curator announces with clear and extreme distaste the command he feels required to resist or, through some imaginative subtlety, to only seem to satisfy:

> The idols of the tribe
> in voices as puissant as the rutting calls
> of a bull crocodile, bellow:
> "We
> have heroes! Celebrate them upon our walls!"

He notes musingly, in keeping with his assumption that "Art / is not barrel copper easily separated / from the matrix," that Rembrandt's pool was a Dutch canal, not Siloam, and "Milton's Lucifer was a Cavalier— / his God a Roundhead." But he concludes that these are:

> dramatis personae of the ethos
> miracled to befool
> the hubris of the tribe.

He acknowledges the insidious power of Beelzebub, "whose graven images of blood and class . . . / infix the heart of an Ishmael / with the cold and yellow eyes / of the elite of serpent complexity." A nod from the bulls of Bashan "is worse than a brief / from Diable Boiteux." The power of the bulls to influence belief threatens to fix "the center of gravity of the man inside." The very extravagance of this power to tempt the artist from his authentic God-given function is cause for weeping. Nevertheless, despite the formidable power of the bulls, punningly instanced by the Sicilian Bull (the torture device described by Pliny) and Sicilian Vespers (the thirteenth-century massacre of the French at Easter),

Art's
yen to beard in the den
deep down under root and stone
fossick gold and fossiling
stands out
like a whale's
backbone.

This concluding tribute to the truth-seeking nature of art serves as a stage upon which a truth-seeking artist will appear in "Zeta," the next section.

John Laugart is the "savage-sanitive" artist the Curator's generalizations about art and milieu prepare us for. He is

—a Jacob that wrestles Tribus and sunders bonds—
discovers, in the art of the issues
of Art, our pros, as well as our cons,
fused like silver nitrate used
to destroy dead tissues.

The Curator calls at Laugart's obscenely impoverished Harlem flat, sees Laugart's painting *Black Bourgeoisie*, and knows at once that his responsibility as a Curator is fated. As a scholar-critic, he sees the painting with the joy of making a great discovery. As an administrator of a gallery, dependent upon the support of Philistines, he knows that he is in trouble. Laugart's painting "will wring from their babbited souls a Jeremian cry!"

The Curator concludes "Zeta" with a postscript telling that Laugart was robbed and murdered in his flat. The news, however, is anticlimactic. The Curator's initial picture of Laugart is of an artist mugged by the neglect and antagonism of the world in which he lives and paints. Wearing his rags proudly, Laugart nevertheless acknowledges, as he sits on his rickety bed: "The eagle's wings, / as well as the wren's, grow weary of flying." But Laugart's faith in the power and durability of his work in contrast to his own life is staunch:

> A work of art
> is an everlasting flower
> in kind or unkind hands;
> dried out,
> it does not lose its form and color
> in native or in alien lands.

And the integrity of his commitment never wavers: "I shall never sell / mohair for alpaca / to ring the bell." The Curator has no choice but to acknowledge the power and authority of both painter and painting. Upon seeing the painting, it is as if he has been transported to John's exile on the Isle of Patmos, and he is filled with a sense of prophecy:

> *Here emerges the imago*
> *from the importance of the chrysalis*
> *in the dusk of a people's dawn—*

The scene shifts in "Eta" to Aunt Grindle's Elite Chitterling Shop where the Curator meets Dr. Obi Nkomo, "the alter ego / of the Harlem Gallery." Nkomo, as alter ego, serves not in opposition to the Gallery, but rather as a Socratic questioner of its functions. He has as much respect as the Curator for art and the artist. When the newsboy announces the death of General Rommel, the Desert Fox (thus dating the action of the poem to 1944), Nkomo is moved to comment: "The lie of the artist is the only lie / for which a mortal or a god should die." Since Nkomo is "unharassed by the *ignis fatuus* of a lost job," he is not easily intimidated. Thus Mr. Guy Delaporte III and others have difficulty knowing how to deal with him. The Curator suggests that his disinterested concern for humanity, his "*All hail to man*," causes him to function as a touchstone separating the pretentious and the prideful from the genuine. But his tempered skepticism, his insistence on seeing man as a product of the tridimensionality that Tolson himself often referred to, is not to be confused with cynicism or absurdism. He defines a masterpiece as the artist's *vis viva*, either "A virgin or a jade . . . / to awaken one, to pleasure one— / a way-of-life's aubade," a mildly ironic echo of the Curator's opening description of the Gallery awakening him "at a people's dusk of dawn."

Nkomo's reference to an imaginary "virgin or jade" as the subject of an artistic masterpiece is then comically counterpointed by the appearance of the wife of Dipsy Muse, a realistic jade, who flies into a formidable rage at the sight of her husband's dissipation. Nkomo makes this scene a matter of humorous philosophic speculation, "O Romeo O Casanova, / *prithee*, what is chivalrous—what, barbaric?" Then implying the question is not worth great worry, he answers it indirectly by another tribute to the life-fulfilling or, in the truest sense, *civilizing* value of art:

From Chattel to Esquire

When a caveman painted a rubric
figure of his mate with a gritstone,
   Eros conquered Thanatos.

Nkomo ironically suggests that, because he has made the cultural journey from native veldt to Harlem in one lifetime, he is not as likely to become entangled in the half-assimilated, self-defeating preconceptions of his Western friends.

His confidence draws a wondering challenge from another customer: "Mister, *who* are you?" He answers the question with his name, but rebukes its superficiality by changing it to "*what* am I," a question that tests "the will / of Solon and Solomon." That question leads him to remember a story told him as a Zulu lad of an eagle raised among chickens. The eagle had to be encouraged several times to fly because his wings were made useless by his assumption that he was truly a chicken. Nkomo then pointedly asks his challenger, "*what* am I? / Mister, *what* are you?" While he insists that he does not know the answer, the challenge is clear.

Nkomo "eyes / the needle of the present to knit the future's garb." He speaks "to the man Friday in Everyman / boned and lived and veined / for the twelve great fatigues to the Promised Land." He has found his way between the "black Scylla—and white Charybdis." And, although experience has taught him to be skeptical, he has "not forgot / the rainbows and the olive leaves against the orient sky." It is Gibbons, the historian, not Thomas of Celano, the lyric tenor, who "hymns the *Dies Irae!*"

"Theta" is written ex cathedra. Presumably it is a meditation of the Curator's, but there seems little reason to distinguish between author and character. The meditation concerns race and art and ultimately makes an important distinction between the pleasure derived from art and the more immediately vivid attractions of "Happiness." The section opens with an imaginary castle of vanity, in which "Black Keys and White Keys," designed by art to complement each other, as "Changs and Engs" in nature, are nevertheless at odds. "Their hostess, / Marquise de Matrix," whose name is self-explanatory, attempts to smooth over the argument by paraphrasing Robert Frost: "Something there is in Art that does not love a wall." Echoing Blake, she also mocks the futility and pretension of trying to separate what has in fact already been genetically united: "What dread hand can unmix / pink and yellow?"

Both Nature and Art are thus "dedicated to oneness." In the long view they "ignore / the outer and inner / of a person, a place, a thing." As alma maters, another name for Marquise de Matrix, their "eyes unbridled," they "explore / the whole of the *rete mirabile*." Art is pictured as a woman with enough respect for herself to demand respect from others. As "the woman

Pleasure," she "makes no blind dates, but keeps the end of the tryst with one." She is distantly related to "Happiness," but happiness is capricious and of dubious virtue. By implication the dire warnings about happiness, "a bitch who plays with crooked dice / the game of love," reinforce the stern demands and the ultimate rewards of art as pleasure, the end of the tryst. Happiness, though related, cannot be trusted as art can be.

Following this allegorical meditation, "Iota" places us in the Harlem Gallery on its opening day, with the Curator and Dr. Nkomo as "Hrothgarian hosts / closemouthed and open-eyed." If the Curator and Nkomo are guarded in what they say to those entering the Gallery, the Curator nevertheless provides the reader with an uninhibited description of the exhibit in the Gallery. True to the Curator's opening description of the Gallery as an Afric pepper bird awakening him at a people's dusk of dawn, this exhibit is intentionally free of reassuring "nightingales of the old Old World." The exhibit's "flats and sharps of pigment—words— / quake the walls of Mr. Rockefeller's Jericho / with the new New Order of things." The prophetic power of art is the organizing principle.

The exhibit is divided into four sections, each in a separate wing. The East Wing houses murals ("waterglass / on dry plaster"), which represent "paeans and laments of identities / signed in the thought and felt hinterlands of psyches," and watercolors, which "echo the monastic archetypes / of a haunted master" in their simplicity ("fig leaf and barebone"), free of the "Purse pride" of gold, silver, or brass. The "oddly odd or oddly even / of reality and fable" are represented to illuminate "the new New Order of things," which requires one to face "fate fating / Now" so that the accents and nuances of success and disaster are newly subdued and vivified.

The West Wing offers no calm relief. Synaesthetically "the tomtoms of Benin" and "fetishes unseen" via the artistic experiments of Paris and Harlem can be heard and seen among the moderns. In oils, street and alley scenes hidden from view by the blindness induced by the idols of the tribe are now seeable and made to speak to us "in our cis—Apocalypse." The stage of our world is reset in beauty and in terror.

The North Wing's "burnt-in portraits . . . / enmesh Negroid diversity," including "its Kafiristan gaucherie" and "its Attic wit and nerve." "This is Harlem's Aganippe," its fountain of inspiration, in sharp contrast with the way white America has constantly represented black America as a "problem," "America's itching aitchbone." The biological and cultural diversity of Harlem is celebrated, and here creative imagination is revealed working in conjunction with biological and social realism:

> All shapes and sizes and colors of boots
> from the ape cobbler's last

for every actor in the Harlem cast
    entertain, absorb, or vex
    as the egg trot in the design
    goes awry or toes the line
      while trafficking,
      in the human comedy,
    with *Bios* and *Societas* and *X*
      as well as the divine.

The South Wing houses the Curator's concession to the demands of the bulls of Bashan. Here are the heroes that the idols of the tribe demand, the "dusky Lion Hearts" in fresco and secco. Nkomo points out the irony of this exhibit as he refers to this "Heralds' College" as *"afterwit's aftermeat."* He also reiterates a skeptical comment about the pretensions of a feudal reverence for genealogical history that Tolson once aimed at the pretensions of racial purity assumed by Hitler and his vaunted Aryanism, although Nkomo's comment is with indulgent humor:

        If
a Bourbon should shake his family tree
    long enough . . . he
    —beyond a Diogenic doubt—
would kneel at a mourners' bench,
      dressed in black crepe,
      as cannibal and idiot,
        rapist and ape,
        tumble out.

These "unsynchronized opposites, / gentlemen and galoots," are nevertheless "authentic as a people's autography." But, the Curator adds,

      this immaturity,
     like the stag tick's
     will disappear
     like its wings,
when it settles upon a red red deer.

The Curator closes the tour by praising Balzac, who "surpasses the Zolas, old and new," as a *de*-fetishist "in frescoes of bourgeois reality."

In "Kappa," Guy Delaporte III, the chief representative of the bulls of Bashan, is mockingly pictured with his wife as he makes his way through the Gallery until he stops in angry resentment before John Laugart's *Black Bourgeoisie*. He "takes his stand, / a wounded Cape buffalo defying everything and Everyman!" Nkomo observes the confrontation from a distance and calls it to the attention of the Curator. Nkomo's opening comment with its echo of Hughes's *Montage of a Dream Deferred* makes clear the threat Delaporte represents: "Is it not / the black damp of the undisturbed pit / that chokes the vitals—damns the dream to rot?" The Curator acknowledges Nkomo's point: "On its shakedown cruise, / The *Black Bourgeoisie* runs aground / on the bars of the Harlem Blues." But Nkomo insists that the painting is doing its work:

> This work of art is the dry compound
> fruit of the sand-box tree,
> which bursts with a loud report
> *but* scatters its seeds quietly.

The Curator expands Nkomo's comment by likening this confrontation to the historical drama of André Derain leaving his compatriot Fauves to organize a famous collection of modern French masters for Crown Prince Wilhelm's palace:

> *A night like this, O Watchman,*
> *sends a Derain to Weimar*
> *to lick the Brissac jack boots*
> *of Das Kapital that hawks things-as-they-are.*

But the Curator also notes that Derain's perfidy

> did not crush like a mollusk's shell,
> in café and studio,
> the *élan* of Courbet, Cézanne, and Monet,
> nor did the self-deadfall of the Maginot
> palsy the hand of Chagall,
> Matisse,
> and Picasso.

In "Lambda," Hideho Heights arrives at the Gallery and boisterously breaks the tension for the Curator. Heights is named after one of Tolson's Wiley debaters, and his apology for being late hints at the disillusion that Tolson felt with the Communist party's insensitivity to racial politics in America:

> Sorry, Curator, I got here late:
> my black ma birthed me in the Whites' bottom drawer,
> and the Reds forgot to fish me out!

Heights as a poet, "the vagabond bard of Lenox Avenue," enters the Gallery with a competitive challenge, "In the beginning was the Word / . . . not the Brush!" He ignores the exhibit and launches immediately into an enthusiastic description of his just concluded visit to the Daddy-O Club and then into reading a poetic tribute to Louis Armstrong, which he wrote as a consequence of that visit. Later in the poem, in "Chi," the Curator will

From Chattel to Esquire

reveal "the split identity / of the People's Poet." His tribute to Satchmo, "the racial ballad in the public domain," will be contrasted to "E. & O. E.," "the private poem in the modern vein." That distinction suggests that Hideho's tribute to Satchmo is a poetic compromise similar to the pictures of Lion Hearts in the South Wing. His public poem is written for the horizontal audience, his private for the vertical.

The scene shifts for the next five sections, "Mu" through "Xi," from the Harlem Gallery to the Zulu Club, a Harlem nightclub often as reminiscent of the twenties as it is of the forties or fifties. On one occasion Hideho passes liquor to the Curator under the table as if Prohibition were still the law, although the Wits are also served potently alcoholic Zulu Chief cocktails. Here a mix of congenial artists and intellectuals enjoys the popular pleasures, the ritual sexual games, the music synthesizing with eloquent power the aspirations and the blues of its audience, and even the recitation of poetry. At the same time, this shifting but congenial group of Wits conducts a revealing private discussion of personal, racial, and aesthetic considerations that reveal many of the dilemmas and the possibilities of black American art in the midtwentieth century. That Tolson named this club the Zulu Club, the same name he had given to the recreation room in his Langston home, and that one of the more prominent characters is named after a former Wiley debater and the theme of a band leader who achieved popularity in the thirties suggest how strongly Tolson's representation of this Harlem scene was rooted in his own early experience of Harlem and the countless discussions with friends about race and art over a period of many years. Although no portions of the earlier *A Gallery of Harlem Portraits* survive in this later poem, the tendency to broad caricature with a heavy dependence on pathos marks the kinship of the two books and bridges the years between.

Both the Curator and Hideho Heights are very comfortable at the Zulu Club: "like the brim of old hats," they "slouched at a sepulchred table." Snakehips Briskie and an "ebony Penthesilea" join in an erotic dance to the "complex polyrhythms" of the Indigo Combo. Hideho savors the scene and the cumulative history of jazz and its creators as he sardonically remembers Gertrude Stein's apparently disparaging comment: "Did the High Priestess at 27 rue de Fleurus / assert, 'The Negro suffers from nothingness?' " While pondering his own rhetorical question, he offers not too confidently, "Jazz is the marijuana of the Blacks." The Curator counters, "Jazz is the philosophers' egg of the Whites." But the Indigo Combo of Frog Legs Lux has the last word, and the Curator draws a historical analogy lightly underscoring again the emergence of a more proletarian culture from a bourgeois past:

> Just as
> the bourgeois adopted

243

the lyric-winged piano of Liszt in the court at Weimar
for the solitude of his
aeried apartment,
Harlem chose
for its cold-water flat
the hot-blues cornet of King Oliver
in his cart
under the
El pillars of the hoop.

The Master of Ceremonies introduces "the poet laureate of Lenox Avenue," and the audience explodes in applause. Hideho, on his way to the microphone, compliments "a tipsy Lena" with a friendly slap on the buttocks and assumes a mockingly impressive brown pose as "the laughing Philosopher." The Curator, however, ominously sees Hideho "as a charcoal Piute Messiah / at a ghetto / ghost dance." The Piutes' faith in Wovoka and his ghost dance led them to catastrophe in nineteenth-century America. The Curator, like Tolson, questions whether the vox populi can be trusted to voice the true interests of the people.

Hideho entertains his audience with "The Birth of John Henry." (As mentioned earlier, when the original manuscript of the *Libretto* once seemed too short to make a book, Tolson planned to couple it with a poem about John Henry.) The Curator sincerely admires Heights's performance despite the reservation of his initial premonition. He watches the creative impulse leap "from Hideho's lips to Frog Legs' fingers," and he muses:

> *the birth of a blues,*
> *the flesh*
> *made André Gide's*
> *musique negre!*

When Hideho nears the end of his recitation, Vincent Aveline, sports editor of the *Harlem Gazette* and close personal friend of the Curator, joins his table. Trouble is clear in his face and words, and it is counterpointed by Hideho's closing stanzas of "John Henry," which point up again the Scylla and Charybdis of race in America:

> *Ma taught me to pray. Pa taught me to grin.*
> *It pays, Black Boy; oh, it pays!*
> *So I pray to God and grin at the Whites*
> *in twenty-seven different ways!*
>
> *I came to Lenox Avenue*
> *Poor Boy Blue! Poor Boy Blue!*

From Chattel to Esquire

I came to Lenox Avenue,
but I find up here a Bitchville, too!

While the Curator tries to guess Aveline's problem, Joshua Nitze regales the Zulu Club Wits with a story about a black stevedore ordering a platter of chitterlings in a high-hat restaurant in the South, proving "White Folks ain't ready for integration!" After the laughter dies, Aveline chills the Curator with the news that Aveline has caught his wife and Guy Delaporte III in "between the sheets / of his Louis XIV bed!"

Black Diamond, policy-king and former student of the Curator's in Waycross, Georgia, appears at the table. He "vilifies the Regents of the Harlem Gallery" and assures the Curator of his considerable protection if the Regents threaten the Curator's position. This "ghetto Robin Hood" publicly displays his loyalty and friendship for the Curator and jots down his six private telephone numbers to make sure that he is available to the Curator. In Tolson's frequent battles with college administrators, he probably received similar, if less blatant, demonstrations of loyalty from his students.

Shadrach Martial Kilroy, president of Afroamerican Freedom, then begins a pointedly racial discussion with the statement, "The White Man is the serpent / in Dolph Peeler's *Ode to the South*." Dolph Peeler's *Ode to the South* is probably a reference to Tate's "Ode to the Confederate Dead," and Kilroy's statement echoes Tolson's argument in a letter to Tate that his ode "is a flagrant deviation from the ante-bellum Party Line!" But the reference to Tate's poem is only incidental. Kilroy's statement leads to a contest of choosing animal images to represent the racial dilemma. Lionel Matheus offers the Afroamerican as a frog, "the harder the frog tugged outward, / the deeper it became impaled / on the inward-pointing fangs of the snake." Nkomo adds, "The little python would not let go the ass of the frog—so the big python swallowed both." Nkomo's metaphor implies Tolson's continuing belief that class is a greater issue than race.

These images pose the dilemmas of race and class. The Curator senses "thoughts springing clear of / the *terra firma* of the mind— / the mettled forelegs of horses / in a curvet." But the discussion begins to drag as the white magic of John Barleycorn assumes control. Nevertheless, Tolson has two of his characters make statements that underscore his own often-stated beliefs. Kilroy, in response to Matheus's mockingly ironic, "Almost thou persuadest me to be a nigger-lover," soberly sighs: "It is hard for a phobic camel to go / through the eye of a needle of truth." And apparently drinking has caused Nkomo to brood in increasing isolation, for he interposes with little relation to anything previous in the conversation:

Nationalism,
the Sir Galahad of the African republics, has

        severed the seventh
    tentacle of the octopus of imperialism.

The scene closes with Hideho Heights in a drunken stupor slobbering,

        My *people,*
        my people—
    they know not what they do.

   The Zulu Club belongs to the people in a sense that the Curator can only
at this point aspire to for the Gallery. The intellectual elite, represented by
the Wits, may come here and feel perfectly at ease. Perhaps their comfort
even stems from the fact that what goes on here is determined by and repre-
sentative of a collective popular taste. The Curator and his friends also rec-
ognize and appreciate that in the music, the dances, and Hideho's poetry
aimed at a popular audience there is often a very powerful and subtle art-
istry and wit. Yet the manner in which Tolson closed this scene suggests a
significant critical reservation. The artist and the people are by no means
completely in tune. The artist is giving his audience what they think they
need. He does not have sufficient confidence in them to give them the truth
as he sees it. This is a good-time place. The lotos-vision, represented by John
Barleycorn, prevails. Hideho's closing lament blames the people, but his
drunkenness confesses his own responsibility as well.
   "Omicron" and "Pi" are again meditations by the Curator stimulated by
pungent comments on art and culture by Dr. Nkomo. In comparison to
"Theta," the Curator here celebrates the sustaining and life-giving values of
art and the prophetic nature of the artist, particularly in a time of crisis and
confusion. "Omicron" begins with a quotation from Nkomo: "Life and
art . . . beget incestuously." Art is not something in itself. Tolson consis-
tently resisted the tendency of the New Critics to distinguish art from its
milieu. From primitive man to the most sophisticated periods of civiliza-
tion, the artist is dependent on the world into which he is born for what he
can create. This raises a specific question for the Afroamerican artist:

        Is *Homo Aethiopicus* doomed,
            like the stallion's beard,
        to wear the curb of the bridle?

   The Curator answers the question confidently:

        The melon feeds the imago of the ladybird . . .
            the heritage of Art . . .
                nurtures everywhere
        the wingless and the winged man.

The Curator, as Tolson himself, assumes an ultimate realization of universal democracy in history:

> Unseen,
> perhaps,
> unheard,
> low heels will overtake high heels,
> to reach the never-never travelers' rest,
> a democracy of zooids united by a stolon
> but separated by a test.

The individual artist, however, need not project such ultimate vision. He makes what he can. Each work asserts, "I am that I am." He leaves the rest to such pedants as the Curator. Yet inevitably the artist in order to make merry while living "in the tenderloin's maw" must "add a head and a wing and a claw / to the salamander of Gerry." He must create a Gerrymander. Likening the artist's creation to the politician's may imply an unnecessarily high compliment to the latter, but it also suggests that the artist must be tough and have the wit to make what he can out of a demanding and resistant world.

The present age calls for a Bacon to clarify the past, present, and future. Tolson alludes to the story of Bacon's brass head, which was reputed to be omniscient and to possess the power of speech. According to the story, Bacon believed the success of an experiment would be confirmed if he could hear the head speak. One night he ordered a servant to stay up to hear the head if it spoke. The servant fell asleep, and the head spoke at half-hour intervals: "Time is; Time was; Time is past." Then it fell to the floor and shattered. The brass head's fall is associated in this poetic context with the Baconian collapse of the idols of the tribe, or the end of class and race distinctions, often invoked by Tolson. This age that "ties / tongues and stones irises" cries out for the release and clarification that the fall of these idols would signal.

The Curator details the restricting and distorting effect of these idols on the artist's vision:

> The idols of the tribe
> make the psyche of the artist lean
> inward like an afferent blood vessel,
> or turn its view
> —an adjusting iris diaphragm—
> toward the backyard of the Old
> or the front yard of the New.

When the time is right, or "good," the artist sees clearly the prophetic utopian vision:

As a skiascope views the changes
of retinal lights and shadows,
the élan-guided eye, in good time, ranges
a land of the leal
that no longer estranges.

In art creeds can accept difference and variation without making them bar-
riers to love:

In the magnetic field of Art, the creed
of the exploring coil discovers
diatonic nuances of taste
and vintage varieties that need
no philter for lovers.

Assuming a world freed from the tyranny of false idols, the Curator then
spells out the net consequences for the artist. The artist loses the alms of the
rich, but that is no loss at all since, while they may console "the *hoity
toity*," they leave "the pocketbook of his art / the poorer." The artist profits
from the surgical removal of "the art-fetish" from the flesh of the world: art
is to be integral and ordinary, intrinsic in our living. Having implied that he
would profit overall, the Curator concludes the section by celebrating the
characteristics of the artist that resist or combat the thanatos-influence of
the idols and those that nurture the eros-vision into historical reality:

The pride of the artist
is
the leach of green manure
that slows down
the sleet and snow and ice
of an age's scorn.

The élan of the artist
is
the rain forest sapling
which pushes upward
through bog and snarl
to breathe the light.

The school of the artist
is
the circle of wild horses,
heads centered,
as they present to the wolves
a battery of heels,
in the arctic barrens where

no magic grass of Glaucus
gives immortality.

The grind of the artist
is
the grind of the gravel in the gizzard
of the golden eagle.

The temperament of the artist
is
the buffer bar of a Diesel engine
that receives the impact
of a horizontal of alpine and savanna
freight cars drawn along in the rear.

The sensibility of the artist
is
the fancier of the Brahman and Hamburg and Orington,
the Frizzle and Silky—but
everlastingly he tests to discover
new forms and strange colors,
nor does he balk to wring the neck
of Auld Lang Syne
in any breed.

The esthetic distance of the artist
is
the purple foxglove
that excites
the thermo receptors of the heart
and the light receptors of the brain.

"Pi" is one of the most ambiguous sections of the poem, yet it is also one of the most crucial. The Curator discusses the sources of the power of art and the reasons it is often so difficult to recognize. He begins negatively. The last word is not simply, "*I like.*" Given the chaos resulting from the oppressive power of class rule disguised in racial terms, the artist must retain his respect for measure, his will to refrain. But even when the idols of the tribe have fallen and "his world is ours and ours is his," even then the egoism of the artist will cause his work, like the art of God, to be strange and foreign to all save "the hedonistic." The last is a surprising designation. In what sense *hedonistic?* The opening of the section clearly suggests that the Curator has little respect for self-indulgent pleasure. In "Theta" the promise of art as the woman Pleasure, who keeps her tryst, although she makes no blind dates, thus distinguishing her from the bitch Happiness, informs us of a more virtuous pleasure. This reference is confirmed a few lines after the

Curator's reference to "the hedonistic" when he describes a work of art as "a domain" of a particular race, time, place, and psyche, that nevertheless has an Al Sirat, or bridge to Paradise, of its own where "the ritual of / light and shadow, / idiom and tone, / symbol and myth, / pleasures the lover of Art alone." These are apparently visionary hedonists who are not mystified by the artist's messiahlike egoism. They know art as a peak experience whether the artist is "an ape-god of Eros or Thanatos." The Curator longs for such a moment in history and sees the key to it as the end of the power of money and its resultant bourgeois values:

> O son of profits,
> when does the hour come to sight
> the anchor? When will the parasitic crater
> stifle the bulls of Bashan in the night?

Prior to such an event, however, the Curator asks those in a position of power to let the remembrance of things past remind them of the need for tolerance. The babble of the times calls for a clear, strong voice. As examples, Dr. Nkomo invokes Robert Frost, at the Kennedy inauguration when he gave meaning to the motto of the Great Seal of the United States, and Paul Cezanne, "a Toussaint L'Ouverture of Esthetics," hailed by Zola, Renoir, Degas, Gauguin, Van Gogh, and Rodin. But Nkomo adds a disillusioned note that the "*vox populis* and red-tapedom / remained as silent as spectators in a court / when the crier repeats three times, 'Oyez!' " These instances parallel the lament Tolson voiced in *Caviar and Cabbage* over the failure of the public to respond to Richard Wright's achievement in *Uncle Tom's Children*.

The Curator's remarks about critics are generally disparaging; however, he notes, "Sometimes / a critic switches the dice and gambles on / his second sight." Given that the artist's credo is of necessity so amorphous, "*now* a riding light . . . / *then* a whistling buoy in / a Styx' night," such a switch is sane, if, unfortunately, rare. Dr. Nkomo upset many potential patrons of the Gallery by suggesting that the Critics' Circus refuses to recognize the social relevance of art, another reference to that stream of the New Criticism from which Tolson wished to divorce himself. It "grants an artist / a passport to / the holy of holies . . . or a whorehouse; / but never to Harpers Ferry or Babii Yar or Highgate."

The Curator also dismisses the critic of art as a dissonant force, but then describes his searching personal response in terms that imply a very healthy and comprehensive critical perspective:

> I visit a work of art: in the garden How
> I pluck the pansy; blink the weed;

fish in the dark tarn Auber for the Why:
seek out the What and trace its breed.

The road to the magical world of Xanadu is not lit by "the Hamburg grape."
Neither God, nor his ape, the artist, would be such a fool. While the giant
Philistine world wallows in self-indulgence, the misunderstood and misused
"harlot Now the master paints / aspires to hang in the gallery Hence." The
present reality longs to be graced into the future, to transcend time, through
the artist's power.

"Rho," "Sigma," "Tau," and "Upsilon" tell the story of Mister Starks, pi-
anist, composer, and poet, and his manuscript, *Harlem Vignettes*. The Cu-
rator begins the story in media res describing how Hedda Starks telephoned
him from the Harlem police station on New Year's Day promising to turn
over to him the manuscript of *Harlem Vignettes* as Mister Starks has com-
manded in his will. Then the Curator sketches the biography of Starks, in-
cluding the story of how he came to be named *Mister*, his marriage to
Hedda, alias Black Orchid, a "striptease has-been" who used his artistic
achievements to climb "the aerial ladder / of the black and tan bourgeoisie,"
and her subsequent affair with Guy Delaporte as a cause for Mister Starks's
suicide, a Hardyesque beau geste.

In "Sigma," Ma'am Shears, Proprietress of the Angelus Funeral Home,
receives Starks's last will and testament in the mail and guesses his intention.
She calls and tries to dissuade him: "It's not like Black Folks to commit sui-
cide." Mister Starks responds with cool irony, "Aren't we civilized yet?"
Ma'am Shears is puzzled. "Civilization and suicide?" he affirms, "Soil and
plant. . . . Masaryk speaking-in Vienna," referring to Tomas Masaryk's
Suicide and the Meaning of Civilization (originally published in 1881),
which argued that the increasing incidence of suicide in nineteenth-century
Europe was evidence of a cultural crisis. Starks plays his role with polished
deliberateness as he makes an appointment to meet Ma'am Shears, and oth-
ers, "at Archangel Gabriel's hangout / on Elysian Boulevard." But the su-
perintendent to Starks's apartment later finds the .38 that killed Starks in
Crazy Cain's toilet bowl, which suggests that Starks may well have been
murdered. At any rate, Tolson sardonically dramatizes Miss Bostic, Ma'am
Shears's assistant, as savoring the profit and publicity the Angelus Funeral
Home will reap from Starks's death. Hedda, arrested at a marijuana party
"and haunted in her cell," buys peace for herself by turning over her hus-
band's manuscript, *Harlem Vignettes*, to the Curator.

The major artistic achievement of Mister Starks's life was his musical
composition, *Black Orchid Suite*. He conducted the Harlem Symphony Or-
chestra in its premiere. The Curator points up the ironies of the remarkable

achievement and the grotesque indifference, if not antipathy, the artist finds in this world by invoking these images of a tragically relentless fate:

> O spindle of Clotho,
> O scroll of Lachesis,
> O scales of Atropos,
> the black ox treads the wine press of Harlem!

The final image merits special consideration. References to the fateful tread of black oxen can be found in Hesiod and Deuteronomy. Sir Walter Scott repeated the image in "The Antiquary," and these references often suggest a misfortune caused by a near relative or friend. But Tolson probably had in mind Yeats's lines from *The Countess Cathleen:*

> The years like great black oxen tread the world,
> And God the herdsman goads them on behind,
> And I am broken by their passing feet.

Gertrude Atherton reinforced the image with her popular novel *Black Oxen,* published in 1927. But Tolson added to the image by linking the black oxen with the wine press, anticipating his use of wine and winemaking as a symbol for the development and ripening of a culture later in the poem. Here it eloquently suggests that Mr. Starks's art is the distilled product of his painful personal experience.

If the premiere of the *Black Orchid Suite* was "sunrise on the summit" for Starks, it by no means indicated the boundaries of his talents. He was a shrewd observer and an accomplished caricaturist-poet. His *Harlem Vignettes* reminds us of Tolson's own *Gallery of Harlem Portraits.* He draws poetic portraits of ten of the most important characters in *Harlem Gallery,* including himself, Heights, John Laugart, Dr. Nkomo, and the Curator. His portraits of some of the minor characters, particularly that of Crazy Cain, add significant information about the narrative action of the poem. By its focus on the wits and artists, his collection of portraits suggests a microepic of the artist-seer's dilemma living in a community made culturally insecure by a barbaric and lengthy legacy of racism, and too readily tempted to seek relief from this legacy by worshiping the bourgeois fetishes and pleasures of its racist exploiters, a community too insecure and too preoccupied to justly value the beauty and truth created and perceived by its artists and seers.

Starks has made two inscriptions on the manuscript, wrapped in mamba's skin with a snapping turtle pictured on the back: "In the sweat of thy face shalt thou make a work of art," and "I should have followed-perhaps-*Des Imagistes* / down the Macadam Road. / But I'm no Boabdil / at the last sigh of the Moor." Tolson, too, often stressed that writing demanded as much perspiration as it did inspiration. He also often regretted his belated discovery of modernist writers, but, unlike Starks, he did belatedly follow them down the Macadam Road. Thus Starks as a poet seems a projection of the early Tolson. Starks's poetry is relatively straightforward and prosaic, and it is directly concerned with social issues even as he laments the social response to his and others' art. However, since Starks was a recognized, successful musician, he did not pander to the horizontal audience as a poet. His poetry was a private affair. The Curator sees Starks's poems as plucked by chance, "a few oysters / from a planter's bed—a site located in Harlem / strewn with layers of shells, slag, cinders, gravel," a site where art is fiercely engaged in challenging the mind-numbing complacency of the ruling powers.

Harlem Vignettes opens with a self-portrait in which Starks disavows his popular success as a musician: "My talent was an Uptown whore; my wit a downtown pimp." However, as a composer of music, his principal talent, there is no question that Starks aims for the vertical audience. He scornfully repeats the proverb of Alcuin's letter to Charlemagne that Tolson previously referred to in "A Long Head to a Round Head": "(God help *vox populi*— *vox Dei!*)." He approvingly quotes John Laugart: "A work of art is a moment's / antlers of the elaphure in the hunting lodge of time." This echoes an entry Tolson himself made in his notebook:

> Reason for *Gallery*: A poet, consciously or unconsciously, etches the differentiae of his time. The *Gallery* is an attempt to picture the Negro in America before he becomes the great auk of the melting-pot in the dawn of the twenty-second century.

Starks's expressed intention of etching "a few / of the everybodies and somebodies and nobodies in Harlem's *comedie larmoyante*" was later echoed by Tolson in *Book Week* early in 1966: "Harlem is a multiple jack-in-the-box. No Negro novelist has yet pictured Harlem in its diversity—not James Baldwin, not Ralph Ellison, not Richard Wright. It will take a black Balzac to do Harlem's *comedie larmoyante*."[6]

Starks is not a full-fledged Balzac, but, recognizing how the dice are loaded against him as "a Negro, a Harlemite, an artist," he feels free to hunt heads without compromising restraint in his portraits. He studied in Europe and knew the exciting possibilities of mixing sophisticated jazz and contemporary classical music, but he did not return to the States burdened with regret. He tried "to poise that seesaw between want and have." But the intoxicating lure of Black Orchid was too much for him. He pressed the *Black Orchid Suite* out of the grapes of his experience, and, although even the musicians of the orchestra seemed unimpressed, he treasures the premiere as an experience that "will forever stir my dust and bones."

Starks does not know Hideho Heights's "bifacial nature" as a poet. Only the Curator has read "E. & O. E." For Starks, the poet laureate of Lenox Avenue "is a man square as the X in Dixie, / in just the right place / at just the right time, with just the right thing." Starks's tribute to Heights, however, recognizes that Heights's very rightness to his time and place brings him inevitably into conflict with the bulls of Bashan: "To the black bourgeoisie / Hideho was a crab louse / in the pubic region of Afroamerica." Heights is, however, complacently indifferent to such class antagonism.

Dr. Obi Nkomo is also sketched heroically. A mix of "Barbarus and Culture," he has made an odyssey from the Christ present in the African veld to the Morgan collection of art and artifacts by way of the Statue of Liberty and Wall Street. His odyssey, as that of Afroamericans, is incomplete, poised before fulfillment or fruition: "stopped like fermentation checked / by alcohol / in the must of grapes." But what he stands for, what he believes in, is clear to all. Starks records Nkomo in dialogue with the other Zulu Club Wits. First Dr. Shears pictures him as a St. John, "who envisions / humanity as a thick mass of bees / with hairs on their legs— / by which they carry the collected pollen / to a collective hive." Nkomo returns Shears's compliment by describing him as sharing Whitman's healthy disillusion with Western materialism:

> Bedded in the Democratic Vista Inn,
> the Good Gray Poet discovered
> the materialism of the West was a steatopygous Jezebel
> with falsies on her buttocks.

Hideho Heights takes his turn at characterizing Nkomo in a parallel tribute to his idealistic prophetic searching:

> Obi Nkomo is a St. John who envisions
> a brush turkey that makes
> a mound of the Old World's decaying vegetables
> to generate heat and hatch the eggs of the New.

Nkomo accepts and acknowledges the compliment by responding, "Only an Aristotelian metaphorist . . . / could conjure up an image like *that!*"

We learn more of Nkomo in Starks's poetic portrait of the Curator, which begins with a series of images reflecting how the gallery is perceived by a variety of Harlem citizens. The series assumes an identification between the Curator and the gallery, and the incongruous perceptions of the citizens lead Starks to deduce the Curator as "a *strange* bird." But, as if apologizing for the extravagant verbal play, Starks follows this with a left-handed, but substantial, tribute:

> Sometimes
> the Harlem Gallery

was in bad odor; however—
it was not the smell of bad ideas
unembalmed and unburied.

The Curator is represented as in a continual sparring match with Guy Delaporte III, both because of the latter's flabby misperceptions about art and because of his personal antagonism toward the Curator. But these problems of the Curator do not stir him as deeply as the desertion of a student prodigy, Richard Fairfax, who "knuckled under as a gigolo / of Black and Tan Skin-Whiteners, Inc." The Curator's rage is likened to that of Cellini watching Luigi Pulci embrace the whore Pantasilea. But Starks's climactic compliment to the Curator, seconded by Nkomo, points to his staunch defense of the gallery and his insistence that it serves a disturbing but vital social function:

The Harlem Gallery his *Malakoff*,
I can imagine his saying to
anyone
who advised him to leave,
J'y suis, j'y reste.

Following this, Starks remembers speculating that if he knew the differences between the Curator and Nkomo, he would "know the ebb and flow of tides of color." Then, one night at the Zulu Club, after hours, he witnessed a revealing exchange between the Curator and Nkomo that was sparked by the janitor, "an ex-chaplain from Alabama Christian College" and an ex-Freedom Rider, who observed:

Gentlemen,
when any Old Ship of State
rams a reef of history,
the passengers
as well as the sailors
are involved.

As the Wits "chewed the quid of this," Nkomo slyly formed a leading question for the Curator, "Why cream, O Nestor, instead of milk?"

The Curator, sensing the challenge, prepares a careful answer, an answer Starks describes as carrying "Time's smell of the laboratory." As the Curator's position unfolds, he is clearly contrasted to Nkomo by his careful, almost scientific adherence to what is, while Nkomo is impatient to proclaim the world as it might or should be. The Curator stakes out his position:

I remain a lactoscopist
fascinated by
the opacity of cream,

the dusk of human nature,
'the light-between' of the modernistic.

The Curator is an observer and a historian who recognizes there is much that he does not understand but is fascinated with what rises to the top. He is implicitly an elitist, and this arouses Nkomo's attack: "You brainwashed, whitewashed son / of bastard Afroamerica!" The hyperbole in Nkomo's name-calling is well understood: "the nettle words were stingless." But they still mark out the grounds of the controversy. Nkomo sees the Curator's metaphor as carrying repugnant racist implications: "Barbed in the purple of metaphors, / the Nordic's theory of the cream separator / is still a stinking skeleton."

But the Curator, undisturbed by Nkomo's vehemence, responds, "Since cream rises to the top . . . , / blame Omniscience not me. . . . / Perhaps Omniscience deigns to colorbreed!" Since the Curator is so light-skinned that he is described as a "voluntary Negro," and Nkomo is pure African, this latter statement is particularly taunting; Dr. Nkomo, recognizing the game, plays his "shocked" role "with Lionelbarrymorean gestures."

But at this point the ex-chaplain intercedes. He points to the prevalent white assumption that it only takes one drop of African blood to turn "the whitest Nordic into a Negro." Then he suggests an ironic corollary:

Gentlemen,
perhaps there is a symbolism
—a manna for the darker peoples—
in the rich opacity of cream
and the poor whiteness of skim milk.

While the implication that racial mixing produces cream indirectly supports the Curator's stance, the skimming process is here suggested at the expense of what is left, poor white milk, and that aims the barb not at black people, but at the racially defensive whites.

The metaphoric argument is by no means completely resolved, but the janitor's wit makes Starks, the Curator, and Nkomo sit back and search for responses. Starks is bemused, "as the sex image of a Mary of Magdala / with kinky hair and a creamy complexion / hula-hulaed across my mind." The Curator gloomily focuses on what he sees as the contemporary historical dilemma: "Between the ass and the womb of the two eras . . . / *table* the milk of the skimmed / and *sip* the cream of the skimmers." And Nkomo righteously quotes Virgil's *Aeneid* to the effect that a mind conscious of the right "is not a hollow man who dares not peddle / the homogenized milk of multiculture, / in deadends and on boulevards / in green pastures and across valleys of dry bones." The argument dissipates in the desolation of the deserted Zulu Club. The "oddest hipsters on the new horizon of Harlem" sit staring into space.

The Curator and Nkomo's mutual respect and close personal friendship suggest that neither Starks nor Tolson sees them as essentially opposed but rather as positions in a dialectical argument. The popular inability to recognize and sustain much of what is most telling and valuable in art coupled with, and often caused by, the poisonous distinctions of race and class create the differences between the two about how one reaches the goal, desired by both, of a democratic world free of the prejudices of race and class and deeply appreciative of the essential beauty and pain of the human experience.

There is yet another anecdote richly developed in *Harlem Vignettes* that bears upon some of the same issues. It is an experience Starks had while working as a pianist in a speakeasy owned by Big Mama. Big Mama and Dutch Schultz are first described as recognizing a class kinship that crosses race. Then one of Schultz's men, one of "the Derbies," leans on the piano Starks is playing. Sentimentally he admits that he wanted to be a Caruso. Starks checks his contempt for the man's self-pity and enters the conversation. But he resents that the thug offers comradeship while retaining his sense of superiority enforced by his race and his gun. Starks reviews in his mind what all Negroes know:

> a white skin was the open
> sesame to SUCCESS— . . .
> Hadn't a white poet said when they cut off his leg,
> "I am the master of my fate . . ."?
> So, the class struggle was a myth
> manufactured in Moscow by the Red White Russians.

But his piano leads him elsewhere, "a new rhythm and melody vistaed before me: / the tones feathered into chords / and leafed and interlaced / in fluxing chromatic figures." Through cigarette smoke he envisions "not only the Derby but . . . / the African who had dramatized integration as / the notes of white keys and black keys / blended in the majestic *tempo di marcia* of Man." Tolson's manuscript "Key Words" suggests that he had Dr. Aggrey in mind, but the image of the piano keys was also introduced in "Theta." Starks's extempore composition commands the attention of all present. He names it *Rhapsody in Black and White* and sees it as "an answer to / Tin Pan Alley's blues classic." He feels, "like every other artist / an incorrigible gambler. / The stakes? / Caesar or God!"

Yet, as if the gamble were too audacious, he abruptly stops, grabs a bottle of bootleg whiskey "As Caesar seized Alesia," and flees to the street. Starks remembers a comment of Nkomo's as an editorial intrusion on his own story, an intrusion that reminds us again of the winepress theme: "A man is juice . . . pressed from the / apples of life—juice made hard or sweet or bitter." In the street he regains his composure by exposing a vice officer pretending to be a john to a prostitute the officer is about to entrap. Then, ordering a drink in Pisano's café, he spurns Pisano's surreptitious offer of the anti-Semitic *Protoculs of the Wise Men*. Interspersed in these garish incidents the admonitory refrain "Put the notes on the staff, Black Boy!" is repeated in parentheses. The God-given human imperative is clear, but in the particular circumstances of this time and place it is a difficult imperative to risk.

Besides these major portraits, Starks composes poetic sketches of Dr. and Ma'am Shears, Crazy Cain, Mrs. Delaporte, and John Laugart. All add a variety of human details to the collective portrait of a community. But the sketch of Crazy Cain makes an almost surreal comment on the themes of Starks's poetry and music. In "Sigma," Tolson planted the suspicion that Starks's intended suicide was prevented by Cain's murdering him. Now Starks's poetic sketch provides a bizarre but compelling explanation of events. Starks fired Cain from the Harlem Symphony Orchestra "in spite of Mrs. Guy Delaporte's vase of tears." Cain's mixed-racial history, cloaked in disguise and repression, is the flip side of the Curator's. Despite Mrs. Delaporte's concern for his job, Cain knew he was the bastard son of Black Orchid and Mr. Guy Delaporte, "but his knowing fell short of the *Poudres de Succession*." This sexual travesty is represented as a modern sequel to the rape of a Mandingo woman by an Irish fieldhand that began Cain's mixed racial heritage. Cain was also "as ignorant of his people's past / as Charicleia in *Ethiopia*." Thus his bastardy marks his imagination as well as his genetic heritage, and he kills the man who is qualified by talent and vision to be his true father. It is a bizarre and bitter story of the poisonous legacy of race, class, and sex, reminiscent of another epic story with a homophonous title, Jean Toomer's *Cane*.

After reading *Harlem Vignettes*, the Curator feels the need to join Hideho Heights in drink. Apparently referring to Starks's poetic effort to distinguish between him and Nkomo, the Curator feels that Starks "had seen in me / the failure of nerve / Harlem would never see— / the charact in the African / that made / him the better man." Nkomo insists that one should live as if the world were what one believes it should be. One must believe and live in the power of prophecy. The Curator is too skeptical, too ironic, too burdened by his knowledge of how barbarism has too often overwhelmed civilized values, or, more particularly, how his own people have been brutalized and repressed by barbarism masking as civilization. The Curator feels his own "failure of nerve." He seeks a drink and company at the Zulu Club.

Although he has been deeply touched by *Harlem Vignettes*, his critical judgment of it is reserved at best. It is "a smokestack / . . . to prevent / the escape of sparks," a venting of deep feelings before they explode, but it is not likely to pass the extraordinary tests demanded of black American art. It will fetch "no white laurel of joys / no black crepe of regrets." The Curator's judgment on *Harlem Vignettes* probably is infused with Tolson's own stern judgment of his own *A Gallery of Harlem Portraits*. It belongs to a pre-modern style of writing doomed to extinction.

But the episode at the Angelus Funeral Home as well as Starks's manu-script make the Curator feel for the time a strong kinship with such sardonic laughers as Gogol, Dickens, and Rabelais as he is conscious of residing "in the black world of white Manhattan." Moved by this mood he addresses Black Boy directly: "Let no man lie"—sentimentalize or romanticize—"about the Noble Savage who survived the Trek of Tears and the Middle Passage." Legislators and sages of Jim Crow culture obsessively ask, "What is a Negro?" And the effect of their obsession with the question traps Black Boy and the Curator in a false role: "We" are made into something else to suit the appetites or needs of Negro-lovers as well as Negro-haters.

Shadrach Martial Kilroy opens the discussion of the Zulu Club Wits as if he were in tune with the Curator's thoughts by proclaiming that "the specter of *Homo Aethiopicus*," like a "pigmented Banquo's ghost," haunts the Great White World. Nkomo sees Afro-Americans as victims of their poly-breeding, their plural strains. Like Albert Ryder, they are "of many schools / and *none*." But more pointedly, since civil rights are reserved for the unpig-mented,

> the vanity
> of the Iscariots of
> the Republic pancakes
> your star of destiny flat
> as a depressed appetite.

Kilroy persists in developing his opening statement by pointing to the vari-ous meanings of *Negro* throughout the world. But Nkomo dismisses all such nice considerations of race. The central issue is

> As man to man,
> should you and I grovel in dust and ashes because
> of *what* I think of you or *what* you think of me?

Kilroy and Heights acknowledge the power of Nkomo's point.

Then Heights engages the Curator in another discussion of Dolph Peeler's *Ode to the South*. The Curator points approvingly to "the symbol of the pig in the boa's coils," a symbol interestingly enough that Tolson was very proud of in his *Libretto*. Heights, however, is challenged by the Curator's praise for this symbol, and, sparked by the previous discussion, he feels

himself caught in the throes of poetic creation. The Curator's gibes spur
the process until Hideho announces, "This is . . . IT— / Curator," and
launches into the story of the sea turtle and the shark. It is a harrowing
image of "the instinctive drive of the weak to survive":

Driven
riven
by hunger
from abyss to shoal,
sometimes the shark swallows
the sea-turtle whole.
The shy reptilian marine
withdraws,
into the shell
of his undersea craft,
his leathery head and the rapacious claws
that can rip
a rhinoceros' hide
or strip
a crocodile to fare-thee-well;
now,
inside the shark,
the sea-turtle begins the churning seesaws
of his descent into pelagic hell;
then . . . *then,*
with ravenous jaws
that can cut sheet steel scrap,
the sea turtle gnaws
. . . and gnaws . . . and gnaws . . .
his way in a way that appalls
his way to freedom,
beyond the vomiting dark,
beyond the stomach walls
of the shark.

Just as the Curator once recognized the authority of John Laugart's paint-
ing, he now recognizes the authority of Heights's poetic analogy: "I knew
his helm was in line with his keel / as an artist's helm should be." The Jamai-
can bartender downs a double shot of Zulu Chief and adds his quiet, but
earnest, approval:

God knows, Hideho, you got the low-down
on the black turtle and the white shark
in the deep South. . . .
And perhaps in many a South in the Great White World!

He also adds a comment that reveals the rich dramatic possibilities Tolson could give to his images. He too hates "Peeler's pig in the boa's coils!" But his comments make clear that he is repelled not by the image in its poetic context but by the historic truth it attempts to picture, the image of a people helplessly victimized by a voracious power. He poses McKay's famous image as a counter: "If we must die, let us not die like hogs."

Heights's achievement lights up the darkness for the Curator. He sees the Zulu Club as "the sunshiniest place / in the black ghetto." It truly *is*

> a city of refuge,
> for those who have fallen from grace,
> for those who are tired of the rat-race
> (the everlasting—*On your mark! Get set! Go!*)
> in the land of the Gray Flannel Suit
> and the Home of the Portfolio!

But Hideho chooses this moment of triumph to confess obliquely to the Curator his misgivings about some of his earlier popular creations. He gives the Curator a glimpse into his private gallery where hangs a painting of "a whore giving birth / to a pimp's son . . . on a filthy quilt." He is happy, in retrospect, that he now sees the picture. But "an artist's travail is like / a woman's." It is

> an issue of the *élan vital* in sweat and blood,
> born on a brazen
> sea and swaddled
> on a raft of life and shaped like a question mark.

The artist, like the birth-giving woman, is so controlled by the creative process that at the time he has no interest in splitting hairs, or making nice distinctions about the propriety of his intentions. Yet, even if he is in retrospect troubled, the authentic artist's creations, his efforts to reach and serve a popular audience, are not to be confused with those abortions produced by the Eddie Jests and Shortfellows "who use no rubbers / when copulating with muses on the wrong side of the tracks."

The Curator's glimpse into Hideho's private gallery reminds the Curator of his secret discovery of "E. & O. E.," Heights's "private poem in the modern vein." The Curator also once overheard Hideho voice his concern of never reaching the vertical audience. The Curator explains to Poor Boy Blue, another name for Black Boy, that it is the Great White World and the Black Bourgeoisie who "have shoved the Negro artist into / the white and not-white dichotomy . . . , / the dialectic of / to be or not to be / a Negro."

In explanation the Curator details his reminiscence of the night that he took Hideho home dead drunk, and, after putting the poet to bed, discovered "E. & O. E." The Curator was astonished upon reading the poem to discover that Hideho had lived in Paris and had known such artists as Salmon, Apollinaire, Mac Orlan, and Picasso. That Hideho had kept this part of his past hidden, that in fact it had had no visible effect on the poetry he was known by, is for the Curator "eyesight proof / that the Color Line, as well as the Party Line, / splits an artist's identity." That is further explained in "E. & O. E." itself when Hideho is represented as feeling "out of square" with his previous fellow expatriates: "I have not said, 'Hippoclides doesn't care.'" Hideho abandoned the relatively free and richly exciting world of Paris to return to the frustrations and limitations that are built into the American scene for the black artist. He came home, but he carried with him questions that he hid from his audience about the rightness of his decision:

> Why place an empty pail
>   before a well
>   of dry bones?
> Why go to Nineveh to tell
>   the ailing that they ail?
> Why lose a golden fleece
>   to gain a holy grail?

Contrasted to the bold confidence of the public poet the Curator has previously known, these questions suggest to the Curator that "the protagonist aped the dubiety / of a wet cake of soap." Yet the Curator remembers an incident in which Hideho had in fact confronted "a puking slop-bowl gobbler," "Bishop" Gladstone Coffin, and gone to jail for exposing the Bishop's Uncle Tom asininity. And from jail Hideho had powerfully and earnestly insisted, "A man's conscience is home-bred" and "Integrity is an underpin."

The Curator does not doubt Hideho's integrity. Thus his discovery of the surprising poem forces him to think in other terms for an explanation. *Time* and *timing* become the issue. Hideho is caught between two worlds. The Parisian world he has abandoned has exposed him to possibilities in art that are not present in the Harlem world he has chosen. But he could not stay in the Parisian world without feeling he had become another Hippoclides, or, to use another Tolson label, a spiritual nudist. Harlem is not as culturally ripe as Paris. Its cultural maturation is hamstrung by the oppressive force of American racism and by its kowtowing embrace of the bourgeois values and consequent class distinctions of capitalism. Thus Tolson has the Curator quote those sections from Tolson's own "E. & O. E." that make the artist's plight in relation to his time seem most lamentable, although Tolson omits the key section that indicates that the poet-protagonist may well accept the burden of living in a far from favorable moment of history with purposeful modesty and dignity:

From Chattel to Esquire

I sought
in a Tarshish nook
neither the Golden Fleece
nor the Holy Grail
but a pruning-hook.

The Curator's memory of discovering Hideho's poem concludes with a quote from the end of Tolson's poem in which the poet-protagonist implies that, despite terrible burdens, he will not resort to Lear's prayer, Barabbas's curse, or Job's cry. His stoic posture seems strained. He is victim of his time, and, given Heights's dramatic role in the poem, that is appropriate. His artistic career illustrates that midtwentieth-century time is still out of joint for the black American artist.

It is then up to the Curator in the final two sections, "Psi" and "Omega," in a direct address to Black Boy and on particular occasions to White Boy as well, to spell out some means of hope and sustenance in the midst of great confusion and threatening disorder. He gathers "the crumbs and cracklings / of this autobio-fragment, / before the curtain with the skull and bones descends." Admitting the incompleteness of much that he has had to say, he nevertheless assures Black Boy that his "psyche escaped the Sodom of Gylt / and the Big White Boss." He draws a verbal picture of Black Boy standing before his heritage, cheated, posing a bleak rhetorical question himself: If the tools of democracy don't work, what can be built with "the trowel / of Uncle Tom?" The Curator then draws for Black Boy the moral of the stories of John Laugart, Mister Starks, and Hideho Heights:

in this race, at the time, in this place,
to be a Negro artist is to be
a flower of the gods, whose growth
is dwarfed at an early stage—
a Brazilian owl moth,
a giant among his own in an acreage
dark with the darkman's designs,
where the milieu moves back downward like the sloth.

Black Boy has not known "the El Dorado of aeried Art," because his artists, as a matter of integrity, disdain the contemptible sustenance and mocking grace offered to them in the world in which they live. The Curator quotes a rhetorical question posed by Nkomo that points up the righteousness of the artists' disdain:

What is he who smacks
his lips when dewrot eats away the golden grain
of self-respect exposed like flax
to the rigors of sun and rain?

263

Melvin B. Tolson

Yet Black Boy can take grim solace from the fact that all groups con-
fronted by a powerful barbarism have characteristically believed their own
death rattle to be "the *Dies Irae* of the world." In a rhetorical ploy the Cura-
tor suggests that a group of anthropologists be summoned to the gravestone
of Bilbo, the archetypal racist Southern senator, to answer the question,
"What is a Negro?" The implication is that the cancer in Bilbo's mouth, his
racist message, will continue to live after he is dead and needs to be objec-
tively examined to be laid to rest. The Curator asks incredulously,

> what's in a name that wries the brain
> like the neck of a barley bird?
> Can sounding brass create
> an ecotype with a word?

But the Curator is compelled to warn Black Boy that the dangers that come
from the creation of this racial myth in the white mind are real. "The Black
Belt White . . . / rabbit-punched old Darrow" because he dared defend
Darwin's science against the racially poisoned interpretations of God's Word
commonly accepted in Tennessee. Darwin's evolutionary concept of man's
descent from the apes is then given an ironic twist by the Curator as he
points to the apelike characteristics of the Nordic, his "thin lips, his aquiline
nose, / his straight hair, / organutanish on legs and chests and head."

This sets the stage for the Curator to quote Nkomo's argument to the ef-
fect that "Nature is on the square / with the African." He points to the ad-
vantages of the African's thick hair, skin color, and wide nostrils, physical
characteristics that American racists ignorantly caricatured as signs of in-
feriority. These examples lead Nkomo to suggest that if the black man gets
outside the Great White World he will find the sustenance he needs for
faith in himself and his people, even as the Jews after crossing the Red Sea,
on their exodus, found first "the bitter waters of Marah" but later "the fresh
fountains of Elim."

But the racial division between black and white is only a "Hardyesque
artistry / of circumstance" for Nkomo. He warns menacingly against build-
ing any cultural ethos on race, caste, or class by suggesting an analogy be-
tween such ideas and

> the bodies of the dead
> eaten by vultures
> in a tower of Silence.
> Let, then, the man with a maggot in his head
> lean . . . lean . . . lean
> on race or caste or class,
> for the wingless worms of blowflies shall grub,
> dry and clean,

the stinking skeletons of these,
when the face of the macabre weather-
cock turns to the torrid wind of misanthropy;
and later their bones shall be swept together
(like the Parsees')
in the Sepulchre of Anonymity.

While Nkomo's message does not bring universal applause from the Zulu Wits, the Curator senses his thoughts were "like Ascher's, after / he'd cleaved the giant Cullinan Diamond." But the Curator takes off on another rhetorical tack. He builds an elaborate analogy for Black Boy between the development of a good wine and a people's development of a rich rewarding culture. Soil, time, and integrity are the basic ingredients for both. Palates sensitive to *salt* and *sugar* can tell when either grapevines or races have been transplanted. Good "wines are peacocky / in their vintage and their age / disdaining the dark ways of those engaging / in the profits / of chemical aging." By implication so are good races. The seasonal process of growth and ripening of the vines is in a sense paralleled by the seasoning process of the wine over years in the vats. It is a natural process that cannot be hurried, but it will happen according to its own nature if adequately cultivated and prepared for.

The Curator warns Black Boy of false labeling. The phrase *Chateau Bottled* does not mean that "the Republic" guarantees "the estate, the proprietor, the quality." Black Boy has often been baffled by this problem: "the white man's law / has raked your butt many a time / with fang and claw." The Curator warns Black Boy that even if by chance he goes into "high-hat places / open to all creeds and races," he must beware of the waiter who wraps a napkin around the label. He should check out the pop of the champagne cork, make sure it pops round and full, not flat "because the bottle of wine / is dead . . . dead / like Uncle Tom and the Jim Crow sign." Beware also that lionhearts white and black do not cause your dreams to become unrealistic expectations, "for we know *without no* / every people, by and by, produces its 'Chateau Bottled.' "

Then the Curator turns his address to White Boy. If the question *what* is a Negro seems philosophically remote, the dangers and absurdities of the question *who* is a Negro need to be recognized immediately. The Curator, who can pass for white, experiences the absurdities personally:

Since my mongrelization is invisible
and my Negroness a state of mind conjured up
by Stereotypus, I am a chameleon
on *that* side of the Mason-Dixon
that a white man's conscience
is not on.

265

Pointing to the fact that he is light enough to be considered white and while Black Boy "is the color / of betel-stained teeth"—a contrast reminiscent of Tolson's surprise when he met his many-hued kin as a boy in Missouri—the Curator concludes:

> he and I
> (from ocular proof
> that cannot goof)
> belong to races
> whose dust-of-the-earth progenitors
> the Lord God Almighty created
> of different bloods
> in antipodal places.

Then, after pointing to the obvious, "that laws defining a Negro / blackjack each other with*in* and with*out* a state," the Curator drives home his point with a rhetorical flourish:

> The Great White World, White Boy, leaves you in a sweat
> like a pitcher with three runners on the bases;
> and, like Kant, you seldom get
> your grammar straight—yet
> you are the wick that absorbs the oil in my lamp,
> in all kinds of weather;
> and we are teeth in the pitch wheel
> that work together.

Warming to his task, the Curator sardonically declares,

> The Negro is a dish in the white man's kitchen—
> to some . . . tasty,
> like an exotic condiment—
> to others . . . unsavory
> and unelegant. . . .
> Just as the Chinese lack
> an ideogram for to be,
> our lexicon has no definition
> for an ethnic amalgam like Black Boy and me.

Add the white man's lust to his racist assumptions and one has a Gordian knot "without / the *beau geste* of an Alexander's sword!":

> For dark hymens on the auction block,
> the lord of the mansion knew the macabre score:
> not a dog moved his tongue
> not a lamb lost a drop of blood to protect a door.
> O
> Xenos of Xanthos,
> what midnight to dawn lecheries,

in cabin and big house,
produced these brown hybrids and yellow motleys?

The Curator tries to bring home to White Boy the legacy of such brutal exploitation and oppression:

Buchenwald is a melismatic song
whose single syllable is sung to blues notes
to dark wayfarers who listen for the gong
at the crack of dawn along
. . . that Lonesome Road . . .
before they travel on.

Describing himself as "A Pelagian with the *raison d'être* of a Negro," the Curator has not freed himself from dread. He is too aware

of the noiseless tread
of the Yazoo tiger's ball-like pads behind me
in the dark
as I trudge ahead,
up and up . . . that Lonesome Road . . . up and up.

The Curator is a Pelagian apparently in that he, like Tolson, stresses man's own responsibility for his history rather than seeing the hand of divinity in all events, but a black Pelagian living in a white man's world clearly has special problems of belief.

The Curator closes that portion of his remarks addressed to White Boy and the section "Psi," with an image designed to indicate the ultimate absurdity and futility of the white man's efforts to define the Negro. The idol of the tribe is inherently flawed. Its own unreality, once perceived, causes it to crumble. The good ship *Défineznegro* sailing from its Xanthachroid port cannot reach its goal. Its voyage inevitably will prove unhappy to all. Only its doom can prove happy.

In a Vision in a Dream,
from the frigid seaport of the proud Xanthachroid,
the good ship *Défineznegro*
sailed fine, under an unabridged moon,
to reach the archipelago
Nigeridentité.
In the Strait of Octoroon,
off black Scylla,
after the typhoon Phobos, out of the Stereotypus Sea,
had rived her hull and sail to a T,
the *Défineznegro* sank the rock
and disappeared in the abyss

(*Vanitas vanitatum!*)
of white Charybdis.

The Curator concludes his address and the entire poem in "Omega" by speaking to both White Boy and Black Boy. What has happened in recent history to bring us to this crisis has not been the result of wisdom:

> you have played blackjack with Tyche
> you have shot craps with Hap;
> yet, things-as-they-are in the ghetto
> have sported you for a sap.

The wasteful violence and the threat of revolution in the ghetto indicate the failure of social reason. Nevertheless, on occasion the Attic wit of man has found a way out of such social crises, a way out that the Curator describes with an animal image strikingly like Hideho's sea turtle:

> Sometimes,
> a guy born in a house with the graffito
> of doom lucks upon the know-how of a raccoon
> that gnaws off its leg to escape from a trap.

The Curator implies his Harvard Ph.D. may have been of some use in teaching him how to escape ball and chain. Just as the upper classes give their children the keys to the What, How, and Why of the unknown, so curators do the same for the audience of their exhibitions, particularly with a work of genius that demands great patience and persistence to be recognized as a harbinger of the future. The key may lie in apparently insignificant matter. The constellation canis minor may have baffled Palomar, but Schaeberle, by refusing to disdain it, discovered its significance.

If art is the key to escaping the present cultural crisis, then some generalizations about art and artists are in order. By a series of rhetorical questions increasingly obvious in their implied answers, the Curator makes clear that the artist should not take direction from the merchant, should not "Paint an *ignis fatuus of nawhit,* / to win thirty pieces of silver from the elite." A work of art may be so bitter that it must be doled out at intervals or its effect would be overwhelming. But since there are so many tributaries entering the river of art, the pilgrims may "lave the bruises of the Rain of woes" in "the self-heal of the river."

Conscious of the prevalence of illiteracy and ignorance, the Curator uses again the metaphor of milk and cream to pose a question with disturbing class implications:

> Should he
> skim the milk of culture for the elite

and give the "lesser breeds"
a popular latex brand?

Or should he carefully arrange the art he exhibits so that it will be more digestible? These are troubling questions for him as a curator, "but the binnacle of imagination / steers the work of art aright." The artist is an ape of God. As such he, unlike a curator, does what he has to, not what is calculated and deliberate. What he creates comes to have compelling authority independent even of him. Rhetorically addressing the Goddess of Dawn, who signals new possibilities, the Curator acknowledges that he knows of many instances like that of Degas, who in his old age, disoriented, was forced to leave the rue Victor Masse "to make again / a new place for new things and new men." To drive home his point the Curator lists examples that "the dread hand" of God created out of chaos, and he follows these with a list of the creations of "The ape of God," the artist, impersonalized as "mind instinct with design."

The Curator then makes a generalization unlikely to be contested, "freedom is the oxygen / of the studio and gallery," and by implication links it to a defense of the esoteric in art. He registers his own pleasure in studying the magnificence and intricacy of an ego-dwarfing masterpiece and then asks,

Is it amiss or odd
if the apes of God
take a cue from their Master?

It is the critic's role to see that the topmost mast of art is indeed "an argosy of plunder / from the kingdoms of race and caste and class," for all too often a state creates "a rubber-stamped pyramid of Art" to glorify its own idols. The Curator quotes Nkomo's tribute to Monet, who "gives us new roads / out of the Jardin d'Eau and across the anthroposcape." He expresses a wish that the beholder of the "fruits of the first Harlem harvest" be struck with a similar sense of surprise and renewal. The Curator confesses without regret that he personally no longer has the force of a pioneering discoverer nor "the levitation / to sustain a work of art." He is only a pilgrim "to the cross street . . . / where curator and creator / meet."

But the Curator is confident that the gallery represents the central role of black America in the drama of history even while white America remains willfully and suicidally blind to it:

The moving finger in the Harlem Gallery
paints dramatis personae in the dusk of dawn,
between America's epigraph and epitaph;
yet,
only half an eye has the other half
of the Great White World,

where,
at the crack of doom,
potbellies laugh.

When the Curator has most difficulty with the Regents, when they are grinding his spirit, he fortifies himself by recalling the words of Archbishop French: "The present is only intelligible in the light of the past." The Curator is resigned to the fact that he will see no Haroun-al-Rashid welcome the avant-garde of Harlem and usher in a legendary golden age. The beastly antagonism the artist must expect instead is often frightening, even if its beastliness proves pretentious and absurd, only "a monkey with a lion's tail."

Half playfully the Curator uses these projections to plea for financial support, but then the argument turns dead serious as he acknowledges that even if the gallery becomes a cause célèbre, he is powerless to defy

the dusky Regents who,
tasteless as oxygen,
as colorless, too,
can knot the golden purse strings,
while closeted in the Great Amen,
and mix the ingredients of Sycorax' brew!

Despite the grinding problems of Harlem, there is no doubt in the Curator's mind that the white heather and white almond, the flowers of hope, grow in the ghetto. And while the idols of the tribe rule, the hyacinth and the asphodel, the flowers of death and decay, blow in the white metropolis. In an interview with Jack Bickham, Tolson said of this passage: "I say that the flowers representing decay and death are found in the white metropolis, but the flowers of hope grow in the black belt. I speak here of the masses of poor people. They are on the move. Most American writers are cynical. But even in the violence of Richard Wright there is something that lifts you. There is no despair."[7]

And the Curator ends the poem with a confident and proud tribute to the achievements of the gallery:

Our public may possess in Art
a Mantegna figure's arctic rigidity;
yet—I hazard—yet,
this allegro of the Harlem Gallery
is not a chippy fire,
for here, in focus, are paintings that chronicle
a people's New World odyssey
from chattel to Esquire!

XI

ARS LONGA, VITA BREVIS EST

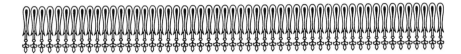

Tolson was reading the proofs for *Harlem Gallery* before his operation for gallstones in April 1964, the operation during which his doctor unexpectedly discovered abdominal cancer. The doctor's diagnosis was bleak and shocking, approximately six months to live. Tolson was not immediately told the bad news. There are conflicting memories of who broke the news and when. However, the prescribed chemotherapy caused a precipitant loss of appetite and weight and a dramatic darkening of the skin. A special program was organized by Langston students to honor Tolson for his achievement and service on 11 May, one month after the operation. He sat on the stage too weak to rise, scribbled the following poem, and read it while remaining seated:

> How could I miss
> Cleopatra's kiss
> Or a night like this?
> You've heard about me
> And my poetry
> From A to Z.
> As the love feast ends
> A NEW CHAPTER BEGINS.
> So good night dear friends,
> Good night. GOOD NIGHT.

Considering Tolson's long-standing fear of cancer stemming from its history in his family, he almost certainly began suspecting the worst early. When the diagnosis became a matter of open discussion in the family, Tolson, on the advice of a former student since become a medical doctor, decided to consult Dr. William Strickland, a cancer specialist in Dallas. Late in December, Dr. Strickland performed an operation that kept Tolson on the table for five hours but probably prolonged his life for eighteen months. Tolson was recuperating from that operation in St. Paul's Hospital when Karl Shapiro's prepublication review of *Harlem Gallery*, taken from his introduction to the book, was featured in *Book Week*, both in the *New York Herald Tribune* and in the *Washington Post*. The front-page prominence given the review must have been both satisfying and tonic to Tolson in his Dallas hospital room. Tolson was back in his classroom at Langston within a month. Joy Flasch remembered:

> President William H. Hale and Tolson's chairman, Mrs. Moxye W. King, arranged a first-floor classroom for him, but the irrepressible little professor could not stay there when most of his colleagues had offices on the second floor. It was a familiar sight to see him slipping upstairs in his red house shoes—the one concession he made to his convalescent state.[1]

Shapiro's introduction heavily influenced the reception of *Harlem Gallery* for some time after its publication. In October, Shapiro had sent a note to Tolson accompanying a copy of his introduction: "Please disregard the brevity, if it seems brief. Maybe the Tate piece unconsciously guided me. I think I said all I had to say: being averse as you know to explication and analysis I could not bring myself to textual criticism, which would be way out of place in a book of this stature anyhow." Shapiro was increasingly at critical odds with Tate by the time he wrote the introduction; thus, while he welcomed the opportunity to praise Tolson and his poetry, welcomed it certainly with greater enthusiasm than did Tate, he also wanted clearly to distinguish his position from that of his predecessor.

His introduction opens with a statement that has nothing to do with his quarrel with Tate: "A great poet has been living in our midst for decades and is almost totally unknown, even by the literati, even by poets." Shapiro's praise and admiration for Tolson and his poetry were deeply felt and lasting. As recently as 1981, he has continued to claim greatness for Tolson.[2] Yet in his introduction his quarrel with Tate is very close to the surface. While Tate admitted that Tolson's subject may be "Negro," he claimed Tolson's artistry as a poet to be nonracial and that it is ultimately his artistry that matters. Shapiro, on the other hand, insisted that Tolson's greatness stems from his "writing in Negro." Shapiro attempted to accept, even embrace, the racial dimension of Tolson's art, in contrast to Tate's effort to minimize it.

In spite of saying in his October note to Tolson that he had said all he had to say in his introduction, he did soon expand his argument in an article published in the *Wilson Library Bulletin* just a few months after *Harlem Gallery* was published. There he contends explicitly with Tate, whom he characterized as "a Confederate of the old school who has no taste for Negroes but who will salute an exception to the race." He argued that Tate's "refusal to see that Tolson's significance lies in his language, Negro," resulted in a falsification of Tolson's achievement:

Karl Shapiro and Melvin B. Tolson in 1965.

The falsification I speak of is that of trying to assimilate Tolson into the tradition when he was doing the opposite. The fact that Tolson's *Libretto* is unknown by white traditionalists gives the lie to the critic's assertion that Tolson has risen above Negro experience to become an "artist." The facts are that Tolson is a dedicated revolutionist who revolutionizes modern poetry in a language of American negritude. The forms of the *Libretto* and of *Harlem Gallery*, are the Negro satire upon the poetic tradition of the Eliots and Tates. The tradition cannot stand being satirized and lampooned and so tries to kick an authentic poet upstairs into the oblivion of acceptance.[3]

In his introduction Shapiro argued: "The history of the Negro places him linguistically at the center of American culture, as it does no other nationality or 'race.' Negro survival had depended upon the mastery of the gradations of English; the Negro has in his possession a *Gradus Ad Parnassum* of culture which no other minority or majority can conceivably encompass." Thus he intended a high compliment to Tolson when he said that Tolson "writes and thinks in Negro, which is to say a possible American language. He is therefore performing the primary poetic rite of our literature. Instead of purifying the tongue, which is the business of the Academy, he is complicating it, giving it the gift of tongues. Pound, Eliot and Joyce did this; but with pernicious nostalgia that all but killed the patient. Tolson does it naturally and to the manner born." The latter distinction almost certainly pleased Tolson, since he so earnestly saw himself as looking to the future and so earnestly wished to dissociate himself from the reactionary social convictions of many of the most prominent modernist writers. But Shapiro's description of Tolson as a "dedicated revolutionist who revolutionizes modern poetry in a language of American negritude" raised a good many critical hackles. In fact critics who felt compelled to challenge Shapiro's statements found it difficult to be fair to *Harlem Gallery* and to Tolson.

Laurence Lieberman described trying to interest his students at a college in St. Thomas—students whose mother tongue is English and whose racial heritage is African—in *Harlem Gallery* with negative results: "They do not understand him [Tolson]. He simply does not speak their language. How then can it be said that Tolson writes *in Negro?*" Lieberman added: "While it is true that often Tolson successfully ridicules the cultural establishment from which he derives so much of his imagery, more often he is too steeped in that tradition to work against it. . . . The tradition that the poem supports *is* basically that of the 'Graeco-Judaic-Christian culture,' and not a distinctly Negro heritage."[4]

If one assumes that the Greco-Judeo-Christian culture is a white culture—surely a racist act of the historical imagination—and that a revolution in the name of black people must hence be within a totally different cultural matrix, then clearly Tolson is not a revolutionary poet. Tolson committed himself to a revolution against class and racism, and, since he saw both as a product of capitalism, he envisioned a world based on egalitarian principles that made capitalism as we know it anachronistic. He did not see the plight of black people as determined solely by race. Race was a part of economic exploitation. The Greco-Judeo-Christian culture had created false gods in place of true gods with which he had no quarrel. Over and over again he pointed out that Christ was betrayed by the mouth-Christians, and there is little doubt that he felt similarly about Greco-Judaic cultural ideals. He did not see these cultures as at odds per se with black or any other nonwhite peoples. However, the true Greco-Judeo-Christian values cried out for redemption, and a revolution by oppressed peoples against the false idols would effect such redemption.

Gwendolyn Brooks responded to *Harlem Gallery* with much greater fairness and appreciation, but she too registered her concern with Shapiro's "amazing introduction." She also pointedly referred to Shapiro as writing " 'in Jew' to the extent that Tolson writes—quoting Shapiro—'in Negro.' " She began her assessment by saying, "Melvin Tolson is a member of the Academy," although "many of his fellows do not concede his presence there." She acknowleged that Shapiro also made this point and that other respected poets, John Ciardi and Theodore Roethke, had tried unsuccessfully to win for Tolson his deserved acceptance in the academy. The failure of their efforts, however, only pointed up the obduracy of racism. She then briefly, but accurately, characterized *Harlem Gallery* and Tolson's particular contribution:

> Melvin Tolson offers this volume as a preface to a comprehensive Harlem epic. Its roots are in the Twenties, but they extend to the present, and very strong here are the spirit and symbols of the African heritage the poet acknowledges and reverences. He is as skillful a language fancier as the ablest "Academician." But his language startles more, agitates more—because it is informed by the meanings of an inheritance both hellish and glorious.

She noted as well the book's "much embroidered concern with Art" and its "many little scheduled and cleverly twisted echoes from known poetry." But her faith in a distant true reading of the poem's intricacy implied that it might have to wait for its vertical audience to develop: "Although this excellent poet's news certainly addresses today, it is very rich and intricate news indeed, and I believe that it will receive the careful, painstaking attention it needs and deserves when contemporary howl and preoccupation are diminished."[5]

Writing a few months after Tolson's death, Sarah Webster Fabio made Tolson's poetry incidental to her direct challenge to Shapiro's claims for the Negro quality of Tolson's language. While acknowledging the difficulties of sorting out Tolson's ironies and parodies and admitting that Tolson's statement "all but defies paraphrase," Fabio asserted, "Melvin Tolson's language is most certainly not 'Negro' to any significant degree. The weight of that vast, bizarre, pseudo-literary diction is to be placed back into the American mainstream where it rightfully and wrongmindedly belongs." She saw Tolson as a pathetic victim of cultural lag, certainly not a pioneer for young black writers to follow:

> Melvin Tolson was not a beat poet; he was a part of the neoclassical scene who—although as able as any to attempt the Quixotic feat of reviving a dead horse, albeit a Trojan horse—was denied a rightful place in this theatre of the absurd. Like many Negroes of this period he was told to go back and perfect the art, and, then, in the great democratic tradition, he would be accepted into the society of the neo-classicists.
>
> He accepted and perfected the art of classical reference as a pillar for an American tradition in literature but became victimized by the cultural lag that is common between the white and Negro worlds. About this time Allen Tate, the Nashville Agrarian poets, and other champions of this movement, gave up this vain pursuit of doing battle with tilting windmills. Therefore, while Tolson busied himself out-pounding Pound, his fellow poets forgot to send him the message that Pound was out.[6]

While Fabio was unwilling or unable to give *Harlem Gallery* a careful reading, the question she raised about Tolson's place in the literary tradition is important. Tolson too saw himself as victimized by "the cultural lag that is common between the white and Negro worlds." This was part of the dilemma of the black artist in *Harlem Gallery*. In his own career he belatedly came to accept the modernist literary experiments embodied in the poetry of Eliot, Pound, Crane, Stevens, and Williams as an accomplished and essential advance in the literary tradition. As Fabio pointed out, by the time *Harlem Gallery* was published, there was an unquestionable reaction against the dominance of these poets as literary models. But Tolson bet on a future in which man would become increasingly sophisticated, increasingly aware of the cultures of the world, particularly those of Africa and Asia. He used the technical examples of Pound and Eliot to build a poetic pathway to a world quite different from that envisioned by either Pound or Eliot. But from the time that Tolson deliberately changed his style to write the *Libretto* in the late forties, he often did project himself as in the vanguard of a host of younger black writers who would claim their place in world literature essentially by "out-pounding Pound," by assimilating the technical verbal brilliance of Pound in the service of a very different cultural ethos. Free of the racial blindness of their white contemporaries, more sensitive to the democratic aspirations of oppressed peoples everywhere in the world, these poets would astonish the world with their comprehensive learning and their responsiveness to human needs. This dream of Tolson's has not happened. Tolson is not well known, let alone broadly emulated, among young black writers. Yet his own poetic achievement is real and substantial, and there is growing, if still slender, evidence that Gwendolyn Brooks's prediction is coming true. His work is beginning to receive "the careful, painstaking attention it needs and deserves when contemporary howl and preoccupation are diminished."

The contemporary reaction to *Harlem Gallery*, however, did include voices not concerned with Shapiro's claims. Dolphin G. Thompson wrote a most enthusiastic review for *Phylon*. After listing some of Tolson's recent honors, he praised:

> His new book, *Harlem Gallery: Book I, the Curator,* justifies every honor given him and should be the basis for the highest awards the literary world can give.
> The book is "Gibraltarian" in content and apogean in scope. He has done in poetry what Marian Anderson did in song; what Jackie Robinson did in baseball, and what George Washington Carver did in science. He has taken the language of America and the idiom of the world to fashion a heroic declaration of, about and for Negroes in America. It is a book that should be on every shelf.[7]

From quite a different quarter an anonymous reviewer wrote in *Muhammad Speaks:*

> Tolson brings new richness to the English language. By comparison the writers of poetry in America seem to be pale ghostly writers using language that is dead and afraid to create new symbols of visual excitement that can make the reader feel that life is vibrant and worth the challenge.

This review concludes by recalling Langston Hughes's description of Tolson during his days at Wiley, a description that is apt despite the seeming paradox created by the esoteric qualities of *Harlem Gallery:* " 'Tolson is no highbrow. Students revere him and love him. Cowpunchers understand him. . . . He's a great talker. There is only one Tolson.' And he [Hughes] is right!"[8]

An anonymous reviewer for the *London Times* gave a sound summary of *Harlem Gallery*, although he assumed a too complete identification between the Curator and Tolson:

> An academic love of displayed literary and mythical erudition makes the work difficult, in the tradition of Pound and Eliot, and the linguistic complexity and use of involuted metaphors call for a reading in the line of Hart Crane, but the gist of these 170 pages is clear. In one sense the artificially

created idiom is itself the poet's theme: the nature of Negro art in a white culture, "the phoenix riddle" of "this allegory of the Harlem Gallery," "a people's New World odyssey from chattel to Esquire!" . . . Gradually the analytical wit and sensuous humour move towards a final mocking, serious criticism of blackness, whiteness and the Lost Gray Cause, tinged with self-reproach as a "Judas" who needs and knows European culture and yet realizes the need for Negro re-invention.[9]

Robert Donald Spector, writing for the *Saturday Review*, pointed to the dramatic diversity and richness of *Harlem Gallery*:

> Tolson stands apart from and above contemporary poetic accomplishment. For comparison with what he has done, it is necessary to turn to the novel, to that wildly imaginative world, with its language both earthy and symbolic, in Paul Goodman's *The Empire City*. Yet Tolson's poetry, unlike Goodman's prose, creates its bizarre atmosphere in a disciplined esthetic form. Out of the terse structure of the ode, Tolson manages a narrative that puts in motion and sets at odds his *dramatis personae*—extending from the curator of the Harlem Gallery down to the policy racketeer, and including every recognizable type.

The dramatic richness of Tolson's poem was an answer to Gertrude Stein's charge that the Negro "suffers from Nothingness." After giving some illustrations of Tolson's inventive achievement, Spector concluded:

> But what of the fantastic way in which discussions of esthetics are turned into social comment? What of the incredible manner in which Tolson ranges over every field of art, plays adroitly with language? These require pages of demonstration. Sufficient to say that whatever his reputation in the present critical climate, Tolson stands firmly as a great American poet.[10]

Josephine Jacobsen took issue with Karl Shapiro's introduction, but she did so in a manner that reflected positively on Tolson's achievement. She suggested why Tolson's work failed to gain immediate broad recognition:

> The reasons for the unquestionable lack of wide appreciation—as distinct from critical appreciation—of Mr. Tolson's stature as poet are certainly more complex than the bizarre simplification Mr. Shapiro suggests. One factor, possibly major, is an admirable characteristic of Mr. Tolson's own work—his refusal to be pushed into an inflexible stance, his ground held between two schools of absolutists. Not only does his work do nothing so simplistic, and irrelevant to his poetry, as "contravene" an entire culture; he considers, tragically, wittily and with great flexibility, the underside of that culture's accomplishment. He is less interested in howling, "Moloch!" than in considering the agonies, distortions, victories, and disasters of the individual caught in the turn of giant change in thought, in belief, in objectives.

After paying tribute to the eloquence with which Tolson represented the dilemma of the artist in the midtwentieth century, "one of the most appalling areas in which the human spirit has had to struggle," and after paying tribute to the vividness of Tolson's cast of Afro-Americans, Jacobsen concluded:

Mr. Tolson has true wit, he can convey disgust, violence or vituperation, without clamor. He seems to have everything essential to sustain the weight of a major work. He has above all two things: élan (which he characterizes as "the artist's undivorceable wife"), and a ruthless perception of the artist's basic necessities: *The school of the artist / is / the circle of wild horses, heads centered, / as they present to the wolves / a battery of heels, / in the arctic barrens where / no magic grass of Glaucus / gives immortality.*[11]

With the exception of Fabio's comments, published late in 1966, these are samples of the reviews Tolson himself read. The enthusiastic and often discerning praise must have been both satisfying and tonic for a man who had successfully resisted the most immediate threat of death. The critical respect for Tolson has continued and grown, although it is still by no means clear whether the academy will grant him a position commensurate with that claimed for him by many of his most ardent advocates.

Since then, over the last sixteen years, there have been a number of critical examinations of Tolson's work. Robert J. Huot prepared a critical edition of *Harlem Gallery* for his Ph.D. dissertation at the University of Utah in 1971. In 1980, Mariann Russell completed *Melvin B. Tolson's "Harlem Gallery": A Literary Analysis*, which examines *Harlem Gallery* "from the focus of its relationship to the Harlem community," particularly its "double image of cultural capital and ghetto." Joy Flasch's dissertation, "Melvin B. Tolson: A Critical Biography," done at Oklahoma State University in 1969, became the source of her book, *Melvin B. Tolson*, published in 1972. Jon Stanton Woodson completed his dissertation, "A Critical Analysis of the Poetry of Melvin B. Tolson," which makes *Libretto* the key to Tolson's poetic vision, at Brown University in 1978. And Wilburn Williams finished "The Desolate Servitude of Language: A Reading of the Poetry of Melvin B. Tolson" at Yale University in 1979. Two book-length collections of Tolson's writings have also been published posthumously: *A Gallery of Harlem Portraits* in 1979, Tolson's first book of poems and his original effort to represent Harlem in epic form, and *Caviar and Cabbage* in 1982, a selection of Tolson's columns written for the *Washington Tribune* between 1937 and 1944.

Not all of the attention paid to Tolson has been by literary critics. T. J. Anderson, a former colleague of Tolson's at Langston, who had moved to Atlanta as composer-in-residence to the Atlanta Symphony, composed "Variations on a theme by M. B. Tolson," a musical composition with a text made of excerpts from *Libretto* and *Harlem Gallery*. On 27 May 1970, Anderson's composition was performed by the Atlanta Symphony with soprano Bernardine Oliphint giving what one critic described as "a haunting performance." Anderson's composition has also been recorded on a Nonesuch record, *Spectrum: New American Music*, volume 5.

This is at least the second attempt to put Tolson's poetry to music. Earl Robinson, some thirty years earlier, had composed a score for "Dark Symphony." Robinson is best known for his "Ballad for Americans," which attracted much public attention when it was performed on the CBS Sunday afternoon program *Pursuit of Happiness*, 5 November 1939. It was later recorded featuring Paul Robeson as soloist.

In addition to the noted book-length literary commentaries, there have been shorter critical pieces on Tolson's work. One of the most promising is "Ellison, Gordone and Tolson: Some notes on the Blues, Style and Space," by Ronald Walcott, in *Black World*, December 1972. Taking "the individual as stylist" as his point of comparison, Walcott quoted Charles Keil's *Urban Blues* to the effect that what is seen from the white point of view as entertainment is seen

> from the Black or theoretical point of view as ritual drama or dialectical catharsis. Ritual itself is a highly stylized structure laid out and perceived in space. Accustomed to, and perhaps most at home, participating in ritual, the stylist is a performer, a man who moves in space, who attracts attention and employs it in defining himself. These stylists, or bluesmen, or representatives of the soul tradition, as Keil calls them, are all identity experts, specialists in changing the joke and slipping the yoke, for one can find in their performances—be they athletes, singers, musicians, preachers, comedians, writers, disc jockeys, *etc.*—the essentials and defining features of Black culture as a whole.[12]

Walcott then described *Harlem Gallery* as a significant new development in this tradition:

> Tolson's epic poem, *Harlem Gallery*, in which the stylist, too, is hero, signals a radical departure from the tradition articulated in *Invisible Man* and carried on through *No Place to Be Somebody*, though, like them, it is the "auto-bio-fragment" of an artist. For Melvin Tolson, the victories attainable through style are not only real, considerable and worthy of record, but they are indicative as well of his people's invincible sense of the possible. Tolson's "auto-bio-fragment" also operates out of the blues tradition, but its hero, the poet himself is confident of his perception of the relationship between style and substance: that style, if one takes it seriously as an expression of vision, *is* substance, insofar as it reflects and determines one's experience, assessment and response being what experience, after all, is about.[13]

Describing *Harlem Gallery* as "an epic undertaking owing as much to Eliot, Pound, Yeats, Crane and Stevens as it does to Billie Holiday, Bessie Smith, Satchmo, Langston Hughes, and Ol'Red Taylor," Walcott confidently claimed:

> Incorporating elements of the very best of contemporary poetry and informed with a truly impressive grasp of learning, *Harlem Gallery* is an unabashed tribute to Black tradition, tradition which has inspired the vigor and human diversity it is the poem's stated purpose to render. Its characters— Hideho, the Curator, Professor Nkomo, Mister Starks, Guy Delaporte III and wife, Black Orchid, and all the rest of the gallery, are very much grounded in their own history, at home in it and recreating it daily with their outlandish, inspiring, totally unself-conscious uniqueness. For them, truly, style is what one is.[14]

Walcott concluded by pointing out the revolutionary implications in Tolson's concern with the artist:

> In the Harlem Gallery the Curator hears the alarm birds announcing revolution, not only the revolution of politics but that of poetics; he hears "a dry husk-of-locust blues / descend the tone ladder of a laughing goose." The blues and jazz, we see, are to figure, and prominently, in the revitalization of Western aesthetics. . . .
>
> Called, there is to be no turning away for the Black artist, for to do so is to turn away from the possibilities of affirmation, of celebration, lying within art and the self. If the artist is to be sustained, and he must be, it is to be by what Ellison has called the traditional sense of style which stands behind every artist "a sense of the felt tension, indicative of expressive completeness; a mode of humanizing reality and of evoking a feeling of being at home in the world." Tolson's artist is at home everywhere in the world: "the gaffing 'To ti?' of the Gadfly girds / the I-ness of my humanness and Negroness." In this world, there are no either/or polarities. The very dialectical opposition which tore Gabe Gabriel apart; the ambiguity which was synonymous with life, and just as bewildering, for the invisible man are here signs of the complexity and versatility of human experience, accessible to the artist through his sense of self and style, his concern for the human being. For him, Tolson reminds us, there always exists that special space in which "the plain is twilled and twilled is plain."[15]

Dudley Randall, in an article titled "The Black Aesthetic in the Thirties, Forties, and Fifties," grouped Tolson with Robert Hayden and Gwendolyn Brooks "as poets conscious of technique, who were familiar with and learned from the modern experimental masters such as Hart Crane, Eliot, Pound, and Yeats, and not from minor poets such as Housman or Edna St. Vincent Millay, or traditional poets such as Keats, all of whom influenced Countee Cullen." Curiously Randall had little to say about *Harlem Gallery*. Instead he repeated the story that Tolson had told him about extensively revising *Libretto* after Tate refused to write a preface for the original version. This story does not square with evidence in the correspondence between Tolson and Tate and will be discussed more completely later in relation to a separate Randall interview of Tolson. As repeated by Randall and referred to by Fabio, however, this story implied that Tolson foolishly submitted to an outdated white authority. Thus Randall completed this unfortunate circle by echoing Fabio: "The irony is that, about this time, the New Criticism was declining, and the Beat poets, with their lesser, freer, more emotional language and form, were coming into popularity. In any case, the learned allusive language is not the spontaneous speech of the Negro people."[16]

Eugene B. Redmond, in his amazingly detailed critical history of Afro-American poetry, *Drumvoices*, responded to Randall's statement that reading *Libretto* is like reading "other learned poets, such as Milton and T. S. Eliot," with this comment: "However, reading Tolson is not *exactly* like reading other poets, for he places black information in front of the reader. He bends the ode into an Afro-American musical structure and celebrates the black past."[17] As for *Harlem Gallery*, Redmond had strong praise:

> A staggering poem, *Harlem Gallery* "is a work of art, a sociological commentary, an intellectual triple somersault." (Flasch). It meets the vigorous intellectual, scholarly, and stylistic whims of modern poetry, but at the same time is "impossible to describe." Yet it is Tolson's crowning achievement in more ways than one. First it continues his fascination with black and general history. Second, it pursues his intense interest in the psychodynamics of both the Afro-American character and the artist; he is particularly concerned with the plight of the twentieth century black artist (hence *Book I, the Curator*). Third, it provides one of the most powerful and authentic links between the Harlem Renaissance and the Black Arts Movement of the 1960's and 1970's. The very title of *Harlem Gallery* gives it a black setting; and the fact of its being conceived and initially drafted during the renaissance indicates that Tolson labored over the years (from the standpoint of memory, technique, and subject matter) in the afterglow of the literary flowering watered by McKay, Cullen, Toomer, Hughes, Fisher, Johnson and Locke.[18]

Redmond also noted:

> We do not know what would have been Tolson's fate as a poet had he come to his own comfortable style as a young man in the Harlem Renaissance. He was nearly fifty when he sent Tate the manuscript for *Libretto*. And fifty is quite an old age for a poet still to be at odds with his craft—or to have it overseen by a patronizing critic. Nevertheless, Tolson, not admitted (as Shapiro noted in black poets) to the "polite company of the anthology," had to get his voice "together" without the immediate financial and emo-

tional aid available to the "Fugitives" or those in other molding centers of the modern poetry. Few black poets at the time were attempting Tolson's feat—Blacks' interest in poetry declined during the forties and fifties—and there is much evidence that Tolson generally intimidated other black scholars and intellectuals with his vast knowledge and great talents. Like poets of other generations, he was a part-time poet, expending much of his energies on students and school-related work. Randall has pointed out that unless black poets imitate Tolson—and thus keep him apparent and interesting—he will not exert a major influence on Afro-American poetry. But as Barksdale and Kinnamon note, a poet of Tolson's range and power cannot go unnoticed for long.[19]

A few years later, in 1979, Nathan A. Scott, Jr., surveyed black literature for the *Harvard Guide to Contemporary American Writing*. He chose Tolson, Brooks, and Hayden as the most distinguished poets of a group of "gifted writers of the present and recent past" standing aside from the new "street" poetry. Noting that Tolson "has remained a figure obscure and unregarded, withal the high praise that has occasionally come from such poet critics as Allen Tate and Karl Shapiro," Scott concluded,

the general neglect of his work [is] but another instance perhaps of the profound reluctance of the literary intellectual community to reckon seriously with the Negro writer who asks to be considered as something other than merely a special case of ethnic ferment. And, of course, it is precisely the largeness of Tolson's response to the literary world of his time that has guaranteed his disfavor amongst those espousing the esthetic doctrines of black separatism—who are inclined to render something like the verdict of Sarah Webster Fabio, that his complex and difficult rhetoric represents only a 'bizarre, pseudo-literary diction' that he misguidedly took over the 'American mainstream where it . . . belonged' and where it should have been allowed to remain.

Scott was careful to hedge his praise, but ultimately he paid Tolson high tribute:

The heavily declamatory fustian of his early writing had by the time he undertook his remarkable *Libretto* . . . given way to a language which, at its best, is marked by an extraordinary richness and intensity. True, the brilliance of the *Libretto*, like that of *Harlem Gallery*, is—in a way that recalls Pound's *Cantos*—an affair of arresting fragments: the *effort* to which Tolson committed himself may remind us of *The Waste Land* and of *Paterson* and of *The Anathemata*, but he had not the kind of systematic intelligence that sustains the long poem; yet, again and again, in the poems on Liberia and Harlem . . . one meets evidences of a gift that justifies Tolson being spoken of in relation to the major poets of his time who used the English language.[20]

One other piece of extraordinary critical praise for Tolson has met with surprising silence. In 1973 an article by Roy P. Basler on Tolson was published in *New Letters* emphasizing the future orientation of Tolson's vision, an emphasis that would have undoubtedly pleased Tolson. Basler began by characterizing his own perspective as conditioned by "Thomas Jefferson's 'prospective,' as opposed to John Adams' 'retrospective,' concept of history and culture." He also assumed the centrality of the issue of race in our time: "one must face the fact that literary study today is affected willy-nilly by the racial febricity in our sick society." With these assumptions clear, he stated his thesis:

> Tolson is perhaps the poet of our era who best represents, or comes nearest to representing, in his comprehensive humanity, the broadest expanse of the American character, phrased in the richest poetic idiom of our time. Better than his contemporary peers, he knew the span from low-brow to high-brow in both life and literature, and he loved the American English language, from gutter to ivory tower, better than any of them. His poetic diction is a natural blend of home words and hall words, where *hearth* and *bema* sing side by side. He is the natural poet who cultivated his nature, both root and branch, for the flower and the seed, for it was the seed more than the flower, Ruskin to the contrary, that Tolson the poet believed art grew for—yes, the "yellow wasps of the sun swarm down," but when Tolson's "New Negro" speaks for "his America," the word is more American perhaps than any of his great contemporaries have spoken.[21]

About the *Libretto* and Tate's introduction Basler wrote:

> The *Libretto for the Republic of Liberia* is not only one of the great odes in the English language, it is in many respects one of the finest poems of any kind published in the English language during the twentieth century, so far as my acquaintance goes. Allen Tate's minor caveats are meaningless to me in the presence of Tolson's afflatus and Jovian humor. . . . And the "irony," which Tate comments on, that an American government has never, could never have, commissioned such an official poem to be read in Washington only reminds me that I agree with Tolson that "these truths," of which Jefferson wrote, are bearing and will bear fruits for which white Americans must yet acquire the taste.[22]

But it is *The Harlem Gallery* that Basler saw future scholars salvaging from libraries of this era in order to guess what manner of men we were. For it is in *The Harlem Gallery* that "the heart of blackness with the heart of whiteness lies revealed. Man, *what* do you think you are is not the white man's question but the black man's rhetorical answer to the white man's question."

Basler acknowledged as basic Albert Murray's statement in *The Omni-Americans* that American culture is neither white nor black, but mulatto.

Thus, "However Eliotic the retrospective tradition may seem to those who understand only what they have been taught, the Tolsonian prospect lies certainly, and I think clearly, ahead."

Art is "the means by which . . . not only an individual poet but also mankind could transcend, in some measure, both the past and the present in the future, if mankind put art to its highest use in recreating human life." Thus Basler concluded:

> Tolson has written of American life as it is and will be. He has taken our white-black culture and imagined it into a new thing more representative of the modern human condition than any of his contemporary peers among poets has managed to create, and it is not "negritude," although he has plenty of that, but "humanitude" that enabled him to accomplish the feat. I do not expect anyone to accept this judgment until he has read and appreciated Tolson's poetry for himself, and I do not expect professors of American literature to accept it generally for perhaps a quarter century, but Tolson's recognition will come as surely as has Whitman's.[23]

According to Joy Flasch, as well as members of Tolson's family, Tolson was consistently confident that his poetry would some day achieve a significant audience. But Flasch's account of her commitment to write her book includes a revealing description of Tolson's state of mind in December 1964, just before *Harlem Gallery* was published and just before he went to Dallas for his second operation. Flasch had begun teaching at Langston in January 1964. Three weeks after she had begun, Tolson bounded into her office and introduced himself. She would often later think of this moment as if it were somehow predetermined, as if a door were opened and there was no choice but for her to walk through. He had heard that she was a writer. She protested that she was not. She had two small children. She lived with them and her husband on a nearby farm. But Tolson insisted that she not be intimidated by the idea of writing and encouraged her to try. He asked if she knew his work, and when she confessed that she did not, he gave her a copy of *Rendezvous with America*. Harold, her husband, was deeply moved when she read him poems from *Rendezvous* that evening. She took the book to her teachers at Oklahoma State University, where she was enrolled in a doctoral program, but met only skepticism and indifference. After Karl Shapiro's review of *Harlem Gallery* was published, some of her teachers were willing to reconsider. But that was after she had already inadvertently committed herself to writing a book about Tolson.

This is how she told the story to me in 1979:

> He had had an operation for cancer in April of 1964, just about three months after I met him, and in December of that year he knew that he would have to have a second operation. He was very depressed. *Harlem*

Gallery had not yet come out, although he had expected that it would by that time. He was afraid that he wouldn't live to see how it was received. He was very anxious to know how critics would accept it. And we were sitting together in old Page Hall, which is a very ramshackle building, a very ancient building on Langston's campus, that December. We both had our coats on, collars turned up, trying to keep warm. And he was talking to me about how difficult life had been for him in many instances. And he was very low, concerned about his health at that point. And so I just wanted to do something to make him feel better. I thought so much of him, admired him so much, thought what a terrible thing it was that here was a man who was a great poet, who perhaps was going to die, and he would not really ever have received the acclaim that I thought he should have and that many poets and critics obviously had felt he should have. And I thought how terrible that this is going to happen and that no one will ever know anything about him. So I just sort of . . . I don't know what made me say it when I didn't think I could write at all, but I said, "Well, Dr. Tolson, I'd like to write a book about you." And it was simply at that moment to try to do something to lift his spirits. And he looked at me and said, "Well, colleague, would you really?" And he had a big smile on his face. And I said, "Well, I really would. I think there is some tremendous material both about your life and your poetry. And someone should do it. I don't know how to write a book, but I'd like to be that someone if you'd like to give me that material." So he said, "I certainly will."[24]

From that point on Joy Flasch diligently began the task of gathering material for what was first her doctoral dissertation and then her *Melvin B. Tolson* of Twayne's United States Authors Series published in 1972. She attended Tolson's classes, when possible, and all his nearby lectures. She talked with him at his home and at the office and took copious notes. She and her husband became close friends of the Tolson family, frequently driving Tolson to the airport or to special lectures. In the process she assembled an impressive collection of information from Tolson about both his life and his writing for which future Tolson scholars will be forever indebted. After the favorable reviews of *Harlem Gallery* appeared prominently in print, several other people expressed interest in writing about Tolson's life, but Tolson firmly indicated that he was committed to providing Flasch whatever biographical material he could.

On at least a few previous occasions Tolson had indicated that he intended to write his own autobiography, but he never made any systematic effort to do so. In fact he firmly resisted his sons' efforts to tape the reminiscences that in later years frequently colored his conversation. But, after December 1964, he was very happy to have such a dedicated colleague recording his reflections and ideas. Melvin, Jr., speculated shrewdly to Joy Flasch that his father thought his biography should be saved for the end, but that implied that if he began to cooperate with a biographer he would be admitting the nearness of the end. Thus he refused to consider seriously a biography until after he had been told that his cancer was terminal, although even then he staunchly refused to believe the doctor's prognosis of only six months to live. He had too much to do. He could not stop for death.

The appearance of Karl Shapiro's introduction as a prepublication review in *Book Week* was also the beginning of another elaborate promotional effort by Twayne to bring a book of Tolson's to public attention. Despite his recent operation, he joined the effort enthusiastically. In fact, the attention he received seemed to give him energy. It certainly fed his will to live. In March he traveled to Detroit, New York, Philadelphia, and Washington, D.C. A partial summary of his activities in New York remains among his papers. On 22 March he arrived shortly after 10 A.M. and was driven to the Plymouth Hotel. At 12:30 he was at the Twayne offices meeting his publisher and staff. At 1:30 he lunched with Jacob Steinberg, Ingram Fox, and McPheeters at the Southern Restaurant. At 3:00 he attended a strategy meeting with McPheeters at the Plymouth Hotel. At 8:15 he arrived with chauffeur at the American Society for African Culture to read his poetry. Horace Mann Bond had invited Tolson to be a member of AMSAC at its inception in 1957. Langston Hughes introduced him, and the audience included such notables as Dr. John Davis, Dr. Joel Spingarn, Dr. Raullerson, Herbert Hill, Wilmer Lucas, Belle Rosenbaum, Muriel Rukeyser, Steve Duncan, and Carl Cowell. Tolson received a standing ovation after his reading, and an informal reception followed an animated question-and-answer period.

The next morning Tolson was interviewed by Bob Potts on WNDT-TV and then went to a business luncheon at the swank Blue Sea Restaurant. There the summary ends, but another note indicates that Tolson was also interviewed by Sheila Duncan on 25 March for the NYU radio series *These Are My Shoes*. Another confidential memo lists "Business Commitments Made" during Tolson's visit to New York City and indicates that Dr. Clarence R. Decker of Fairleigh Dickinson University was to recommend Tolson for membership to the Board of the Poetry Society of America at their 1 April meeting, arrange for Tolson to address the Fairleigh Dickinson student body in October or November for a stipend of from three hundred to five hundred dollars and an open meeting of the Poetry Society on the same visit for another three hundred to five hundred dollars, and finally to arrange for Tolson to compete in the Poetry Society's Concours for a prize of from one thousand to three thousand dollars. Tolson was also to write a chapter for Herbert Hill's book *The Negro Writer in the U.S.A.* for a guaranteed two hundred and fifty dollars plus a prorated percent of the retail sales, depending upon the length of the chapter. This book was probably the one that appeared as *Soon, One Morning*, containing Tolson's poem "Abraham

Lincoln of Rock Spring Farm." Hill was also to arrange for Tolson to address the New School for Social Research on his projected fall visit for three hundred dollars and expenses. Harvey Shapiro of the *New York Times* was to ask Tolson to "write an article of your choosing, 2,500–3,000 words" for a guaranteed one hundred and fifty to four hundred dollars on acceptance. The idea of the "Ballad of the Rattle Snake" was suggested as a topic. Nona Balakian wanted Tolson to write a review for the *New York Times Book Review* and was interested in having a correspondent cover the Langston Festival of Arts. Counsel General Thomas of the Liberian Embassy apparently was considering some significant purchase of books, and Stephen Ruddy, New York City cultural affairs officer, was arranging for copies of *Harlem Gallery* to be sent to the mayor for special inscription. He was seeking to arrange a special presentation for Tolson's visit to New York in June. Leaving New York City, Tolson was invited to present a copy of *Harlem Gallery* to the White House library in Washington, D.C. In sum hardly the kind of program one might expect for a patient convalescing from major surgery.

Tolson had visited Detroit for a few days before going on to Philadelphia and then New York City. It was probably on this occasion that he met Dudley Randall at the home of poet-sculptor Oliver LaGrone, a meeting Randall described in his "Portrait of a Poet as Raconteur," published in January 1966. According to Randall, Tolson told him that "after completing *Libretto for the Republic of Liberia* he asked Allen Tate to write a preface for it, and Tate replied that he wasn't interested in the propaganda of Negro poets. Tolson spent a year studying modern poetic techniques and rewriting the poem so that it said the same things in a different way and then sent it to Tate." Tate then wrote the requested preface. Joy Flasch repeated this story, citing Randall as her authority. Randall indicated early in his account that Tolson had suggested that evening that "he would forget about Jim Crow and concentrate on Old Crow," so it is quite possible that this fictional account may have in fact been allowed to grow in the haze of fantasy that good whiskey often encourages. But it is also possible to see some unintentional significance in the way events were transformed in Tolson's memory and finally became reported as literary history.

When Tolson sent Tate an early draft of *Libretto* on 19 February 1949, he referred to Tate's rejection of a long poem, "The Horns of the Bull," which Tolson had submitted to *Sewanee Review*. Since Tolson wrote Tate again on 9 May 1949 expressing his appreciation that Tate was willing to write a preface for *Libretto*, Tolson's reported account to Randall is clearly in error. It seems likely that either carelessly or forgetfully Tolson many years later confused the rejection of "The Horns of the Bull," for which there is no surviving recognizable manuscript, with a fictional rejection of *Li-*

Ars longa, vita brevis est

Melvin B. Tolson, presenting a copy of *Harlem Gallery* to the
White House library in March 1965.

bretto. The reference to a year between Tate's supposed rejection and Tolson's supposed resubmission of his manuscript also suggests such a confusion. Tolson often was careless with dates. He delighted in a good story. And this story indicates that Tolson felt it necessary to deal with Tate with all the duplicity that blacks have characteristically used in dealing with authoritarian white, to in fact change the joke and slip the yoke. Unfortunately, what Tolson probably made up either consciously or unconsciously, as a tale to indicate his folk shrewdness, then became an anecdote that Tolson's severest critics would point to as evidence of his kowtowing to a dead tradition.

But Randall's portrait of Tolson in this article is much more sympathetic than his later critical appraisal of Tolson's work included in *Modern Black Voices* and summarized above. In fact he reported another anecdote that Tolson told with considerable appreciation. Tolson remembered meeting a white Northern club woman distressed because a Southern member of her club said that Negroes steal chickens:

> Instead of abruptly denying this, Tolson asked, "Did you ever see movies of a Southern mansion with a huge dining hall and chandeliers and a linen-covered table where old Colonel sat to dinner with his family?"
>
> "Yes," she answered.
>
> "And did you see a black butler in a white coat bringing in a platter of fried chicken balanced high in the air with one hand?"
>
> "Yes."
>
> "Well, black Sam served the chicken. And who cooked the chicken?"
>
> "His wife, I guess."
>
> "Yes, black Mandy sweated over the stove to cook the chicken. And who fed and watered and took care of the chicken?"
>
> "His daughter, I suppose?"
>
> "Yes, little Cindy raised that chicken. And who grew the corn and the crops that fattened the chicken so the Colonel could eat it?"
>
> "The butler's son?"
>
> "Yes, black Junior toiling in the fields raised the corn to fatten that chicken. But, who ate the chicken?"
>
> By this time the clubwoman had begun to see the point and was smiling. "The Colonel, of course."
>
> "Yes, the Colonel ate that chicken, but somewhere on that plantation was a black Patrick Henry who said, 'Give me liberty, or give me—chicken!' Now, did the Colonel give him his liberty?"
>
> "No," the woman answered with a smile.
>
> Then, as Tolson described with mock-Freudian symbols how the slave captured the hen by tickling its rump with a long pole, the woman shook with laughter, and, he says, she was never again disturbed by the Southern woman's allegations that Negroes stole chickens.

Randall also joined the chorus of friends and acquaintances who were amazed by Tolson's energy, even during these final months of debilitating illness:

> Tolson has great gusto as a talker. The night I met him, LaGrone and I left early, as he was convalescing from a major operation. But we found out later that he had learned that James Farmer, one of his students, was in Detroit, and telephoning until he located him, he had gone out and spent the night in talk and had not returned to his sister's home until five o'clock the next morning.[25]

Tolson and James Farmer had much to talk about, not only the years they shared at Wiley as teacher and student, coach and debater, director and actor, but also the drift of racial politics in the 1960s and what it meant for the dreams in which both men had invested so many years of their lives. Farmer's leadership of CORE was increasingly being challenged by militant nationalists. He was to resign at the end of the year to take on a new and different challenge in public life, heading an antipoverty venture backed by government and foundation funds.

While Tolson was in New York in March 1965, just after seeing Farmer in Detroit, he was also named to the *New York Herald Tribune* Book Review Board. On 30 May 1965, Tolson reviewed Robert Penn Warren's *Who Speaks for the Negro* along with Erskine Caldwell's *In Search of Bisco*. At the end of his review of the Warren book Tolson noted the author's choice of Adam Clayton Powell as "perhaps their [Negroes'] greatest spokesman." Obliquely mocking such a game and acknowledging that Warren logically protected himself slightly with the word *perhaps*, Tolson nevertheless seized the occasion to speak up for his friend and former student, James Farmer: "Since Mr. Warren has taken the inductive hazard, I might as well follow suit. My choice is James Farmer of CORE." On 20 February 1966, the *Herald Tribune* also published Tolson's review of Farmer's *Freedom— When?* Tolson was extremely proud of Farmer and the work he had done, and Farmer considered Tolson one of the major influences on his life.

When Tolson returned to Langston after his promotional trip to New York and Washington, Langston University continued the celebration of Tolson's achievement by dedicating the spring Fine Arts Festival to him. Karl Shapiro came from Lincoln, Nebraska, for the occasion, and Tolson and he both gave readings. On 15 April, Shapiro wrote Tolson: "I've been trying to think of some way to write you to make sense after my wonderful stay with you—it was overwhelming for me, one of the few great moments of my life. You're scary and unscathed, really heroic to me, a great man (word I always try to shun). I hope to come back when the Writers deal is set up, which I think will happen."

Melvin B. Tolson

Melvin B. Tolson in 1965.

At the time it was commonly assumed that Tolson was sixty-five, the usual year for retirement, although in fact he was sixty-seven. Hence on 17 May, Tolson, along with two other colleagues, addressed a banquet arranged to honor their retirement from Langston University. But Tolson had no intention of retiring. Through the efforts of another former student and now chair of the English department of Tuskegee, Dr. Youra Qualls, he had already been offered the Avalon Chair as visiting distinguished professor of humanities for the following year, and there was little doubt of his acceptance.

The honors and recognition were now rolling it. Lincoln University was quick to add an honorary Doctor of Humane Letters to the Doctor of Letters it had previously awarded its distinguished alumnus. The ceremony noted that Tolson merited the honor "because he has demonstrated that true creative ability is not limited by artificial barriers like race and that belated recognition need not stifle the artist's creativity." Tolson's place of birth occasioned a comparison with another writer from the same state: "Although a long-time resident of Texas and Oklahoma, Melvin Beaunoru Tolson, born in Moberly, Missouri, at the turn of the century, has never lo several of the distinguishing characteristics of a citizen of the 'Show M state: loquaciousness, imagination, inventive genius, an innate sense of h mor, and forthrightness—the same qualities possessed by Mark Twain, a other literary son of Missouri."

Apparently, however, Tolson did not attend an alumni reunion at Lincc scheduled for June. In an undated letter, Horace Mann Bond wrote that I "sense of deprivation at not attending was greatly alleviated" by Tolso decision not to attend, particularly since, "after all, those of the noble cl of '23 whom I most treasured, are gone to their reward already—all but yo

The same summer that Joy Flasch was gathering most of her informat from Tolson for her biography, Dan McCall came from Cornell to teacl Langston. McCall was obviously deeply impressed by both Tolson and work. He published a very perceptive article on Tolson's *Libretto*, discus above, that fall in *American Quarterly*. His first novel, *The Man Says* published in 1969, the same year that his critical study *The Exampl Richard Wright* was published, contains a character clearly based on son. Henri Prudhomme is an aged professor, dying of cancer, brave shrewd, fighting the last battle of his life to rid Bundy University of a tr nical, but effective, president, whose excessive drinking, womanizing, physical abuse of his wife outrage common decency.

A letter from Dan and Dorothy McCall to Tolson dated 23 Septei 1965 clearly indicates the basis for McCall's quasi-fictional plot. After tl ing Tolson for opening his "home and bottles and Zulu Club to us f

pinks from the North" and commenting, "Langston turned out to be the best summer of our lives—mainly because you were there," the McCalls referred to a recent investigation of President William H. Hale of Langston:

> Word from your blood-brother at Langston is that King Louis came out of that investigation "unscathed." We want to know what's happened lately; we heard from Achille back in August. Did you folks hear anything new? We talked to a member of the Association of American University Professors' Investigating Team and he said he doesn't think an academic body is going to do any good. Where That Man can be got at is in the courts. Why the Hell doesn't someone who has been assaulted or injured file a suit and get the case to a Grand Jury?[26]

McCall apparently decided That Man could also be "got at" in fiction. Hale appears in the novel as Achille T. Washington, president of Bundy University. But most pertinent here is McCall's depiction of Tolson in the character of Henri Prudhomme. There are several slight, but revealing, incidents in the novel, in addition to the climactic confrontation between the professor and the president.

Early in the novel Prudhomme has to set straight young Beaunorus Green, the protagonist of the novel, whose name suggests Tolson's pervasive presence—Beau's wife is also named Ruth. Beau is a Ph.D. from Stanford, and he has lost touch with Southern racial politics. Thus Prudhomme gives him a lesson in Tolson-talk that makes ironic light of Tolson's effort to reconcile Marx and Christ:

> "Boy, you're lookin' at a charter member of the Anti-Tex-ass Legion. Many a time the vigilantes tried to feed me to the Little Dixie alligators. . . . What do you know? They used to sell niggers in the Galveston market by the pound. They burned niggers at the stake, and first they chopped off their fingers and toes and sold 'em as souvenirs. And you sit there all miseducated and Northern and tell me it's taken 'your' people a long time to make their move?"
> Then he said, "Now I knew I couldn't dance around this Baptist empire quoting Marx." I looked up, and he had put on a sweet smile; deeply he said, "Old Marx tells us to have all our things in common and sell your possessions and goods and part them to all men as every man has need. Now that's Marx. Isn't that Marx, Mr. Phi Beta Kappa?"
> "In the flesh."
> "The hell it is." He dropped his hands. "You illiterate black college man, that's Saint Luke. . . . Oh how I studied my Bible when I was working for the NAACP. Forget the talented tenth; I was out there with the sharecroppers. That's how you don't get kicked out of town as a Bolshevisky. Say Jeesus said it."[27]

A little too glib to be a completely fair representation of Tolson's views of Marx and Christianity, this is still an earnest and sensitive attempt to catch the flash of Tolson's wit.

Another effort to catch Tolson's manner occurs in a sermon that Prudhomme gives in a store-front church. It begins with a name used as a statement: "I-mman-uel Kant. I-mman-uel Kant asks you, Do you exist?"[28] Tolson was good at such rhetorical games, and he enjoyed making his audience reach for his point.

But McCall's most deeply felt tribute to Tolson is in the climactic scene of the novel. Prudhomme has adroitly instigated an investigation of the president by the state police. The evidence is overwhelming, but the president pulls the necessary political strings, and the investigation is stopped. The president gets drunk and comes for the professor with a gun. Prudhomme, his stomach distended from cancer and chemotherapy and wearing red felt slippers, the same slippers Joy Flasch noted Tolson wore after his first Dallas operation, walks out on the front porch to face the drunken president. After the first shot, Prudhomme "reached to his neck and he slowly wrapped ten fingers around the pajama shirt and—the noise crackling, low like a brush fire—he began to rip. He ripped the pajama shirt open, and it slid from his little shoulders, down off his arms, down onto his porch. The bronze abdomen jutted out. 'Put a bullet in the cancer. Archie, put a bullet'—and for the first time his voice, obscene—'*in the Can-cer.*' "[29] Prudhomme did not win his battle to bring down the president, and Tolson lost to cancer, but McCall created a fictional tribute to Tolson's bravery and his enduring social zeal.

When Melvin and Ruth packed for Tuskegee late in the summer of 1965 there was no thought of making a permanent move. They retained their home in Langston. And amid all the attention, honors, and the medical concerns that would seem to fill an ordinary life, Tolson characteristically continued to write. There are several manuscripts marked with his address at Tuskegee, 109 Bibb Street. He apparently did not relinquish his plans to complete the other four books of *Harlem Gallery*. They were to be titled *Book II, Egypt Land; Book III, The Red Sea; Book IV, The Wilderness;* and *Book V, The Promised Land*. There is an eight-page manuscript of an uncompleted poem titled "Dark Laughter," which may have been intended as some part of this epic, since it is written in the centered lines Tolson used so successfully in *Book I, The Curator*. The poem is set in a veldt village in modern Africa, where a tribal chief and a council of elders are entertaining two poets, one black and one white, who are close friends. The Zulu lord was "born on the veldt / but bred on a hill above the Seine." The other was born and bred in Kentucky but made his way through Greenwich Village and the Latin Quarter. The Chief proposes a friendly contest between the poets to determine *"what* land the Great God has blessed / with the strongest wine!"* The Zulu poet "straddled the question with / *ethnic two-ness*,"* and the Chief sneers, "The loins of a straddler cry for a kola nut!" The Kentucky poet winks sympathetically at his chastened friend and tells tall tales of his own mountain youth that strike a responsive chord in his audience. The Chief acknowledges, "In truth you *are* a bard" and accepts his fables as a tribute to his land. Then, feeling his own land has not been adequately represented by the Zulu bard, he tells a tale himself, "shuttling between what *is* and what *was*." But the Kentucky poet challenges the ethnic purity of his tale, finding evidence in it of an "USA movie in a ghost town of the Old West." When his companion poet protests, "Are you accusing The Good Gray Chief of theft?," the westerner responds, "Poets know all men are thieves. . . . After all, it's One World—isn't it?" Thus the

> dark laughter,
> beguiles the tribal censor,
> cheats the governess, reason,
> with Falstaffian relief from stock responses to
> paramount chief and witchdoctor,
> debauchee and maligner.

The poem is rough; it does not have the studied density of reference of *Book I*, but it indicates something of the direction of Tolson's imagination in these final months.

Tolson apparently did not attempt all the speaking engagements planned for New York in the fall, but he did go to Washington, D.C., in October to read his poetry at the Library of Congress under the auspices of the Gertrude Clarke Whittall Poetry and Literature Fund. The reading was tape-recorded, and his voice on the tape is firm and full, but the morning after his reading, as previously planned, he flew to Dallas for a third operation to check the growth of cancer. He apparently took this operation in stride, for one week before Thanksgiving found him back in Washington for another reception in his honor at the Liberian embassy.

On 14 February 1966, Tolson returned to Oklahoma, where he was the prnicipal speaker at a banquet of the Arts and Sciences College at Oklahoma State University in Stillwater. On 6 March he was in New York City, as the mystery guest, joining Sammy Davis, Jr., Harry Belafonte, Duke Ellington, and others in a tribute to James Farmer at Philharmonic Hall. Fourteen March marked a different kind of special event at Tuskegee—Dr. Wiley Wilson was named the first Carver Foundation Fellow Lecturer. In 1959 Wiley had received the Superior Performance Award for his research in steroid hormones at Walter Reed Army Institute of Research.

Ars longa, vita brevis est

In April, Fisk University held a writers' conference to celebrate its centennial year. Tolson appeared on a panel with Arna Bontemps, Robert Hayden, and Margaret Walker representing "Poetry from the Negro Renaissance Till Today." David Llorens described the conference for *Negro Digest*:

> One attends a writers conference anticipating new ideas, pertinent criticisms, enhanced perspectives—a touch of the inexplicable as well as the profound—but one also secretly hopes for that person who will rise to the occasion and provide the emotional stimulus that transforms writers conferences into good old "down home" Baptist conventions—for at least a little while!
> That stimulus was provided by Melvin B. Tolson, poet laureate of Liberia.

Llorens described Robert Hayden as setting the stage for "the stimulus" that Tolson gave to the conference. Visibly disturbed, Hayden rejected the label *Negro poet* and insisted that he was "a poet who happens to be Negro." Expecting opposition, he challenged those who did not accept his position by concluding, "Baby, that's your problem, not mine." One can imagine Tolson, long conditioned by his years and years of debate and platform experience, responding to such a challenge even if Hayden had taken the opposite side of the question. As Llorens reported, Hayden "created a perfect setting for the entrance of Mr. Tolson."

Tolson began with a favorite story about a visit to an old poet's grave. On the tombstone was engraved: *I am dead as all can see, ye bear you all to follow me!* These words gave him pause before he responded: *To follow you I'm not content, until I know which way you went!*:

> And as laughter filled the hall, Tolson rose from his chair with the energy of one of his pupils, and in a sweeping gesture and a booming voice that rocked Jubilee Hall, he roared: "Nobody writes in a vacuum or out of a vacuum—when a man writes, he tells me which way he went in society."

A poet's nature is determined by his tridimensionality: "A man has his biology, his sociology, and his psychology—*and then he becomes a poet.*" Tolson then played upon Hayden's phrase, "happens to be":

> "Hap, hap . . . let me see, hap means accident. Is someone going to make M. B. Tolson an accident? You'll never make me an accident" and by this time his voice was blazing to the rafters as he exclaimed: "I'm a black poet, an African-American poet, a Negro poet. I'm no accident—and I don't give a tinker's dam what you think."

After discoursing on the origins of the word *negro*, Tolson observed that "there was no stigma attached to it 'until the coming of Christian civilization.' Tolson blamed capitalism for the world's race problem." Tolson then underscored this statement by alluding to LeRoi Jones's *The Toilet*: "Every-

297

one thinks he was talking about a toilet in Harlem; he wasn't talking about a toilet in Harlem—he was talking about an entire civilization that has become a commode. When the intellectuals and the artists condemn a civilization, that doesn't mean that that civilization is in trouble—*it means it's on its way out!*"[30]

Robert Hayden was unfairly steamrollered by a vintage Tolson performance. It is appropriate to note, however, that Tolson responded to the question of racial identity that Hayden raised by reiterating his longstanding belief in nurture over nature and in capitalism being responsible for the world's race problem. Hayden may have expected an attack from young nationalists, but he must have been surprised at all this thunder coming from a man fifteen years his senior.

In June, Dudley Randall wrote Tolson about what a pleasant surprise it had been to run into him at Fisk: "David Llorenz [*sic*] was very taken with you. He wrote me, 'Tolson, not Cassius, is the Greatest.' " Randall at the same time announced that he was sending under separate cover the manuscript of a collection of poems for which Tolson was to write an introduction. Randall had received permission from Twayne to print Hideho Heights's poem, "The Sea Turtle and the Shark," from *Harlem Gallery* as a broadside. Randall also announced that he was writing a master's thesis titled "African Influences on Tolson's *Libretto* and Ellington's *Liberian Suite*."

Meanwhile, William Melvin Kelley apparently was also very impressed when he met Tolson at the Fisk writers' conference. On 5 May 1966 he sent Tolson a copy of his second novel, *A Drop of Patience*, and wrote: "I have only known you for a short time, but already I feel as if we have known each other for 300 years now, all our years in bondage. You are a part of my proud past—the past that my white man's education kept from me. You are a great man. And that word MAN is a very heavy word. Somehow in the James Baldwins and the Leroi Joneses I have never been able to find that MAN, and I didn't expect to find one at Fisk either, and I am moved that I did. Keep going; you're going great."[31]

On 8 May, Tolson addressed the Fortieth Scholarship Night Convocation at Tuskegee. Dean A. P. Torrence wrote later to thank him for the "inspiring address": "The thunderous applause that followed your address indicated clearly the admiration that the audience had for you and the acceptance of your magnificent presentation. Tuskegee is honored to have such a distinguished person as you to serve as its first Avalon Professor of Humanities."

On 25 May, Tolson was back in New York City to be honored with a $2,500 award as poet and playwright by the American Academy of Arts and Letters. The affair was posh, with George Kennan presiding over the award ceremonies. Other writers honored that evening included William Alfred, John Barth, James Dickey, H. E. F. Donahue, Shirley Hazzard, Josephine Herbst, Edwin Honig, and Gary Snyder.

It was another proud moment for Tolson, but an incident occurred at the reception prior to the ceremony that touched him deeply and clearly distracted him from the pleasure he should have taken in the honor. It is impossible to tell whether Tolson was being unduly sensitive or not, but he felt the incident deeply enough to write about it and to discuss it with Joy Flasch and with Ruth. These are Tolson's notes, titled "Comments on *Invisible Man* & Ellison":

The Brotherhood in *I. M.* is defeatist.

Only embarrassing moment I've had all year—Ellisons and T.'s [Tolsons] only Negroes at reception before Academy presentations. Allan Nevins had come up at cocktail party to talk; Felicia Geffes, secretary, had been very gracious since we arrived early. This is hard for me to describe. I was talking to Dr. Nevins, who was writing down his address and telling me to apply for Huntington fellowship. I saw Ralph and waved my hand. He nodded rather formally. Later he was talking to Felicia and Dr. Nevins left; Ellison came around on my left side and formally shook hands.

I knew Ellison when he was a Communist and have been to his flat. Mrs. E. came up and Mrs. T. said, "I've known your distinguished husband for a number of years, but this is the first time I've had the pleasure of meeting you." She said, "It's nice to meet you, too," and drifted off to hug some white ladies.

I tried to strike a conversation. I asked Ellison if he had read my book. He said, "Yes, I bought a copy three weeks ago."

Both of us were in radical movement years ago. He and I understood Negro society as no other writers do. I can read between the lines. He can't get involved in the Negro movement.

The ideological battle is the most bitter and devastating battle there is. Ex-Communist turns on Communist. Ellison knows that I know; but he knows I cannot be bought. I haven't changed; he has.

Ten years ago in this room we argued about the individual vs. Socialist. He doesn't know to what extent I may go in joining other writers in attacking him. I have to write an article on Negro writers. Our social approach is different. In *H. G.* I write about an opulent society serving the Belshazzarian feast. He is an individualist. I am a social writer. Ellison claims he is a descendant of Emerson. He says the Negro endures; I say he advances. He and I have debated long. I don't want to write an Alger story of a Negro who succeeded. I have a social approach to man's problems.[32]

Tolson's statement that "he and I understood Negro society as no other writers do" suggests his deep respect for Ellison's writing and a sense of kinship in their both having traveled the sometimes obscure pathway from radical leftist politics to modernist literary concerns. It is likely that Tolson saw his own position in poetry as analogous to Ellison's in fiction—an assumption encouraged by the flattering recognition that *Harlem Gallery* was then winning for Tolson. Thus it is likely that he anticipated a particularly warm clasp of literary comradeship from the only other black writer in this sea of white faces. Thus he perceived a double slight: Mrs. Ellison's turning away from Ruth's warm gesture and Ellison's seemingly pointed laconic reply to Tolson's eager question about *Harlem Gallery*, "Yes, I bought a copy three weeks ago." It started the bitter juices to flow. Poor Boy Blue was told to stay in his place again. So he looked once more at his own beliefs and those of Ellison and he drew a revealing proud distinction. Ellison "is an individualist. I am a social writer." Unlike Ellison, Tolson had remained true to his past.

On 1 September 1966, after Tolson's death, Ellison wrote a letter of condolence to Ruth expressing his grief both as a friend and as an Oklahoman at her husband's death. He noted that he had no idea that Tolson was ill when they met at the ceremonies in May. He wrote of his early memories of Tolson's debating teams and the standard of excellence they achieved, of his respect for him as a college professor, and of the many exciting evenings of intellectual discussion they had shared during the 1940s. He acknowledged that Tolson along with Roscoe Dungee and his sister Drusella had helped shape his life as a writer, but there is only a slight reference to Tolson's achievement as a poet. There is no other apparent indication in the letter that he was aware that Tolson felt deeply slighted by him at the May ceremonies. Ellison returned to Oklahoma City in November as one of the guest speakers at the inauguration of the Oklahoma Council of Arts and Humanities. Ruth Tolson attended, in spite of what she, too, remembered as a very definite slight. She knew her husband would have expected her to go. He did not believe in holding personal grudges.

Melvin and Ruth returned to Langston in early June 1966 to see Arthur Tolson awarded his Ph.D. at the commencement exercises of the University of Oklahoma, the last of the three sons to earn his doctorate. Ruth Marie had earlier earned her master's degree in Library Science. All of the boys now had more substantial protection against the rise and fall of the capitalistic economic ferris wheel than Tolson had ever enjoyed, but he still delighted in challenging them before any who would listen, "It doesn't matter how many doctor's degrees you boys get—you won't ever catch up with your old man. He has a headstart on you—and as long as he's around he intends to keep it."

Just a few days after Arthur's graduation, Tolson returned to Dallas and entered St. Paul's Hospital for the last time. Ironically, a letter that was already sent to his Tuskegee address and later was sent again to his Langston

Ars longa, vita brevis est

Melvin B. Tolson in 1965.

address from Gerald Freund of the Rockefeller Foundation announced that a grant of $5,000 had been recommended for Tolson's living and travel costs for four months during 1967 to support his writing.

In the next two months Dr. William Strickland performed three operations on Tolson. It was only during the third operation that it was discovered that the cancer had metastasized and there no longer were grounds for hope. The last operation was 24 August, a Tuesday morning. M. B. Tolson died Sunday evening, 29 August. On that Sunday afternoon his condition had seemed stable and his eyes were clear. Melvin, Jr., left the hospital to return to Norman. Ruth and her daughter stayed longer but left the hospital about 5:30 P.M. Two attendants were in the room talking with their patient about 9:30 P.M. when they suddenly became conscious that he was not responding to their talk. They were surprised to discover that he had passed.

His extraordinary will to live had almost convinced his wife and his children, no matter what the doctor said, that death could not claim him, but he relinquished life peacefully, content at last to live in the memories of family and friends and in the words he had woven with such passion and humor and care for the world that would succeed him, content to wait for the vertical audience to nurture his carefully wrought ironies into truths that would crumble the idols of the tribe and bond mankind instead in the promise of universal democratic brotherhood.

NOTES

Chapter I: Jockeying Down the Years on Pegasus

1. *Caviar and Cabbage: Selected Columns by Melvin B. Tolson from the "Washington Tribune,"* 1937–1944, ed. Robert M. Farnsworth, p. 246.

2. Dan McCall, "The Quicksilver Sparrow of M. B. Tolson," p. 538.

3. A letter Tolson wrote in 1955 requesting a birth certificate from the Bureau of Vital Statistics, Randolph County, in order to obtain a passport for his forthcoming trip to Liberia suggests that he was then not absolutely certain about the year of his birth: "It seems that I was born in Moberly, Missouri, February 6, 1900—or thereabout." Tolson probably was born in Moberly since the *Journal of the Thirteenth Session of the Central Missouri Conference of the Methodist Episcopal Church* (29–31 March 1899–) lists his father's ministerial appointment at Higbee, which is very close to Moberly. Unfortunately, the birth records for Randolph County for this period were all lost in a fire.

4. Joy Flasch, *Melvin B. Tolson*, p. 20.

5. "The Odyssey of a Manuscript," pp. 5–6.

6. "Melvin B. Tolson: An Interview," in *Anger and Beyond*, ed. Herbert Hill (New York: Harper and Row, 1966), p. 193.

7. Thomas Whitbread refers to this same anecdote in explaining Tolson's inspiriting vitality and the power of his words in a poetic tribute to Tolson after his death:

> He loved life so much
> That knowing him was almost to be his cancer,
> Devouring him.
> He and words were twins, at one.
>
> In one of his favorite anecdotes
> He told of a train delayedly stopping, a Frenchman getting off,
> The Frenchman seeing his twelve-year-old paintings, the
>   Frenchman asking him to come to Paris,
> His mother barring the door for over a week thereafter.
>
> That was how, he said, he turned to poetry.
> He turned to it with vengeance. He wrote words
> He could say with tremendous power
> And accuracy.
>
> I remember Tolson, summer of '65
> Throwing a half-eaten McDonald's hamburger, in its
>   paper, out the window
> Of a moving car
> And later describing that hamburger as white America.

"In Praise of M. B. Tolson," in *Whomp and Moonshiver* (Brookport, N.Y.: Boa Editions, 1982), p. 45.

8. *All Aboard*, Tolson Manuscripts, Library of Congress, p. 214.

9. *Melvin B. Tolson*, p. 22.

10. *Caviar and Cabbage*, p. 258.

11. "The Odyssey of a Manuscript," p. 7.

12. Ibid., pp. 7–8.

13. *Caviar and Cabbage*, p. 260.

14. *Washington Tribune*, 13 July 1940. This *Caviar and Cabbage* column and others from which I quote are not included in the collection I edited in 1982. These columns will be noted only by their dates and may be found on microfilm in the Moorland-Spingarn Research Center at Howard University.

Notes

15. *Washington Tribune*, 21 January 1939.
16. Tolson Manuscripts, Library of Congress. Obvious syntactical and spelling errors have been corrected.
17. *Washington Tribune*, 21 September 1940.
18. *Caviar and Cabbage*, pp. 263–65.
19. Ibid., p. 239.
20. Letter from Samuel J. Washington to Robert M. Farnsworth, 18 September 1980.

Chapter II: Harlem Visited

1. "My Early Days in Harlem," in *Harlem: A Community in Transition*, ed. John Henrick Clarke (New York: Citadel Press, 1969), p. 62.
2. "Melvin B. Tolson: A Critical Biography," pp. 11–12.
3. "The Harlem Group of Negro Writers," M.A. thesis, Columbia University, 1940, p. 8.
4. Ibid., p. 80.
5. Ibid., p. 84.
6. Ibid., p. 82.
7. Ibid., p. 27.
8. Ibid.
9. Ibid., p. 31.
10. Ibid., pp. 36–39.
11. Ibid., p. 33.
12. *Pittsburgh Courier*, 2 February 1933, pp. 10–11.
13. *Caviar and Cabbage*, pp. 255–56.
14. "The Harlem Group of Negro Writers," pp. 120–21.
15. James O. Young, *Black Writers of the Thirties* (Baton Rouge: Louisiana State University Press, 1973), pp. 3–5.
16. "Odyssey of a Manuscript," pp. 8–9.
17. Interview with Mariann Russell, 8 June 1975.
18. "The Harlem Group of Negro Writers," p. 39.
19. *Melvin B. Tolson's "Harlem Gallery,"* p. 54.
20. Hobart Jarrett, "Adventures in Interracial Debates."
21. *Caviar and Cabbage*, p. 240.
22. Ibid., pp. 240–42.
23. *Caste, Class and Race* (Garden City: Doubleday, 1948), p. 198.
24. *Good Morning, Revolution: Uncollected Writings of Social Protest*, ed. Faith Berry (New York: Lawrence Hill, 1973), p. 125.
25. "Odyssey of a Manuscript," pp. 16–17.
26. *Negro Voices*, ed. Beatrice M. Murphy, p. ii.
27. "The Cultural Barometer," *Current History*, February 1938, p. 56.
28. "A Man Against the Idols of the Tribe," p. 32.
29. Ibid., p. 31.
30. Ibid., pp. 30–31.

Chapter III: Recognition and World War II

1. "The Omega Fellowship and Scholarship Awards," *The Oracle*, October 1940, page numbers unavailable on reprint used.
2. Tolson Manuscripts, Library of Congress.
3. An undated clipping from an unidentified newspaper saved by Arthur Tolson.
4. *Caviar and Cabbage*, pp. 104–6.
5. Ibid., p. 125.
6. Ibid., pp. 151–52.
7. Ibid., p. 107.

Notes

8. Ibid., pp. 107–8.
9. Ibid., p. 127.
10. Ibid., pp. 29–31.
11. Ibid., pp. 131–32.
12. Many years later Tolson told Prof. Cliff Warren at Central Oklahoma University that he got the idea for this poem from an old Negro who worked for a white family. A friend of the family, a judge, would visit and try to drink himself senseless in an effort to drown his guilt at having attained his position as judge through what he had done to an innocent Negro. Jay Flasch manuscript note.
13. Mary Lou Chamberlain failed to understand this line on first reading (letter, 4 February 1944, from Chamberlain to Tolson). *Vertical* here means standing up with proud and moral self-assertion. *Horizontal* is its opposite. After 1958 Tolson used these terms principally in reference to the *immediate* and *future* audiences for poetry that John Ciardi described in the *Saturday Review of Literature*, 22 November 1958, pp. 12, 42.
14. *Francis Bacon* (Los Angeles: University of California Press, 1962), pp. 291–93.

Chapter IV: A Time to Move

1. "Books in Brief."
2. Quoted from a collation of comments on *Rendezvous* in Tolson Manuscripts, Library of Congress. Attributed to *New Adventures into Poetry*, a title I have not been able to identify.
3. Quoted without note of publication in *Wiley College Reporter*, May 1945.
4. "Book Review: Lyrico-Dramatic."
5. "Among the New Volumes of Verse."
6. "Two Powerful Negro Poets."
7. "The Poet Speaks."
8. Quoted in collation of comments on *Rendezvous with America*, Tolson Manuscripts, Library of Congress.
9. "Key Words," p. 3, in the Tolson Manuscript Collection, Library of Congress.
10. Arthur L. Tolson, *The Black Oklahomans, A History: 1541–1972* (New Orleans, 1974), p. 94.
11. Zella J. Black Patterson, *Langston University: A History* (Norman: University of Oklahoma Press, 1979), p. 5.
12. John Ciardi, "Dialogue with an Audience," *Saturday Review of Literature*, 22 November 1958, pp. 12, 42.

Chapter V: Novels and Plays

1. Sterling A. Brown, Arthur P. Davis, and Ulysses Lee, eds., *The Negro Caravan* (New York: Arno Press, 1941), p. 398.
2. Letter from Professor Edward Boatner to Robert M. Farnsworth, 13 October 1980.
3. George S. Schuyler, *Black No More* (New York: Negro Universities Press, 1969), p. 46.
4. "Our Struggle: The Story of Montgomery," in *Black Protest Thought in the Twentieth Century*, ed. August Meier, Elliott Rudwick, and Francis L. Broderick (Indianapolis and New York: Bobbs-Merrill, 1965), p. 294.

Chapter VI: Publishing *Libretto*

1. *Collier's* did not publish the poems, but they probably eventually appeared as "Abraham Lincoln of Rock Spring Farm," in *Soon, One Morning*, ed. Herbert Hill.

2. Letter from Tolson to Tate, 1 June 1949, in Allen Tate Collection, Princeton University Library.
3. *Modern Quarterly* 8: 1 (1933): 17–24.
4. *Modern Quarterly* 8: 6 (1934): 372–73.
5. "Notes on the Trombone of the West," pp. 51, 52.
6. "Modern Poetry under the Microscope," pp. 113–14.
7. See "Portrait of a Poet as Raconteur," pp. 54–57, and Joy Flasch, *Melvin B. Tolson*, p. 74.

Chapter VII: Writing for the Vertical Audience

1. Tolson Manuscript Collection, Library of Congress.
2. *Caviar and Cabbage*, pp. 90–92.
3. *Washington Tribune*, 21 January 1939.
4. *Caste, Class and Race* (Garden City: Doubleday, 1948), pp. 238–39.
5. *Renascent Africa* (New York: Negro University Press, 1969), pp. 9–11.
6. It is perhaps appropriate here to remember Duke Hands, whose last name tells a story and who makes up a ballad commemorating the Pullman car as a combination of vision and craftsmanship: "Duke grinned as Uncle George's vision unfolded in sky-climbing grandeur. He closed his eyes and there stood the midwestern giant with great horney hands around him—hands ready to build a miracle of civilization" (*All Aboard*, p. 155).
7. Selden Rodman, "On Vistas Undreamt."
8. John Ciardi, "Recent Verse."
9. J. Saunders Redding, "Book Review."
10. Tolson Manuscripts, Library of Congress.
11. Howard P. Fussiner, "A Mature Voice Speaks," pp. 96–97.
12. Arthur P. Davis, "Negro Poetry." On 24 January 1954, William Stanley Braithwaite also wrote Tolson a supportive letter after seeing Rodman's review in the *New York Times*. Braithwaite had not at the time read the *Libretto*. He apparently felt that Tolson's conversion of Allen Tate was sufficient cause for congratulation: "This is a different Allen Tate than I knew twenty-five years or thirty years ago who did not accept the Negro artist on the higher level of excellence. It is, apart from anything else, a great achievement to have converted this critical authority to the single standard by which all artists irrespective of race or color should be judged. With patient industry and concentrated devotion you have achieved an art that adds a glory to contemporary American literature" (letter among Tolson Manuscripts, Library of Congress).
13. Lorenzo D. Turner, Review of *Libretto for the Republic of Liberia*.
14. S. E. Hyman, "The Negro Writer in America: An Exchange," p. 207.
15. "A Poet's Odyssey," in *Anger and Beyond*, ed. Herbert Hill, p. 185.
16. "The Decolonization of American Literature," p. 853.
17. In addition to Dan McCall's and Jon Stanton Woodson's criticisms, Nathan A. Scott, Jr., in "Black Literature," praised the *Libretto*. See *Harvard Guide to Contemporary American Writing*, ed. Daniel Hoffman (Cambridge: Harvard University Press, 1979), p. 376.
18. Dan McCall, "The Quicksilver Sparrow of M. B. Tolson."
19. Jon Stanton Woodson, "A Critical Analysis of the Poetry of M. B. Tolson," p. 107.
20. Ibid., pp. 107–8.
21. Ibid., p. 114.
22. Ibid., pp. 183–84.
23. Ibid., p. 186.

Chapter VIII: Bridging the Peaks

1. *A Gallery of Harlem Portraits*, pp. 8, 209–10.

Notes

Chapter IX: Langston–The Hub of a Universe

1. See *Arna Bontemps–Langston Hughes Letters, 1925–1967*, pp. 261–63.
2. "The Foreground of Negro Poetry," pp. 33–34.
3. Tape recording of Tolson's AMSAC reading, in possession of Robert M. Farnsworth.
4. "State Poet Recalls Robert Frost," *Daily Oklahoman*, 10 February 1963.
5. *Oklahoma Black Dispatch*, 29 March 1957.
6. "Modern Poetry under the Microscope," pp. 113–15.
7. Letter from Wiley Wilson Tolson to Robert M. Farnsworth, 26 October 1982.

Chapter X: *Harlem Gallery:* From Chattel to Esquire

1. *Caviar and Cabbage*, p. 198.
2. Ibid., p. 200.
3. Ibid., p. 199.
4. Howard Brotz, ed., *Negro Social and Political Thought: 1850–1920* (New York: Basic Books, 1969), p. 485.
5. *The Souls of Black Folk* (New York: Peter Smith, 1964), p. 69.
6. "Miles to Go with Black Ulysses," p. 12.
7. "Flowers of Hope," *Oklahoma's Orbit, The Magazine of the Sunday Oklahoman*, 29 August 1965, pp. 6, 9.

Chapter XI: *Ars longa, vita brevis est*

1. *Melvin B. Tolson*, p. 40.
2. See "The Critic Outside."
3. "Decolonization of American Literature," p. 853.
4. "Poetry Chronicle," pp. 456–57.
5. "Books Noted," pp. 51–52.
6. "Who Speaks Negro?," pp. 55–57.
7. "Tolson's *Gallery* Brings Poetry Home."
8. "Books in Review," *Muhammad Speaks*, 13 August 1965.
9. *TLS*, 25 November 1965, p. 1049.
10. "The Poet's Voice in the Crowd."
11. "Two Volumes of Contemporary Poetry."
12. Ronald Walcott, "Ellison, Gordone, and Tolson: Some Notes on the Blues, Style, and Space," p. 9.
13. Ibid., p. 26.
14. Ibid., p. 27.
15. Ibid., pp. 28–29.
16. "The Black Aesthetic in the Thirties, Forties, and Fifties," in *Modern Black Voices*, ed. Donald B. Gibson, p. 40.
17. *Drumvoices*, p. 254.
18. Ibid., pp. 257–58.
19. Ibid., p. 262.
20. Nathan A. Scott, Jr., "Black Literature," in *Harvard Guide to Contemporary American Writing*, ed. Daniel Hoffman, pp. 325–26.
21. "The Heart of Blackness—M. B. Tolson's Poetry," pp. 64–65.
22. Ibid., p. 67.
23. Ibid., p. 76.
24. Interview of Joy Flasch, 7 June 1979, Langston, Oklahoma.
25. "Portrait of a Poet as Raconteur," pp. 54–57.
26. Tolson Manuscripts, Library of Congress.
27. *The Man Says Yes*, pp. 64–65.

28. Ibid., p. 119.

29. Ibid., p. 217.

30. "Seeking a New Image: Writers Converge at Fisk University," *Negro Digest*, June 1966, pp. 54–68.

31. Tolson Manuscripts, Library of Congress.

32. Ibid.

BIBLIOGRAPHY

Published Works of Melvin B. Tolson

Books

Caviar and Cabbage: Selected Columns by Melvin B. Tolson from the "Washington Tribune," 1937–1944. Edited by Robert M. Farnsworth. Columbia and London: University of Missouri Press, 1982.
A Gallery of Harlem Portraits. Edited by Robert M. Farnsworth. Columbia and London: University of Missouri Press, 1979.
Harlem Gallery: Book I, The Curator. New York: Twayne Publishers, 1965.
Libretto for the Republic of Liberia. New York: Twayne Publishers, 1953.
Rendezvous with America. New York: Dodd, Mead and Co., 1944.

Poems, Articles, and Reviews

"Abraham Lincoln of Rock Spring Farm." In *Soon, One Morning: New Writing by American Negroes,* edited by Herbert Hill, pp. 57–77. New York: Alfred A. Knopf, 1963.
"African China." *Voices* 140 (Winter 1950): 35–38.
"All Aboard!" *New Letters* 39: 4 (Summer 1973): 3–37.
"Alpha," "Beta," "Gamma," "Delta," "Epsilon," "Zeta," "Eta" (*Harlem Gallery*). *Prairie Schooner* 35: 3 (Fall 1961): 243–64.
"The Auction." In *Negro Voices,* edited by Beatrice M. Murphy, pp. 152–53. New York: Henry Harrison, 1938.
"The Black Rapist." *The Oracle,* October 1938, pp. 14, 15, 18.
"The Braggart" (*Rendezvous with America*). *Common Ground* 4: 4 (Summer 1944): 74.
"The Breadline." In *Sonnets: An Anthology of Contemporary Verse,* edited by Ralph Cheyney, p. 97. New York: Henry Harrison, 1939.
"The Cabin's Victim." *The Lincolnian* (Yearbook, Lincoln High School, Kansas City, Missouri), 1917, pp. 52–55.
"Caviar and Cabbage," *Washington Tribune,* 9 October 1937–24 June 1944. On microfilm, Moorland-Spingarn Research Center, Howard University.
"Claude McKay's Art," *Poetry* 83: 5 (February 1954): 287–90.
"The Contributors' Column." *Atlantic Monthly* 168: 3 (September 1941): v.
"Dark Symphony" (*Rendezvous with America*). *Atlantic Monthly* 168: 3 (September 1941): 314–17.
"Dr. Harvey Whyte" (*A Gallery of Harlem Portraits*). *Modern Monthly* 10: 7 (August 1937): 10.
"E. & O. E." *Poetry* 78: 7 (September 1951): 330–42, 369–72.
"Five Essays" (*Caviar and Cabbage*). *New Letters* 48: 4 (Summer 1981): 103–19.
"Five Poems" (*A Gallery of Harlem Portraits*). *New Letters* 42: 4 (Summer 1976): 164–69.
"The Foreground of Negro Poetry." *Kansas Quarterly* 7: 3 (Summer 1976): 30–35.

Bibliography

"Goodbye Christ." *Pittsburgh Courier*, 26 January 1933, pp. 10–11; 2 February 1933, pp. 10–11.

"Hamuel Gutterman" (*A Gallery of Harlem Portraits*). *Modern Monthly* 10: 5 (April 1937): 7.

"Harlem" (*A Gallery of Harlem Portraits*). *The Arts Quarterly* 1: 1 (April–June 1937): 27.

"Jacob Nollen" (*A Gallery of Harlem Portraits*). *Modern Monthly* 10: 6 (May 1937): 10.

"Kikes, Bohunks, Crackers, Dagos, Niggers" ("The Underdogs," *A Gallery of Harlem Portraits*). *The Modern Quarterly* 11: 4 (Autumn 1939): 18–19.

"From *Libretto for the Republic of Liberia*." *Poetry* 76: 4 (July 1950): 208–15.

"From *The Lion and the Jackal*." *Okike* 1: 5 (May 1967): 8–16.

"A Long Head to a Round Head." *Beloit Poetry Journal* 11: 4 (Summer 1952): 19–21.

"A Man Against the Idols of the Tribe." *The Modern Quarterly* 11: 7 (Fall 1940): 29–32.

"The Man from Halicarnassus." *Poetry* 81: 1 (October 1952): 75–77.

"Miles to Go with Black Ulysses." *New York Herald Tribune Book Week*, 20 February 1966, pp. 2, 12.

"Modern Poetry under the Microscope." *Midwest Journal* 7: 1 (Spring 1955): 113–15.

"The Negro Scholar," *Midwest Journal* 1: 1 (Winter 1948): 80–82.

"The Note." In *Eros, An Anthology of Modern Love Poems*, edited by Lucia Trent, p. 69. New York: Henry Harrison, 1939.

"Notes on the Trombone of the West." *Voices* 140 (Winter 1950): 50–52.

"The Odyssey of a Manuscript." *New Letters* 48: 1 (Fall 1981): 5–17.

"The Past, Present and Future." *The Lincolnian* (Yearbook, Lincoln High School, Kansas City Missouri), 1918, p. 31.

"A Poet's Odyssey." In *Anger and Beyond*, edited by Herbert Hill, pp. 181–95. New York: Harper and Row, 1966.

"Quotes or Unquotes on Poetry." *Kansas Quarterly* 7: 3 (Summer 1973): 36–38.

"Rendezvous with America" (*Rendezvous with America*). *Common Ground* 2: 4 (Summer 1942): 3–9.

"Retrospection." *The Lincolnian* (Yearbook, Lincoln High School, Kansas City, Missouri), 1917, pp. 28–29.

"Roland Hayes." In *Negro Voices*, edited by Beatrice M. Murphy, pp. 151–52. New York: Henry Harrison, 1938.

"Richard Wright: *Native Son*." *The Modern Quarterly* 11: 5 (Winter 1939): 19–24.

"She Can't Take It." *Flash* (Washington, D.C.), 31 August 1939, p. 6.

"Six Poems" (*A Gallery of Harlem Portraits*). *New Letters* 43: 3 (Spring 1977): 11–18.

"Recipes of the Success of Black Men." *The Oracle* (date and issue unknown).

"A Song for Myself" (*Rendezvous with America*). *Phylon* 4: 4 (1945): 351–52.

"The Tragedy of the Yarr Karr." *The* (Wiley College) *Wild Cat* (1926), pp. 193–98.

"Uncle Walt" (*A Gallery of Harlem Portraits*). *Modern Quarterly* 10: 7 (March 1938): 10.

"Unpublished Poems of Melvin B. Tolson" (*A Gallery of Harlem Portraits*). *Y'Bird* 1: 2 (1978): 82–97.

Bibliography

"Vergil Ragsdale" (*A Gallery of Harlem Portraits*). *Modern Quarterly* 10: 7 (Winter 1939): 48.

"Wanderers in the Sierra." *The Lincolnian* (Yearbook, Lincoln High School, Kansas City, Missouri), 1918, pp. 20–26.

"Wanted: A New Negro Leadership." *The Oracle*, September 1937, pp. 10–11.

"Will the Real Moses Stand Up." *New York Herald Tribune Book Week*, 30 May 1965, pp. 5, 8.

"The Wine of Ecstasy. In *Negro Voices*, edited by Beatrice M. Murphy, p. 153. New York: Henry Harrison, 1938.

"*Woodcuts for Americana*: 'Old Man Michael,' 'The Gallows,' 'The Man Inside,' 'When Great Dogs Fight' " (*Rendezvous with America*). *Common Ground* 3: 3 (Spring 1943): 38–43.

On Tolson's Life and Works

Books

Flasch, Joy. *Melvin B. Tolson*. New York: Twayne Publishers, 1972.

Russell, Mariann. *Melvin B. Tolson's "Harlem Gallery": A Literary Analysis*. Columbia and London: University of Missouri Press, 1980.

Dissertations

Flasch, Joy. "Melvin B. Tolson: A Critical Biography." Oklahoma State University, 1969.

Huot, Robert J. "Melvin B. Tolson's 'Harlem Gallery': A Critical Edition." University of Utah, 1971.

Williams, Wilburn. "The Desolate Servitude of Language: A Reading of the Poetry of Melvin B. Tolson." Yale University, 1979.

Woodson, Jon Stanton. "A Critical Analysis of the Poetry of M. B. Tolson." Brown University, 1978.

Reviews and Articles

On *Rendezvous with America*

Benet, William Rose. "Two Powerful Negro Poets." *Saturday Review* 28: 12 (24 March 1945): 34–36.

Burke, Arthur E. "Book Review: Lyrico-Dramatic." *The Crisis* 52: 2 (February 1945): 61.

Davis, Frank Marshall. Review of *Rendezvous with America*. Quoted in a collation of comments on *Rendezvous* among Tolson Manuscripts, Library of Congress. Attributed to *AN Preview*.

Garrison, W. E. "Books in Brief." *The Christian Century* 61: 38 (20 September 1944): 1078–79.

Hilyer, Robert. "Among the New Volumes of Verse." *New York Times Book Review*, 10 December 1944), p. 29.

I., E. D. "Songs for All America by a Gifted Negro." *Kansas City Star*, 23 September 1944, p. 12.

Lowe, Ramona. "Poem 'Rendezvous with Ameria' Wins Fame for Melvin Tolson." *Chicago Defender*, New York Bureau, 24 February 1945.

Bibliography

K., J. "Unprejudiced Poems." *Raleigh Observer*, 8 October 1944.

Newsome, Effie Lee. "Melvin B. Tolson, *Rendezvous with America*." *Negro College Quarterly* 2: 4 (December 1944): 171–72.

Tillman, Nathaniel. "The Poet Speaks." *Phylon* 5: 4 (Fourth Quarter 1944): 389–91.

Walker, Margaret. Review of *Rendezvous with America*. Quoted in a collation of comments on *Rendezvous* among Tolson Manuscripts, Library of Congress. Attributed to *New Adventures in Poetry*.

On *Libretto for the Republic of Liberia*

Ciardi, John. "Recent Verse." *The Nation* 178: 7 (27 February 1954): 183.

Davis, Arthur P. "Negro Poetry." *Midwest Journal* 6: 2 (Summer 1954): 74–77.

Fussiner, Howard P. "A Mature Voice Speaks." *Phylon* 15: 1 (First Quarter 1954): 96–97.

McCall, Dan. "The Quicksilver Sparrow of M. B. Tolson." *American Quarterly* 18: 3 (Fall 1966): 538–42.

Redding, J. Saunders. "Book Review." *Philadelphia Afro-American*, 23 January 1954.

Rodman, Selden. "On Vistas Undreamt." *New York Times Book Review*, 24 January 1954, p. 10.

Turner, Lorenzo D. Review of *Libretto for the Republic of Liberia*. *Poetry* 86: 3 (5 June 1955): 175–76.

On *Harlem Gallery*

Anonymous. "Books in Review." *Muhammad Speaks*, 13 August 1965.

———. Review of *Harlem Gallery*. *Times Literary Supplement*, 25 November 1965, p. 1049.

Bickham, Jack. "Langston Poet May Signal New Era." *Sunday Oklahoman*, 23 May 1965, p. 10.

Brooks, Gwendolyn. "Books Noted." *Negro Digest* 14: 11 (September 1965): 51–52.

Conroy, Jack. "Tolson: A Poet to Appreciate." *Chicago Sun-Times*, 18 July 1965.

Delancey, Rose Mary. "Tolson Hailed as a Great Poet." *Fort Wayne News-Sentinel*, 24 April 1965, p. 4–A.

Fabio, Sarah Webster. "Who Speaks Negro?" *Negro Digest* 16: 2 (December 1966): 54–58.

Jacobsen, Josephine. "Two Volumes of Contemporary Poetry." *Baltimore Evening Sun*, 2 November 1965, p. A–20.

Lieberman, Laurence. "Poetry Chronicle." *Hudson Review* 18: 3 (Autumn 1965): 455–60.

Miner, Virginia Scott. "A 'Great Poet' Unknown to Our Own Midwest." *Kansas City Star*, 25 July 1965, p. 5D.

Sherwood, John. " 'Architect of Poetry': Harlem Poet's Epic Out 30 Years Later." *Washington Evening Star*, 31 March 1965, p. E–2.

Spector, Robert Donald. "The Poet's Voice in the Crowd." *Saturday Review* 48: 32 (7 August 1965): 29.

Thompson, Dolphin G. "Tolson's *Gallery* Brings Poetry Home." *Phylon* 36: 4 (Winter 1965): 408–10.

Tulip, James. "Afroamerican Poet—M. B. Tolson." *Poetry Australia* 10 (June 1966): 37–39.

Bibliography

On *A Gallery of Harlem Portraits*

Anonymous. Review of *A Gallery of Harlem Portraits. Forum for Modern Language Studies* 16: 4 (October 1980): 381–82.
———. "Poetry of Former Kansas Citian Tells of Life in Harlem During Jazz Age." *Kansas City Call*, 1–7 February 1980, p. 10.
Bone, Robert. "A Poet with a Fame Deferred." *Change* 11: 7 (October 1979): 65–67.
Cargas, Harry James. "University Presses: Some Important Contributions." *Catholic Library World* 52: 8 (March 1981): 344–45.
Fabre, Michel. Review of *A Gallery of Harlem Portraits. AFRAM Newsletter* 10 (April 1980): 21.
Payne, James R. Review of *A Gallery of Harlem Portraits*, Melvin B. Tolson's "Harlem Gallery," and *Caviar and Cabbage. World Literature Today* 57: 1 (Winter 1983): 110.
Rampersad, Arnold. Review of *A Gallery of Harlem Portraits. Yearbook of English Studies* (1983): 354–55.
Webster, Thomas A. "Missouri Poet Rediscovered." *Kansas City Star*, 10 February 1980, p. 14 E.

On *Caviar and Cabbage*

Fabre, Michel. Review of *Caviar and Cabbage. AFRAM Newsletter* 17 (September 1983): 27.
Miller, E. Ethelbert. "A Black Columnist's Contribution." *Washington Works*, no. 6 (Fall 1983).
Payne, James R. Review of *A Gallery of Harlem Portraits*, Melvin B. Tolson's "Harlem Gallery," and *Caviar and Cabbage. World Literature Today* 57: 1 (Winter 1983): 110.
Webster, Thomas A. "Collection Restores Author to His Rightful Literary Place." *Kansas City Star*, 25 April 1982, p. 11K.

Miscellaneous

Anonymous. "Langston Hears Poet's Odyssey." *Daily Oklahoman*, 9 April 1965, p. 16.
———. "Lauded Oklahoman Poet Working Hard after Battle with Cancer." *Daily Oklahoman*, 4 February 1965, p. 11.
———. "Let's Erect a Monument." *Wiley Reporter*, 23 August 1948.
———. "Liberia Honors Poet Laureate from Oklahoma." *Daily Oklahoman*, 24 November 1965, p. 10.
———. "Poets Thieves by Listening, Tolson Says." *Daily Oklahoman*, 15 February 1966.
———. "State Poet Recalls Robert Frost." *Daily Oklahoman*, 10 February 1963.
———. "Tolson Draws Praise." *Dallas Times Herald*, 17 January 1965.
———. "Tolson Speaks on Negro History in Convocation." *The Fisk University Forum*, 26 February 1965.
Basler, Roy P. "The Heart of Blackness—M. B. Tolson's Poetry." *New Letters* 39: 3 (Spring 1973): 63–76.
Bickham, Jack. "Flowers of Hope." *Sunday Oklahoman, Orbit*, 29 August 1965, pp. 6–9.

Bibliography

————. "A Superbly Successful Human Being." *Oklahoma Courier*, 9 September 1966, p. 5.

Bontemps, Arna–*Langston Hughes Letters, 1925–1967*. New York: Dodd, Mead and Co., 1980.

Calverton, V. F. "The Cultural Barometer." *Current History* 48: 2 (February 1938): 56.

Cansler, Ronald Lee. " 'The White and Not-White' Dichotomy of Melvin B. Tolson's Poetry." *Negro American Literary Forum* 7: 4 (Winter 1973): 115–18.

Editorial on Tolson as Mayor. *Oklahoma Black Dispatch*, 29 March 1957.

Farnsworth, Robert M. "Preface to Tolson's Essays." *New Letters* 42: 4 (Summer 1981): 101–2.

————."What Can a Poet Do? Langston Hughes and Melvin B. Tolson." *New Letters* 47: 1 (Fall 1981): 19–29.

————. "Tribute to Tolson." *New Letters* 46: 3 (Spring 1980): 125–27.

Flasch, Joy. "Humor and Satire in the Poetry of M. B. Tolson." *Satire Newsletter* 7: 1 (Fall 1969): 29–36.

————. "A Great American Poet." *Oklahoma Librarian* 18: 4 (October 1968): 116–18.

Fuller, Hoyt W. "Negro Writers and White Critics." *The Progressive* 30: 10 (October 1966): 36–39.

Hyman, Stanley E. "The Negro Writer in America: An Exchange, The Folk Tradition." *Partisan Review* 25: 2 (Spring 1958): 197–211.

Jarrett, Hobart. "Adventures in Interracial Debates." *Crisis* 42 (August 1935): 240.

Kline, Betsy. "Tolson Took Pulse of 'Renaissance.' " *Kansas City Star*, 10 February 1980, p. 14E.

Littlejohn, David. "M. B. Tolson." In *Black on White: A Critical Survey of Writing by American Negroes*, pp. 81–83. New York: Grossman, 1966.

Llorens, David. "Seeking a New Image: Writers Converge at Fisk University." *Negro Digest* 15: 8 (June 1966): 54–68.

McCall, Dan. *The Man Says Yes*. New York: Viking Press, 1969.

————. "Tolson 65." *Negro Digest* 15 (September 1966): 66.

Oringeriff, Nora Bell. "Langston Honors Retiring Professor." *Sunday Oklahoman*, 11 April 1965.

Price, Libby. "A.-S. Faculty Hears Tolson." Oklahoma State University *O'Collegian*, 16 February 1966.

————. "Honors Paid to Langston's Great Poet, Melvin Tolson." *Stillwater Daily-News Press*, 11 April 1965.

Randall, Dudley. "The Black Aesthetic in the Thirties, Forties, and Fifties." In *Modern Black Voices*, edited by Donald B. Gibson. Englewood Cliffs: Prentice-Hall, 1973.

————. "Portrait of a Poet as Raconteur." *Negro Digest* 15: 3 (January 1966): 54–57.

Rohrer, Bob. "Anderson Premiere Haunting." *Atlanta Constitution*, 27 May 1970.

Redmond, Eugene B. *Drumvoices*, pp. 247–63. Garden City: Doubleday, 1976.

Richardson, Jack. "The Black Arts." *The New York Review of Books* 11: 2 (19 December 1968): 10–13.

Bibliography

Scott, Nathan A. "Black Literature." In *Harvard Guide to Contemporary American Writing*, ed. Daniel Hoffman, pp. 287–341. Cambridge: Harvard University Press, 1979.

Seamster, Cynthia. "Laureate Poet Explains Principles at Banquet." *Daily O'Collegian* 61: 90 (16 February 1965): 1.

Shapiro, Karl. "The Decolonization of American Literature." *Wilson Library Bulletin* 39: 10 (June 1965): 843–53.

———. "The Critic Outside." *American Scholar* 50: 2 (Spring 1981): 197–210.

Walcott, Ronald. "Ellison, Gordone, and Tolson: Some Notes on the Blues, Style, and Space." *Black World* 22: 2 (December 1972): 4–29.

Whitbread, Thomas. "In Praise of M. B. Tolson." In *Whomp and Moonshiver*, pp. 45–46. Brockport: BOA Editions, 1982.

White, Chappell. "Anderson 'Variations' Shows Writer's Skill." *Atlanta Journal*, 27 May 1970.

INDEX

A

African Charter, 71–72, 153
Aggrey, Dr. James E. Kwegyir, 71, 230, 257
Alcuin, 191, 253
Alfred, William, 299
American Academy of Arts and Letters, 298–99
American Negro Exposition in Chicago, 63; Tolson poetry prize, 64
American Society for African Culture, 203, 222, 287
Anathemata, The, 283
Anderson, Marian, 277
Anderson, Maxwell, 202
Anderson, T. J.: "Variations on a Theme by M. B. Tolson," 279–80
Antar, 8
Armstrong, Louis, 242–43, 281
Ashmun, Jehudi, 154–55
Askia, 153
Attucks, Crispus, 8
Auden, W. H., 213, 223
Avalon Chair, Tuskegee University, 216, 293, 298
Azikiwe, Nnamdi, 151; *Renascent Africa*, 159

B

Bacon, Francis, 1, 223, 247; "The Idols of the Tribe," 87–88
Balakian, Nona, 288
Baldwin, James, 253, 298; *Notes of a Native Son*, 220
Barksdale, Richard, 283
Barth, John, 299
Basler, Roy P., 284–85
Bates, Ernest Sutherland, 143
Belafonte, Harry, 296
Bell, Benjamin, 51, 54, 60, 63, 79, 103–4, 145–46, 175, 202, 224–25
Benet, Stephen Vincent, 141
Benet, William Rose: review of *Rendezvous*, 96
Bickham, Jack, 270
Bishop, John Peale, 143
Blackmur, R. P., 167
Blake, William, 239
Blok, Alexander, 167
Blues, 171, 280–81

Boatner, Edward, 124
Bond, Horace Mann, 24, 138, 139, 140, 146, 151, 177, 222, 287, 293; role in Tolson becoming poet laureate, 106–8; history of Lincoln University, 215–17
Bontemps, Arna, 34, 64, 97, 202, 297
Boswell, Hamilton, 60
Braithwaite, William Stanley, 205, 306
Bread Loaf Writers Conference, 205–9
"Bridge, The," 165, 166, 170, 171, 176. *See also* Brown, Richard L.
Brooks, Gwendolyn, 141, 277, 281, 283; review of *Harlem Gallery*, 275
Brown, Richard L., 133, 206
Brown, Sterling, 34, 41, 95, 203, 204
Browning, Elizabeth Barrett, 143
Bryant, William Cullen, 12
Bunche, Ralph, 41
Burke, Arthur E.: review of *Rendezvous*, 95–97

C

Cagliari, Paolo: *Sodom*, 233
Caldwell, Erskine: *In Search of Pisco*, 291
Calverton, V. F., 57–61, 63, 64, 80, 105, 125, 142, 143, 150, 214
Campbell, Simms, 227
"Cantos, The," 176
Carlyle, Thomas, 11
Carver, George Washington, 148, 228, 277
Cellini, Benvenuto, 255
Cerf, Bennett, 57
Cezanne, Paul, 250
Chamberlain, Mary Lou, 64, 89, 305
Christy, Arthur, 40, 42
Churchill, Winston, 71–72
Ciardi, John, 133, 145, 151, 206, 215, 275; definition of "horizontal" and "vertical" audiences, 111–13; review of *Libretto*, 165–66
Clark, Felton, president of Southern University, 212, 216
Cobo, Albert E., mayor of Detroit, 220
Cole, Lois Dwight, 57
Conroy, Jack, 97
Cowell, Carl, 210, 287
Cox, Oliver Cromwell, 55–56, 105, 215; *Caste, Class and Race*, 158–59; *Foundations of Capitalism*, 213–14

Index

Index

Index

Index

Sitwell, Edith, 143
Smith, Bessie, 281
Smith, Huston: *The Purposes of Higher Education*, 222–23
Snyder, Gary, 299
Socrates, 167
Spector, Robert Donald: review of *Harlem Gallery*, 278
Spenser, Edmund, 167
Spingarn, Dr. Joel, 40, 287
Songhai, 153
Southern Agrarians, 137
Star of Africa, awarded to Tolson, 205, 206, 210, 217
Stein, Gertrude, 8, 10, 61, 116, 243, 278
Steinberg, Jacob, 151, 205, 210, 215–16, 217, 220, 224, 225, 287
Stevens, Wallace, 167, 181, 276, 281
Stevenson, Coke, governor of Texas, 104
Strickland, Dr. William, 271, 302
Swift, Jonathan: *Journal to Stella*, 161

T

Tate, Allen, 24, 152, 167, 168, 169, 170, 171, 172, 174, 190, 205, 272, 274, 276, 282, 283, 284, 288–89, 306; preface to *Libretto*, 138–42, 146–51. *See also* "Ode to the Confederate Dead"
Taylor, Ol' Red, 281
Tennyson, Alfred Lord, 73; "Parliament of Men," 163
Thomas of Celano, 239
Thompson, Dolphin G.: review of *Harlem Gallery*, 277
Thoreau, Henry David, 161
Thurman, Wallace, 34
Tillman, Nathaniel: review of *Rendezvous*, 96
Tintoretto: *Paradise*, 233
Tolson, Alonzo, 4–5, 6, 8, 20, 21, 43, 97; marriage of, 7; ministerial assignments of, 7
Tolson, Arthur, 98, 101, 104, 217, 220; birth of, 32; *The Black Oklahomans*, 221; Ph.D., 300
Tolson, Helen. *See* Wilson, Helen Tolson
Tolson, Lera Hurt, 1, 6, 8–9, 70, 75, 116–18, 225; marriage of, 7; death of, 9
Tolson, Melvin B., Jr., 32, 47, 51, 98, 101–2, 105, 220, 225, 286, 302; birth of, 28
Tolson, Melvin Beaunorus: family origin, 4–5; birthdate, 7, 303; high school, 27–28; packinghouse job, 22–23; courtship and marriage, 26–29; Wiley College appointment, 31; debate tradition begins,

32; living in Harlem, 33; debate teams, 50–54; concern for sharecroppers, 54–55; effect of *Rendezvous* on Wiley career, 97; move to Langston, 98, 109–11, 160–64; speech at Rustin, La., 103; 1946 speech at University of Texas, 104; cancer, 140, 206–7, 225–26, 271, 295; embrace of modernism, 142–46; Liberian embassy literary tea, 205; Doctor of Letters degree, 206; mayor of Langston, 210–12; Liberian trip, 217–19; stop in Paris, 219–20; Fine Arts Festival, Langston University, 291; Doctor of Humane Letters degree, 293; A. & S. Banquet, Oklahoma State University, 296; death of, 302
—— Published books. *Caviar and Cabbage*, 3, 4, 11, 13, 14, 22, 23, 28, 35, 36, 40, 41, 48, 53, 59, 62, 71, 73, 74, 105, 114, 121, 157, 158, 165, 227, 230, 250, 279; *A Gallery of Harlem Portraits*, 9, 40, 42–50, 58, 62, 63, 66, 92, 139, 179–82, 229, 252, 529, 279; *Harlem Gallery*, 2–3, 35, 48, 49, 51, 54, 67, 72, 139, 170, 171–72, 179, 182–84, 201, 211, 220–21, 223, 224, 226, 228–70, 271–85, 301; *Libretto for the Republic of Liberia*, 5, 24, 66, 67, 72, 124, 138–39, 146–67, 185, 189–90, 193, 194, 201, 205–6, 212, 216, 218, 220–21, 225, 226, 229, 230, 233, 244, 259, 274, 276, 279, 282, 283, 284, 288–89, 293, 298; *Rendezvous with America*, 64, 66, 67, 77–92, 93–97, 198, 285
—— Individual poems. "Abraham Lincoln of Rock Sring Farm," 177, 194–98, 287–88; "African China," 139, 177, 179–82; "Alexander Calverton," 44; "The Auction," 58; "Aunt Tommiezene," 45; "Babylon," 64, 87; "The Ballad of the Rattlesnake," 54–55, 84, 288; "The Bard of Addis Ababa," 69–70, 72, 86; "The Black Man's Burden," 218–19; "The Breadline," 63; "Damascus Blade," 86; "Dark Laughter," 295–96; "Dark Symphony," 63, 81–82, 96–97, 140, 217; "Dr. Harvey Whyte," 57–59; "E. & O. E.," 104, 136, 139, 177, 182–90, 192, 195, 243, 254, 261–63; "Edna Borland," 46; "Esperanto," 80–81; "An Ex-Judge at the Bar," 80, 305; "Flora Murdock," 44–45; "Freemon Hawthorne," 46–47; "The Gallows," 31, 85, 96; "A Hamlet Rives Us," 96; "Hamuel Gutterman," 57; "Harlem," 49, 57; "The Horns of the Bull," 138, 190, 288; "The Idols of the Tribe," 88–

320

Index